Programming with C#.NET

Graham Hall

Lecturer in Computing
Coleg Meirion-Dwyfor, Dolgellau, Gwynedd

Copyright © 2015 Graham Hall. All rights reserved.

Published by Lulu.com

ISBN: 978-1-291-53631-7

FRONT COVER IMAGES

Welsh cottage, Margaret Hall

District line Train at Earl's Court, Paul Robertson on Flickr
http://www.flickr.com/photos/pauliewoll/5532264790/

Theatre interior, Guillermo Arévalo Aucahuasi from Wikimedia Commons
http://commons.wikimedia.org/wiki/File:Interior_del_Gran_Teatro_Nacional_del_Per%C3%BA_cazuela.JPG

Contents

Introduction	2
1. Camera	4
2. Calculator	11
3. Railway Tickets	17
4. Solitaire	31
5. Airport	49
6. London Underground	59
7. Estate Agent Database	83
8. College Courses	117
9. Fast Food	149
10. Theatre Bookings	162

Introduction

The purpose of the second edition of this book is to provide a simple introduction to C#.NET programming with Microsoft Visual Studio 2013. This book was designed initially for students of the Glyndŵr University Foundation Degree in Applied Computing who are undertaking the module 'Object Oriented Programming' in the second year of their course. These students will have completed a module in text-based Java programming in which a variety of console applications were developed. They should be familiar with basic programming structures such as loops, conditionals and arrays, and will have been introduced to object oriented concepts of classes, properties and methods.

Visual Studio provides a very wide range of programming and database tools for software development. It is therefore possible to solve the same software problem in a number of different ways, and each individual programmer is likely to develop their own preferred techniques and methods of working. The solutions demonstrated in this book are not necessarily claimed to be the 'correct' or 'best' programming approaches, but have been found to work reliably and to be relatively easy to understand.

For reasons of space, comment lines have not been included in the program listings, although programming techniques are explained in the accompanying text. Students are strongly encouraged to add their own comment lines to the program listings, both as a way of checking their understanding of the program and as a way of easily identifying sections of code which can be copied into other projects as standard modules.

By working through the example programs in this book, students should gain an understanding of basic interface construction, processing and database operations in an object oriented C#.NET environment. Students are encouraged to develop the programs further by adding extra functionality, or to create their own similar projects which incorporate the programming techniques demonstrated here. Programming is a very practical activity, requiring extensive practice to develop a high level of skill.

Grateful thanks are due to students of Coleg Meirion-Dwyfor who have helped in the design and testing of the example programs in this book. However, the author accepts sole responsibility for any errors in the work.

Chapter outline

The initial chapters **Camera** and **Calculator** demonstrate the construction of graphical user interfaces in Microsoft Visual Studio from toolbox components. Conversion between string and numeric data formats is explained, and the TRY...CATCH error handling structure is introduced.

The program **Railway Tickets** represents a more substantial application, with data values passed between the forms. Boolean variables are used in conjunction with radio button groups.

The **Solitaire** game demonstrates the creation of a two dimensional array of buttons at run time, to produce an interactive game board display. Algorithm logic is developed to check for valid moves during the game.

Airport introduces the techniques for setting up a database table, accessing the database from a C# program at run time, and displaying the table data in grid view on a form.

The **London Underground** route finding program explores the techniques for drawing graphics in C# at run time, and provides further practice in handing database tables and arrays. A more complex algorithm is developed, involving multiple nested loops.

The **Estate Agent Database** program demonstrates a full range of file handling operations for a multiple table database: creating, displaying, editing and deleting records, and selecting particular records by means of SQL queries.

College Courses introduces an object oriented approach to representing entities in a data model. The program defines object classes for students, courses and registrations within an administrative system.

Fast Food is a small program demonstrating how picture images can be stored directly into a database table in binary format, then reloaded for display on screen.

The final program project, **Theatre Bookings**, brings together many of the techniques developed in earlier chapters. Again there is an emphasis on object oriented design, with classes representing theatre events, customers and bookings. Bookings are made via interactive seating plans of the theatre, and extensive use is made of database operations to handle booking records.

1 Camera

The first program we write will display a picture on a Windows screen, with buttons to make the picture appear and disappear.

Begin by loading **Microsoft Visual Studio 2013**. From the introduction screen, choose '**New Project**':

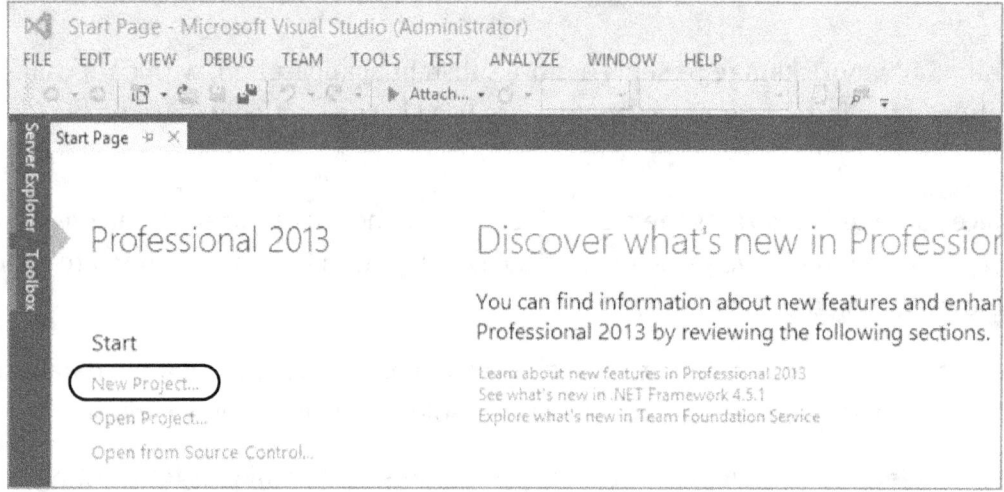

At the next page, select '**Windows Forms Application**'. Choose a location on your computer where you wish to store the program, and give it the name '*camera*':

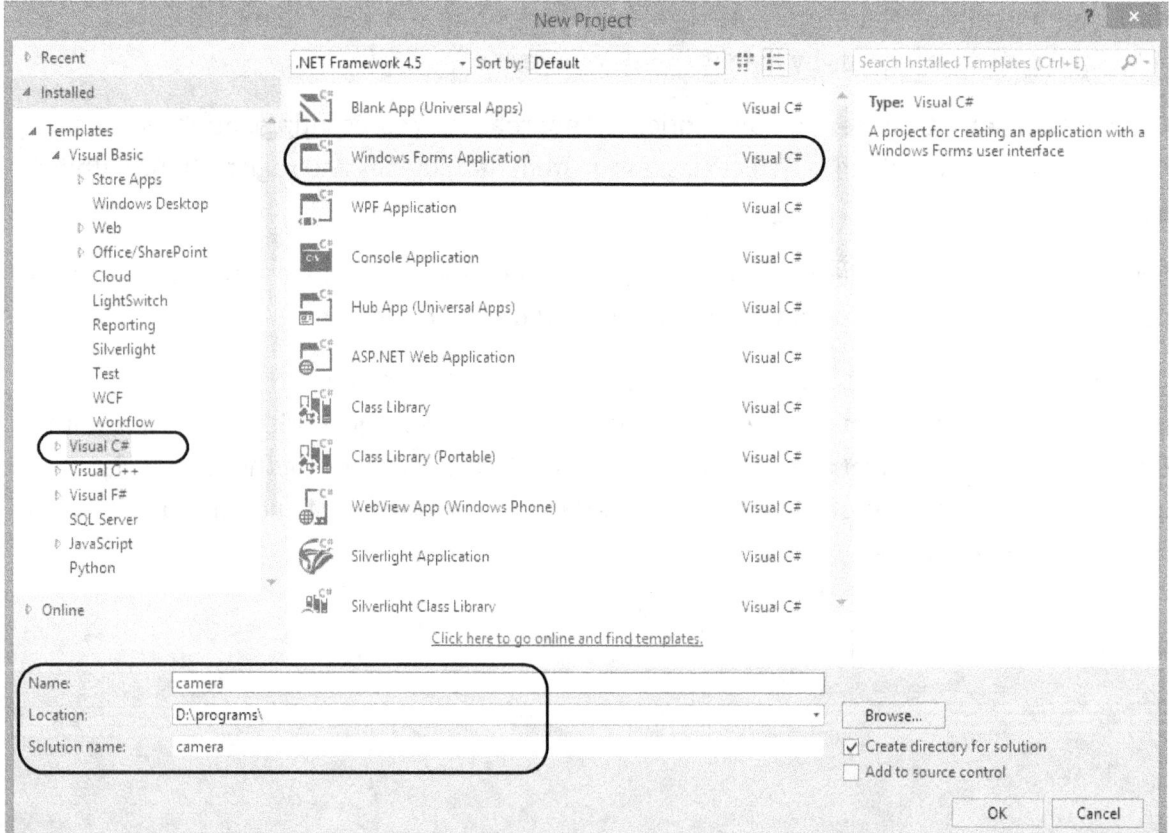

C# programs consist of a number of files, and Visual Studio will create a folder called '**camera**' in which all the necessary files will be stored. Click '**OK**' and an empty Windows form appears. You can change the size of this by dragging the side or corner.

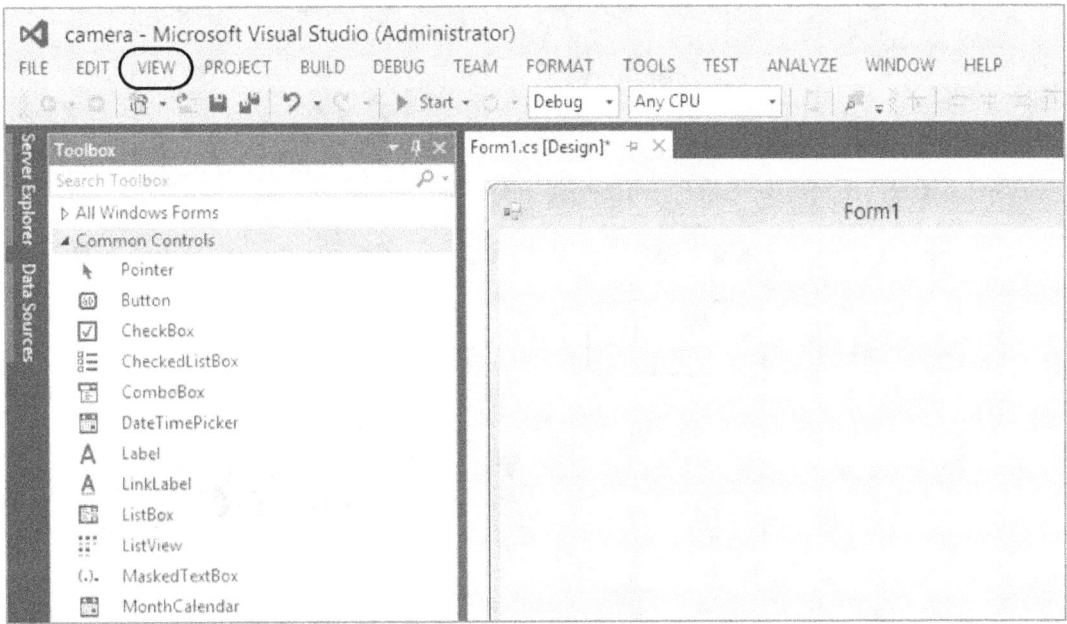

Open the **Toolbox**, either by clicking '**Toolbox**' on the left hand margin of the screen, or by selecting **View / Toolbox** from the top menu line.

In the Toolbox window, click the '**PictureBox**' component. Go to the **Form1** window and drag the mouse to create a PictureBox outline.

In the top right hand corner of the PictureBox frame is a small arrow. Click this to open an options window. Click '**Choose Image**':

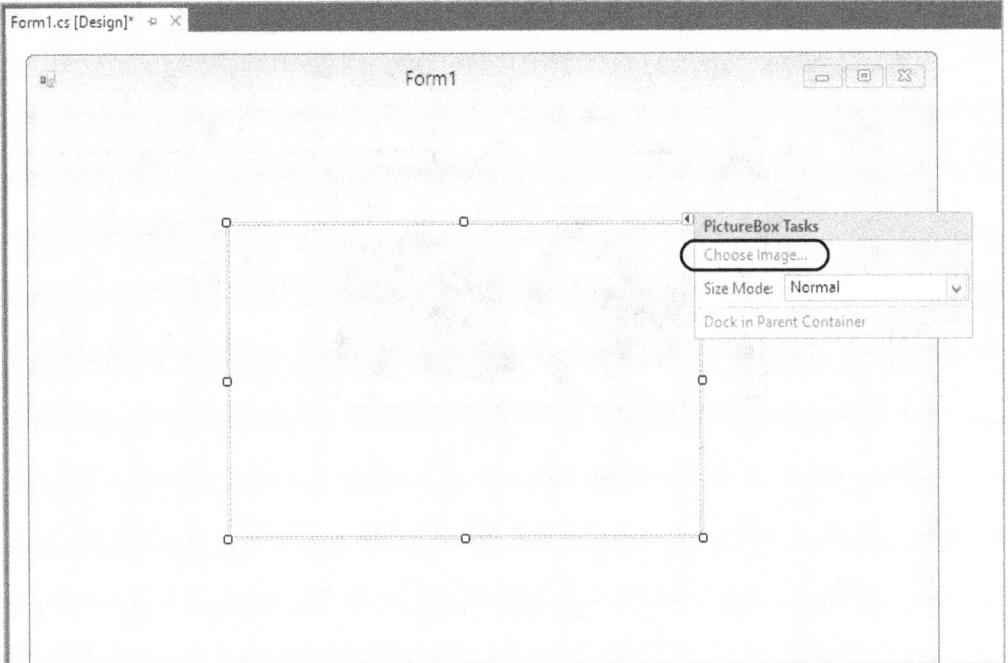

6 Programming with C#.NET

Select '**Local resource**'. Use the file dialog window to locate a suitable picture, then click the '**Import**' button:

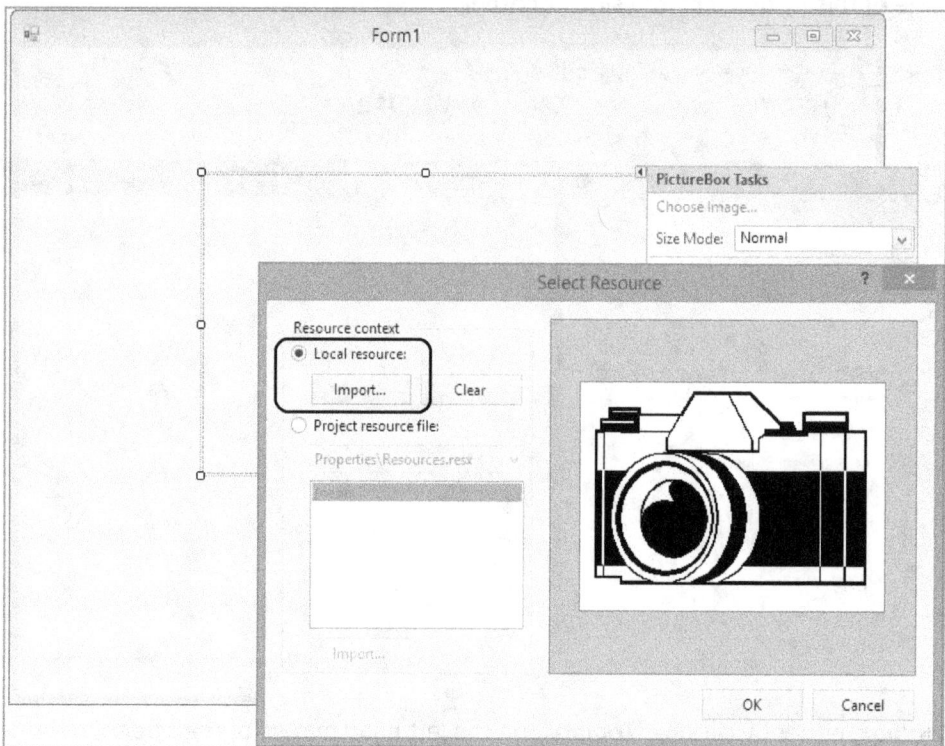

Select '**Size Mode / StretchImage**', so that the image fills the **PictureBox** frame. You can then drag the frame to a suitable size:

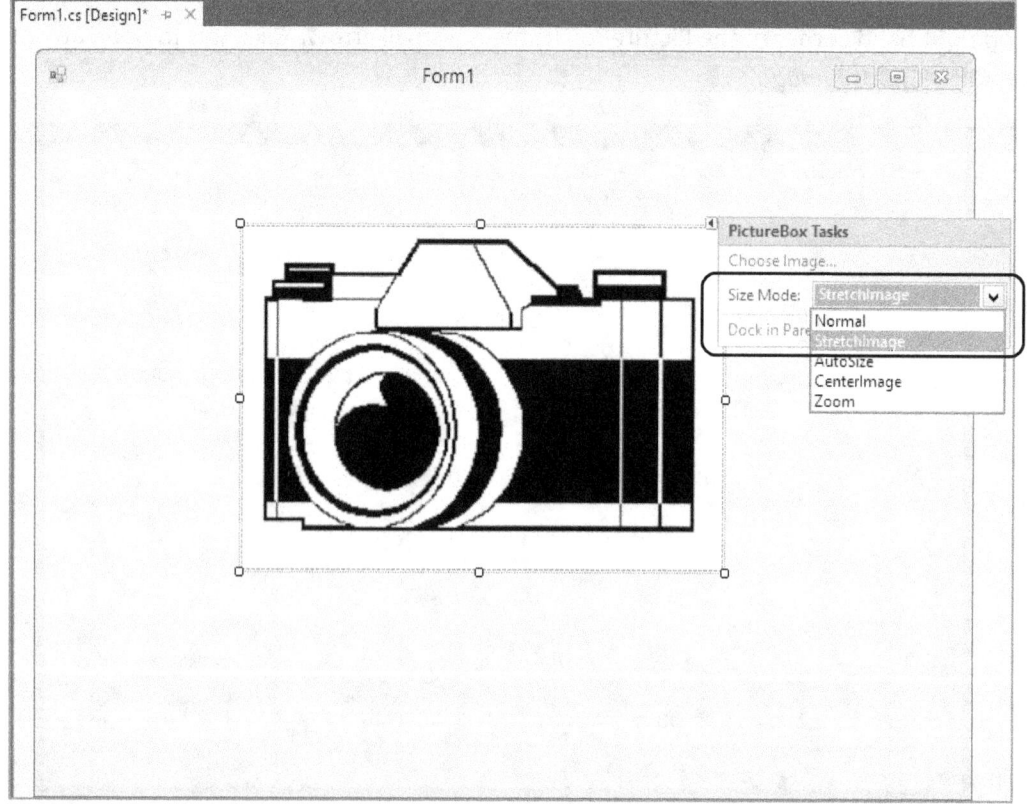

Select the '*Button*' component in the Toolbox. Use the mouse to create three buttons underneath the picture.

We will use the right hand button to close the program. Click once on the button to select it, then go to the '*Properties*' window in the bottom right of the screen. Locate the '*Text*' property in the alphabetical list, then change this to the word '*Close*'. This sets the caption which will appear on the button.

Go to the '*Design*' section of the **Properties** list, and change '*(Name)*' to '*btnClose*'. This will make the programming easier and avoid mistakes by clearly showing the purpose of this button.

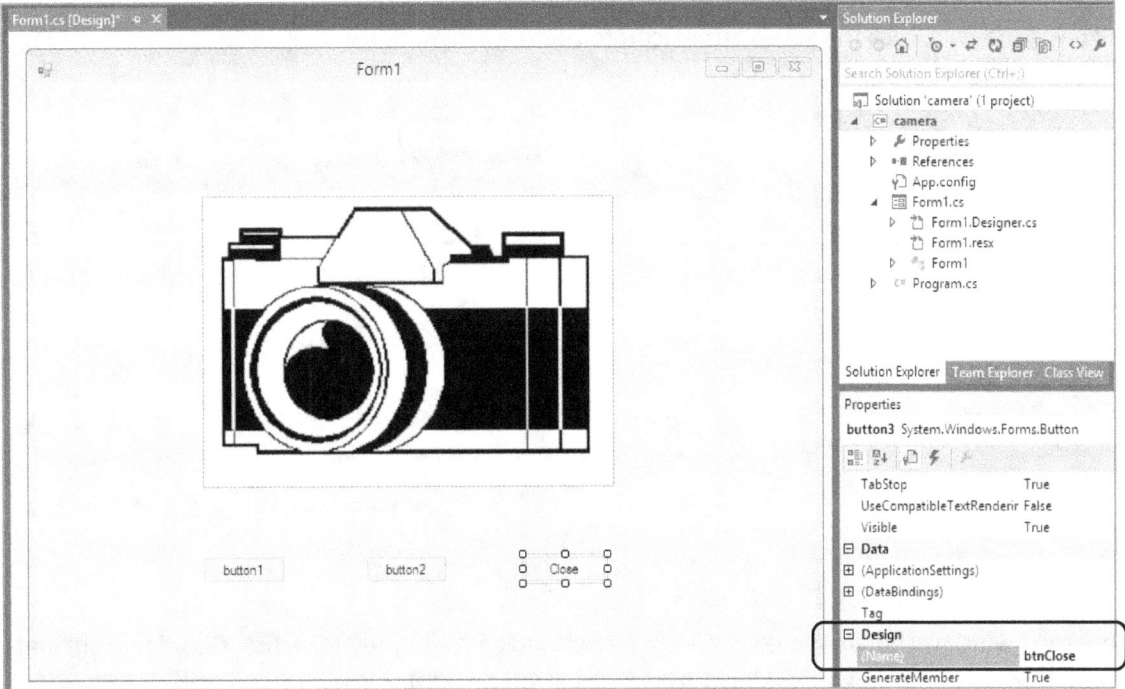

Go back to the **Form1** screen and double click the '*Close*' button. A new window will appear in which our program is being written:

```
namespace camera
{
    public partial class Form1 : Form
    {
        public Form1()
        {
            InitializeComponent();
        }

        private void btnClose_Click(object sender, EventArgs e)
        {
            Close();
        }
    }
}
```

You will see that the computer has already created an empty method '*btnClose_Click*'. We put program code inside this method to carry out any required actions when the button is clicked. In this case, we just want the program to close, so add the command:

Close( );

We can now test the program so far…

Go to the menu line and select **Build / Build Solution**. If there are any errors in the program code, you will receive a message at this point, and you must go back and correct the errors before continuing.

If all has gone well, click the green arrow icon to run the program:

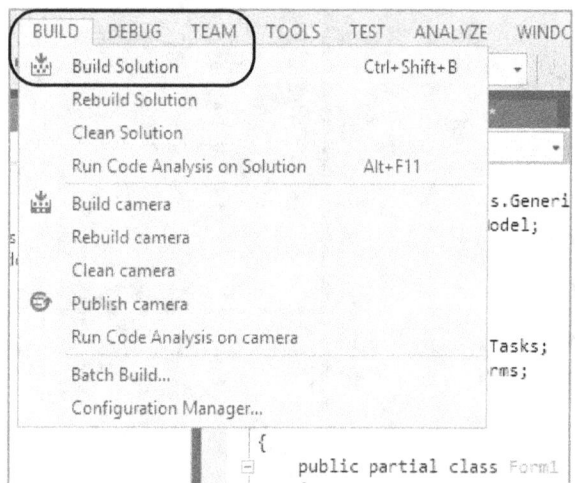 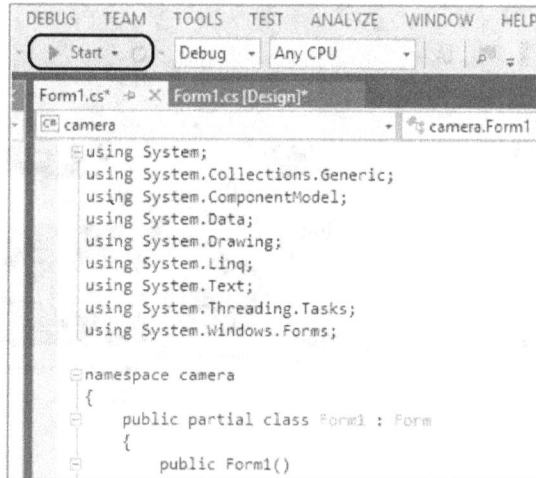

The **Form1** window should appear, with the picture image displayed. Click the '**Close**' button, and the program will end – taking you back to the Visual Studio editing screen.

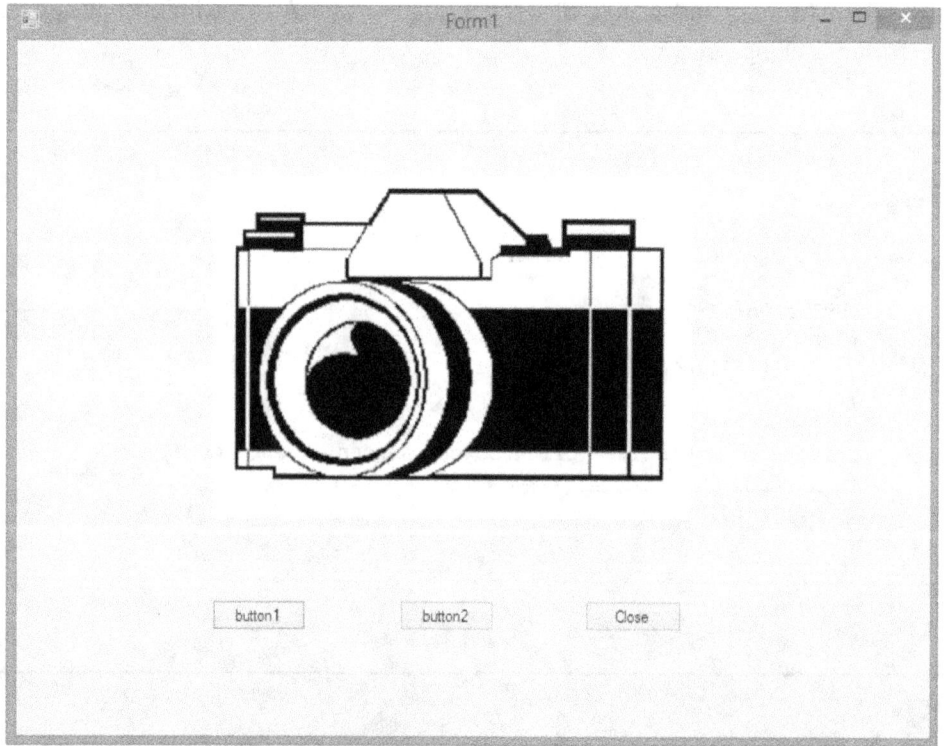

If the Form1 Design screen is not showing, select this by either clicking the '***Form1.cs(Design)***' tab in the programming window, or click the '***Form1.cs***' icon in the '***Solution Explorer***' window.

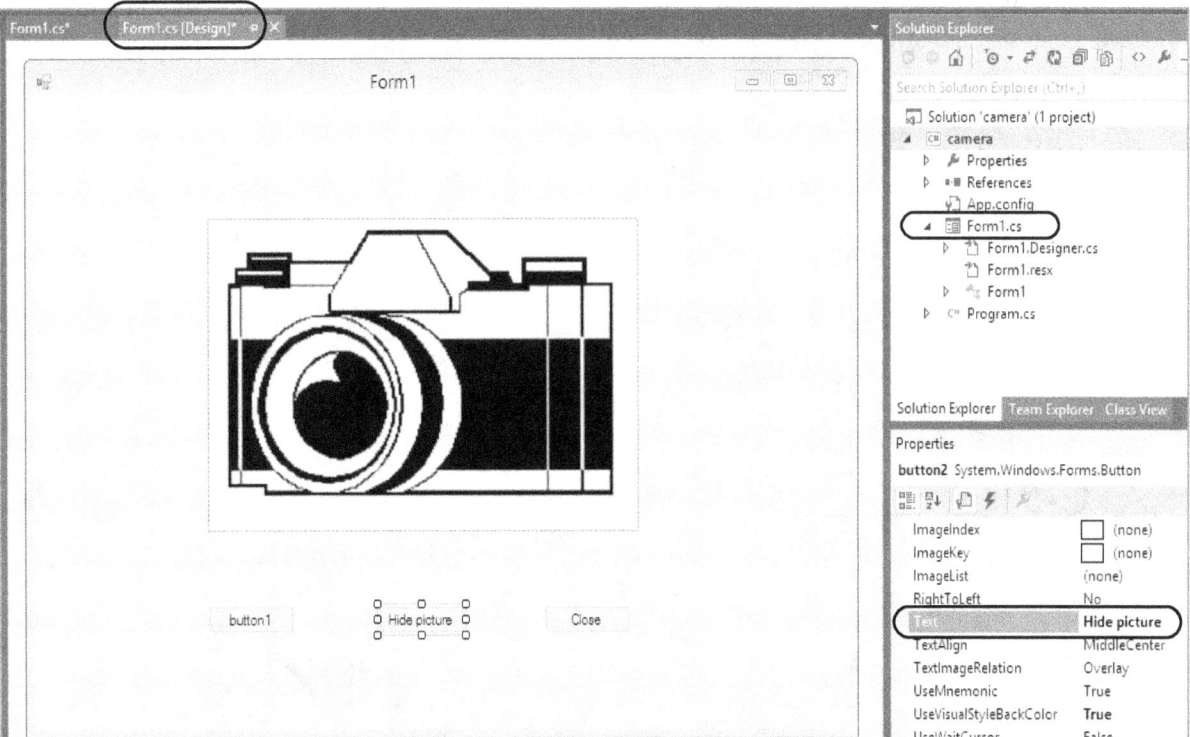

Select each of the remaining buttons in turn, and set the properties:

    Left button   text: '***Show picture***'   name: ***btnShow***

    Middle button   text: '***Hide picture***'   name: ***btnHide***

We are now going to add program code which will make the image appear and disappear when the buttons are clicked.

Double-click each button in turn, and add the lines of program shown below. The computer will create the empty button_click methods for you. Only the lines outlined need to be added:

```csharp
private void btnClose_Click(object sender, EventArgs e)
{
    Close();
}

private void btnShow_Click(object sender, EventArgs e)
{
    pictureBox1.Visible = true;
}

private void btnHide_Click(object sender, EventArgs e)
{
    pictureBox1.Visible = false;
}
```

When you have added the program code, go to the '*File*' menu and select '*Save All*'. The computer will save all the necessary files for creating the program. Always save before running a program, just in case something goes badly wrong and your program files become corrupted. In that situation, you will be grateful that you remembered to save an up-to-date copy.

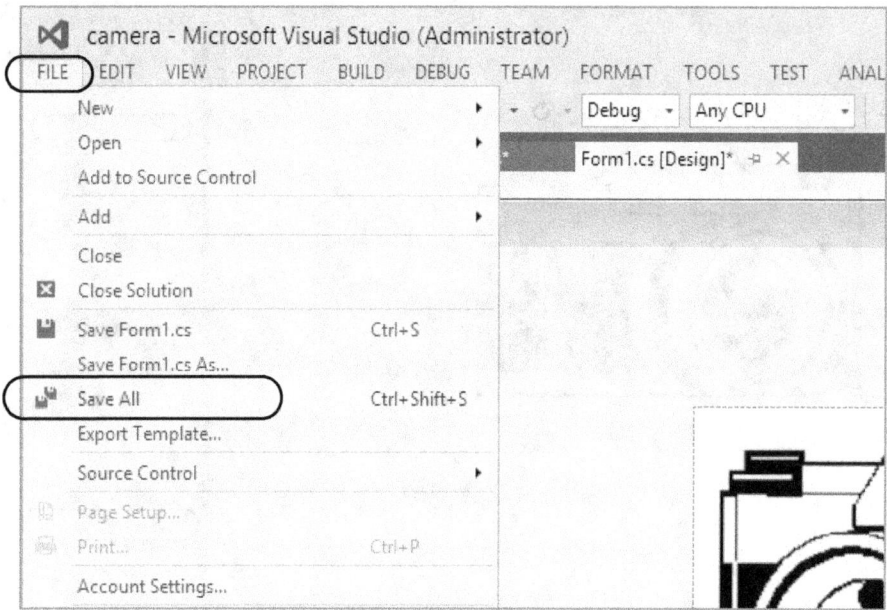

Use the **Build / Build Solution** menu option. If necessary, correct any errors before continuing.

Run the program by means of the green arrow icon.

The picture should appear and disappear when the corresponding buttons are clicked.

2 Calculator

Our next program will allow the user to input two numbers, then carry out basic arithmetic calculations.

Start a new project. If you have just completed the previous program, go to the *File* menu and select '*Save All*', then '*Close Solution*'. You can now select '*New / Project*':

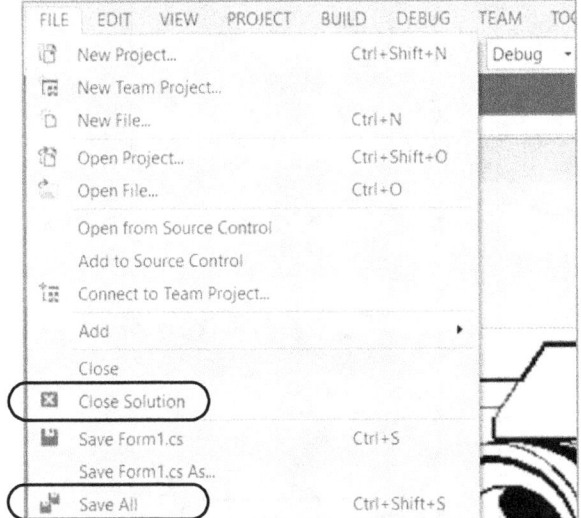 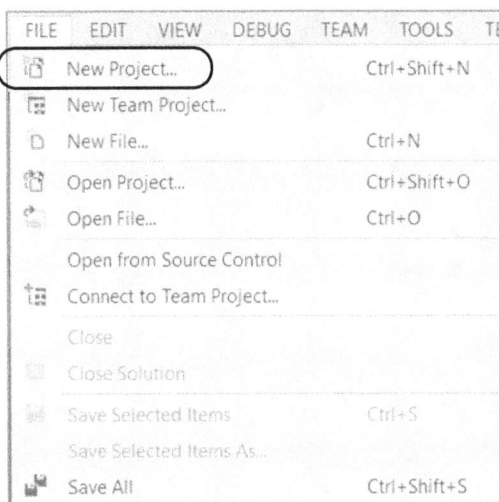

Select '*Visual C# / Windows Forms Application*' and give the name '*calculate*' for the program:

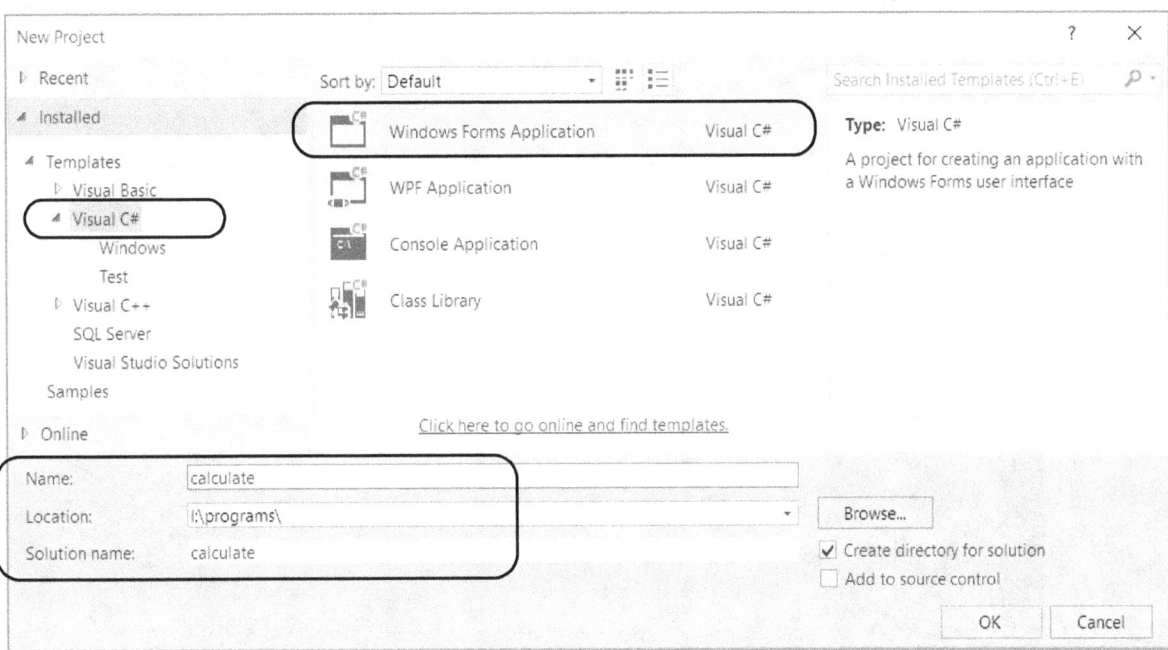

Click '**OK**' and a blank **Form1** screen will appear. Drag the edges of the form to fill the program window.

Select the **TextBox** component in the Toolbox. Drag the mouse to create a TextBox on Form1. When the program runs, the user will be able to type a number into this box.

Go to the **Properties** window, and change the name of the TextBox to **txtA**. This will help to remind us that the number entered into this box is to be stored as the number variable '**A**'.

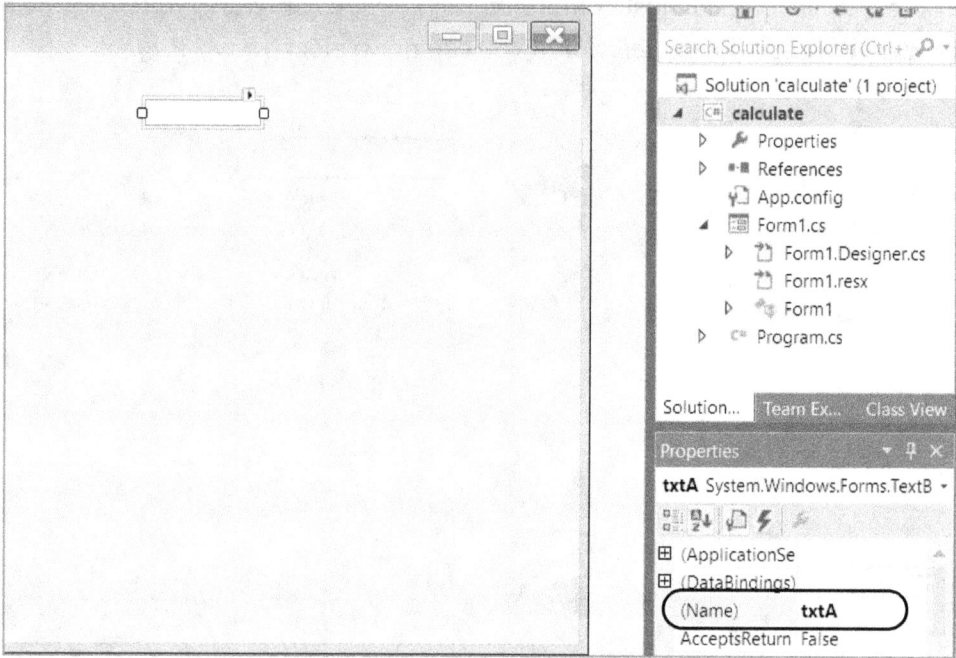

Select the **Label** component in the Toolbox, and drag the mouse to add a label alongside the text box. Change the **Text property** of the label to '**A**'.

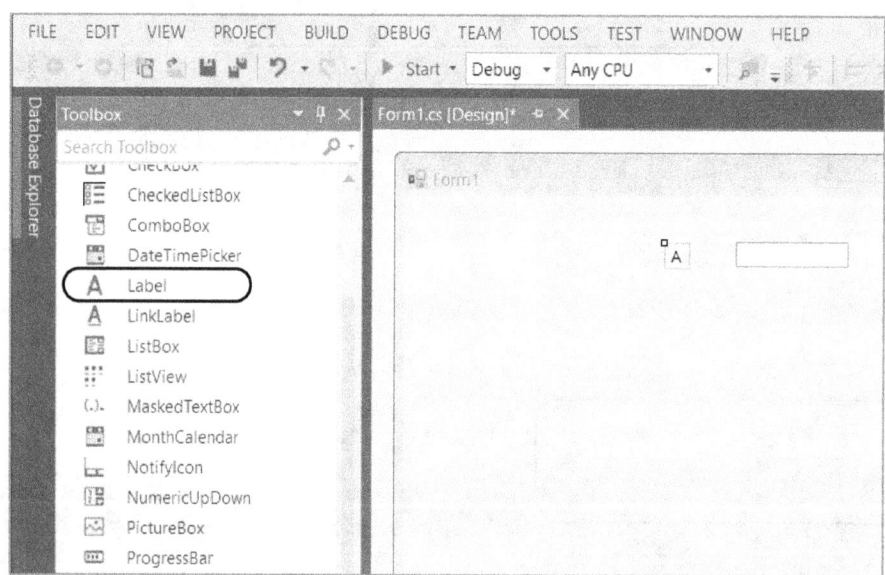

Chapter 2: Calculator   13

Add a second **TextBox** and **Label** component in the same way. Give the second TextBox the name **txtB**, and set the Text property of the second label to '**B**'.

Add a **Button**. Set the **Text** property to '**Calculate**', and change the name to **btnCalculate**.

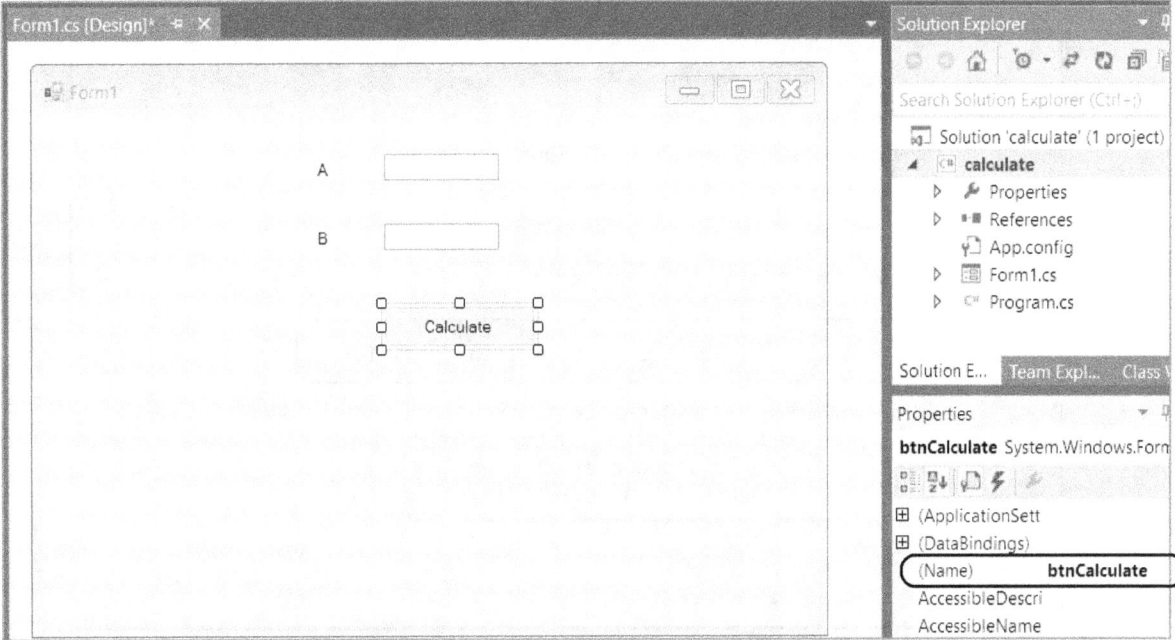

Continue in the same way to add TextBoxes which will display the results when the two numbers **A** and **B** are added, subtracted, multiplied and divided. Set the names of the TextBoxes to be:

txtAdd, txtSubtract, txtMultiply, txtDivide

You may find that the label text is too small. You can adjust the font size by selecting each label and clicking on the '**Font**' property. A font selection window will open.

That completes the user interface design. We are now going to add the program code to carry out the calculations.

Double-click the '**Calculate**' button. The program code window will open, with an empty button-click method created for you. Add the lines of code outlined below:

```
namespace calculate
{
    public partial class Form1 : Form
    {
        public Form1()
        {
            InitializeComponent();
        }

        double A, B, add, subtract, multiply, divide;

        private void btnCalculate_Click(object sender, EventArgs e)
        {
            A = Convert.ToDouble(txtA.Text);
            B = Convert.ToDouble(txtB.Text);
        }
    }
}
```

We begin by setting up some '*double*' variables to hold decimal numbers. *A* and *B* will be the input numbers, and the other variables '*add*', '*subtract*', '*multiply*' and '*divide*' will hold the answers to the calculations.

Inside the *btnCalculate_click* method, add the lines of code which will take the text typed into the TextBoxes and convert these into the decimal number format required for our variables A and B.

Build the program and run it. If correct decimal numbers are typed into A and B and the '*Calculate*' button is clicked, nothing yet happens. However, if an incorrect number format is entered, you will find that the program crashes:

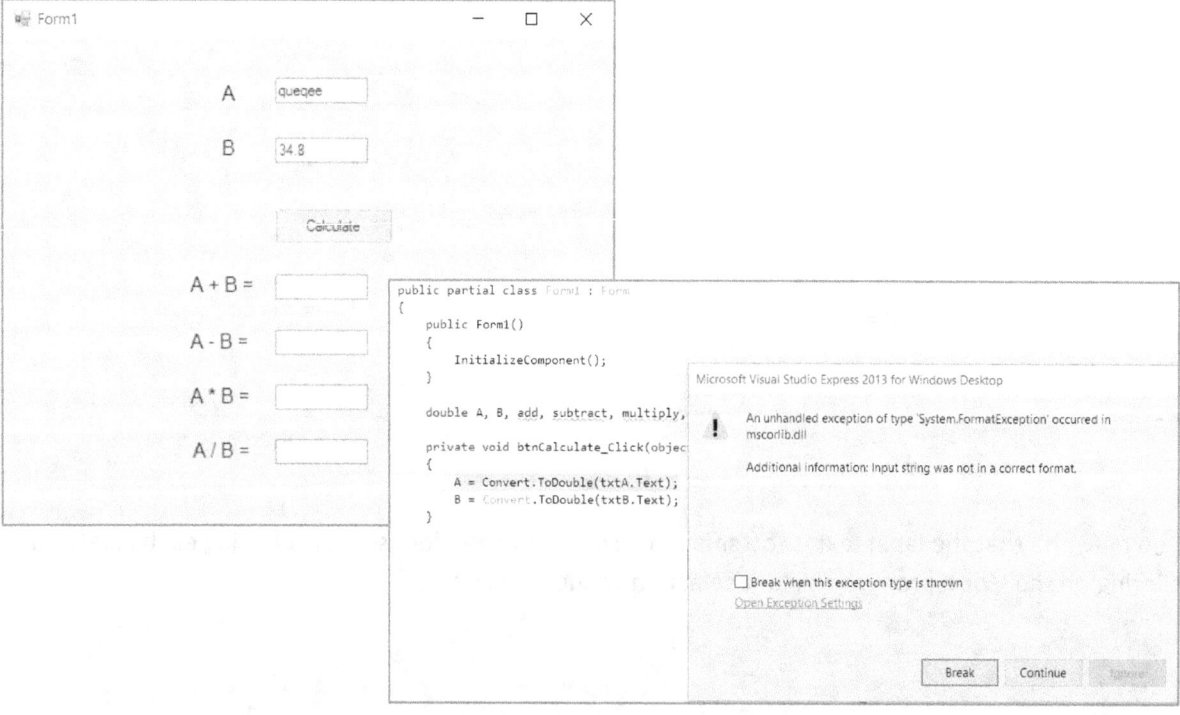

We want our program to be more helpful, and give the user a chance to correct their mistake and continue with the calculation. To do this, we add a **TRY ... CATCH** structure to the program.

```
        double A, B, add,subtract, multiply, divide;

        private void btnCalculate_Click(object sender, EventArgs e)
        {
            try
            {
                A = Convert.ToDouble(txtA.Text);
                B = Convert.ToDouble(txtB.Text);
            }
            catch
            {
                MessageBox.Show("Two decimal numbers must be entered");
            }
        }
```

The program will attempt to convert the TextBox entries into decimal numbers, but if it cannot do this then we will let the program display a message: '*Two decimal numbers must be entered*'.

Add lines of program to the ***btnCalculate_click*** method, as shown above, then run the program.

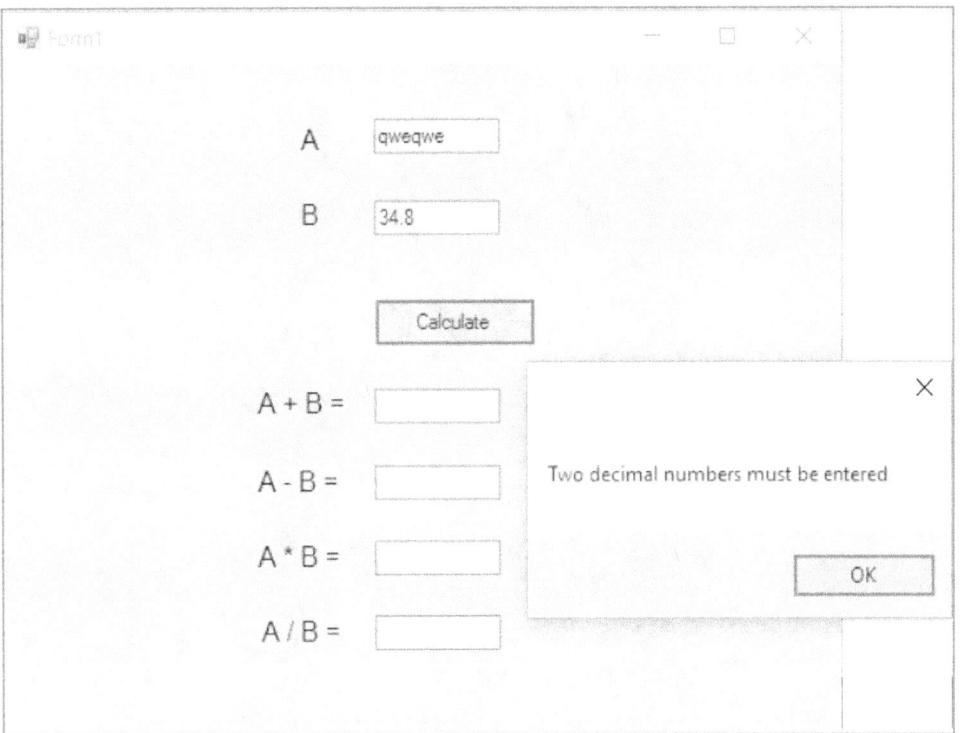

An incorrect entry will now cause the more helpful message to appear, and the user will be able to edit the incorrect data without needing to restart the program.

The only thing left to do now is to calculate and display the results.

Add lines to the **btnCalculate_click** method to calculate the variables '*add*' and '*subtract*', and display these in the TextBoxes '*txtAdd*' and '*txtSubtract*'.

```csharp
private void btnCalculate_Click(object sender, EventArgs e)
{
    try
    {
        A = Convert.ToDouble(txtA.Text);
        B = Convert.ToDouble(txtB.Text);
        add = A + B;
        txtAdd.Text = Convert.ToString(add);
        subtract = A - B;
        txtSubtract.Text = Convert.ToString(subtract);
    }
    catch
    {
        MessageBox.Show("Two decimal numbers must be entered");
    }
}
```

Run the program, and check that correct results are obtained for adding and subtracting the numbers input.

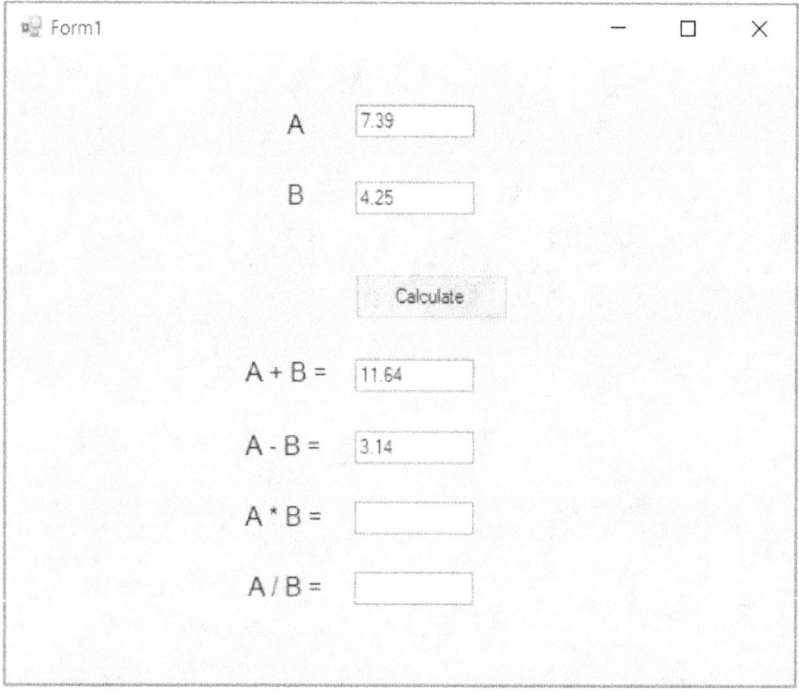

Complete the program by adding lines of code to carry out multiplication and division.

3 Railway Tickets

The next program combines the techniques we have used so far, to produce a ticket program for a narrow gauge railway.

The fare structure for the railway is:

- Single second class adult fare: £6.40
- Return fare is one and a half times the single fare
- All child fares are 60% of the equivalent adult fare
- Each adult or child passenger may pay a £2.00 surcharge to travel First Class for the whole of their single or return journey
- Groups of four or more passengers booking together receive a 20% discount on their total fare

We will begin by starting a new project called '*railway*'

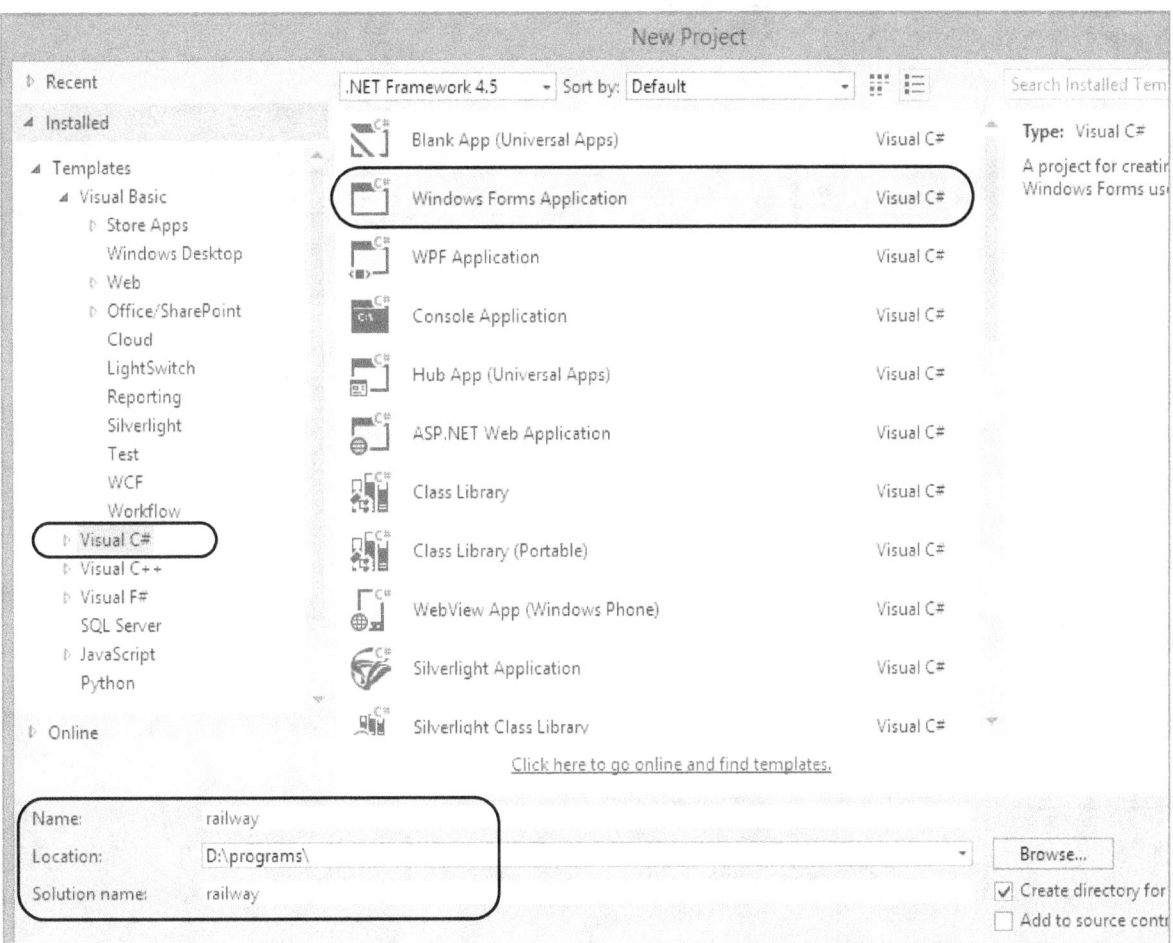

18 Programming with C#.NET

Create two *text boxes* for entering the numbers of adult and child passengers. Give the boxes the names **txtAdult** and **txtChild**. Add labels for the screen display:

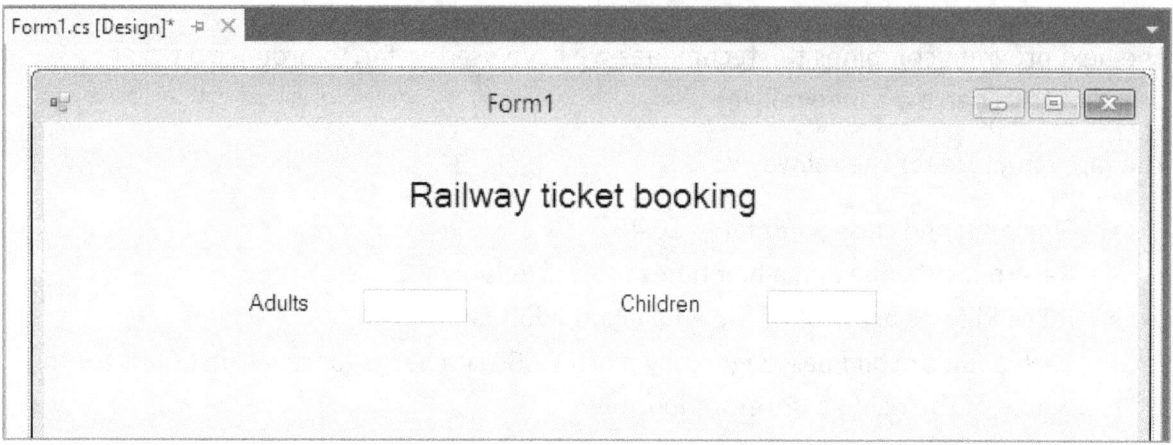

We will now set up buttons for choosing a *single* or *return* ticket.

Begin by selecting the **GroupBox** component in the Containers section of the Toolbox, and drag the mouse to draw a frame. Change the Text property of the GroupBox to '*Journey type*' to create a heading:

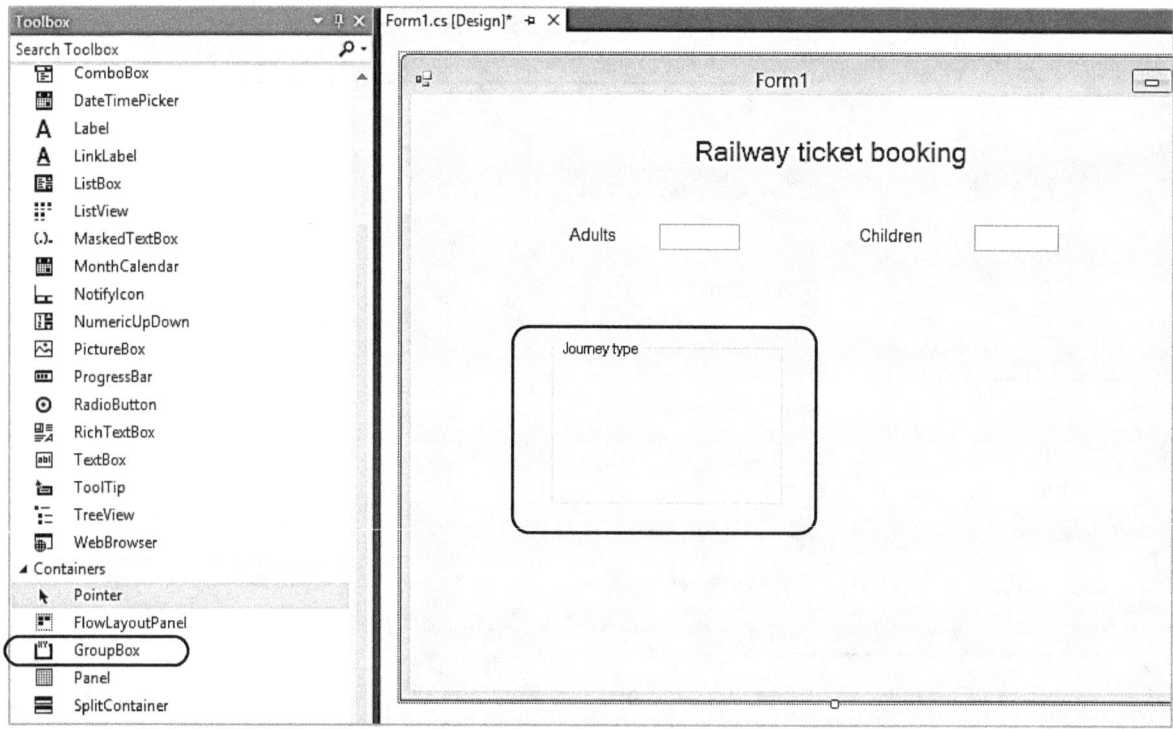

Choose the **RadioButton** component from the Toolbox and drag the mouse to place two buttons inside the group box.

Change the Text properties of the RadioButtons to '*Single*' and '*Return*'.

Give the RadioButtons the names **rbtnSingle** and **rbtnReturn**.

Set the **Checked** property of the 'Single' button to **True**:

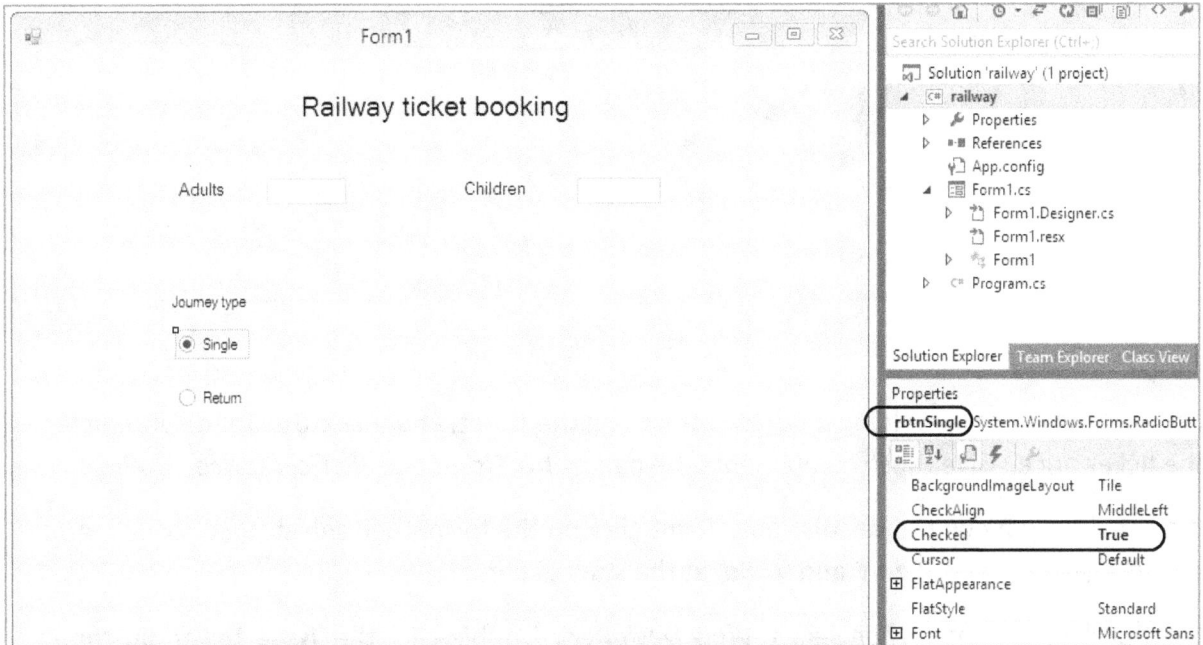

Run the program to test the radio group. If this works correctly, the '*Single*' button should initially be selected. It should only be possible to select one of the options:

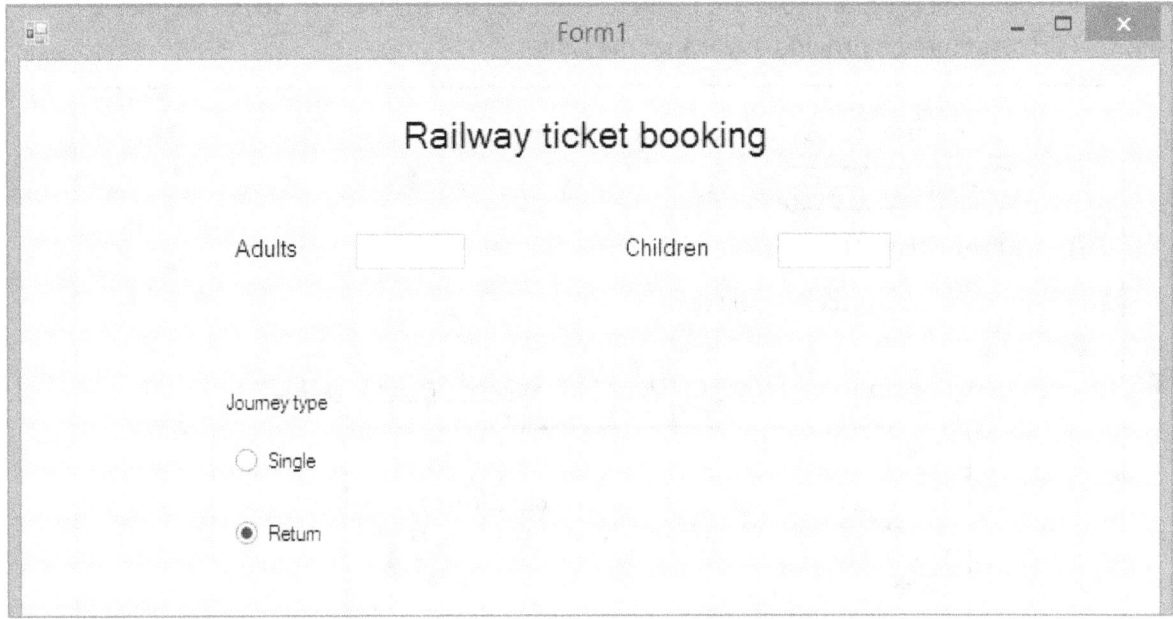

Stop the program by clicking the red cross at the top right-hand corner of the form.

Return to the design screen and add another **GroupBox** and two **RadioButtons** to allow the user to select a '*First class*' or '*Second class*' ticket.

Give the RadioButtons the names **rbtnFirst** and **rbtnSecond**. Set the **Checked** property of the '*Second*' RadioButton to *True*.

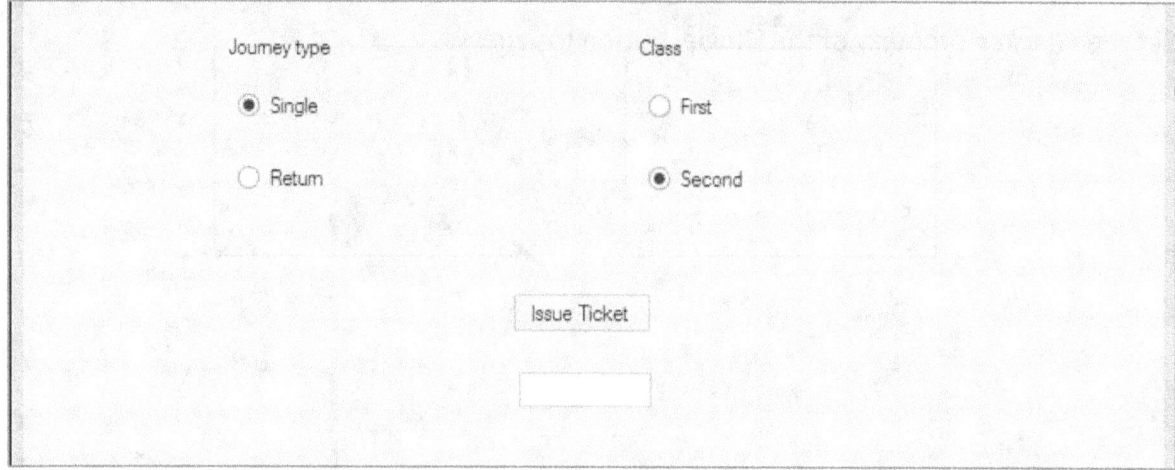

Complete the form by adding a **Button** for issuing the ticket, and a **TextBox** for displaying the ticket price. Give these components the names **btnTicket** and **txtTicketprice**.

We can now work on the calculations. Right-click on the form, then select '*View Code*'. Add two integer variables '*adult*' and '*child*' at the start of Form1.

Right-click on the form, then select '*View Designer*'. Double-click the '*Issue Ticket*' button to create a button_click method. Add lines of code to obtain the numbers of adults and children from the TextBox inputs.

We do not want the program to crash if the user makes an entry error, so we will use a TRY..CATCH structure to provide a warning message:

```
public partial class Form1 : Form
{
    int adult, child;

    public Form1()
    {
        InitializeComponent();
    }

    private void btnTicket_Click(object sender, EventArgs e)
    {
        try
        {
            adult = Convert.ToInt16(txtAdult.Text);
            child = Convert.ToInt16(txtChild.Text);
        }
        catch
        {
            MessageBox.Show("Incorrect entry");
        }
    }
```

Run the program to test the error trapping. This should give an *'incorrect entry'* message if letters are typed instead of a number, but unfortunately the warning also appears if we leave a box blank – for example, if no children are travelling:

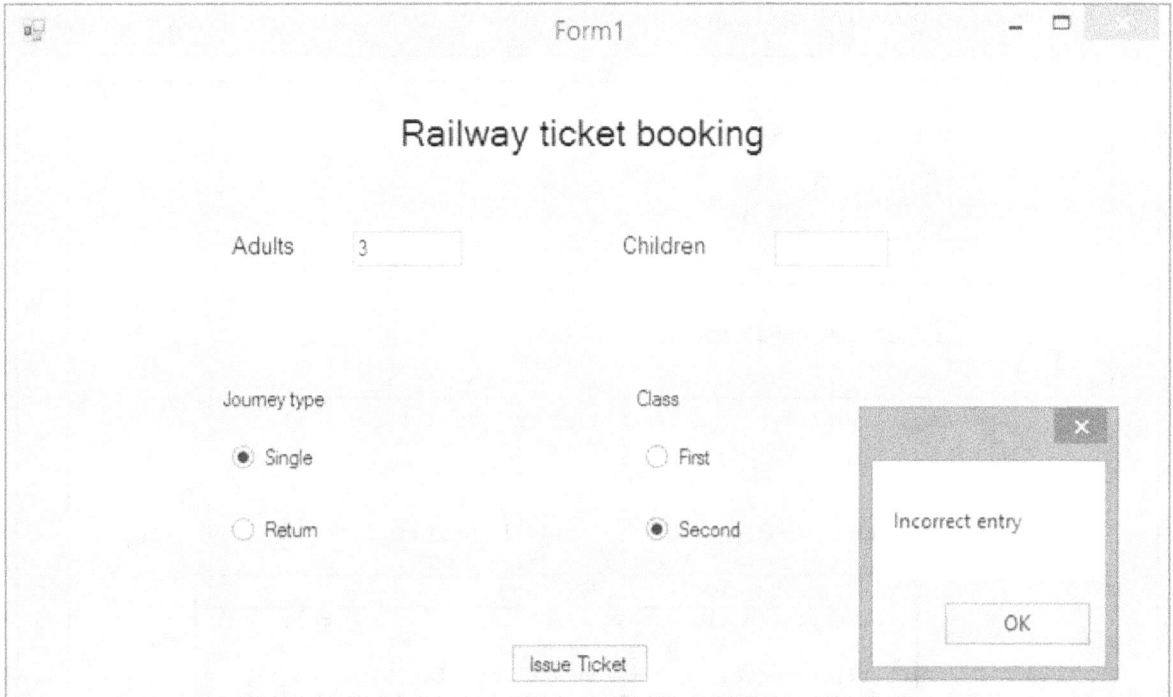

Return to the design screen. Select each of the input TextBoxes in turn, and set the Text property to '*0*'.

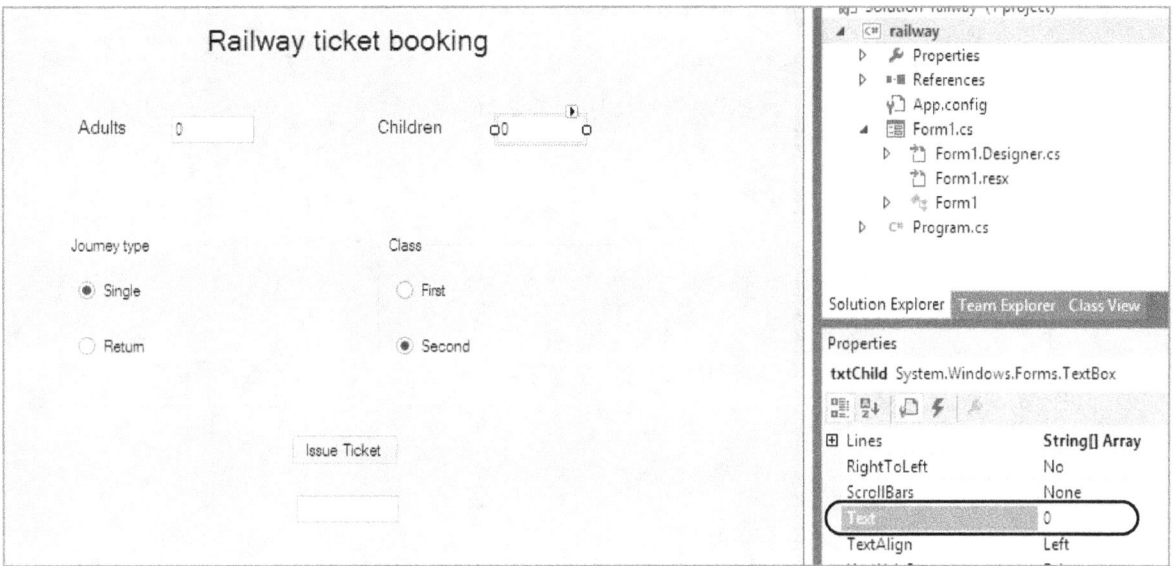

Run the program again and check that no error message appears when booking for one adult travelling on their own. Close the program window and go to the program code.

We can now start work on calculating the ticket cost. Set up a variable '*ticketcost*' which will store this as a decimal number to represent pounds and pence.

The fare structure is quite complex, so it is best to split the calculation into a series of stages, and test the program after each stage. We can begin by working out the cost of the adult and child tickets, assuming a single fare of £6.40, with children paying 60% of the adult cost. The total can then be displayed in the TextBox:

```csharp
public partial class Form1 : Form
{
    int adult, child;
    double ticketcost;

    public Form1()
    {
        InitializeComponent();
    }

    private void btnTicket_Click(object sender, EventArgs e)
    {
        try
        {
            adult = Convert.ToInt16(txtAdult.Text);
            child = Convert.ToInt16(txtChild.Text);
            ticketcost = adult * 6.40;
            ticketcost = ticketcost + (child * 6.40 * 0.60);

            txtTicketprice.Text = Convert.ToString(ticketcost);
        }
}
```

Run the program and check the calculations for different numbers of adults and children (remembering that all tickets are currently *second class single*).

Railway ticket booking

Adults: 2   Children: 0

Journey type:
- ● Single
- ○ Return

Class:
- ○ First
- ● Second

Issue Ticket

12.8

The calculations should be correct, but we have a problem with the display format. In some cases, the pence are not shown correctly with two decimal places.

Go back to the program listing, and alter the code to ensure that the output is always displayed to two decimal places:

```
        try
        {
            adult = Convert.ToInt16(txtAdult.Text);
            child = Convert.ToInt16(txtChild.Text);
            ticketcost = adult * 6.40;
            ticketcost = ticketcost + (child * 6.40 * 0.60);

            string s=ticketcost.ToString("f2");
            txtTicketprice.Text = s;

        }
```

We can now consider the other ticket options. Begin by setting up two **Boolean** (true/false) variables called '*single*' and '*first*':

```
        public partial class Form1 : Form
        {
            int adult, child;
            double ticketcost;

            bool single;
            bool first;

            public Form1()
            {
                InitializeComponent();
            }
```

We will use the '*single*' variable to record the type of journey:

- *single = true*   means   'single ticket wanted'
- *single = false*   means   'return ticket wanted'

An easy way to set the value of '*single*' is just to see whether the '*Single*' RadioButton has been selected. If not, then the user must require a '*Return*' ticket and we add the extra cost as one and a half times the single fare. Add lines to the program as shown:

```
        try
        {
            adult = Convert.ToInt16(txtAdult.Text);
            child = Convert.ToInt16(txtChild.Text);
            ticketcost = adult * 6.40;
            ticketcost = ticketcost + (child * 6.40 * 0.60);

            single = rbtnSingle.Checked;
            if (single == false)
            {
                ticketcost = ticketcost * 1.5;
            }

            string s=ticketcost.ToString("f2");
            txtTicketprice.Text = s;
        }
```

Run the program and test that second class Single and Return fares are now calculated correctly:

Railway ticket booking

Adults: 2   Children: 3

Journey type: ● Return (○ Single)
Class: ● Second (○ First)

[Issue Ticket]

36.48

We will use a similar method to add the First Class charge of £2.00 per person:

```
try
{
    adult = Convert.ToInt16(txtAdult.Text);
    child = Convert.ToInt16(txtChild.Text);
    ticketcost = adult * 6.40;
    ticketcost = ticketcost + (child * 6.40 * 0.60);
    single = rbtnSingle.Checked;

    if (single == false)
    {
        ticketcost = ticketcost * 1.5;
    }

    first = rbtnFirst.Checked;

    if (first == true)
    {
        ticketcost = ticketcost + (adult + child) * 2.00;
    }

    string s=ticketcost.ToString("f2");
    txtTicketprice.Text = s;
}
```

Run the program and check that First Class fares are now calculated correctly.

The final step to complete the ticket calculation is to apply the 20% discount offered to groups of four or more passengers:

```
    first = rbtnFirst.Checked;
    if (first == true)
    {
        ticketcost = ticketcost + (adult + child) * 2.00;
    }

    if ((adult + child) >= 4)
    {
        ticketcost = ticketcost - (ticketcost * 0.2);
    }

    string s=ticketcost.ToString("f2");
    txtTicketprice.Text = s;
```

Run the program and check that group discounts are being calculated correctly.

We will now move on to produce the ticket for the customer …

Begin by creating another form. To do this, right-click on the C# *'railway'* icon in the **Solution Explorer** window, then select *'Add / New Item'*:

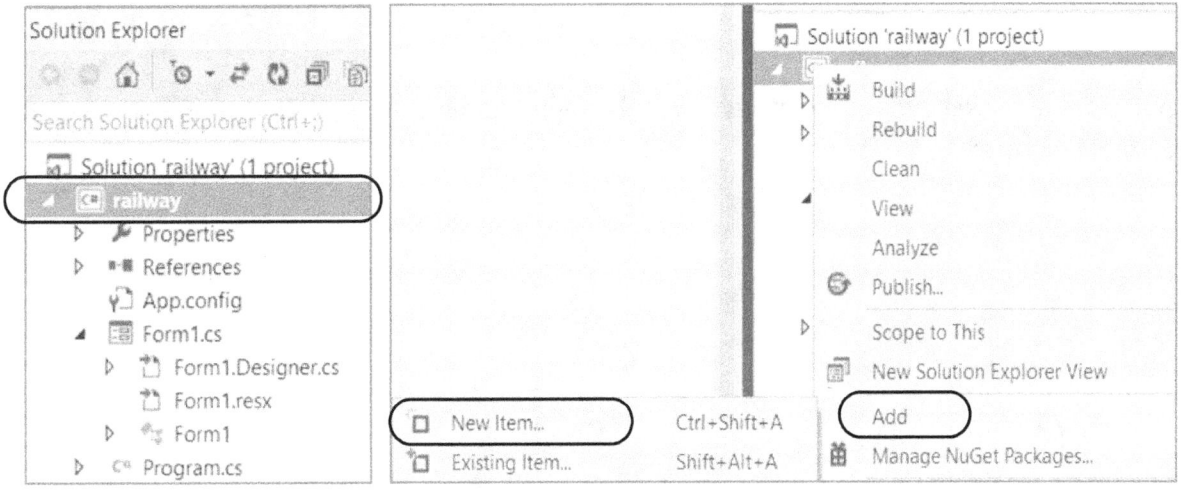

Select *'Windows Form'*, and give this the name *'Ticket.cs'*:

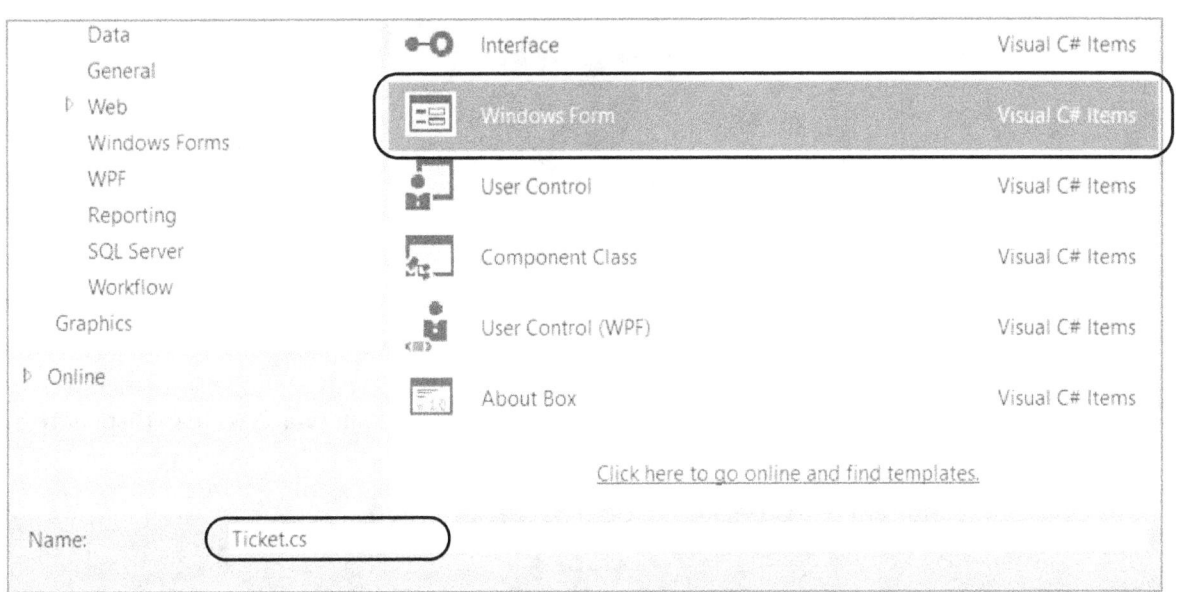

It will be best to use a white background. Click on the form, then go to **BackColor** in the Properties window. Click to open the colour selection palettes, and choose white from the **Custom** palette:

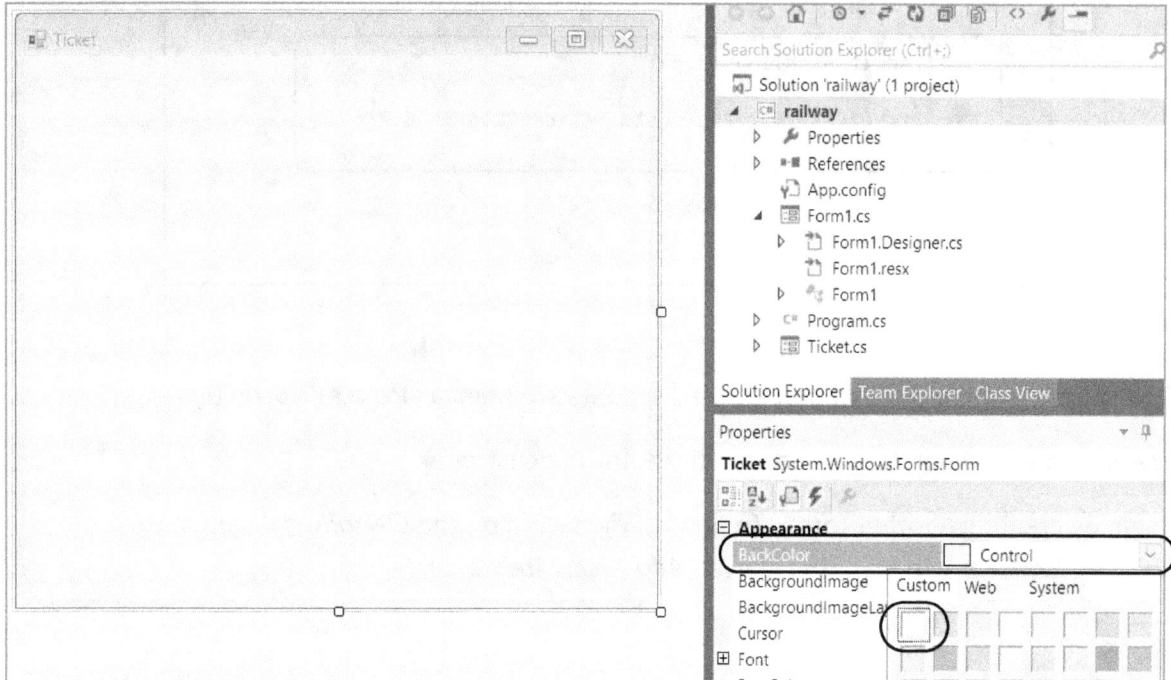

Add a Label '**Ticket**'. Place a **Picture Box** in the right hand half of the ticket area, and insert a suitable picture:

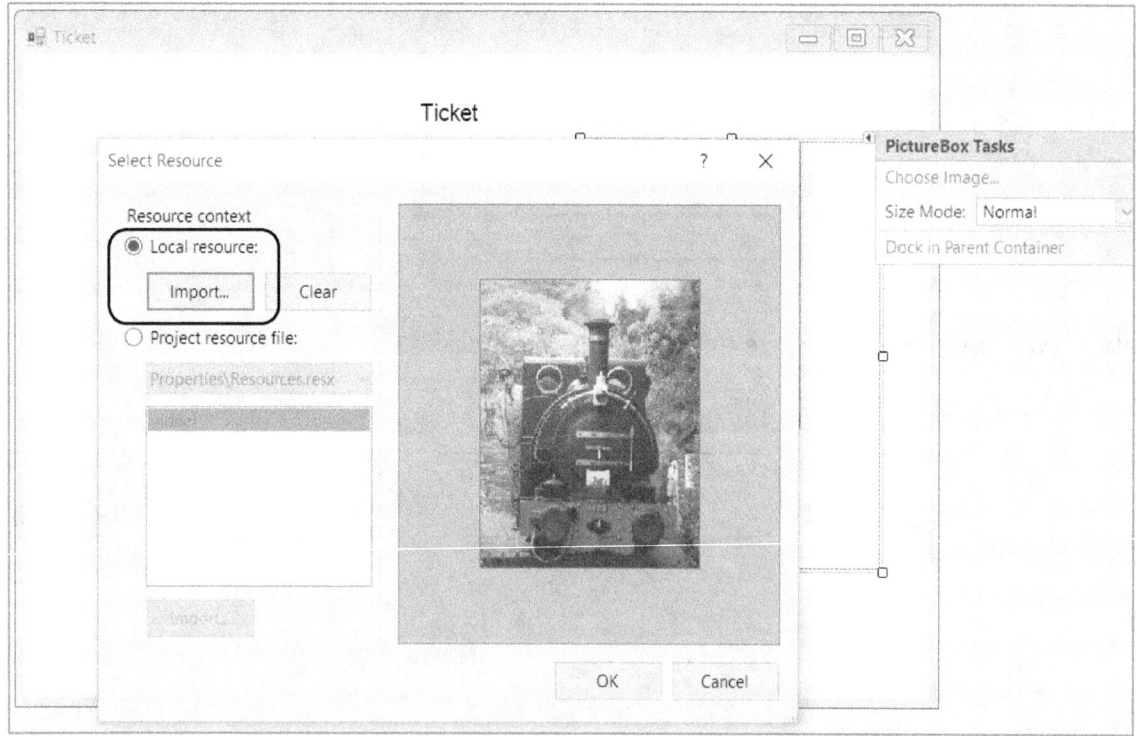

The final component we need to produce the ticket is a **ListBox**, in which we can display the ticket details.

Select the ListBox component in the Toolbox and drag the mouse on the form to produce a box outline. Go to the Properties window, and set the Font property to display a larger point size.

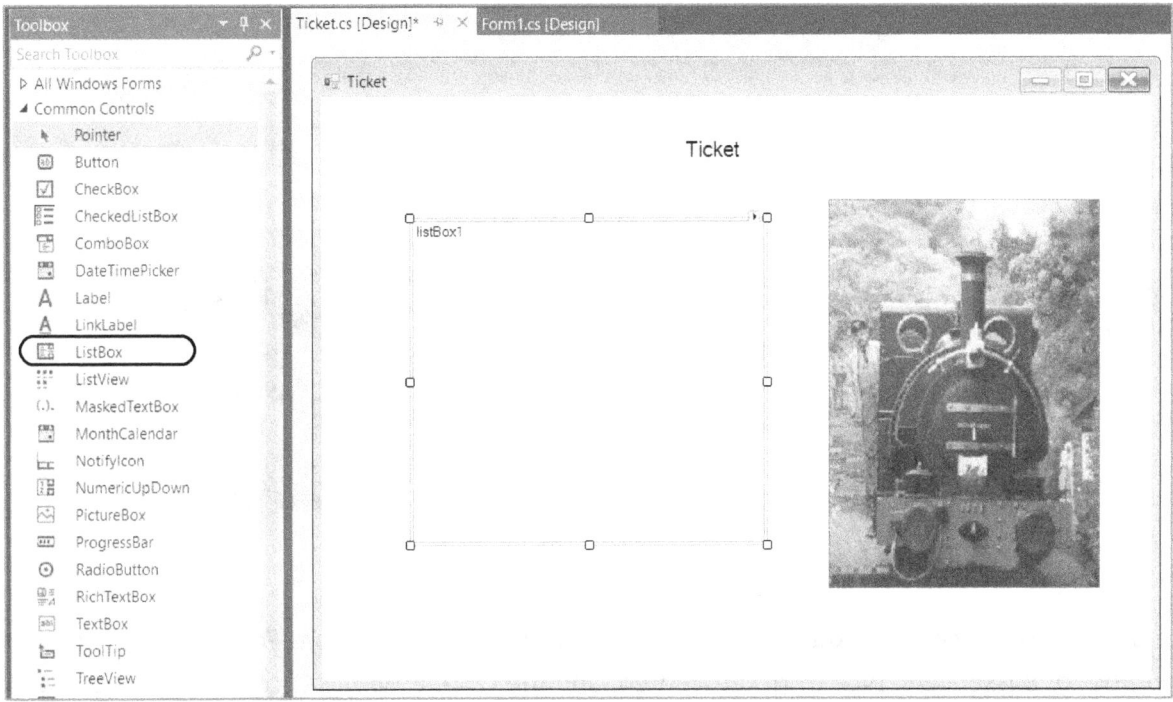

The Ticket form needs to open when the 'Issue Ticket' button is clicked on Form1. To do this, go to the end of the button_click method on Form1, and add the lines of code:

```
        if ((adult + child) >= 4)
        {
            ticketcost = ticketcost - (ticketcost * 0.2);
        }
        string s=ticketcost.ToString("f2");
        txtTicketprice.Text = s;

        Ticket frmticket = new Ticket();
        frmticket.ShowDialog();
    }
    catch
    {
        MessageBox.Show("Incorrect entry");
    }
```

We are using '*Ticket*' to refer to the CLASS we have designed for displaying tickets, whilst '*frmticket*' is one particular OBJECT belonging to this class which we will create when the program is running.

Run the program, enter ticket details, and then click the '*Issue Ticket*' button. If all goes well, the ticket form should open:

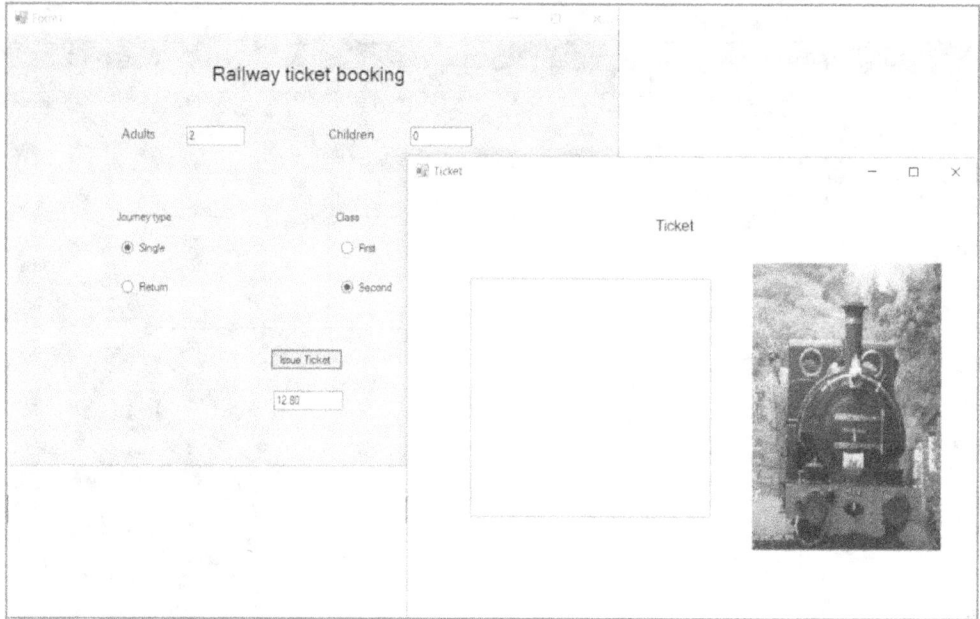

In order to produce the ticket, we need to carry over information from **Form1** about the number of passengers, type of ticket wanted, and the calculated ticket cost. The best way to do this is to set up a method on the '*Ticket*' form which brings in this data as *parameters*. Set up the method '*displayTicket*' as shown:

```csharp
public partial class Ticket : Form
{
    public Ticket()
    {
        InitializeComponent();
    }

    public void displayTicket(int adults, int children, bool single,
                                        bool first, double ticketcost)
    {

    }
}
```

We can now return to **Form1** and add a line of code which will call this method, using the values we wish to transfer as parameters:

```csharp
        string s=ticketcost.ToString("f2");
        txtTicketprice.Text = s;
        Ticket frmticket = new Ticket();
        frmticket.displayTicket(adult, child, single, first, ticketcost);
        frmticket.ShowDialog();
    }
```

Go back now to the '*Ticket*' program code. The data we need should now be available, using the parameter names we have specified in the header of the '*displayTicket*' method.

We can begin by displaying the number of adults. ListBoxes, like TextBoxes, can only display string data, so it is necessary to convert the number into string format.

```
public void displayTicket(int adults, int children, bool single,
                          bool first, double ticketcost)
{
    string s = Convert.ToString(adults);
    listBox1.Items.Add(s + " adults");
}
```

Run the program. Issue a ticket, and check that the correct number of adults is displayed on the ticket:

Return to the '*displayTicket*' method and add lines of code to display the other ticket details. Notice that we have used an **IF** condition to only display the number of children when there are actually children included in the ticket:

```
public void displayTicket(int adults, int children, bool single,
                          bool first, double ticketcost)
{
    string s = Convert.ToString(adults);
    listBox1.Items.Add(s + " adults");

    s = Convert.ToString(children);
    if (children>0)
        listBox1.Items.Add(s + " children");
    if (single==true)
        listBox1.Items.Add("Single");
    else
        listBox1.Items.Add("Return");
    if (first == true)
        listBox1.Items.Add("First class");
    else
        listBox1.Items.Add("Second class");
}
```

Test the program for the different possibilities of: adults plus children or adults only, single or return, first or second class:

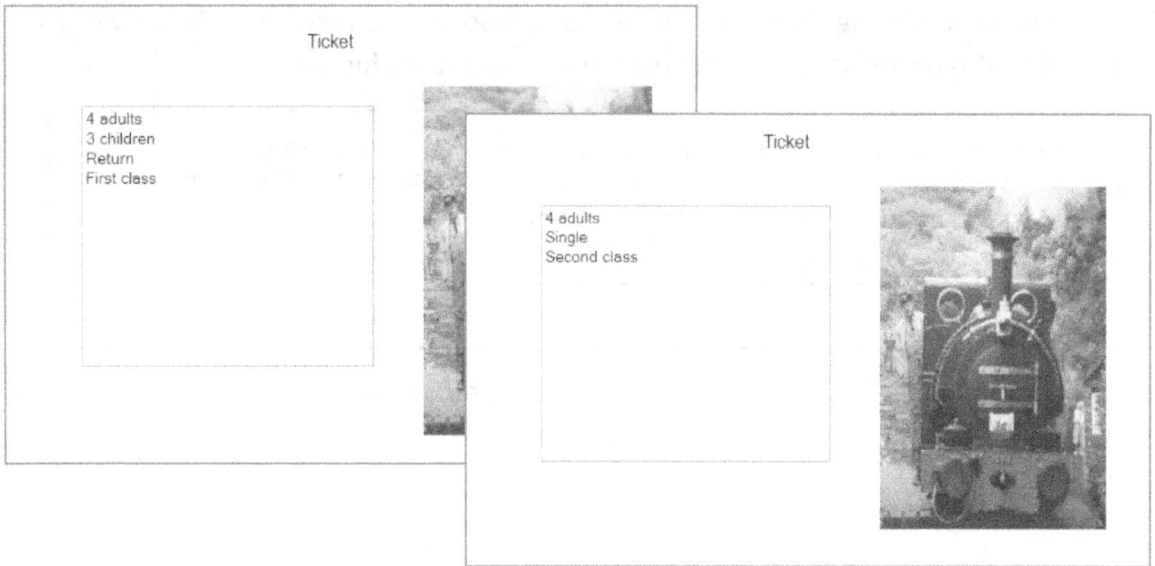

Add code to display discount for groups, and to show the overall ticket price:

```
        if (first == true)
            listBox1.Items.Add("First class");
        else
            listBox1.Items.Add("Second class");

        if ((adults+children)>=4)
            listBox1.Items.Add("20% group discount");
        listBox1.Items.Add("");
        s = ticketcost.ToString("f2");
        listBox1.Items.Add("£"+s);
    }
}
```

Test the finished program. One slight improvement you might try making yourself, is to display the singular word '*adult*' or '*child*' when only one person is travelling, rather than the plural:

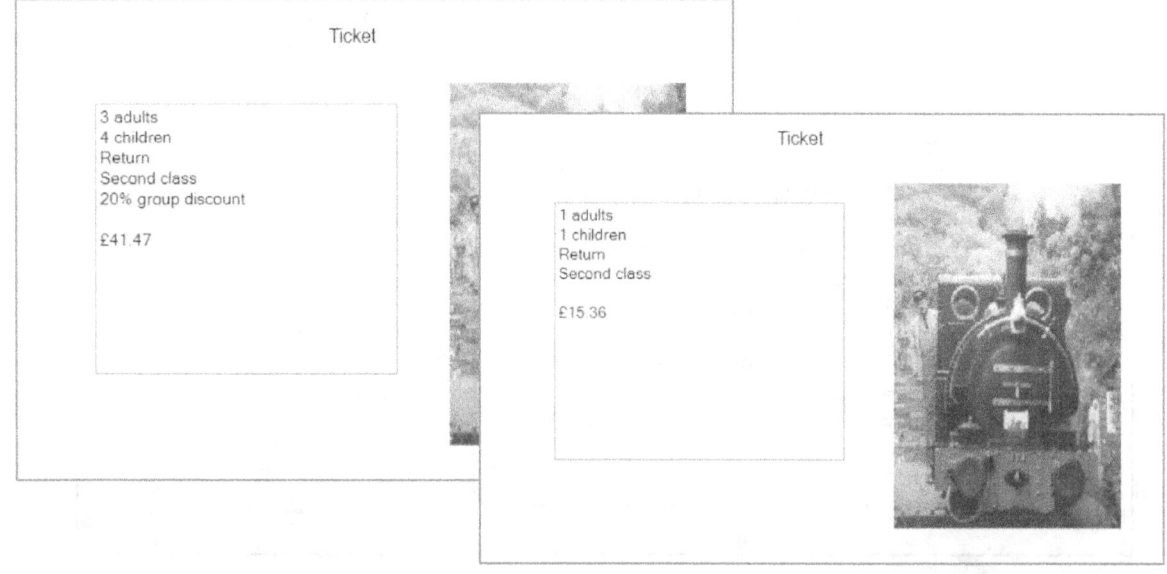

4 Solitaire

For our next application, we will produce an on-screen version of the game Solitaire.

Solitaire is a game for one player. The board consists of a cross-shaped array of holes, into which pegs or other playing pieces are inserted. At the start of the game, all holes are occupied except for the one central position.

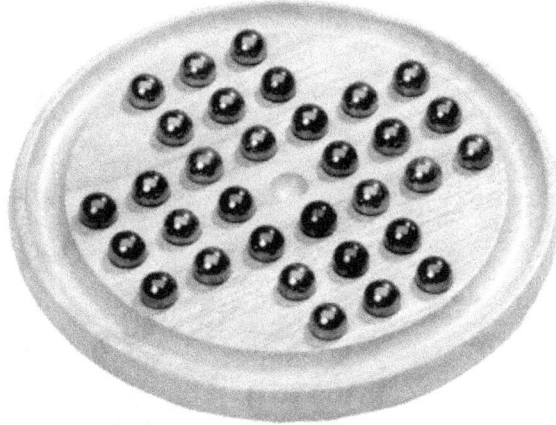

The objective of the game is to remove all but one of the playing pieces, leaving this single piece in the central hole.

A move is made by jumping a playing piece over the top of another piece, to land in a hole. The jumped piece is removed from the board. Moves may occur along the horizontal or vertical lines of the grid, but not diagonally.

In this project, we will produce an interactive graphical program to allow the user to play the game of Solitaire on screen using the mouse. The program should remove jumped pieces from the board automatically, but should only allow valid moves to be made. Begin by setting up a Windows Forms Application. Give this the name '*solitaire*':

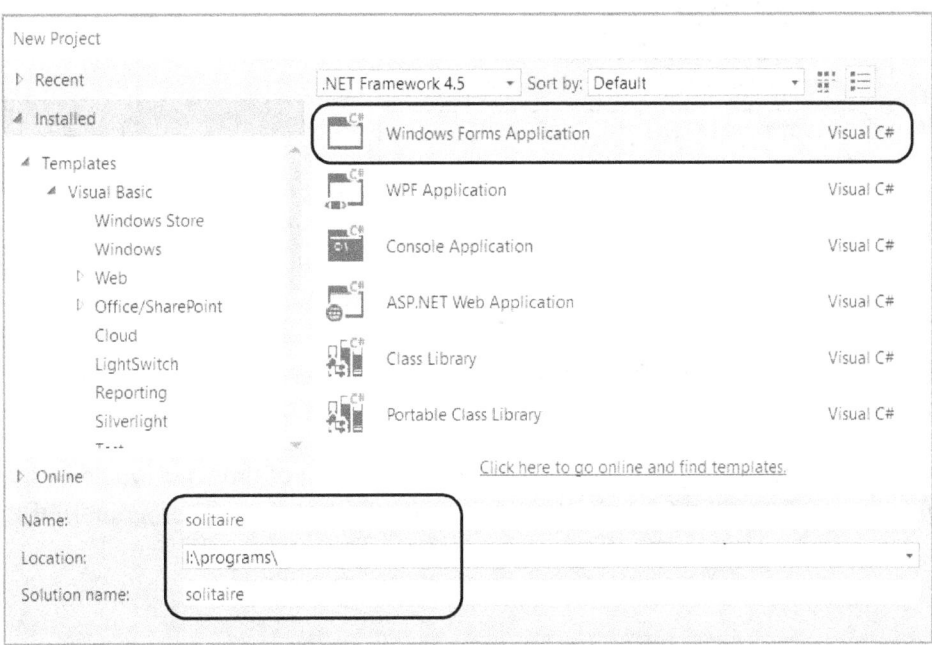

We will begin by putting a **Panel** component onto Form1. Drag the mouse to produce an outline for the playing area. Give the Panel the name '*pnlGame*'

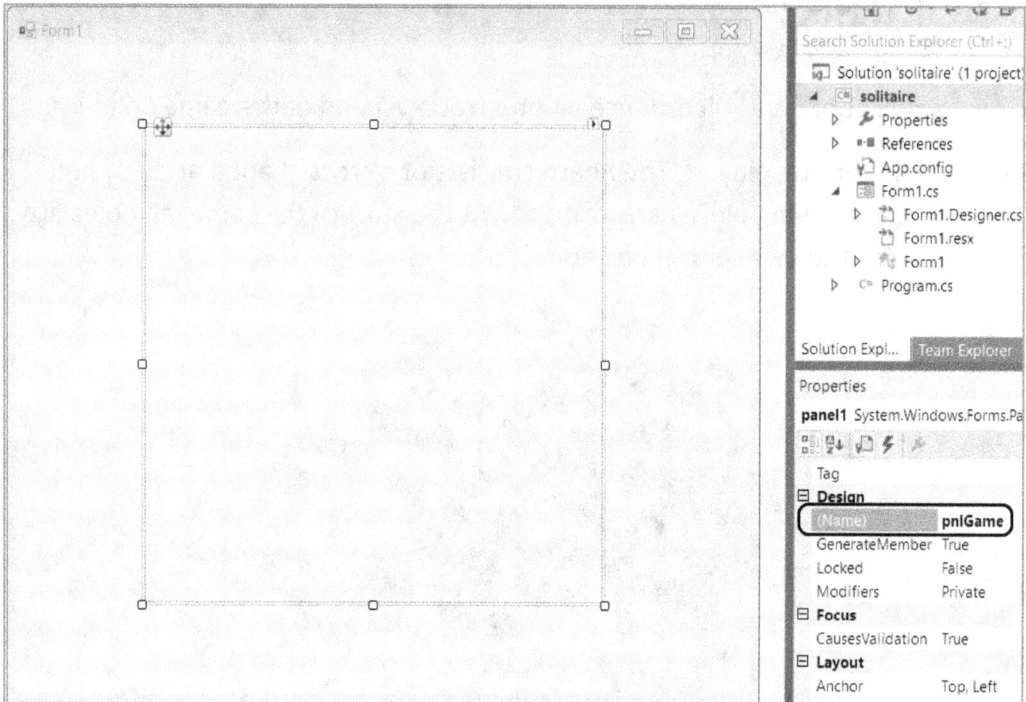

Right-click on Form1 and select '**View Code**'.

Create an empty method called *initialiseBoard( )*. We will add code to this later to display the playing pieces.

Add a line to the **Form1( )** method to call *initialiseBoard( )* when the program starts:

```
namespace solitaire
{
    public partial class Form1 : Form
    {
        public Form1()
        {
            InitializeComponent();
            initialiseBoard();
        }

        private void initialiseBoard()
        {

        }
    }
}
```

A simple way to make the interactive screen for the game is to create a pattern of Button components to represent the grid of playing pieces and holes.

Rather than adding each button by hand, which would take a lot of time and would be inaccurate, we can write program code to set up the buttons automatically when the program runs.

Begin by creating a ***two dimensional array*** of ***Button*** components by adding the line of code above the ***initialiseBoard( )*** method.

Within ***initialiseBoard( )*** we can use two nested loops to produce a rectangular grid of 7 rows and 7 columns of buttons. Each button will have a width and height of 40 pixels, and we change the top left corner position of each button so that it fits correctly into the grid pattern.

```
public Form1()
{
    InitializeComponent();
    initialiseBoard();
}

Button[,] btnGame = new Button[8, 8];

private void initialiseBoard()
{
    for (int i = 1; i <= 7; i++)
    {
        for (int j = 1; j <= 7; j++)
        {
            btnGame[i, j] = new Button();
            btnGame[i, j].Width = 40;
            btnGame[i, j].Height = 40;
            btnGame[i, j].Left = (40 * i);
            btnGame[i, j].Top = (40 * j);
            pnlGame.Controls.Add(btnGame[i, j]);
        }
    }
}
```

Run the program, and a grid of buttons should be created:

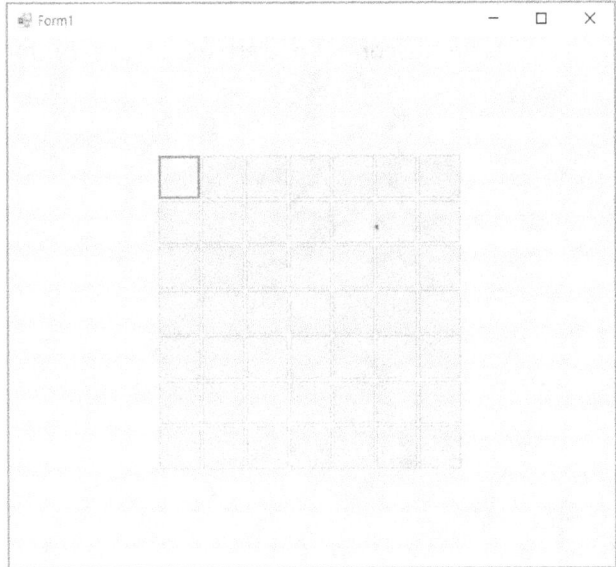

This is a good start, but the playing area is actually in the shape of a cross, with the four corner areas omitted. We can modify the ***initialiseBoard( )*** method to allow for this.

Set up a **Boolean** variable called '***present***'. For any grid position, we will set 'present' to **TRUE** if a button is required, but **FALSE** if that position is to be left blank.

Add the nested **IF..** conditions which will set 'present' to FALSE for each of the corner areas of the cross.

```csharp
private void initialiseBoard()
{
    bool present;

    for (int i = 1; i <= 7; i++)
    {
        for (int j = 1; j <= 7; j++)
        {
            present = true;
            if (i <= 2 || i >= 6)
            {
                if (j <= 2 || j >= 6)
                {
                    present = false;
                }
            }

            if (present == true)
            {
                btnGame[i, j] = new Button();
                btnGame[i, j].Width = 40;
                btnGame[i, j].Height = 40;
                btnGame[i, j].Left = (40 * i);
                btnGame[i, j].Top = (40 * j);
                pnlGame.Controls.Add(btnGame[i, j]);
            }
        }
    }
}
```

Run the program, and we should now have the correct pattern of buttons for the playing area:

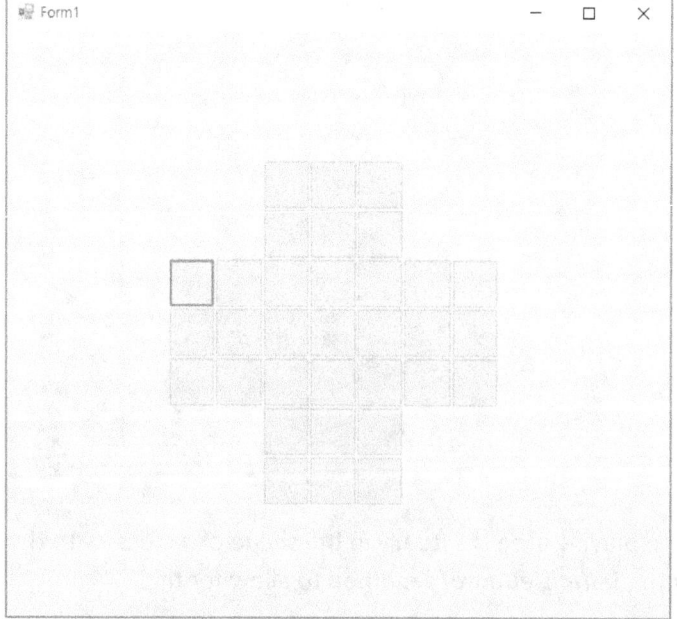

Chapter 4: Solitaire   35

The next step is to make the board look more realistic by adding graphics to represent the playing pieces and holes. Two small graphics images will be needed, which can be displayed on the buttons as appropriate:

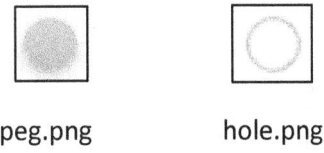

peg.png   hole.png

Create or copy these images, and store them somewhere on your computer.

We will now import the images into the C# project. To do this, go to the Solution Explorer window and right-click on the '*solitaire*' program icon. Select '**Add / Existing Item**'.

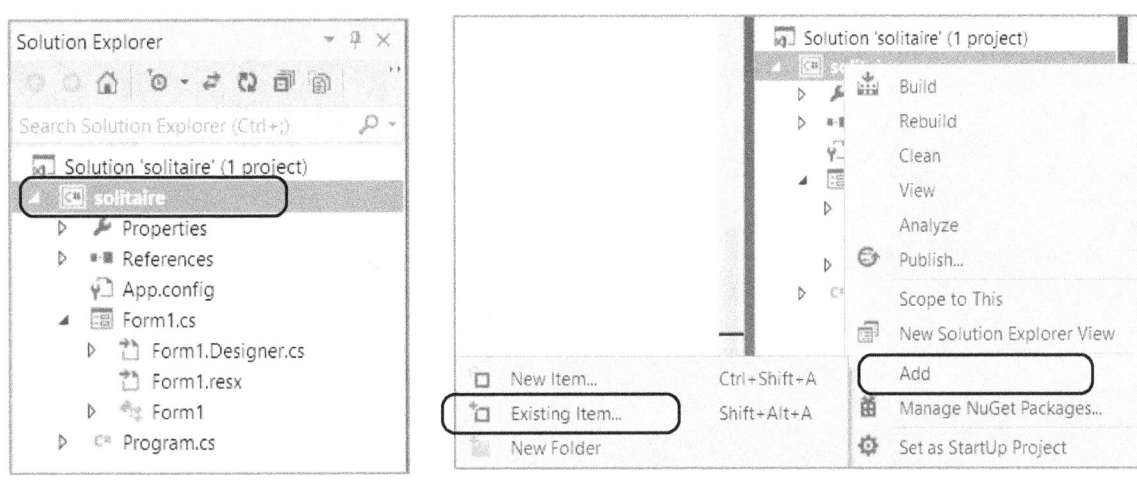

Set the file type to '*All Files*' and navigate to where the graphics images are saved. Click '**Add**' for each image file:

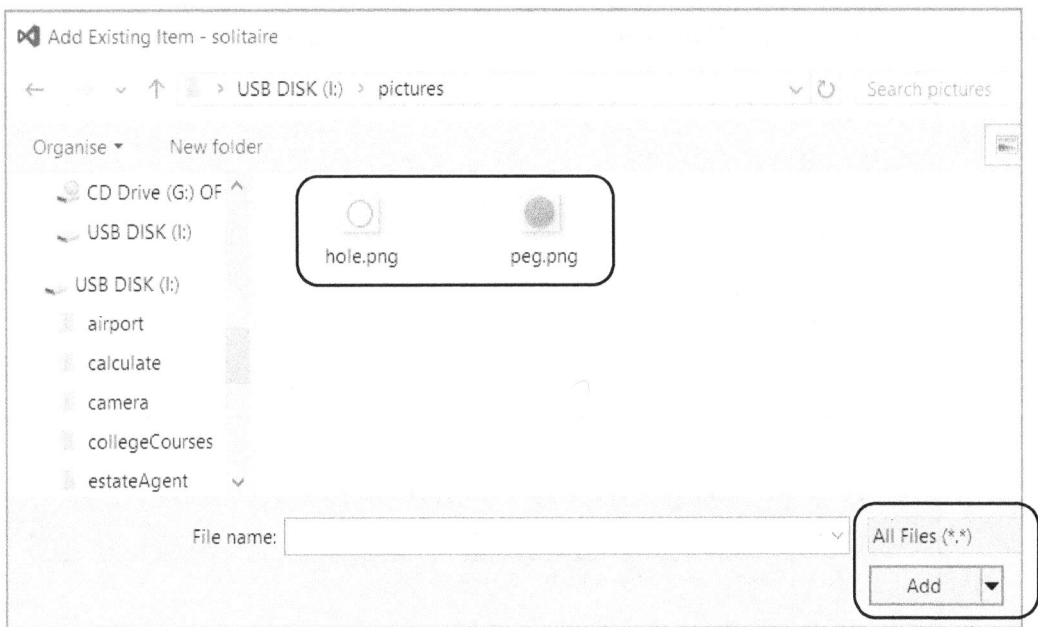

We can now return to the *initialiseBoard( )* method, and add a line of code to display the '*peg.png*' image on each button:

```
if (present == true)
{
    btnGame[i, j] = new Button();
    btnGame[i, j].Width = 40;
    btnGame[i, j].Height = 40;
    btnGame[i, j].Left = (40 * i);
    btnGame[i, j].Top = (40 * j);

    btnGame[i, j].Image = Image.FromFile("../../peg.png");

    pnlGame.Controls.Add(btnGame[i, j]);
}
```

Run the program, and the pattern of playing pieces should appear:

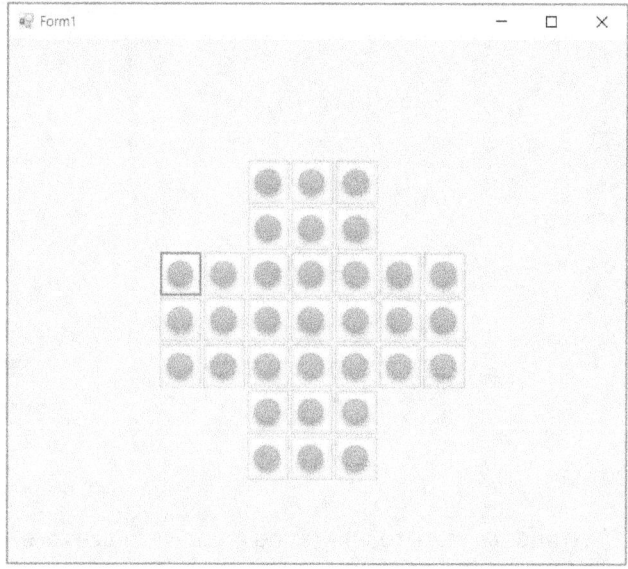

This is almost correct, but we need to begin the game with an empty hole at the centre of the board. Add code to the *initialiseBoard( )* method to treat this as a special case:

```
if (present == true)
{
    btnGame[i, j] = new Button();
    btnGame[i, j].Width = 40;
    btnGame[i, j].Height = 40;
    btnGame[i, j].Left = (40 * i);
    btnGame[i, j].Top = (40 * j);

    btnGame[i, j].Image = Image.FromFile("../../peg.png");

    if (i == 4 && j == 4)
    {
        btnGame[i, j].Image = Image.FromFile("../../hole.png");
    }

    pnlGame.Controls.Add(btnGame[i, j]);
}
```

Run the program and check that the pattern is now correct:

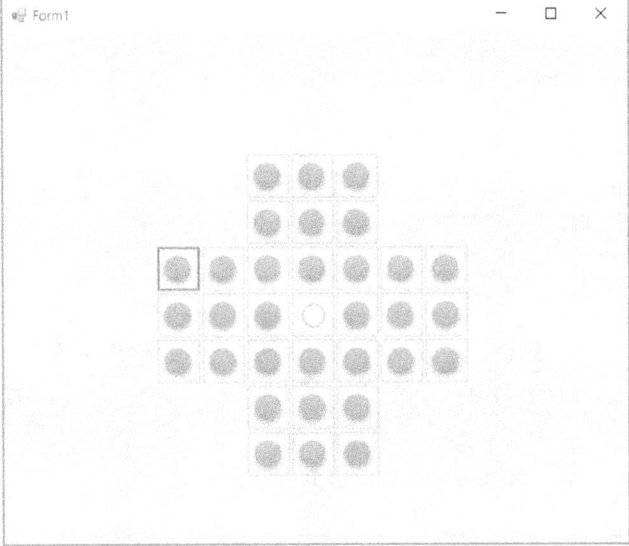

The next stage is to play the game, but before that we must provide the program with a way of recording the positions of the playing pieces and the empty holes. This will be necessary if the computer is going to check for valid moves.

A simple method is to use a two dimensional array of code numbers which correspond to the buttons on the game board. For each button displaying a '*peg*', the equivalent **code value will be 1**. For each button displaying a '*hole*', the equivalent **code value will be 0**.

Start by setting up the array:

```
public partial class Form1 : Form
{
    public Form1()
    {
        InitializeComponent();
        initialiseBoard();
    }

    Button[,] btnGame = new Button[8, 8];
    int[,] play = new int[8, 8];
```

Go to the *initialiseBoard( )* method.

At the point where a button is set to display the '*peg*' image, we will set the corresponding value in the '*play*' array to **1**.

At the point where the central button is set to display the '*hole*' image, we will set the corresponding value in the '*play*' array to **0**:

```
            if (present == true)
        {
            btnGame[i, j] = new Button();
            btnGame[i, j].Width = 40;
            btnGame[i, j].Height = 40;
            btnGame[i, j].Left = (40 * i);
            btnGame[i, j].Top = (40 * j);

            btnGame[i, j].Image = Image.FromFile("../../peg.png");
            play[i, j] = 1;

            if (i == 4 && j == 4)
            {
                btnGame[i, j].Image = Image.FromFile("../../hole.png");
                play[i, j] = 0;
            }

            pnlGame.Controls.Add(btnGame[i, j]);
        }
```

We can now consider the way that the user will play the game, by clicking on the piece which they wish to move, then clicking on the hole to which it should be moved. For this to work, the program must be able to:

- identify which buttons have been clicked, and
- have a method which will process the move.

We will add some code to do these things…

We can allocate names to each button, made up from its column and row position. For example, the button in the middle of the top row will be: '**btn41**', and the button in the centre of the board will be '**btn44**'. The button names are created using the loop counter values **i** and **j**

For the button to respond when it is clicked, we need to create an event handler, and set up an empty button-click method:

```
                if (i == 4 && j == 4)
                {
                    btnGame[i, j].Image = Image.FromFile("../../hole.png");
                    play[i, j] = 0;
                }

                String buttonName = "btn" + i + j;
                btnGame[i, j].Name = buttonName;
                btnGame[i, j].Click += new EventHandler(game_Click);

                pnlGame.Controls.Add(btnGame[i, j]);
            }
        }
    }
}

private void game_Click(object sender, EventArgs e)
{

}
```

Chapter 4: Solitaire

We can now think about the game play. This is quite complex, so we need a way of checking that the program is working correctly. For testing purposes, add a *ListBox* component at the side of the playing grid. This will be removed later when we are sure that the processing is correct.

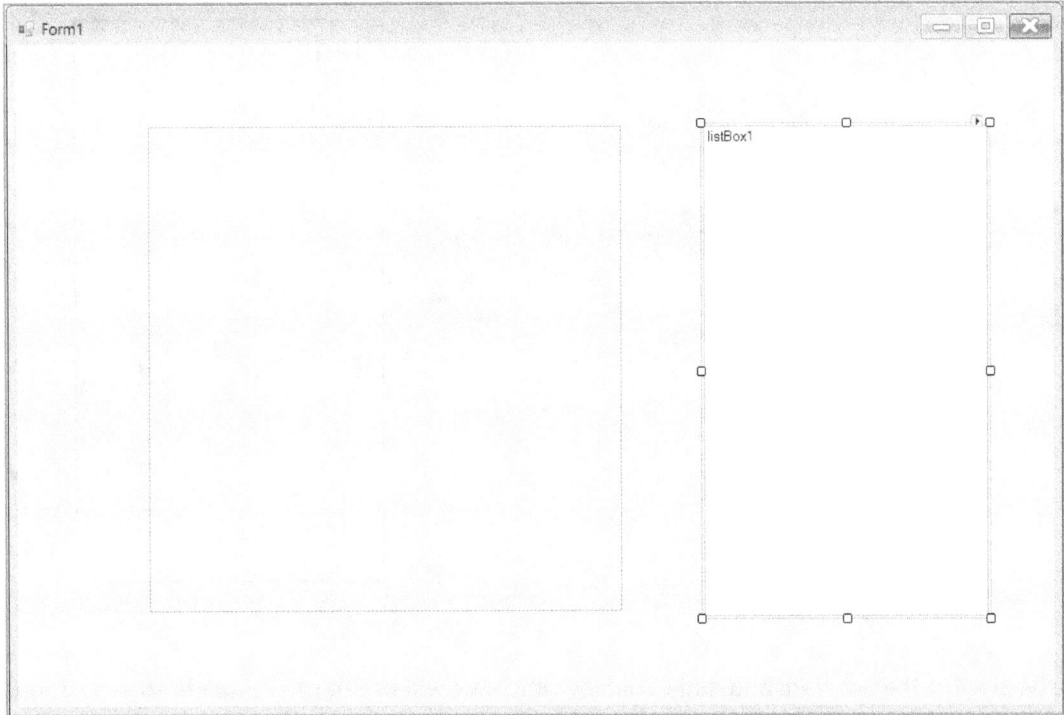

It is important that the program correctly identifies the button that is clicked.

Add code to the *game_Click( )* method which will check the name of the button and use this to determine its column and row number. We will output these values to the *ListBox*, to ensure that they are correct.

```
private void game_Click(object sender, EventArgs e)
{
    Button clickedButton = (Button)sender;

    string s = clickedButton.Name;
    int Ipos = Convert.ToInt16(s.Substring(3, 1));
    int Jpos = Convert.ToInt16(s.Substring(4, 1));

    listBox1.Items.Add("i = " + Ipos);
    listBox1.Items.Add("j = " + Jpos);
}
```

Run the program. Click on different buttons, and check that the correct column and row values are given in each case:

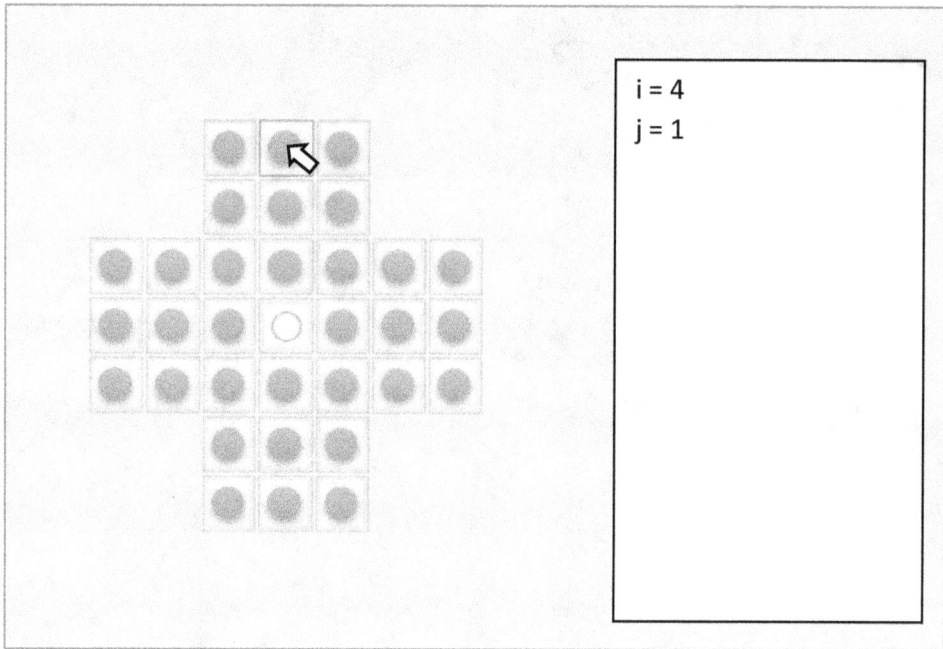

Go to the start of the program and add variables which we will use to record the button positions clicked during a move.

```
public Form1()
{
    InitializeComponent();
    initialiseBoard();
}

Button[,] btnGame = new Button[8, 8];
int[,] play = new int[8, 8];
int startI = 0, startJ = 0, finishI = 0, finishJ = 0;
```

Two buttons must be clicked by the player in order to make a move – firstly on the **piece they wish to move**, and then on the **hole to which it will move**. The following lines of code record the column and row positions of each of the button clicks:

- We begin with the start position undefined, with a column value of zero. When the button is first clicked, the x- and y-coordinates are assigned to the '***start***' variables.
- When the button is clicked again, the coordinates are assigned to the '***finish***' variables.
- The move made by the player can then be checked against the rules of the game, and the move carried out if it is valid.
- The '***start***' column variable is then set back to zero, ready to receive the pair of button clicks during the next move.

Add the lines of code to carry out these actions, and set up an empty method ready for the code which will check and carry out the moves.

```
        listBox1.Items.Add("i = " + Ipos);
        listBox1.Items.Add("j = " + Jpos);
        if (startI == 0)
        {
            startI = Ipos;
            startJ = Jpos;
        }
        else
        {
            finishI = Ipos;
            finishJ = Jpos;
            checkMove(startI,startJ,finishI,finishJ);
            startI = 0;
        }
    }

    private void checkMove(int startI,int startJ,int finishI,int finishJ)
    {

    }
```

Once the program enters the **checkMove( )** method, it should know the start and finish positions for the proposed move. Let's begin by checking that these positions are being identified correctly from the mouse clicks.

Add lines of code to the **checkMove( )** method which will output the start and finish positions to the list box:

```
    private void checkMove(int startI,int startJ,int finishI,int finishJ)
    {
        listBox1.Items.Add("Checking move from: ");

        listBox1.Items.Add("i=" + startI + ", j=" + startJ);

        listBox1.Items.Add("to: ");
        listBox1.Items.Add("i=" + finishI + ", j=" + finishJ);

        listBox1.Items.Add("");
    }
```

Run the program. Click on pairs of buttons, and verify that the correct column and row positions are being recorded in the list box:

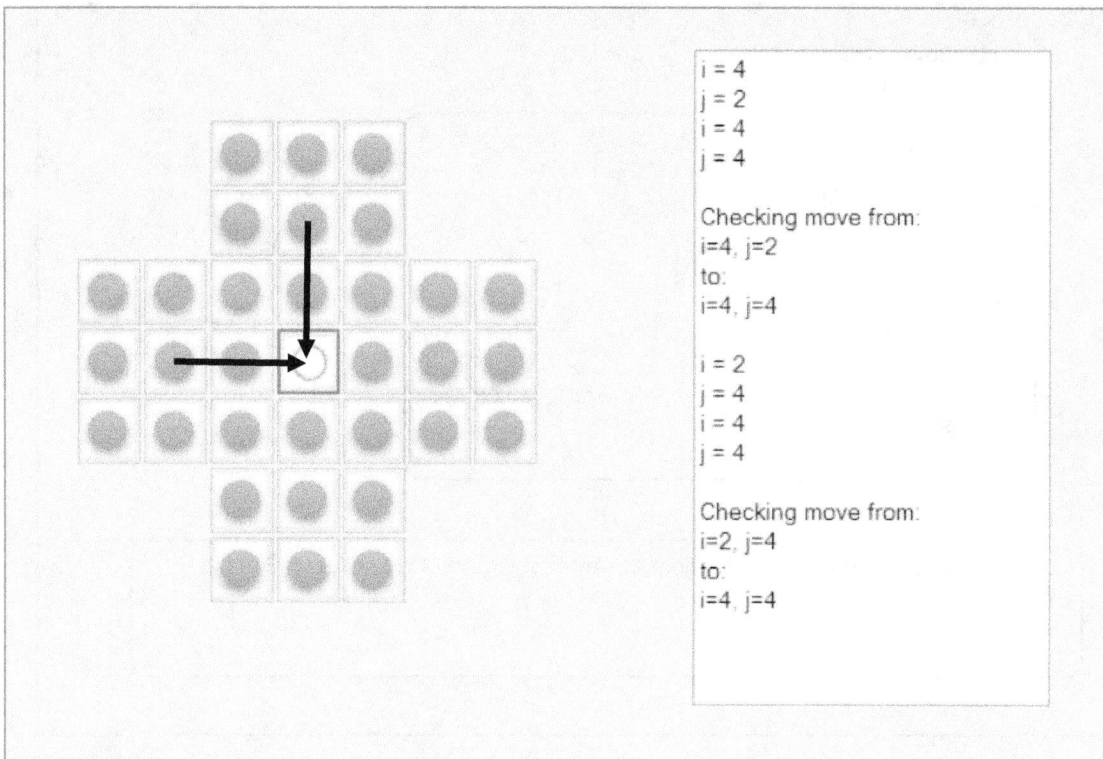

Moves are only valid if the start and finish positions are either on the *same horizontal row*, or in the *same vertical column* of the grid. We can easily check for a horizontal move, by checking that the start and finish j positions are the same. Add a ListBox output line to show this:

```
private void checkMove(int startI,int startJ,int finishI,int finishJ)
{
    listBox1.Items.Add("");

    listBox1.Items.Add("Checking move from: ");
    listBox1.Items.Add("i=" + startI + ", j=" + startJ);

    listBox1.Items.Add("to: ");
    listBox1.Items.Add("i=" + finishI + ", j=" + finishJ);

    if (startJ == finishJ)
    {
        listBox1.Items.Add("Move on a horizontal line");
    }

    listBox1.Items.Add("");
}
```

Run the program, and check that a horizontal move can be detected correctly:

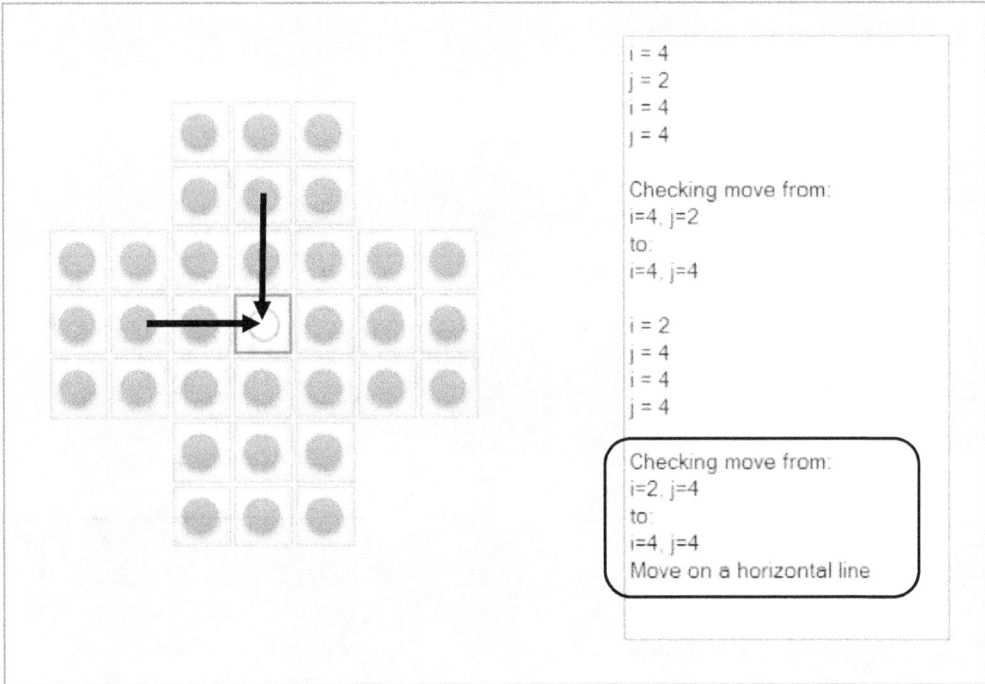

The next requirement for a valid move is that the **start** and **finish** positions must be **two squares apart**, for example: moving along a row from column 2 to column 4, or in the opposite direction from column 4 to column 2.

We can check this by subtracting the finish column from the start column, and checking that the answer is 2 when ***any minus sign is ignored***. This can be done using the **ABSOLUTE** function, which shows any number, positive or negative, as its positive equivalent:

```
if (startJ == finishJ)
{
    listBox1.Items.Add("Move on a horizontal line");

    if (Math.Abs(startI - finishI) == 2)
    {
        listBox1.Items.Add("Positions are 2 squares apart");
    }

}
```

Run the program and check that the computer can detect moves between positions which are two squares apart on a horizontal line.

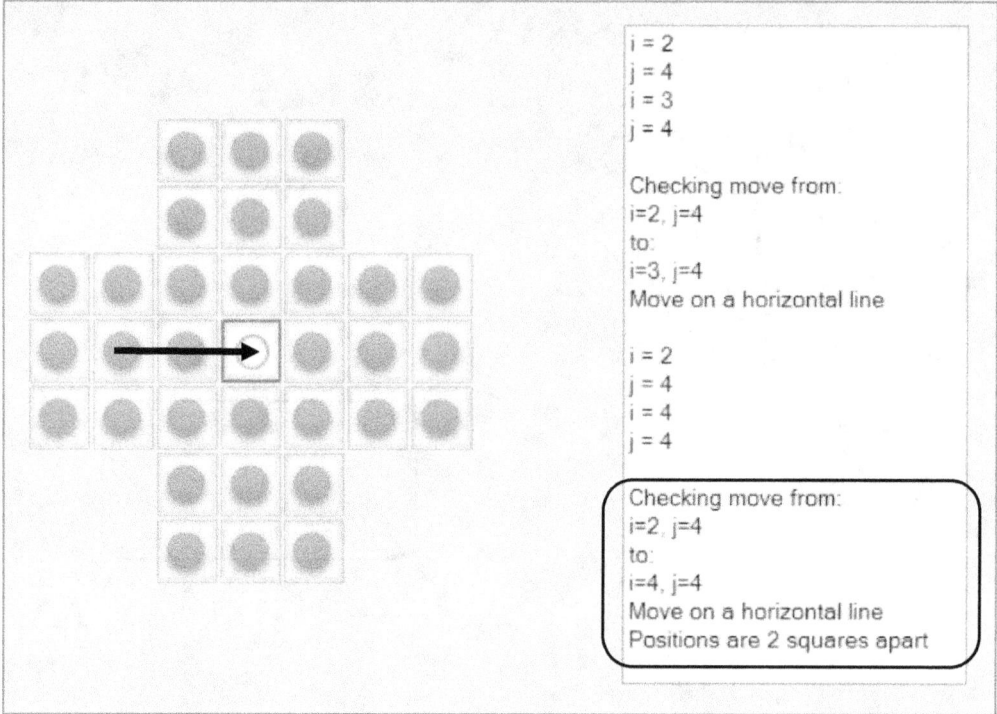

The final condition for a valid move is that the *start* square and *middle* square have playing pieces on them, whilst the *finish* square is empty. This can be checked using the *play[ ] array* values:

```
if (Math.Abs(startI - finishI) == 2)
{
    listBox1.Items.Add("Positions are 2 squares apart");

    int middle = (startI + finishI) / 2;

    if (play[startI, startJ] == 1 && play[middle, startJ] == 1
                                 && play[finishI, finishJ] == 0)
    {
        listBox1.Items.Add("VALID MOVE");
    }
}
```

Run the program, and test that the computer can correctly detect valid horizontal moves:

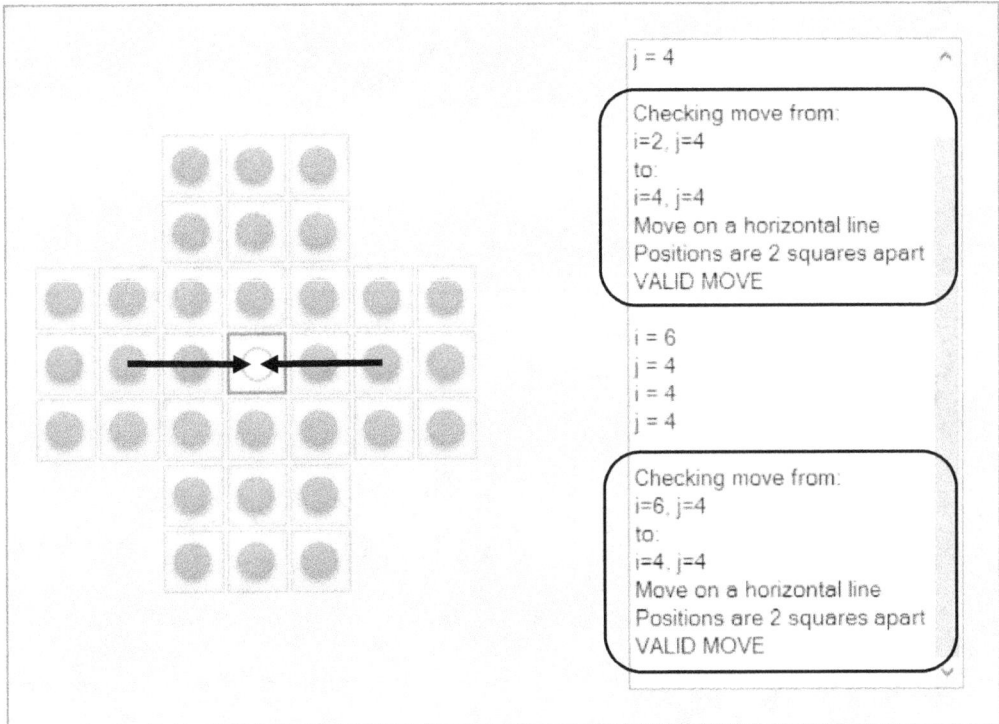

Once a valid move has been made, we can change the pattern of playing pieces on the board accordingly. The **play[ ] array** values can be updated to reflect the new state of the board:

```
if (play[startI, startJ] == 1 && play[middle, startJ] == 1
                                    && play[finishI, finishJ] == 0)
{
    listBox1.Items.Add("VALID MOVE");

    play[startI, startJ] = 0;
    btnGame[startI, startJ].Image = Image.FromFile("../../hole.png");

    play[middle, startJ] = 0;
    btnGame[middle, startJ].Image = Image.FromFile("../../hole.png");

    play[finishI, finishJ] = 1;
    btnGame[finishI, finishJ].Image = Image.FromFile("../../peg.png");
}
```

Run the program again and test that horizontal moves are now displayed correctly:

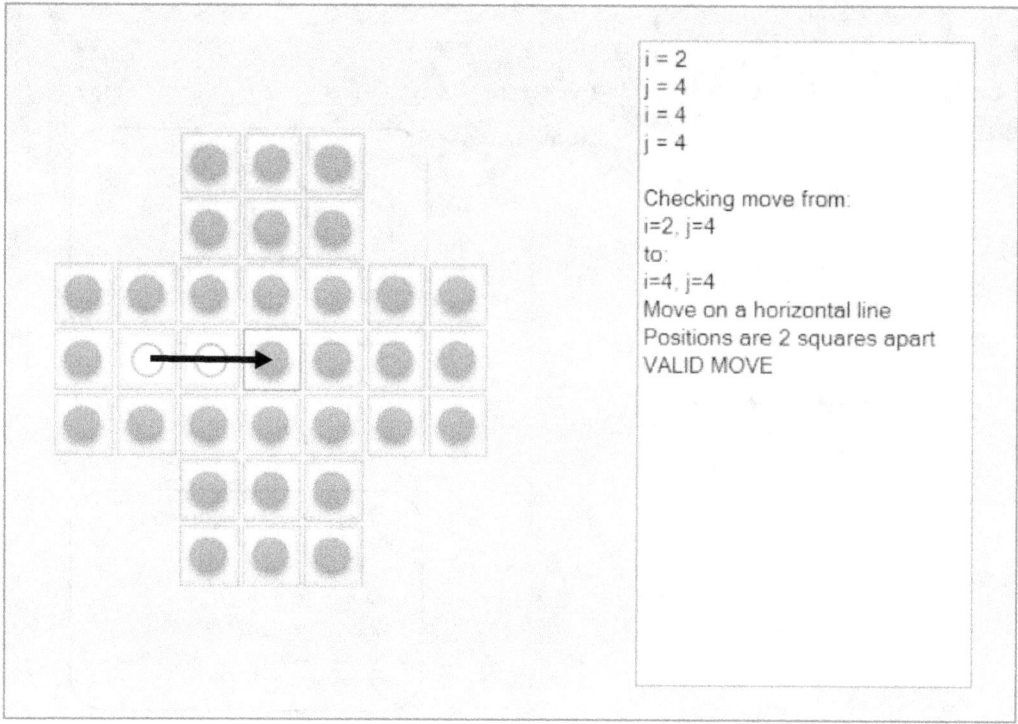

If the procedure for horizontal moves is now working correctly, then the screen display can be tidied by removing the ListBox. The lines in the program which output text to the ListBox can also be removed:

```
private void checkMove(int startI,int startJ,int finishI,int finishJ)
{
    if (startJ == finishJ)
    {
        if (Math.Abs(startI - finishI) == 2)
        {
            int middle = (startI + finishI) / 2;

            if (play[startI, startJ] == 1 && play[middle, startJ] == 1
                                         && play[finishI, finishJ] == 0)
            {
                play[startI, startJ] = 0;
                btnGame[startI, startJ].Image = Image.FromFile("../../hole.png");

                play[middle, startJ] = 0;
                btnGame[middle, startJ].Image = Image.FromFile("../../hole.png");

                play[finishI, finishJ] = 1;
                btnGame[finishI, finishJ].Image = Image.FromFile("../../peg.png");
            }
        }
    }
}
```

Make a copy of the *'horizontal move'* code, and paste this immediately below to make an equivalent *'vertical move'* method:

```
private void checkMove(int startI,int startJ,int finishI,int finishJ)
{
    if (startJ == finishJ)
    {
        if (Math.Abs(startI - finishI) == 2)
        {
            int middle = (startI + finishI) / 2;

            if (play[startI, startJ] == 1 && play[middle, startJ] == 1
                                        && play[finishI, finishJ] == 0)
            {
                play[startI, startJ] = 0;
                btnGame[startI, startJ].Image = Image.FromFile("../../hole.png");

                play[middle, startJ] = 0;
                btnGame[middle, startJ].Image = Image.FromFile("../../hole.png");

                play[finishI, finishJ] = 1;
                btnGame[finishI, finishJ].Image = Image.FromFile("../../peg.png");
            }
        }
    }
}
```

copy

To complete the 'vertical move' procedure, some changes to the code are necessary. These are outlined below:

```
if (startI == finishI)
{
    if (Math.Abs(startJ - finishJ) == 2)
    {
        int middle = (startJ + finishJ) / 2;

        if (play[startI, startJ] == 1 && play[startI, middle] == 1
                                    && play[finishI, finishJ] == 0)
        {
            play[startI, startJ] = 0;
            btnGame[startI, startJ].Image = Image.FromFile("../../hole.png");

            play[startI, middle] = 0;
            btnGame[startI, middle].Image = Image.FromFile("../../hole.png");

            play[finishI, finishJ] = 1;
            btnGame[finishI, finishJ].Image = Image.FromFile("../../peg.png");
        }
    }
}
```

Run the program and test both horizontal and vertical moves are made correctly. It should now be possible to play the complete game of solitaire.

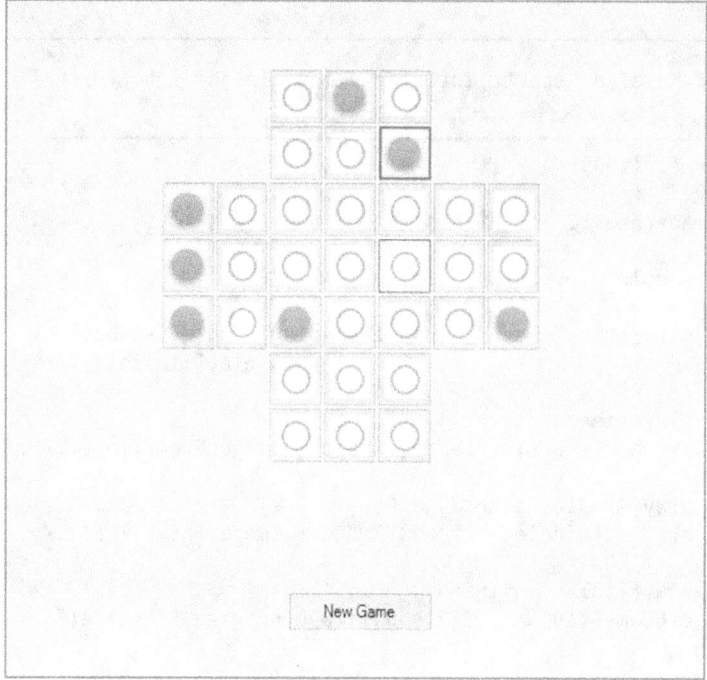

One last improvement that can be made is the addition of a '*New Game*' button, to reset the playing pieces to the start position. Add a Button component to the form and give this the name **btnNewgame**.

To restart the game, it is necessary to remove the current buttons, then call the *initialiseBoard( )* method to set up the playing pieces again in the start position. Add code to the button_click method to do this:

```
private void btnNewgame_Click(object sender, EventArgs e)
{
    int totalButtons = pnlGame.Controls.Count;
    for (int i = 0; i < totalButtons; i++)
    {
        pnlGame.Controls.RemoveAt(0);
    }
    initialiseBoard();
}
```

Run the program. Make some moves, then test that the '*New Game*' method operates correctly.

5 Airport

Most practical applications in C# require data to be stored in a database and accessed by the program. We will examine how this is done by setting up a small database of flights departing from an airport, then writing a C# program to display this data in a table.

Open *Visual Studio*, but do not start a new project yet.

On the menu line, select '*View / Server Explorer*'

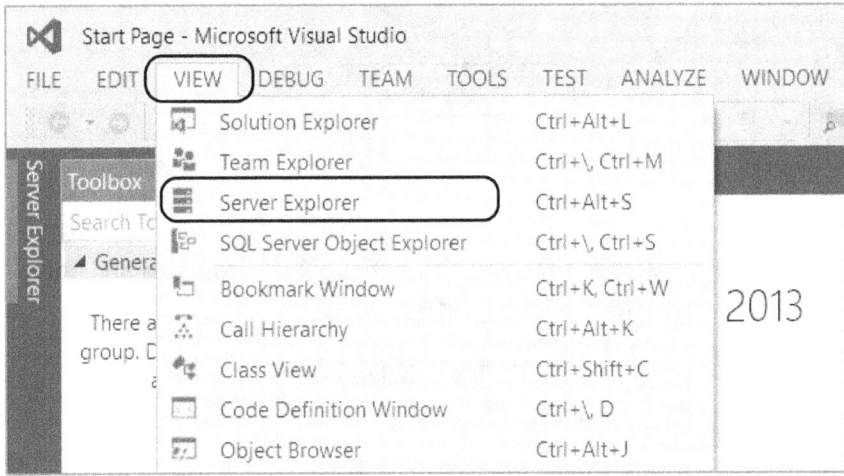

Right-click on '*Data Connections*', then select '*Add Connection*'.

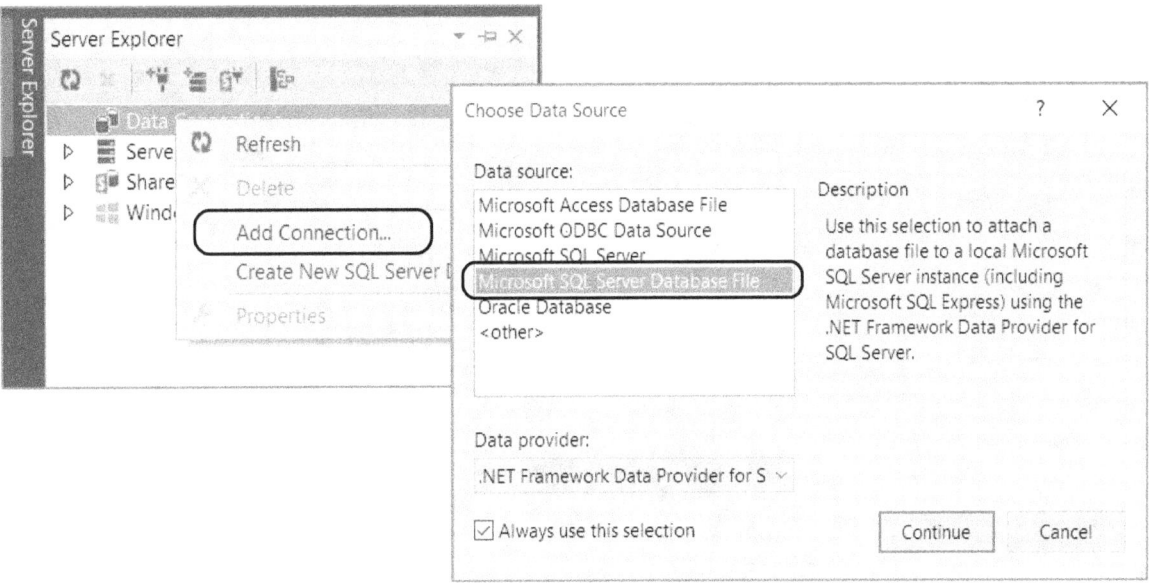

Choose '*Microsoft SQL Server Database File*' as the Data source.

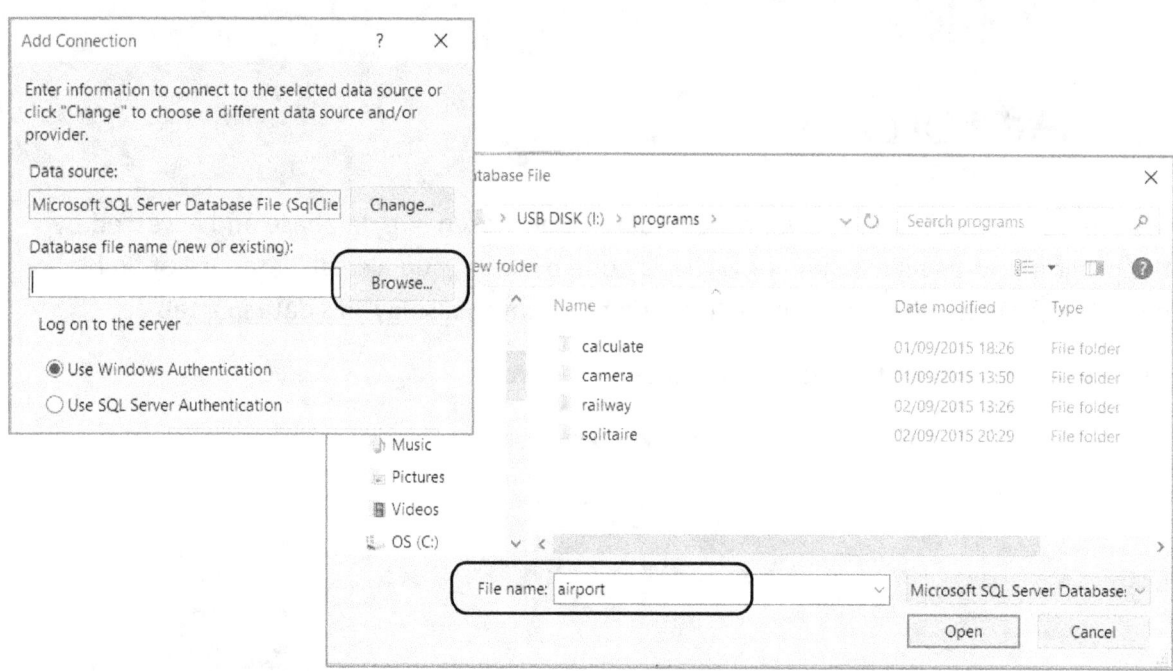

Use the '*Browse*' option to navigate to the location where your C# programs are stored. Give the file name '*airport*' for the database which will be created.

Click '*OK*', then answer '*Yes*' that you wish to create the database file:

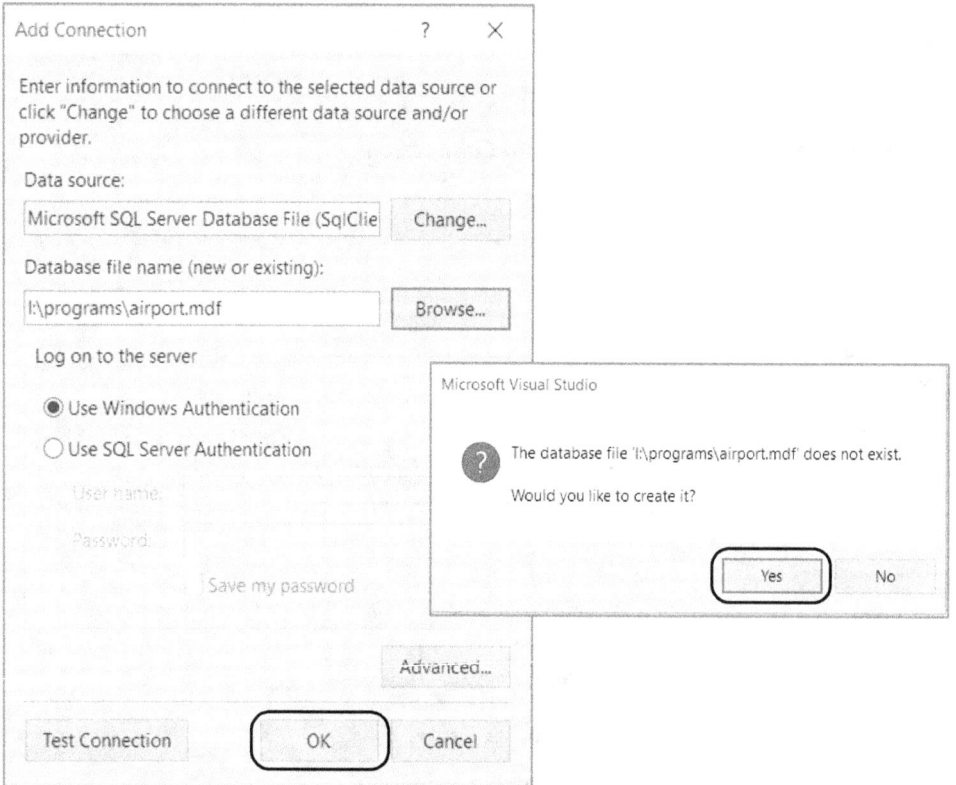

A database icon '*airport.mdf*' should now appear in the Server Explorer window. Click the small arrow symbol to the left of the icon to open a contents list.

Click-right on '*Tables*' and select '*Add New Table*':

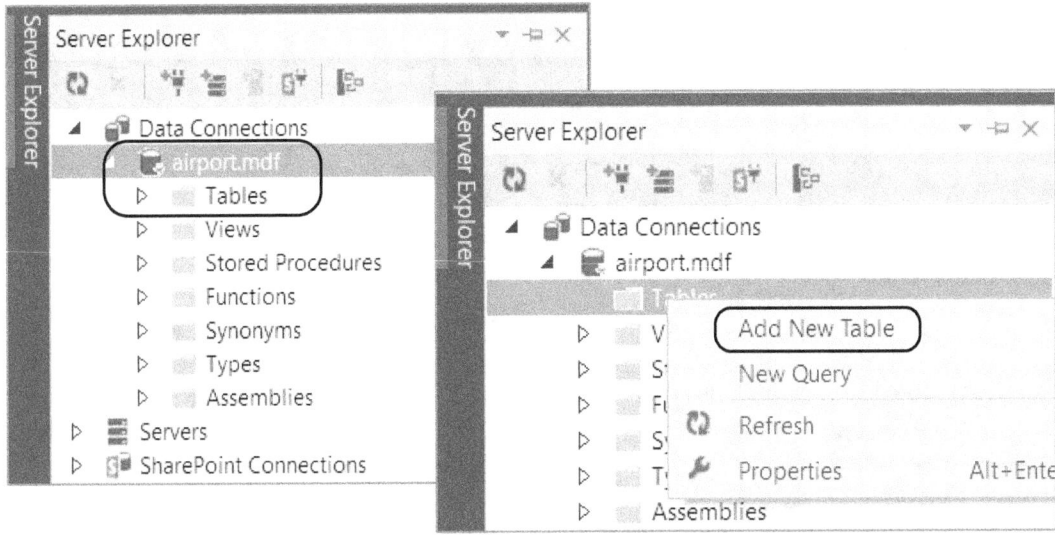

We will include four fields in our database, to record *flight ID*, the *airline*, the flight *destination* and *departure time*. To keep things simple, select '*varchar(50)*' as the Data Type. This allows up to 50 characters to be entered in the field, including both letters and numbers as necessary.

Notice that the first row has a small '*key*' icon. This indicates that it is the *primary key field* of the table. Every record must have a different unique value for the primary key. Leave ticks in the '*Allow Nulls*' box for the other fields.

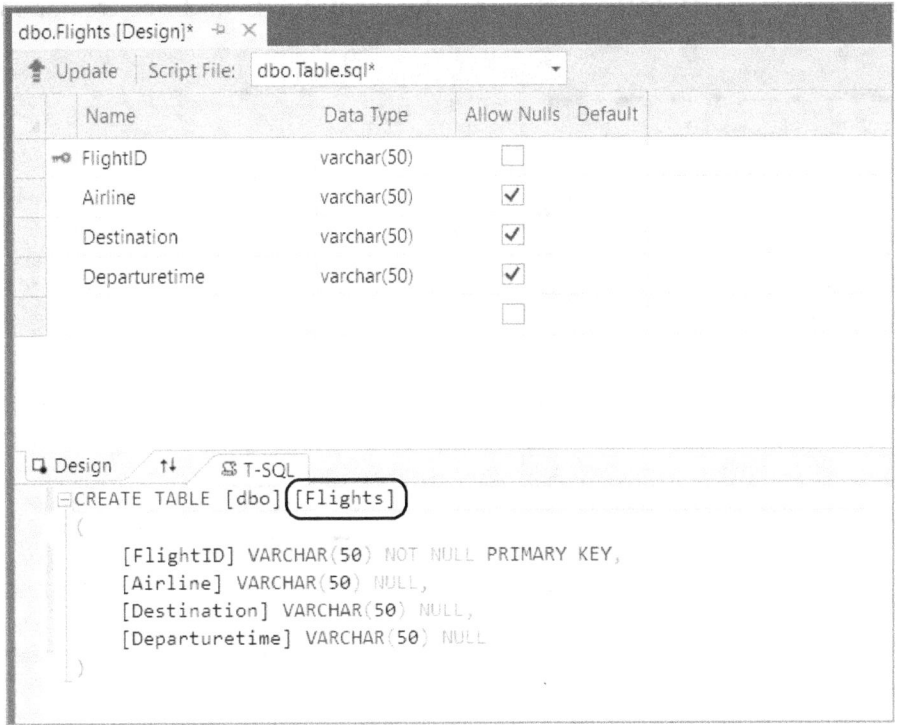

In the lower part of the page you will notice a section of *SQL code* which has been written by the program. This will be used by the computer to create the new table in the database. Go to the *CREATE TABLE* line and change the name of the table to '*Flights*'.

Click the '*Update*' button above the list of fields. When the **Database Update** window appears, click the '*Update Database*' button.

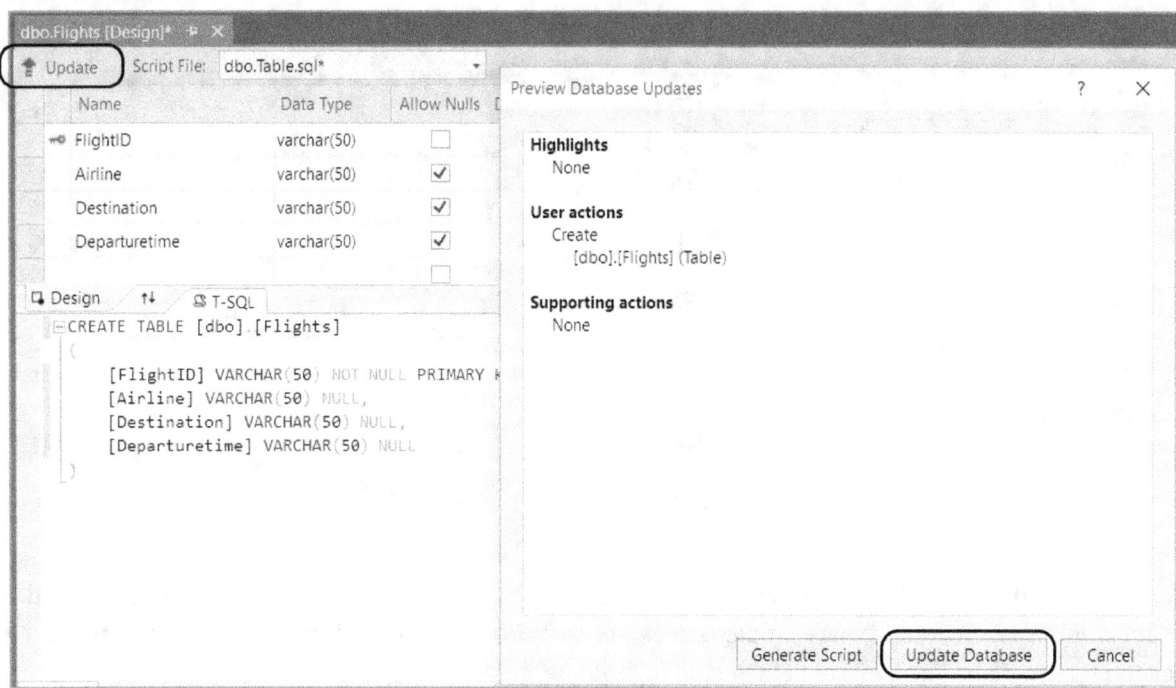

Close the **Flights** table design page and re-open the **Server Explorer** window. Right-click on airport.mdf and select '**Refresh**'.

Click the small arrow to the left of the **Tables** icon. The **Flights** table which you created should now be shown.

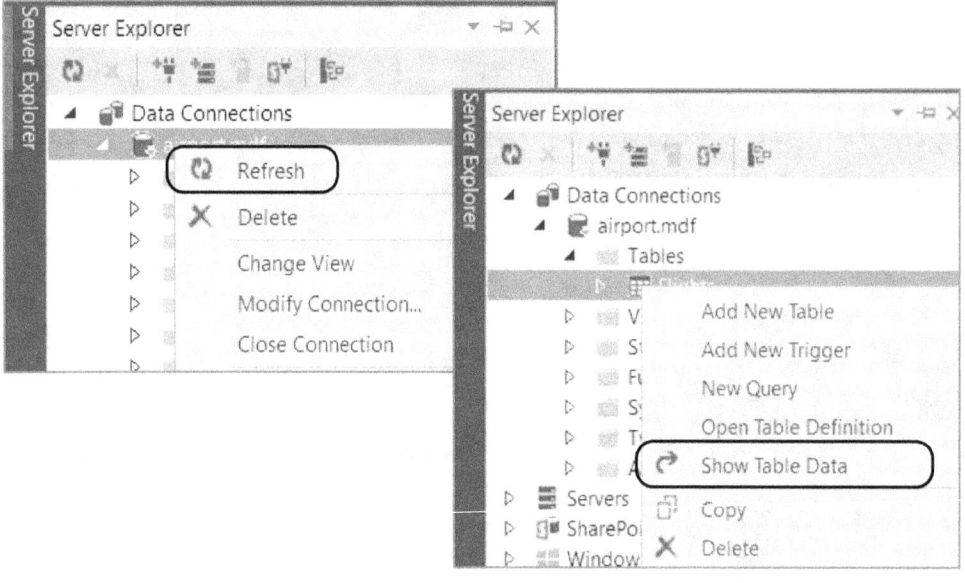

Right-click the **Flights** table, and select '*Show Table Data*'. An empty table will be displayed.

Add test data for a few aircraft departures, then click the cross on the tab to close the table.

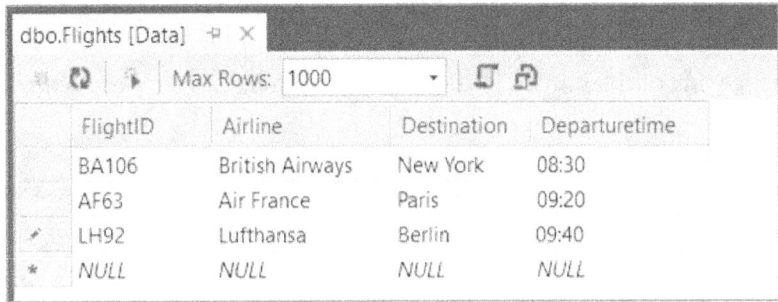

Right-click on '*Flights*' and use the '*Show Table Data*' option again, to check that your records have been saved into the database correctly. Click the cross to close the table again.

We are now going to write a C# program to access the *Flights* table from the database and display the information on screen. It is important to note that the program will not work correctly if the database is open in the *Server Explorer* window, so we will first close the database.

Go to the Server Explorer and right click the *airport.mdf* database icon. Select the '*Delete*' option, and confirm to remove the database connection by clicking '*Yes*'.

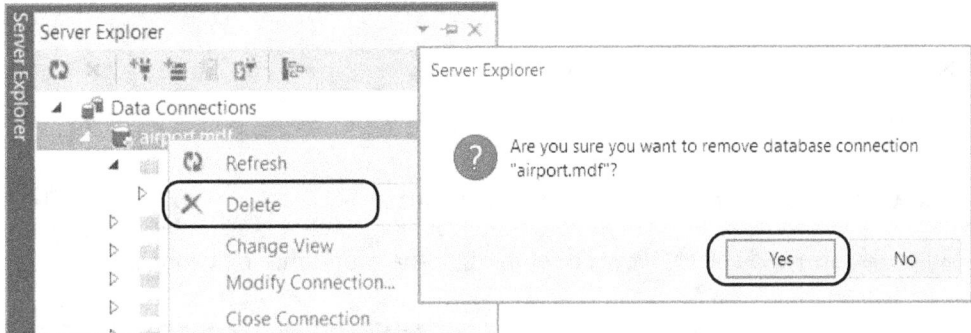

We can now open the *FILE* option on the main menu and select '*New Project*'.

Choose '*Visual C#*' and '*Windows Forms Application*'. Give the name '*airport*'

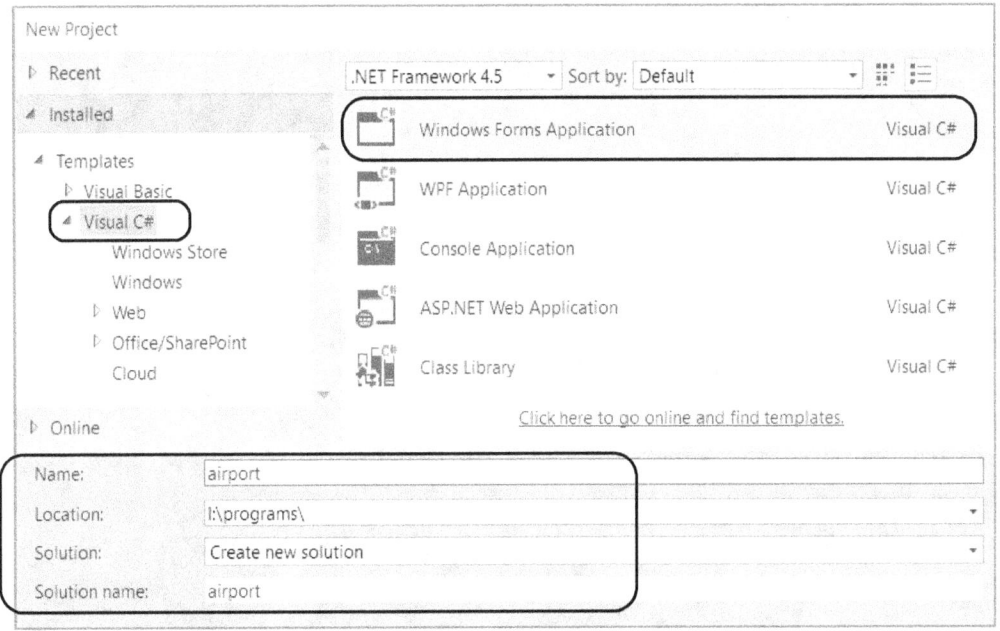

Drag **Form1** to fill the design window. Open the Toolbox and add a '**Departures**' label as a heading.

Go to the '**Data**' section of the Toolbox and select the '**DataGridView**' component. Drag the mouse to position the DataGrid component on Form1 – it will appear only as an empty grey box at this stage. Do not change any of the entries in the list which appears. The '**Data Source**' should remain as '**(none)**'

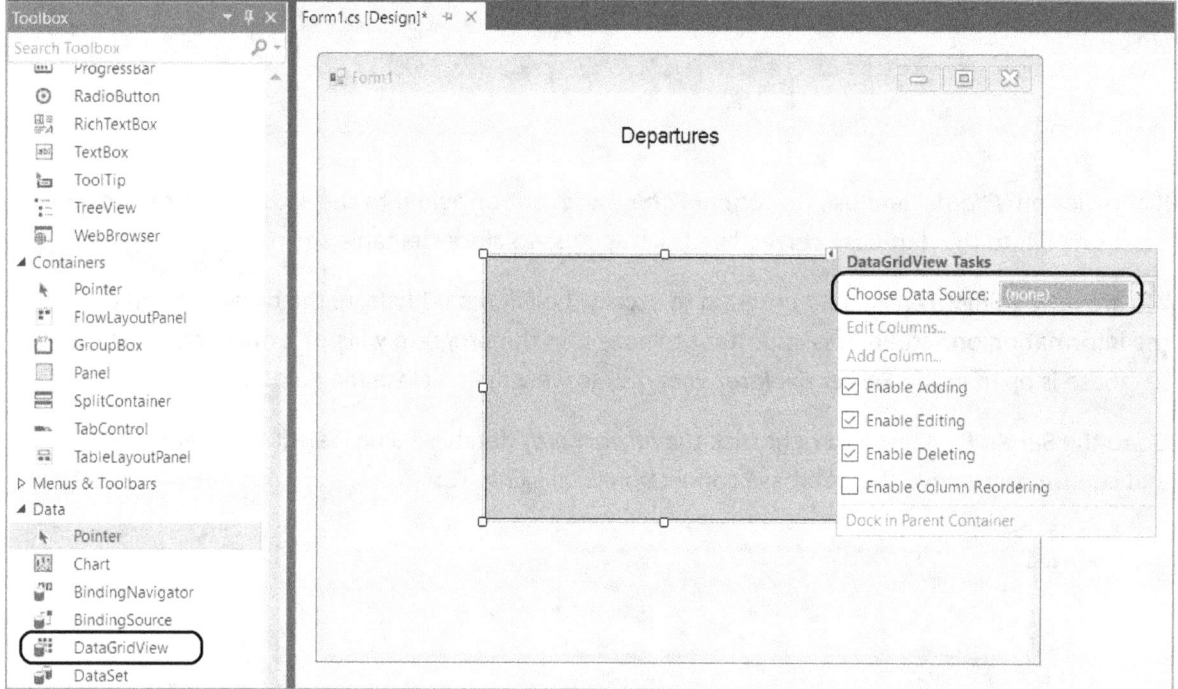

We can now write the program code to access the database.

Right-click on the form and select '**View Code**' to open the programming window

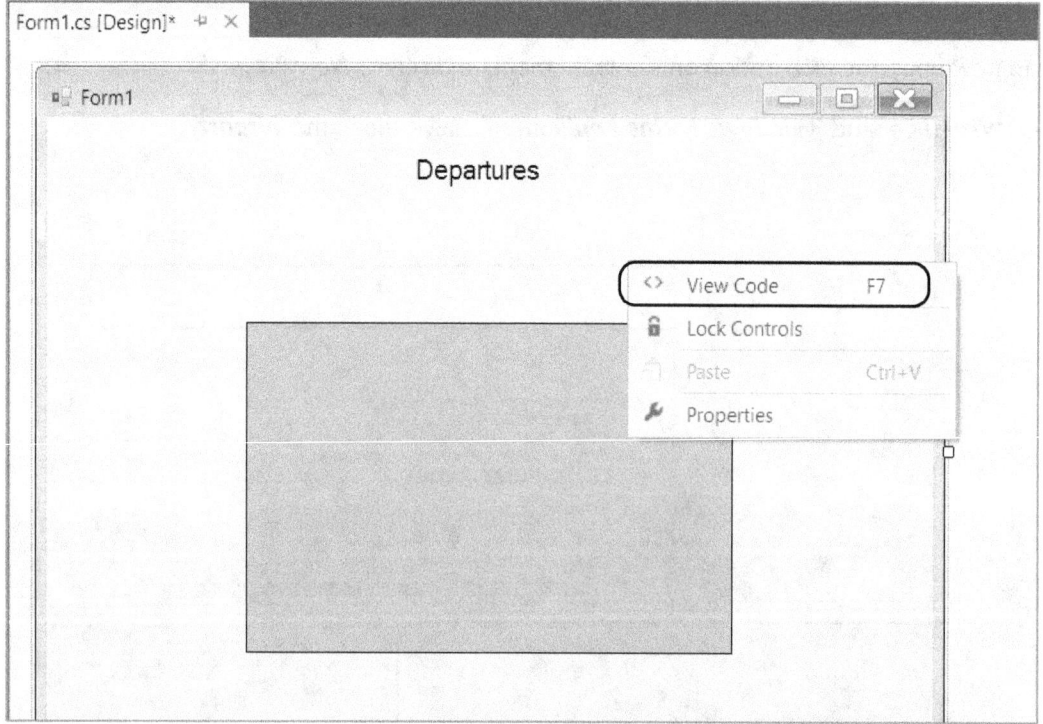

We will begin by creating a method for displaying the flights data. Add a line of code in the **Form1( )** method which will call the **DisplayFlights( )** method when the program runs:

```
namespace airport
{
    public partial class Form1 : Form
    {
        public Form1()
        {
            InitializeComponent();
            DisplayFlights();
        }

        private void DisplayFlights()
        {

        }
    }
}
```

Add a program line at the start of the **Form1** class which gives the name and pathway that you chose for the database on your particular computer. Notice that double back-slash characters must be used. This line has deliberately been placed in a position where it can easily be found, in case the program is transferred to a different computer and the pathway to the database needs to be changed.

```
namespace airport
{
    public partial class Form1 : Form
    {
        string databaseLocation = "C:\\C#\\airport.mdf;";

        public Form1()
        {
            InitializeComponent();
            DisplayFlights();
        }
```

Displaying the database records in a C# program is a two-stage process. Firstly the data has to be read-in from the database on the hard drive or other external memory device. The data is then stored as a *dataset* in the electronic RAM memory, where it is available for display on screen:

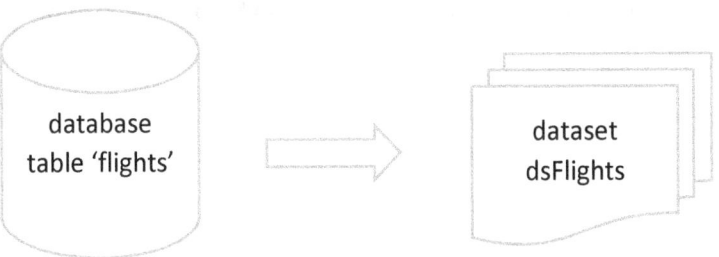

Add a '*using System.Data.SqlClient*' directive to the start of the program, which will make available the code necessary to access the database.

```
using System.Text;
using System.Windows.Forms;

using System.Data.SqlClient;

namespace airport
{
```

We than add lines to the DisplayFlights method. Please note that the line beginning:

SqlConnection con = ...

should be entered as a single line of code with no line breaks.

```
public partial class Form1 : Form
{
    string databaseLocation = "C:\\C#\\airport.mdf;";

    public Form1()
    {
        InitializeComponent();
        DisplayFlights();
    }

    private void DisplayFlights()
    {
        DataSet dsFlights = new DataSet();

        SqlConnection con = new SqlConnection(@"Data Source=.\SQLEXPRESS;
            AttachDbFilename="+databaseLocation + "Integrated Security=True;
            Connect Timeout=30; User Instance=True");
    }
}
}
```

The '*DataSet*' line creates the storage area in the RAM memory to hold the records which we will input from the database.

The '*SqlConnection*' line gives the computer the information which it needs to connect to the database. Apart from the location of the database, we are also telling it what software package to use ('SQL EXPRESS'), and how long to keep trying to access data before giving up with an error message (30 seconds).

Things can often go wrong when accessing a database. To avoid the computer crashing, add a TRY...CATCH block to the DisplayFlights method:

```
private void DisplayFlights()
{
    DataSet dsFlights = new DataSet();
    SqlConnection con = new SqlConnection(@"Data Source=.\SQLEXPRESS;
        AttachDbFilename="+databaseLocation + "Integrated Security=True;
        Connect Timeout=30; User Instance=True");

    try
    {

    }
    catch
    {
        MessageBox.Show("File error");
    }
}
```

We now add lines of code to open the connection to the database and tell the computer what data we wish to retrieve. The command '*SELECT * FROM flights*' means: '*bring back all the data from the Flights table*'

```
private void DisplayFlights()
{
    DataSet dsFlights = new DataSet();

    SqlConnection con = new SqlConnection(@"Data Source=.\SQLEXPRESS;
        AttachDbFilename="+databaseLocation + "Integrated Security=True;
        Connect Timeout=30; User Instance=True");

    try
    {
        con.Open();
        SqlCommand cmFlight = new SqlCommand();
        cmFlight.Connection = con;
        cmFlight.CommandType = CommandType.Text;
        cmFlight.CommandText = "SELECT * FROM flights";
    }
    catch
    {
        MessageBox.Show("File error");
    }
}
```

The final steps are to

- retrieve the data from the database,
- transfer it into the dataset,
- close the database connection,
- then link the dataset to the DataGrid on Form1 so that the records are visible

Add the lines of code shown below:

```
try
{
    con.Open();
    SqlCommand cmFlight = new SqlCommand();
    cmFlight.Connection = con;
    cmFlight.CommandType = CommandType.Text;
    cmFlight.CommandText = "SELECT * FROM flights";

    SqlDataAdapter daFlights = new SqlDataAdapter(cmFlight);
    daFlights.Fill(dsFlights);
    con.Close();

    dataGridView1.DataSource = dsFlights.Tables[0];
}
catch
{
    MessageBox.Show("File error");
}
```

Build and run the program. If all goes well, your database table should appear on screen. It may be necessary to return to the design view and adjust the size of the *DataGrid* component, so that all fields are visible.

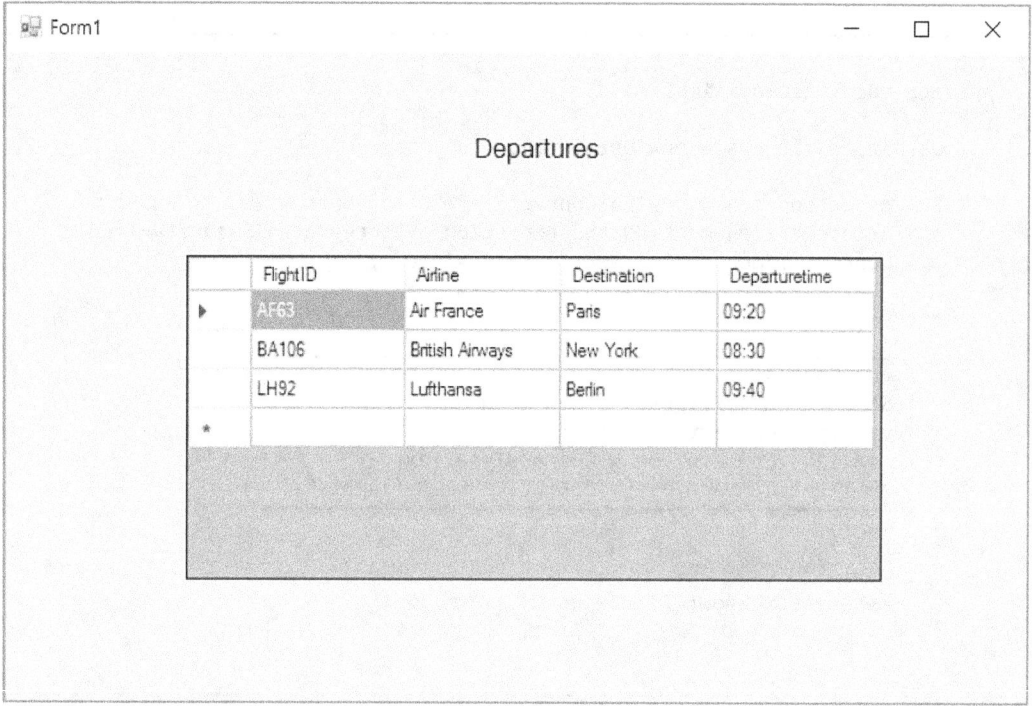

If you receive a '*File error*' message, check very carefully through the lines of code in the *DisplayFlights( )* method, and check the pathway which you entered for your database location. File handling is quite complicated, and it is easy to make an error.

6 London Underground

In the next project we will investigate a more challenging program algorithm, to provide information to travellers about routes between stations on the London Underground system. This program will combine the use of database files and some new techniques for producing screen graphics.

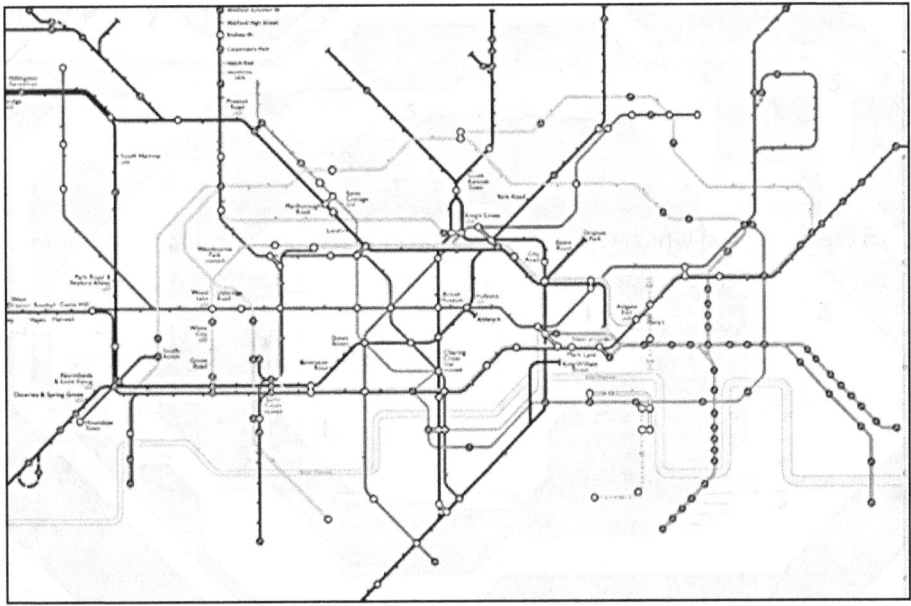

The London Underground is a large system of interconnected lines. To keep our project manageable, we will restrict the program to just four: the **Circle**, **Victoria**, **Central** and **Northern** lines, and we will include only a small sample of stations along these routes. The principles we develop, however, could be extended in a fairly straightforward way to cover the complete network.

We will begin by setting up a database to hold information about the stations and their map locations. Open Visual Studio, and display the *Server Explorer* window. Right-click on *Data Connections* and select '*Add Connection*'. Set up a new *Microsoft SQL Server Database File* called '*underground*' in the same directory as your C# program folders.

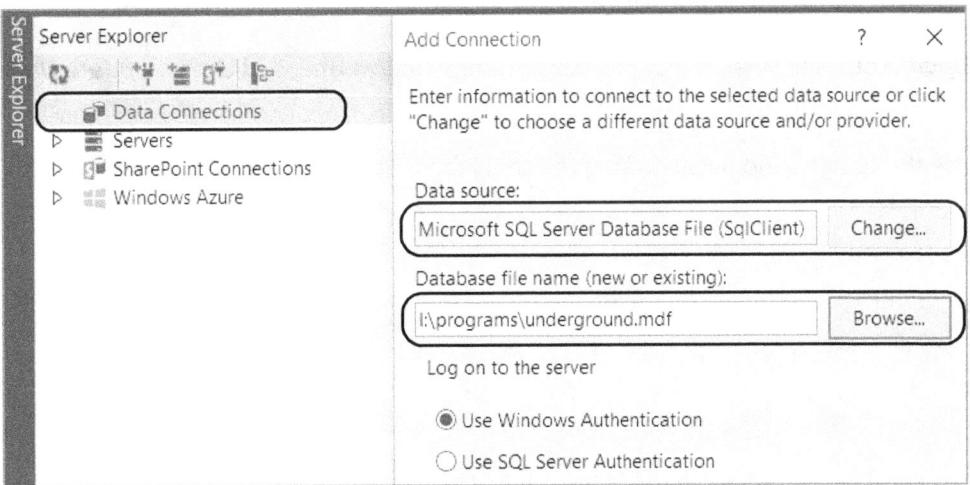

The new database '**underground**' should be listed under the **Data Connections** icon. Click the small arrow to the left to open the database. Right-click on '**Tables**' and select '**Add New Table**'.

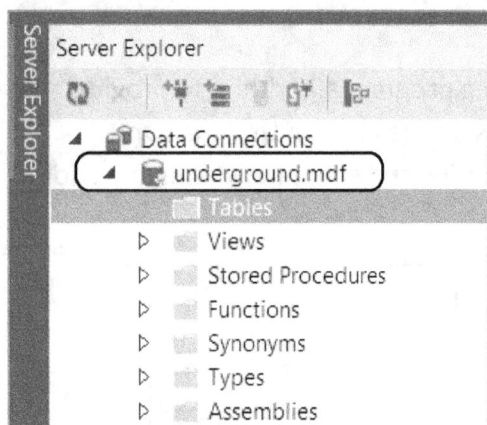 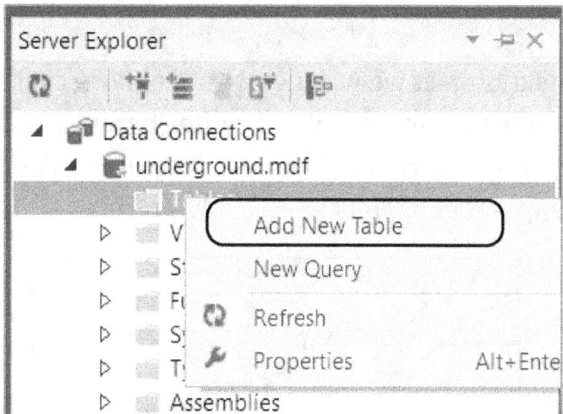

We are going to create a table which will store the names and map coordinates of a number of underground stations. Set up the Column Names and Data Types as shown:

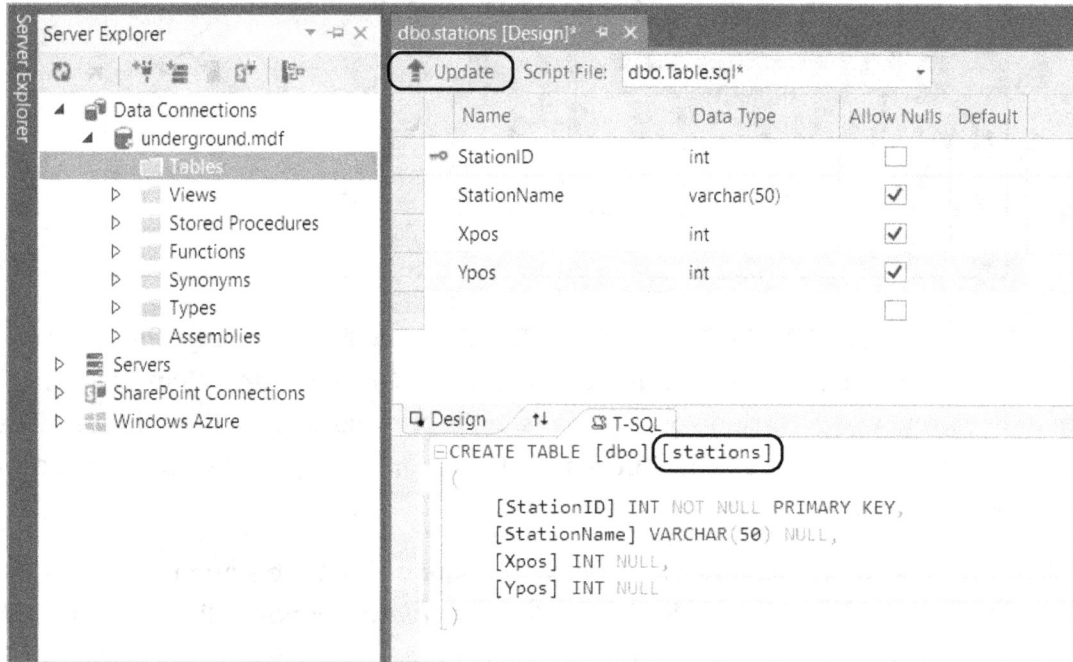

Go to the **CREATE TABLE** line of the SQL code and change the table name to '*stations*'.

Click the **Update** button. When the **Database Updates** window opens, click the '**Update Database**' button.

Finally, close the design window by clicking the small cross above the table.

Right-click on *underground.mdf* in the *Server Explorer* window and select '*Refresh*'.

Click the small arrow to the left of the *Tables* icon to show the '*stations*' table. Right click on '*stations*' and select '*Show Table Data*'. A blank table should appear:

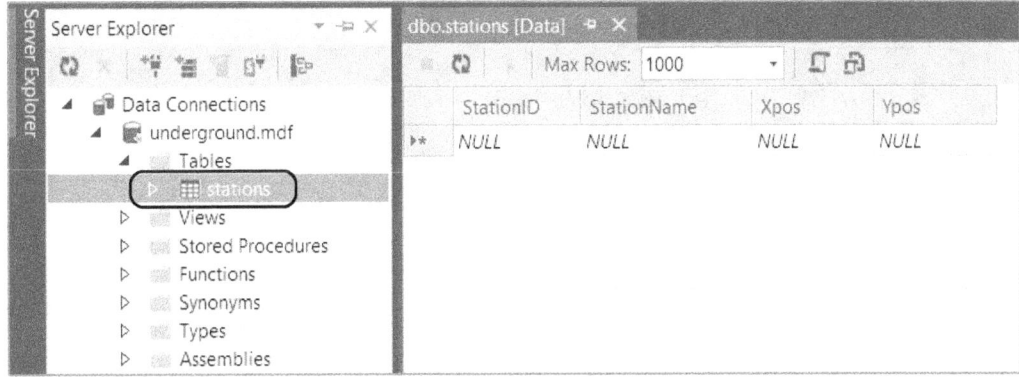

Enter the station information given in the list below. The map coordinates have been found for you by copying the London Underground map into the graphics utility program Paint, then reading off the coordinates as the cursor was moved over each of the required stations.

StationID	StationName	Xpos (pixels across)	Ypos (pixels down)
1	Ealing Broadway	105	269
2	Notting Hill Gate	270	268
3	Paddington	272	221
4	Euston	409	218
5	High Barnet	439	26
6	Oxford Circus	361	267
7	Tottenham Court Road	400	267
8	Embankment	400	333
9	Victoria	342	333
10	South Kensington	280	333
11	Stockwell	383	446
12	Morden	294	535
13	Brixton	410	472
14	Tower Hill	529	299
15	Liverpool Street	531	250
16	Epping	667	11
17	Walthamstow Central	629	119
18	Stratford	667	199
19	Kings Cross	440	218

Check your entries carefully, then close the table. Go to the *Server Explorer* window and delete the connection to the *underground.mdf* database.

We can now set up the C# program. Select '**FILE / New Project**'. Click '**Visual C#**' and '**Windows Forms Application**', and set the program name to '**underground**'.

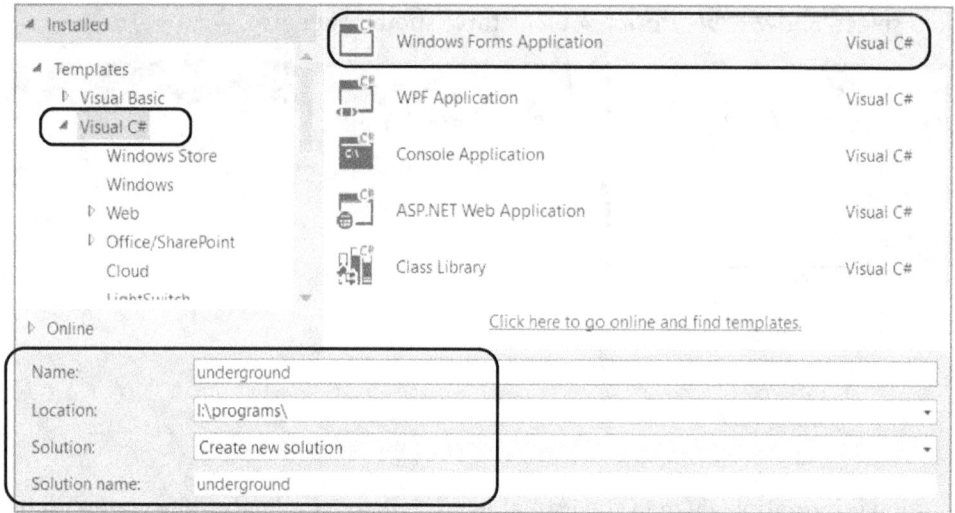

Form1 will be created. Right click the form and select '**View Code**'.

The first stage is to load the station data from the database table.

- Add '**SqlClient**' to the list of '**using**' directives at the start of the program.
- Show the database location,
- Create a **DataSet** for the station data.
- Set up the **GetStations( )** method to load the station data from the database table. This will be very similar to the method you used to load flight data in the Airport program.
- Add a line to the **Form1( )** method to run **GetStations( )** when the program first starts.

```
using System.Windows.Forms;
using System.Data.SqlClient;

namespace underground
{
    public partial class Form1 : Form
    {
        string databaseLocation = "C:\\C#\\underground.mdf;";
        DataSet dsStations = new DataSet();

        public Form1()
        {
            InitializeComponent();
            GetStations();
        }

        private void GetStations()
        {

        }
    }
}
```

Add code to the **GetStations( )** method which will load the data and transfer it to the DataSet. Note that the line beginning:

SqlConnection con =

should be entered as a single line of code with no line breaks.

```
private void GetStations()
{
    try
    {
        SqlConnection con = new SqlConnection(@"Data Source=.\SQLEXPRESS;
            AttachDbFilename=" + databaseLocation + "Integrated Security=True;
            Connect Timeout=30; User Instance=True");
        con.Open();
        SqlCommand cmStations = new SqlCommand();
        cmStations.Connection = con;
        cmStations.CommandType = CommandType.Text;
        cmStations.CommandText = "SELECT * FROM stations ORDER BY stationName ASC";

        SqlDataAdapter daStations = new SqlDataAdapter(cmStations);
        daStations.Fill(dsStations);
        con.Close();
    }
    catch
    {
        MessageBox.Show("File error");
    }
}
```

We have added an instruction '**ORDER BY stationName ASC**' to the SQL command, which will sort the station records into alphabetical order of station name. This will be helpful later when the user is selecting their journey.

Once the data has been loaded, it will be more convenient to transfer it into arrays ready for processing. Set up four separate arrays for the *stationID* numbers, *stationNames*, and the *X* and *Y* map cooordinates. We will also set up an integer variable *stationCount* to record the number of stations for which we have data.

```
public partial class Form1 : Form
{
    string databaseLocation = "C:\\C#\\underground.mdf;";

    int stationCount;
    int[] stationID = new int[20];
    string[] stationName = new string[20];
    int[] stationX = new int[20];
    int[] stationY = new int[20];

    DataSet dsStations = new DataSet();

    public Form1()
    {
        InitializeComponent();
        GetStations();
    }
```

Add code to the *GetStations( )* method to determine the number of stations, and then use a loop to transfer the data for each station into the arrays:

```
        catch
        {
            MessageBox.Show("File error");
        }
        stationCount = dsStations.Tables[0].Rows.Count;

        for (int i = 0; i < stationCount; i++)
        {
            DataRow drStation = dsStations.Tables[0].Rows[i];

            stationID[i] = Convert.ToInt16(drStation[0]);
            stationName[i] = Convert.ToString(drStation[1]);
            stationX[i] = Convert.ToInt16(drStation[2]);
            stationY[i] = Convert.ToInt16(drStation[3]);
        }
    }
```

The next step is to write a method *DrawMap( )* which will display the stations on screen as the basis of a route diagram for the railway system. Add this below the *GetStations( )* method:

```
        for (int i = 0; i < stationCount; i++)
        {
            DataRow drStation = dsStations.Tables[0].Rows[i];

            stationID[i] = Convert.ToInt16(drStation[0]);
            stationName[i] = Convert.ToString(drStation[1]);
            stationX[i] = Convert.ToInt16(drStation[2]);
            stationY[i] = Convert.ToInt16(drStation[3]);
        }
    }

    private void DrawMap()
    {
        Graphics g = this.CreateGraphics();
        Pen black = new Pen(Color.Black, 1);
        SolidBrush white = new SolidBrush(Color.White);
        Font font = new Font("FreightSans Medium", 7, FontStyle.Regular);

        for (int i = 0; i < stationCount; i++)
        {
            g.FillEllipse(white, stationX[i] - 5, stationY[i] - 5, 10, 10);
            g.DrawEllipse(black, stationX[i] - 5, stationY[i] - 5, 10, 10);
            g.DrawString(stationName[i], font, Brushes.Black,
                    new Rectangle(stationX[i] + 3, stationY[i] + 2, 61, 50));
        }
    }
```

This code sets up black line and white fill colours, then draws a circle in the correct X, Y map position for each station. The station name is then added as a caption.

To make the graphics appear when the program runs, it is necessary to add a *Paint( )* method to the form. Change to the form *design view*, click to select Form1, then go to the Properties window. Click the *Events* icon, checking that the *alphabetical list* icon is also selected:

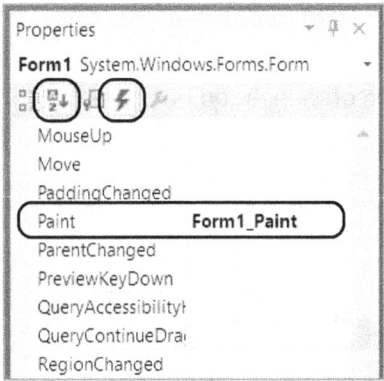

Locate the '*Paint*' event and double click in the right column to create a *Form1_Paint* method. Add the *DrawMap( )* method to this:

```
private void Form1_Paint(object sender, PaintEventArgs e)
{
    DrawMap();
}
```

Run the program. The stations should be displayed in the pattern shown. If the complete map area is not visible then close the program, return to the design view and enlarge the form. If any stations appear in an incorrect position, go to the database table and check that the X and Y cooordinates have been entered correctly.

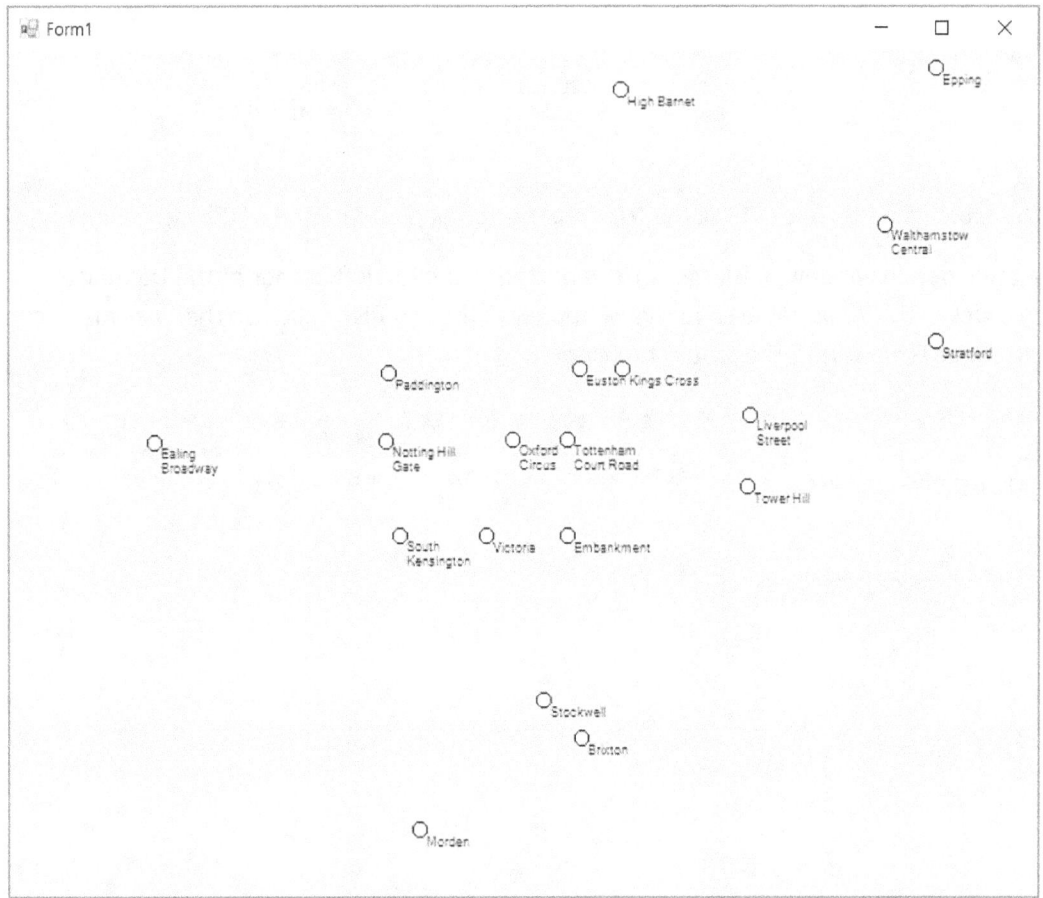

The next task is to connect the stations along each Underground Line. We will need another table in the database to record the sequence of stations along each line. Go to the **Server Explorer** window and right click the **Data Connections** icon. Re-connect the **underground.mdf** database.

Right-click the **Tables** icon. Select '**Add New Table**'. Set up the primary key field as '**LineName**', then add ten integer fields to represent the sequence of stations along the route. These fields are named '**Station1**' to '**Station10**'. For each of the station fields, remove the tick from **Allow Nulls** column and set a **Default** value of **0**.

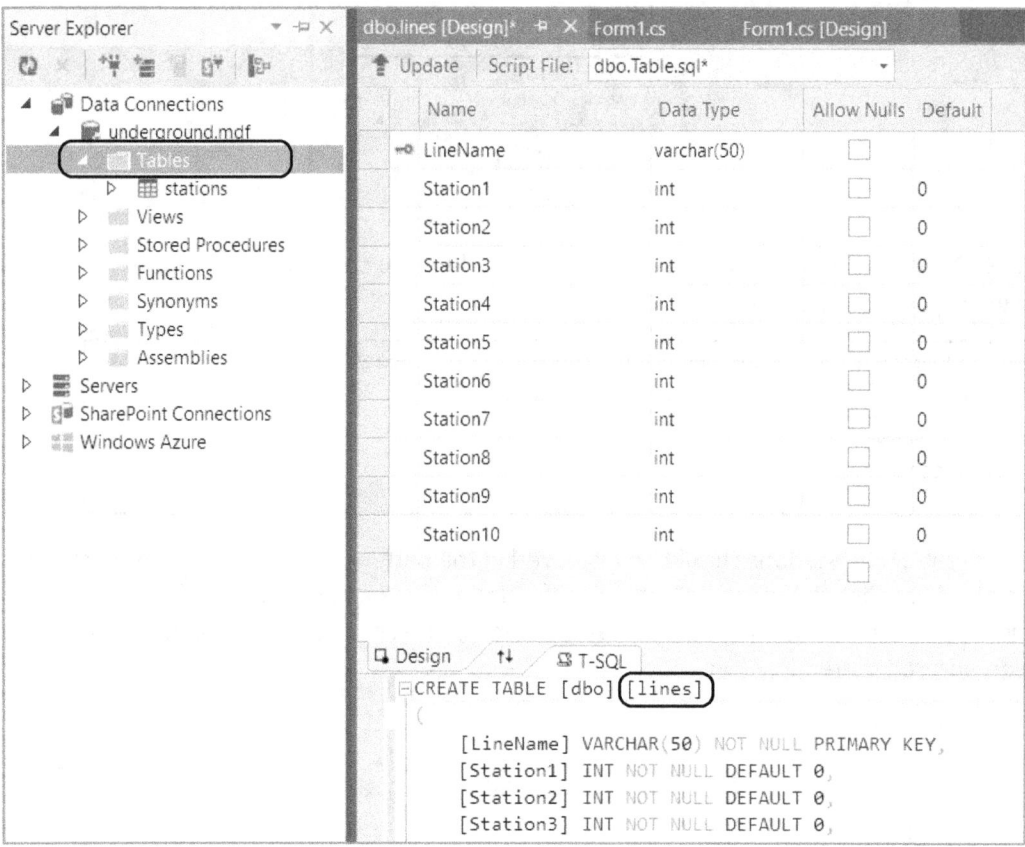

Change the table name to '**lines**'. Click the '**Update**' button and update the database.

Close the table design window. Click the **refresh** button in the top left corner of the Database Explorer window. The '**lines**' table should now appear in the list. Right-click on the **lines** table icon and select '**Show Table Data**'. The empty table opens.

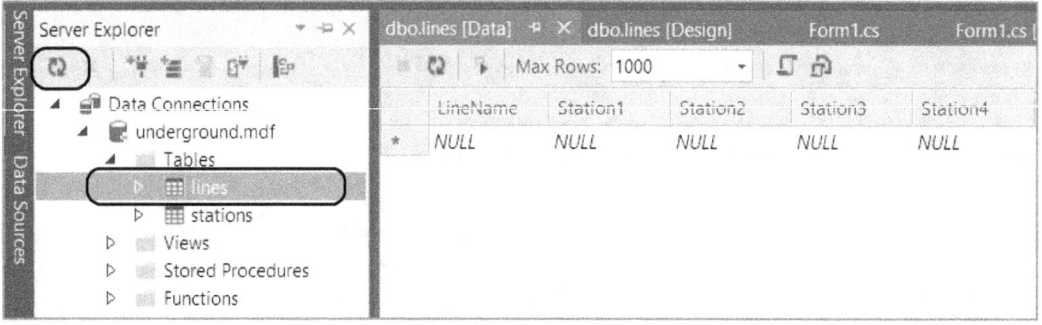

We are going to enter data for four Underground Lines. Each row begins with the name of the line, followed by the ID numbers of the stations along the line. These ID numbers were allocated by the computer when you entered the station data earlier.

LineName	Station1	Station2	Station3	Station4	Station5	Station6	Station7	Station8	Station9	Station10
Central	1	2	6	7	15	18	16	0	0	0
Northern	12	11	8	7	4	5	0	0	0	0
Circle	10	2	3	4	19	15	14	8	9	10
Victoria	13	11	9	6	4	19	17	0	0	0

Close the table when the data has been entered. Go to the Server Explorer window and delete the connection to the *underground.mdf* database.

We need to load the data for the underground lines when the program runs. Add a DataSet to hold the line data, and write a *GetRailLines( )* method. This uses very similar code to the method for loading the stations. You may save some time by copying code from *GetStations( )*, then making the necessary changes.

```csharp
    DataSet dsStations = new DataSet();

    DataSet dsRailLines = new DataSet();

    public Form1()
    {
        InitializeComponent();
        GetStations();
    }

    private void GetRailLines()
    {
        try
        {
            SqlConnection con = new SqlConnection(@"Data Source=.\SQLEXPRESS;
                AttachDbFilename=" + databaseLocation + "Integrated Security=True;
                Connect Timeout=30; User Instance=True");
            con.Open();
            SqlCommand cmRailLines = new SqlCommand();
            cmRailLines.Connection = con;
            cmRailLines.CommandType = CommandType.Text;
            cmRailLines.CommandText = "SELECT * FROM lines";

            SqlDataAdapter daRailLines = new SqlDataAdapter(cmRailLines);
            daRailLines.Fill(dsRailLines);
            con.Close();
        }

        catch
        {
            MessageBox.Show("File error");
        }
    }
```

When the program is running, we want the data for stations and underground lines to be easily available to the program so that a map of the Underground system can be drawn and journeys planned. It is best to hold the data in *arrays* in the fast electronic main memory of the computer, the RAM, where it can be accessed almost instantly.

The station data has already been stored in a set of arrays:

	StationID	StationName	Xpos	Ypos
[1]	1	Ealing Broadway	105	269
[2]	2	Notting Hill Gate	270	268
[3]	3	Paddington	272	221
[4]	4	Euston	409	218
......	......	....	......	......
[19]	19	King's Cross	440	218

These are *parallel* arrays. This means that if we choose data from the same row in each array, the series of data items will all refer to the same station. For example, if we take *row 4* of each array, we know that the station with *stationID = 4* is *Euston*, and its map cooordinates are *Xpos = 409*, *Ypos = 218*.

Notice that the arrays we created for the station data have only one column each. These are called *one-dimensional arrays*.

When we transfer the Underground Lines data into arrays, a different structure will be needed. We can store the *LineNames* in a *one-dimensional array*, but the station ID numbers along each line will need a *two-dimensional array* similar to a spreadsheet grid.

	LineName	Station 1	Station2	Station3	....	Station 10
[1]	Central	1	2	6		0
[2]	Northern	12	11	8		0
[3]	Circle	10	2	3		10
[4]	Victoria	13	11	9		0

Once all the data is available in arrays, it is very easy for the computer to read the *StationID* numbers in sequence along each of the lines, then go to the station data to obtain the name and map coordinates for the station. For example: *Station2* on the *Central* line has ID number 2 and is therefore *Notting Hill Gate*. The map coordinates for this station are *Xpos = 270*, *Ypos = 268*.

	LineName	Station 1	Station2	Station3	....	Station 10
[1]	Central	1	2	6		0
[2]	Northern	12	11	8		0
[3]	Circle	10	2	3		10
[4]	Victoria	13	11	9		0

	StationID	StationName	Xpos	Ypos
[1]	1	Ealing Broadway	105	269
[2]	2	Notting Hill Gate	270	268
[3]	3	Paddington	272	221
[4]	4	Euston	409	218
......	......	....	......	......
[19]	19	King's Cross	440	218

Set up variables near the start of the program to hold the *names of the Underground Lines*, and the sets of *stationID numbers along each line*. Add a call to the *GetRailLines( )* method:

```
DataSet dsRailLines = new DataSet();

int lineCount;
string[] lineName = new string[6];
int[,] stationNumber = new int[6, 12];

public Form1()
{
    InitializeComponent();
    GetStations();
    GetRailLines();
}
```

Go to the end of the *GetRailLines( )* method and add code to transfer the data into the arrays:

```
        catch
        {
            MessageBox.Show("File error");
        }

        lineCount = dsRailLines.Tables[0].Rows.Count;

        for (int i = 0; i < lineCount; i++)
        {
            DataRow drRailLine = dsRailLines.Tables[0].Rows[i];
            lineName[i] = Convert.ToString(drRailLine[0]);

            for (int j = 1; j < 11; j++)
            {
                stationNumber[i, j] = Convert.ToInt16(drRailLine[j]);
            }
        }
    }
```

We now have a lot of variables in use in the program, and it is worth taking the time to construct a reference table, known as a **Data Dictionary**, to remind ourselves of the purpose of each of the variables and the way that the array elements are accessed:

Variable	Data type	Purpose	Examples
stationCount	integer	The number of **station** records in the database	stationCount = 19
stationID	int[20]	One dimensional array storing the stationID numbers allocated to the stations.	stationID[1] = 1 stationID[19] = 19
stationName	string[20]	One dimensional array storing the names of the stations.	stationName[1]="Ealing Broadway" stationName[19]="Kings Cross"
stationX	int[20]	One dimensional array storing the X (across) pixel position of the station on the map	stationX[1] = 105 stationX[19] = 440
stationY	int[20]	One dimensional array storing the Y (down) pixel position of the station on the map	stationY[1] = 269 stationY[19] = 218
lineCount	int	The number of **underground line** records in the database	lineCount = 4
lineName	string[6]	One dimensional array storing the names of the underground lines.	lineName[1] = "Central"
stationNumber	int[6, 12]	Two dimensional array storing the stationID values for stations along each line. First index is the line number. Second index is the station sequence	stationNumber[2,3] = 8 (on underground line 2, the station in position 3 along the line has a stationID value of 8)

By use of the arrays it should be possible to find the sequence of stationIDs along any underground line, then use these stationID values to find the corresponding station names and map coordinates. We can therefore proceed to draw our route map:

Set up a method called **DrawRailLines( )** below the **DrawMap( )** method. Add a call to this method in **Form1_Paint( )**.

We are going to draw the railway map as a series of straight line sections linking pairs of stations. Each line section will begin at the point (startX, startY) and end at the point (endX,endY).

We will set up pen colours to represent the offical colour codes given to the London Underground Lines:

    Central Line: red   ***Northern Line:***   black
    Circle Line: yellow   ***Victoria Line:***   *light blue*

The purpose of the FillRectangle command is to produce a white background for the map area.

Chapter 6: London Underground

```
private void DrawRailLines()
{
    int startX;
    int startY;
    int endX;
    int endY;

    Graphics g = this.CreateGraphics();
    Pen white = new Pen(Color.White, 1);
    Pen blackW = new Pen(Color.Black, 3);
    Pen goldW = new Pen(Color.Gold, 5);
    Pen blueW = new Pen(Color.DeepSkyBlue, 3);
    Pen redW = new Pen(Color.Red, 3);

    g.FillRectangle(white.Brush, new Rectangle(0, 0, 800, 600));
}

private void Form1_Paint(object sender, PaintEventArgs e)
{
    DrawRailLines();

    DrawMap();
}
```

We now add a loop to **DrawRailLines( )** which will repeat for each underground line, and within this a loop which will repeat for each pair of stations. We collect the *stationID*s for the stations:

```
    Pen blueW = new Pen(Color.DeepSkyBlue, 3);
    Pen redW = new Pen(Color.Red, 3);
    g.FillRectangle(white.Brush, new Rectangle(0, 0, 800, 600));

    for (int i = 0; i < lineCount; i++)
    {
        for (int j = 1; j < 11; j++)
        {
            int firstStationID = stationNumber[i, j];
            int secondStationID = stationNumber[i, j + 1];
            if (secondStationID > 0)
            {
            }
        }
    }
```

We will use the *stationID*s to find the map coordinates for each pair of stations, then connect them with a line of the correct colour. For example:

Central line

        Station 1   **Station 2**

stationID = 1: **Ealing Broadway**   stationID = 2: **Notting Hill Gate**

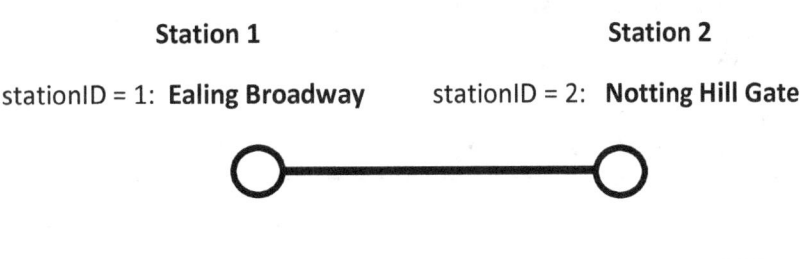

map coordinates   Xpos = **105**, Ypos = **269**   Xpos = **270**, Ypos = **268**

Add lines of code. These use the *stationID*s to find the map coordinates for these stations:

```csharp
for (int j = 1; j < 11; j++)
{
    int firstStationID = stationNumber[i, j];
    int secondStationID = stationNumber[i, j + 1];
    if (secondStationID > 0)
    {
        startX = 0;
        startY = 0;
        endX = 0;
        endY = 0;
        for (int s = 0; s < stationCount; s++)
        {
            if (firstStationID == stationID[s])
            {
                startX = stationX[s];
                startY = stationY[s];
            }
            if (secondStationID == stationID[s])
            {
                endX = stationX[s];
                endY = stationY[s];
            }
        }
    }
}
```

The final step is to draw a line between each pair of stations, using the correct colour for the particular London Underground Line:

```csharp
for (int s = 0; s < stationCount; s++)
{

    if (firstStationID == stationID[s])
    {
        startX = stationX[s];
        startY = stationY[s];
    }
    if (secondStationID == stationID[s])
    {
        endX = stationX[s];
        endY = stationY[s];
    }

}
if (lineName[i] == "Circle")
    g.DrawLine(goldW, startX, startY, endX, endY);
if (lineName[i] == "Northern")
    g.DrawLine(blackW, startX, startY, endX, endY);
if (lineName[i] == "Victoria")
    g.DrawLine(blueW, startX, startY, endX, endY);
if (lineName[i] == "Central")
    g.DrawLine(redW, startX, startY, endX, endY);
}
```

Run the program, and the railway map should be displayed with the stations connected as shown, using the correct line colours. If any stations are not connected correctly, go to the database to check that the stationID numbers have been allocated to stations correctly, and that the stationIDs appear in the correct sequence along each rail line.

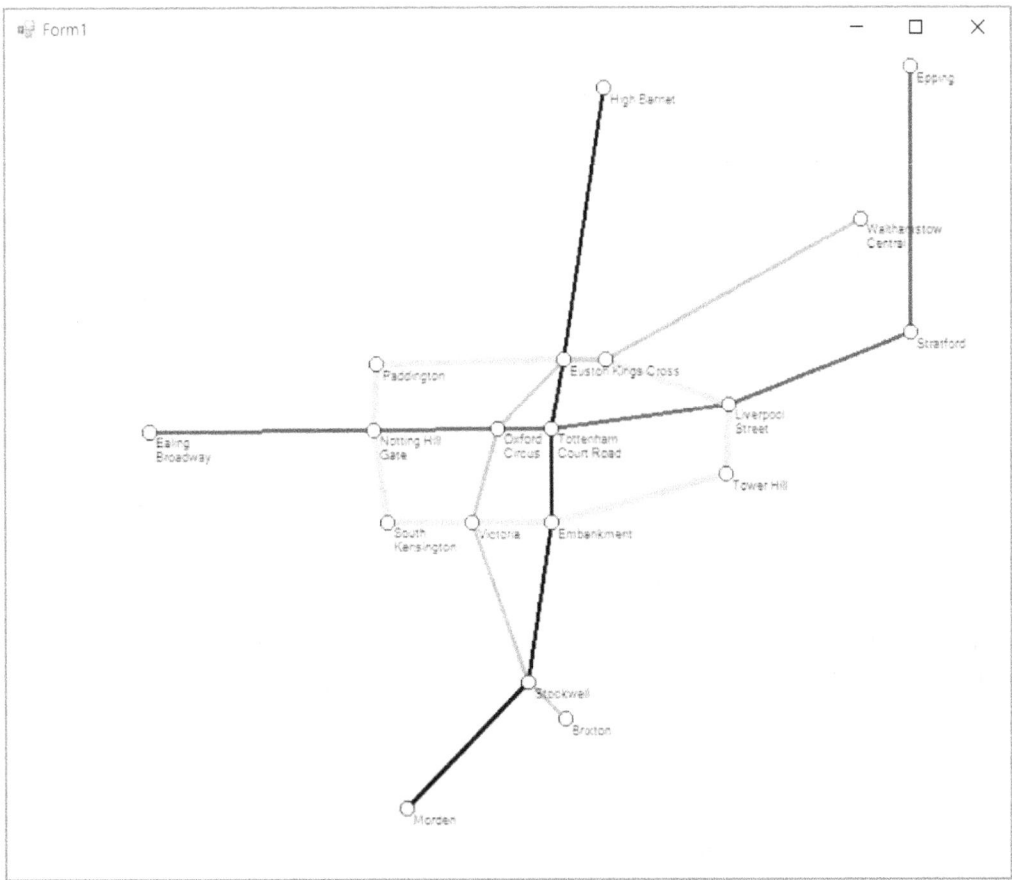

Return to the Form1 design screen and add components to the top right hand corner of the form, beyond the edge of the map, as shown. You will need to extend the form sideways quite a long way to make space for this.

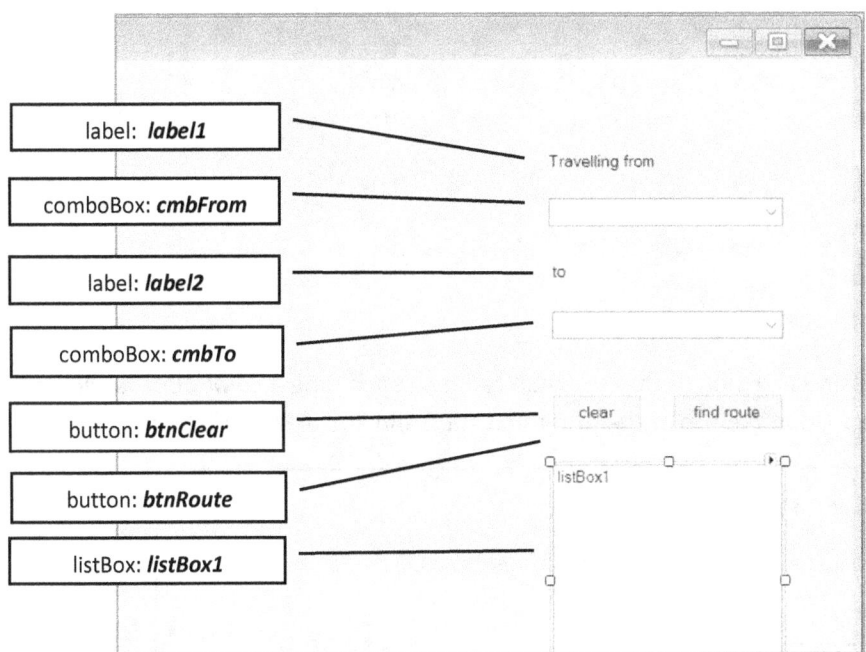

These components will provide a user interface for entering the start and destination stations, and for displaying the route found.

We will give the user the choice of selecting the start and destination stations from drop down alphabetical lists, or by clicking the required stations on the route map.

To produce the drop down lists, go to the **GetStations( )** method. Near the end of the method, add two lines of code to load the station lists into the comboBoxes:

```
for (int i = 0; i < stationCount; i++)
{
    DataRow drStation = dsStations.Tables[0].Rows[i];

    stationID[i] = Convert.ToInt16(drStation[0]);
    stationName[i] = Convert.ToString(drStation[1]);
    stationX[i] = Convert.ToInt16(drStation[2]);
    stationY[i] = Convert.ToInt16(drStation[3]);

    cmbFrom.Items.Add(stationName[i]);
    cmbTo.Items.Add(stationName[i]);
}
}
```

Run the program and check that the station names are listed in the comboBoxes and can be selected by mouse click. If necessary, move the components further to the right so they do not overlap the map.

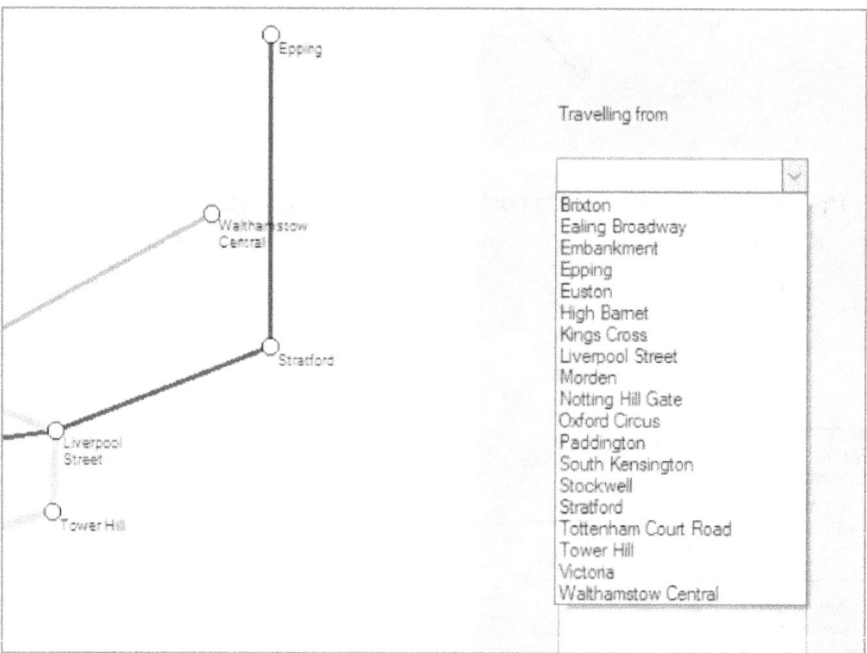

A slight problem, easily corrected, is that the map redraws each time a **comboBox** is clicked, causing the screen to flicker. Go to the top of the program listing and add a **Boolean** (true/false) variable:

```
public partial class Form1 : Form
{
    string databaseLocation = "C:\\C#\\underground.mdf;";

    bool loading = true;
```

Add code to the **Form1_Paint( )** method to ensure that the map is only drawn once, at the time when the program first starts:

```csharp
private void Form1_Paint(object sender, PaintEventArgs e)
{
    if (loading == true)
    {
        DrawRailLines();
        DrawMap();

        loading = false;
    }
}
```

Double click the '**Clear**' button to create a **btnClear_click( )** method, then add code to clear the entries in the comboBoxes and listBox.

```csharp
private void btnClear_Click(object sender, EventArgs e)
{
    cmbFrom.Text = "";
    cmbTo.Text = "";
    listBox1.Items.Clear();
}
```

Run the program to check that the **Clear** button functions correctly.

We can now work on the code to select stations by clicking the route map. Begin by selecting Form1 and going to the Properties window. Change to '**Events**' and double click to create a '**MouseDown**' method:

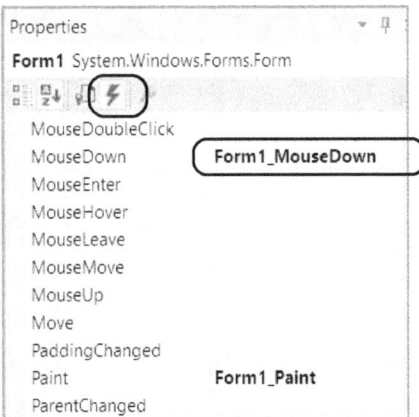

Add code to the **Form1_MouseDown( )** method to find the X and Y position when the mouse is clicked on the form.

```csharp
private void Form1_MouseDown(object sender, MouseEventArgs e)
{
    int X = Cursor.Position.X;
    int Y = Cursor.Position.Y;
    Point p = new Point(X, Y);

    p = PointToClient(p);
}
```

We then use the X and Y cooordinates to look for a station close to this position on the map. The program checks for station cooordinates within 5 pixels of the mouse pointer when the mouse is clicked.

If the first comboBox, recording the starting location, is currently empty then the station name is entered in this box; otherwise it is entered into the second comboBox as the destination.

```
private void Form1_MouseDown(object sender, MouseEventArgs e)
{
    int X = Cursor.Position.X;
    int Y = Cursor.Position.Y;
    Point p = new Point(X, Y);
    p = PointToClient(p);

    for (int i = 0; i < stationCount; i++)
    {
        if (Math.Abs(stationX[i] - p.X) < 5 && Math.Abs(stationY[i] - p.Y) < 5)
        {
            if (cmbFrom.Text == "")
            {
                cmbFrom.Text = stationName[i];
            }
            else
            {
                cmbTo.Text = stationName[i];
            }
        }
    }
}
```

Run the program and check that stations can be selected correctly by clicking on the route map:

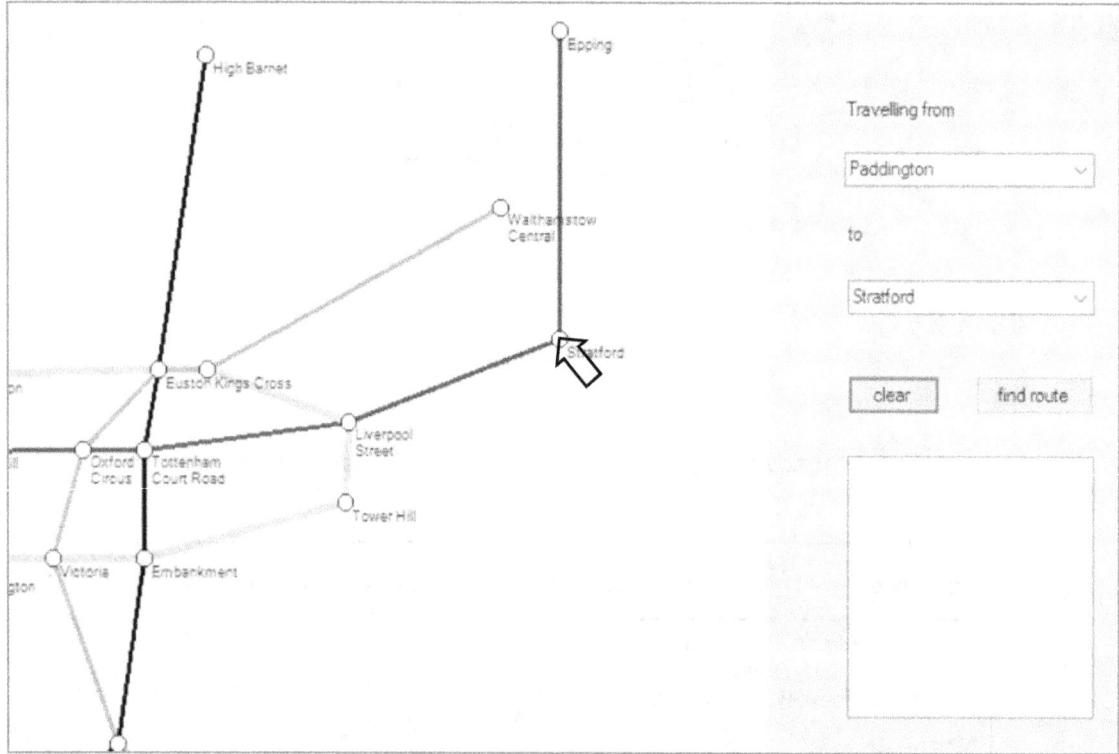

If the user interface is working correctly, we can now begin work on the route finding algorithm.

Close the program and go to the **Form1** design view. Double click the '*find route*' button to produce a **btnRoute_Click( )** method. Add lines of code to collect the names of the departure and destination stations from the comboBoxes and redisplay these in the listBox:

```
private void btnRoute_Click(object sender, EventArgs e)
{
    string startStation = cmbFrom.Text;
    string endStation = cmbTo.Text;

    listBox1.Items.Clear();
    listBox1.Items.Add("Travelling from: " + startStation);
    listBox1.Items.Add("");
    listBox1.Items.Add("Travelling to: " + endStation);
}
```

Run the program and check that the station names are transferred to the ListBox correctly. Increase the width of the List Box if necessary, so that the station names are fully visible.

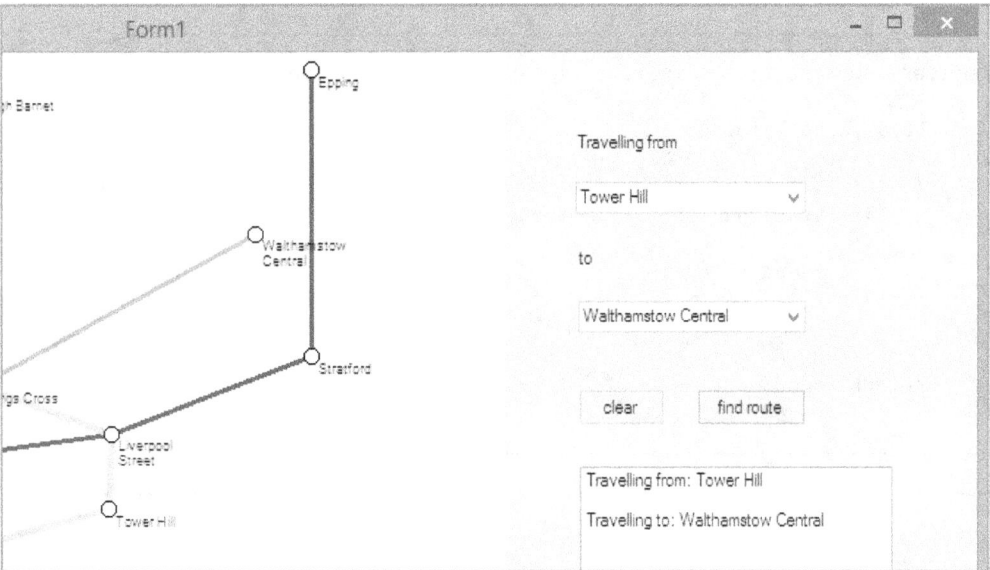

Close the program and return to the C# code page.

We will set up some small methods which will be useful during the route finding process. The first will take the name of a station and **convert it to the equivalent stationID** number. Insert this method above the **btnRoute_click( )** method:

```
private int getStationID(string stationNameWanted)
{
    int stationIDfound = 0;
    for (int i = 0; i < stationCount; i++)
    {
        if (stationNameWanted == stationName[i])
        {
            stationIDfound = stationID[i];
        }
    }
    return stationIDfound;
}
```

Below this we will make another method to do exactly the opposite task, taking a stationID number and *converting this to the equivalent station name*:

```csharp
private string getStationName(int stationIDwanted)
{
    string stationNameFound = "";
    for (int i = 0; i < stationCount; i++)
    {
        if (stationIDwanted == stationID[i])
        {
            stationNameFound = stationName[i];
        }
    }
    return stationNameFound;
}
```

We need to add one more method to check whether a particular station is present on a particular underground line. This will return a result of '*true*' if the station is on the line, and '*false*' if it is not:

```csharp
private bool stationOnLine(int lineNumber, int stationIDwanted)
{
    bool found = false;
    for (int j = 1; j < 11; j++)
    {
        if (stationNumber[lineNumber, j] == stationIDwanted)
        {
            found = true;
        }
    }

    return found;
}
```

Now that we have some useful tools available, we can continue with the route finding procedure.

We know the names of the start and destination stations, so we can use the *getStationID( )* method to find the equivalent stationIDs. Add lines of code to the *btnRoute_Click( )* method.

```csharp
listBox1.Items.Clear();
listBox1.Items.Add("Travelling from: " + startStation);
listBox1.Items.Add("");
listBox1.Items.Add("Travelling to: " + endStation);

int startStationID = getStationID(startStation);
int endStationID = getStationID(endStation);
```

If the stationIDs of both the start and destination stations are present on the same underground line, then it will be possible to make the journey without changing train. We will add code to the **btnRoute_Click( )** method to check for this possibility, making use of the **stationOnLine( )** method:

```
    int startStationID = getStationID(startStation);
    int endStationID = getStationID(endStation);

    bool startFound, endFound;
    string undergroundLine;
    bool directRoute = false;

    for (int lineNumber = 0; lineNumber < lineCount; lineNumber++)
    {
        undergroundLine = lineName[lineNumber];

        startFound = stationOnLine(lineNumber, startStationID);
        endFound = stationOnLine(lineNumber, endStationID);

        if (startFound == true && endFound == true)
        {
            listBox1.Items.Add("");
            listBox1.Items.Add("Travel direct on the " + undergroundLine + " Line");
            directRoute = true;
        }
    }
```

Run the program and test various routes where direct travel is possible:

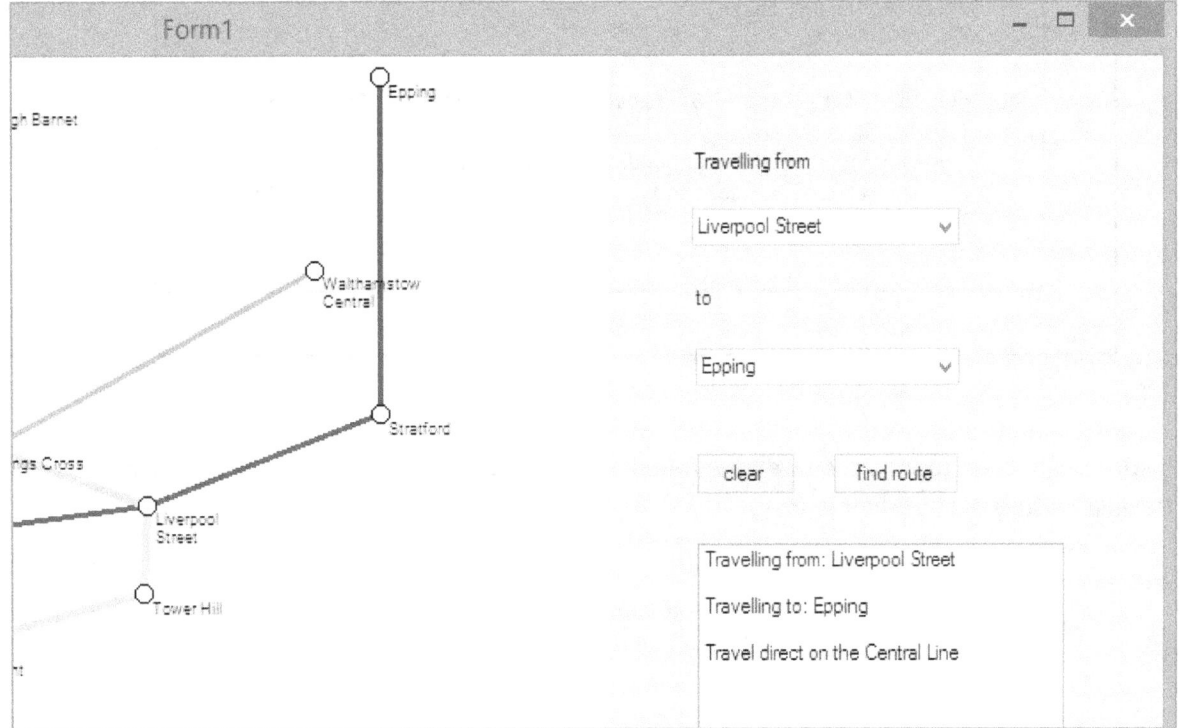

We can now examine the more complicated situation where a change of train is necessary.

If no direct route is found then the following strategy will be adopted:

> 1. LOOP for each underground line
>> 2. LOOP to find if the *start station* is on this line. IF it is…
>>> 3. LOOP for each station along the line – this is potentially a station to *change* trains
>>>> 4. LOOP for each *other* underground line
>>>>> 5. IF the *change station* AND the *destination station* are on this line THEN a route has been found:
>>>>> Display the start line
>>>>> Display the change station
>>>>> Display the destination line

We will begin by adding *loops 1 and 2*, to check each underground line to see if it *contains the start station*:

```
            {
                listBox1.Items.Clear();
                listBox1.Items.Add("Travel direct on the "+undergroundLine+" Line");
                directRoute = true;
            }
        }
        if (directRoute == false)
        {

            for (int firstLine = 0; firstLine < lineCount; firstLine++)
            {
                string startUndergroundLine = lineName[firstLine];
                startFound = stationOnLine(firstLine, startStationID);
            }
        }
```

If *startFound* is set to *true*, then we have found an underground line serving the station where the traveller wishes to start their journey.

We will now consider each of the other stations along this line (*loop 3* in the algorithm above), as it might be a ***possible point to change*** to a different underground line serving the destination.

```
for (int firstLine = 0; firstLine < lineCount; firstLine++)
{
    string startUndergroundLine = lineName[firstLine];
    startFound = stationOnLine(firstLine, startStationID);
    if (startFound == true)
    {
       for (int j = 1; j < 11; j++)
       {
           if (stationNumber[firstLine, j] > 0)
           {
               int changeStation = stationNumber[firstLine, j];
           }
       }
    }
}
```

We can now check each other underground line to see if the ***change station*** and ***destination*** are both on that line (***loops and conditionals 4 and 5*** in the algorithm above):

```
int changeStation = stationNumber[firstLine, j];
for (int secondLine = 0; secondLine < lineCount; secondLine++)
{
   if (secondLine != firstLine)
   {
       undergroundLine = lineName[secondLine];
       bool destination = stationOnLine(secondLine, endStationID);
       bool change = stationOnLine(secondLine, changeStation);
       if (destination==true && change==true)
       {
           string changeStationName=getStationName(changeStation);
           listBox1.Items.Add("");
           listBox1.Items.Add("Travel on the "+startUndergroundLine+" Line");
           listBox1.Items.Add("change at " + changeStationName);
           listBox1.Items.Add("to the " + undergroundLine + " Line");
       }
   }
}
```

Test the completed program, which should now give correct travel options between any starting station and destination. If more than one route is possible, each will be displayed.

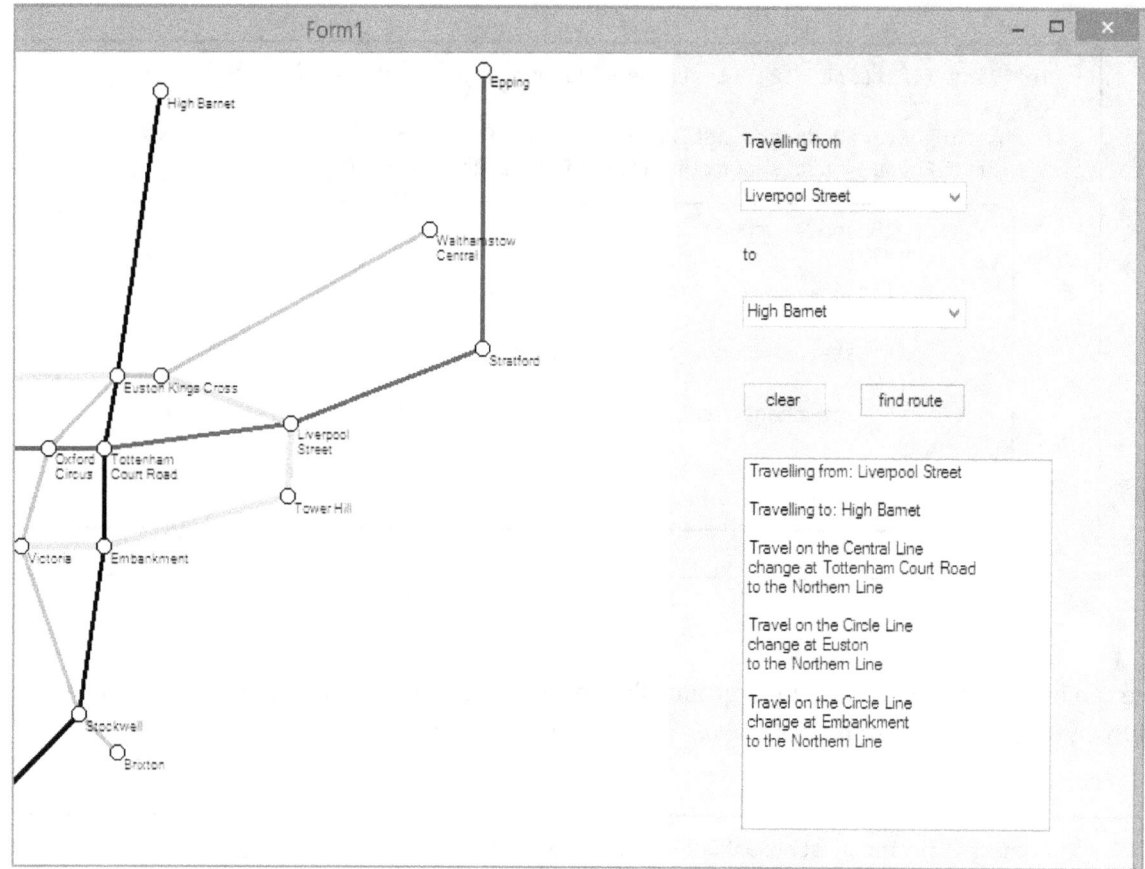

Some programming challenges…

- If more than one route is possible, how could the program select the route through the least number of stations?
- How could the program be developed to include more stations and additional underground lines?
- For a more complex system, more than one change of train might be needed. How could the algorithm be developed to allow for two changes of train?

7 Estate Agent Database

The next program is a complete database application for an Estate Agent, handling properties for sale and customers wishing to find suitable properties. We will look at how C# .NET can **display existing records**, **add new records** to the database, **update records** and **delete records**, as well as carrying out **queries** to find suitable properties for particular customers.

Go to the **Server Explorer** window and right-click on **Data Connection** to set up a new connection. Select **Microsoft SQL Server Database File** as the Data source.

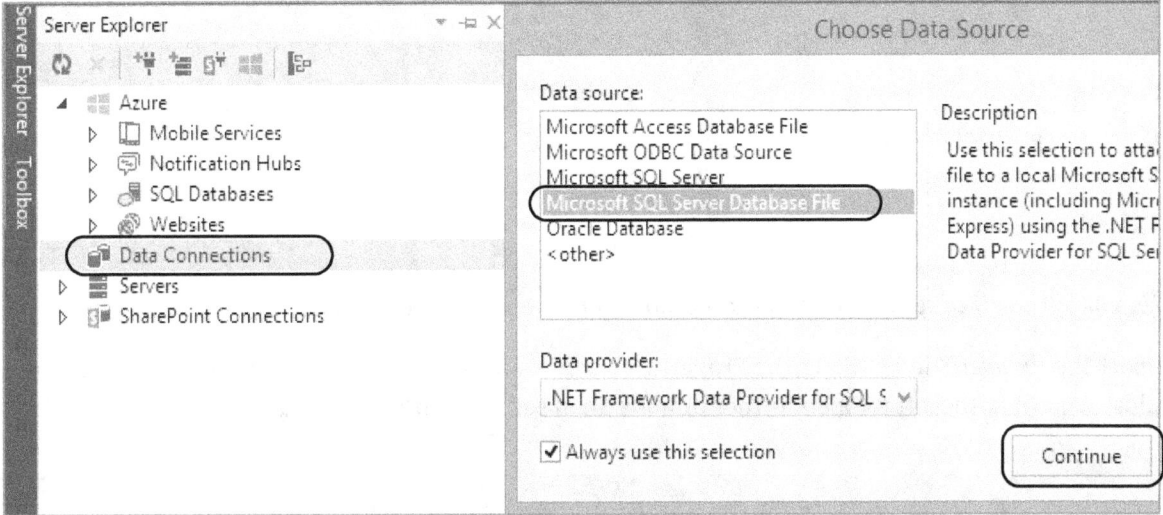

Use the Browse button to select a drive and folder location, then create a database called '*estateAgent*'.

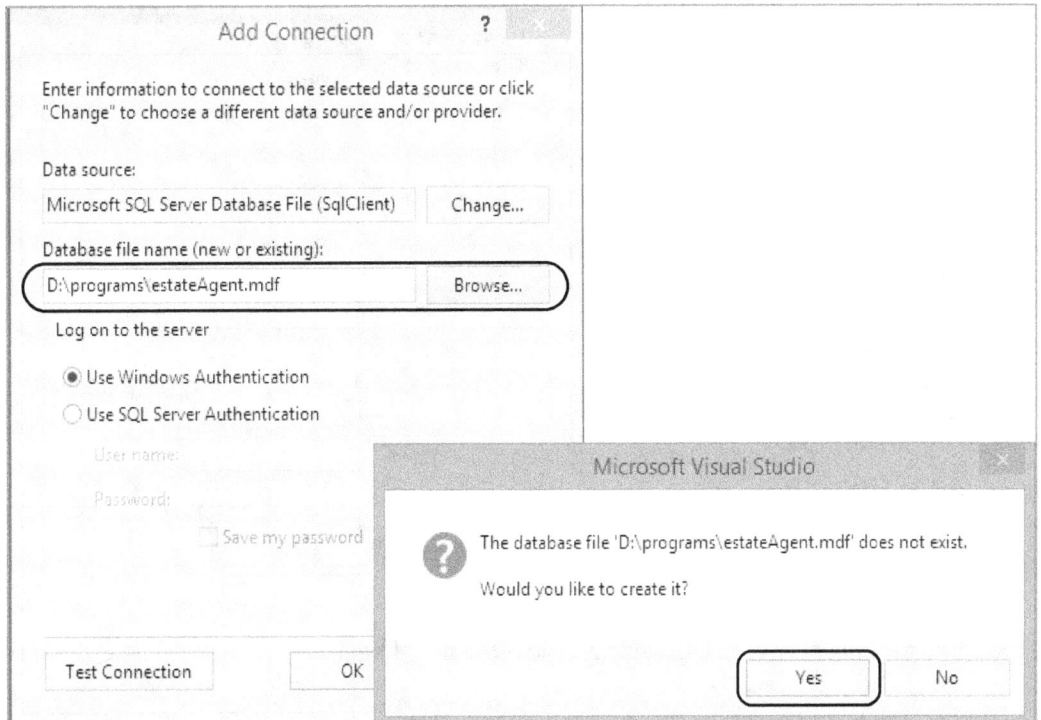

Right-click the **Tables** icon to add a new table to the database. This table will store details of houses for sale.

Add fields to the table as shown. The fields '*propertyType*', '*location*' and '*land*' will be code numbers representing different property descriptions.

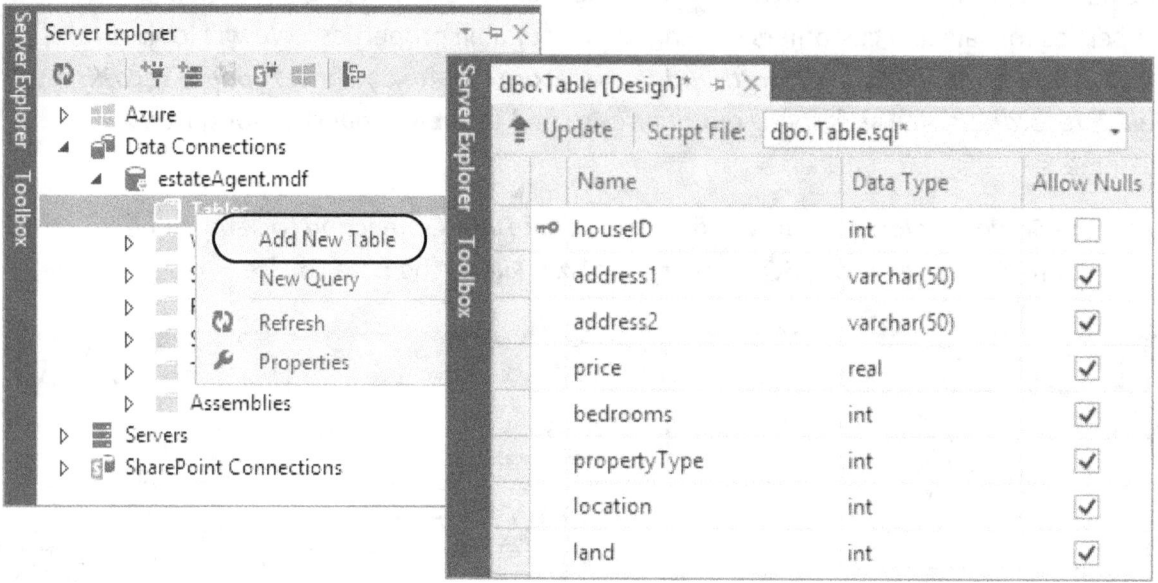

We will set the '*houseID*' to be an auto-number generated by the database.

Select the '*houseID*' field. Go to the Properties window and locate '*Identity Specification*'. Click the 'plus' symbol to the left to open further options, then set '*(Is Identity)*' to '*True*'.

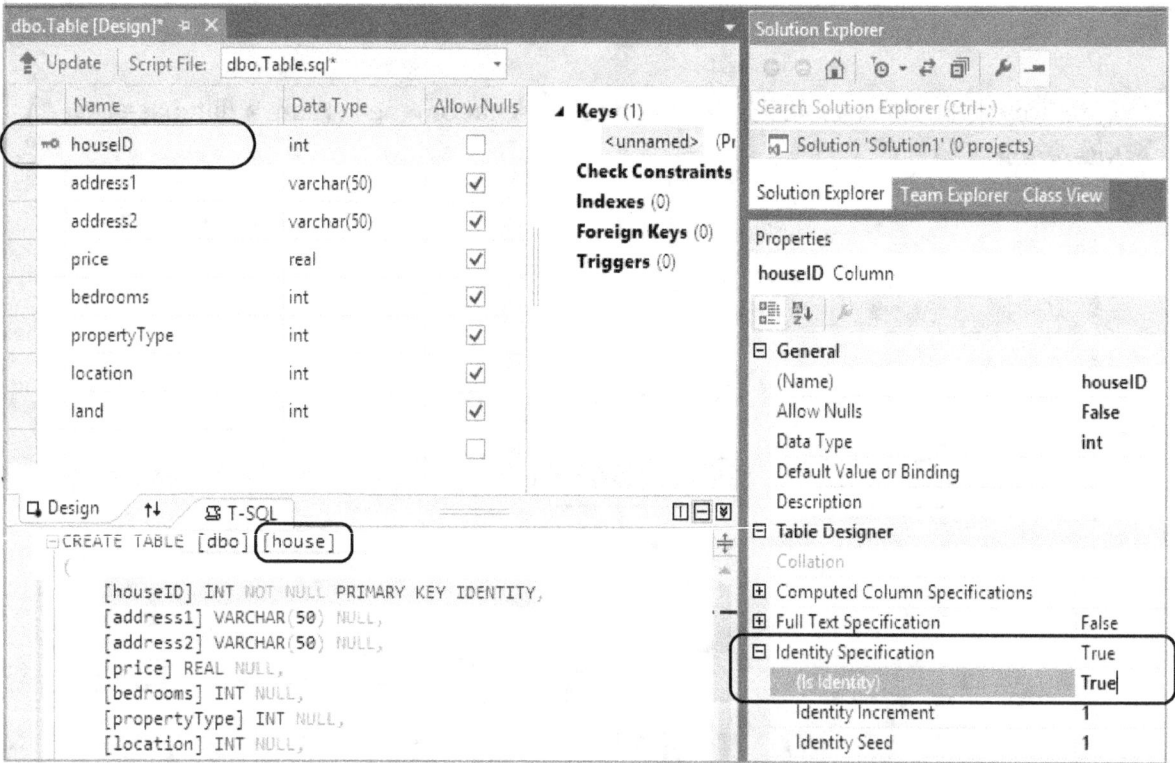

Name the table as '*house*' in the SQL window below the list of fields.

Select the '*Update*' option above the list of fields, then click the '*Update database*' button.

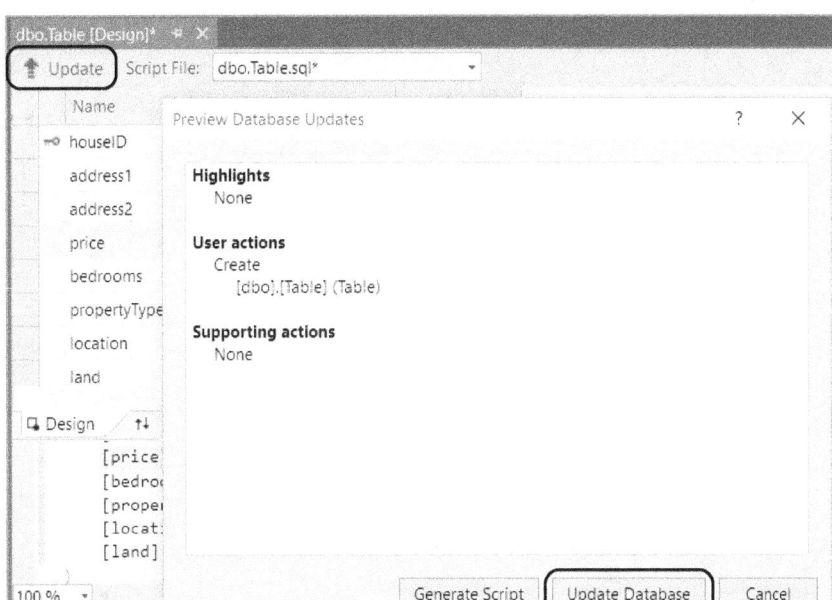

Close the table by clicking the small cross on the tab.

Repeat the sequence of steps above to create another table in the database. This will store details of customers and their requirements. Add the fields shown:

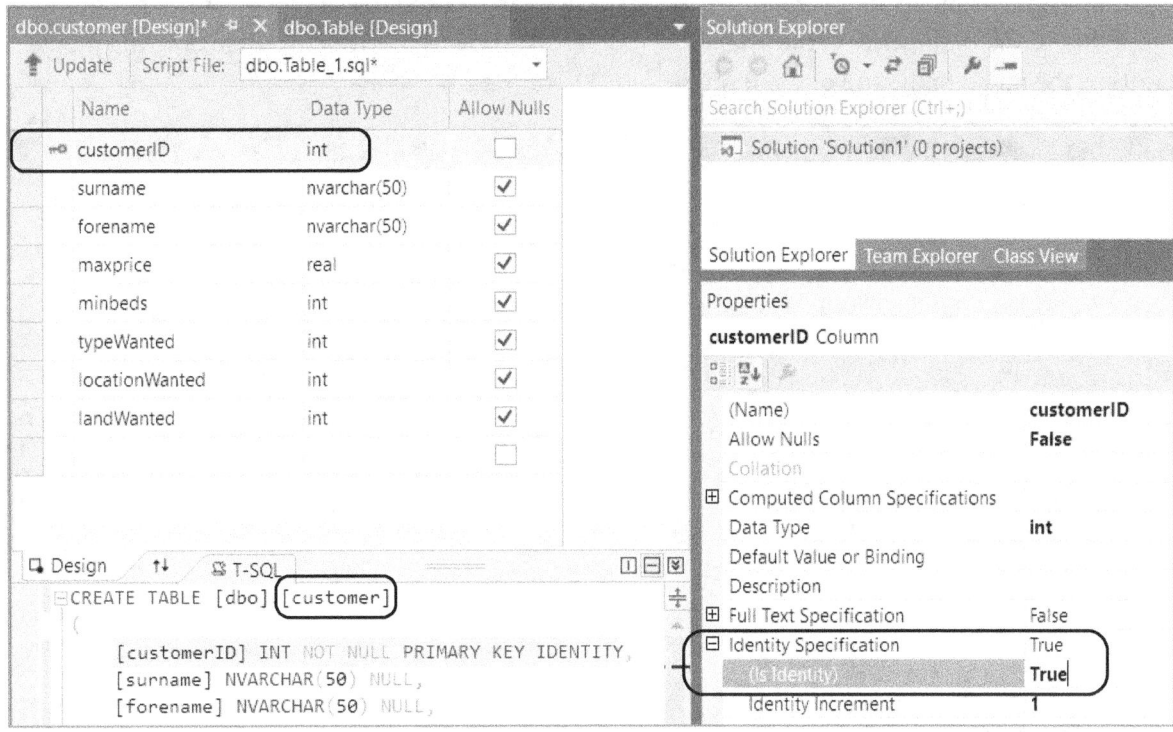

Set the *customerID* field to be an auto-number by setting '*Identity Specification / (Is Identity)*' to '*True*'.

Change the table name to '*customer*' in the SQL panel. Click '*Update*' to save, then close the table by clicking the cross icon above the table window.

We can now begin the C# program which will access the database. Select '**New Project**'. Choose '**Windows Forms Application**', and set the program name to '*estateAgent*'.

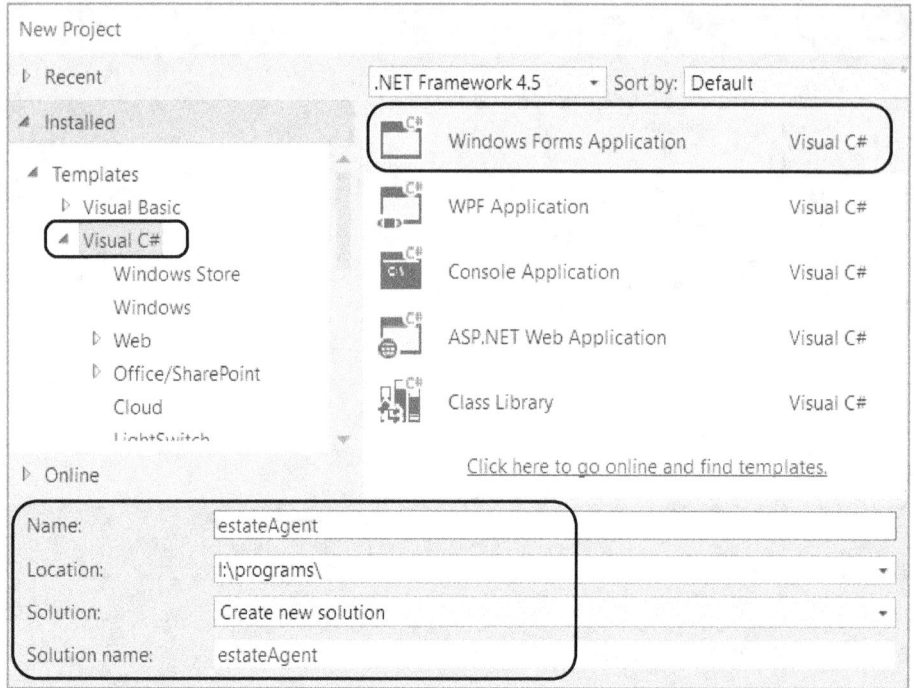

Click '**OK**' to create *Form1*.

We will set up a menu across the top of *Form1* which can be used to select the various program options. Click '*MenuStrip*' in the '**Menus & Toolbars**' section of the Toolbox, then drag the mouse to attach the menu to the top of the form.

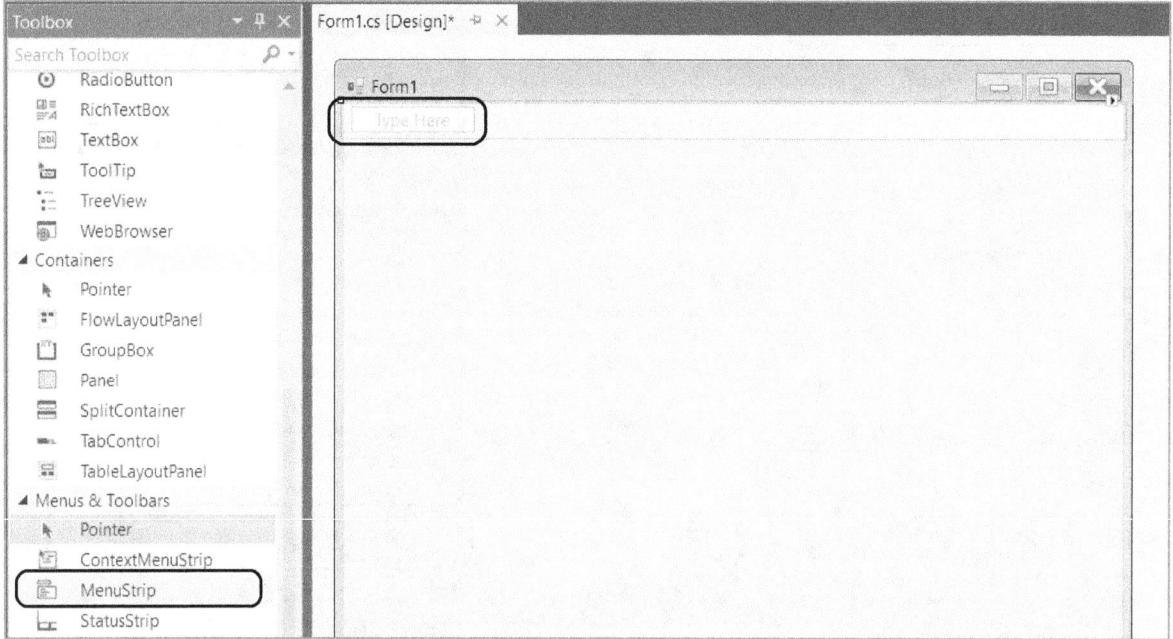

The menu system is started by typing in the box which is displayed. As each menu item is entered, additional boxes appear alongside and below for use if required.

Build up the series of menu options shown below, by typing captions into the required boxes:

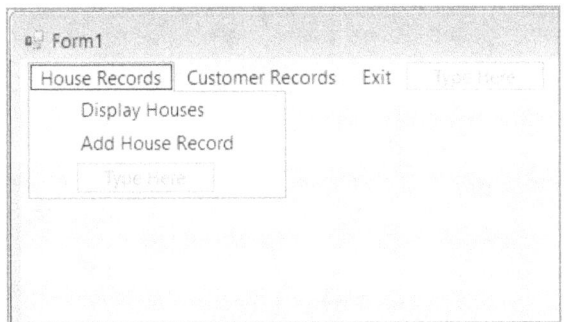
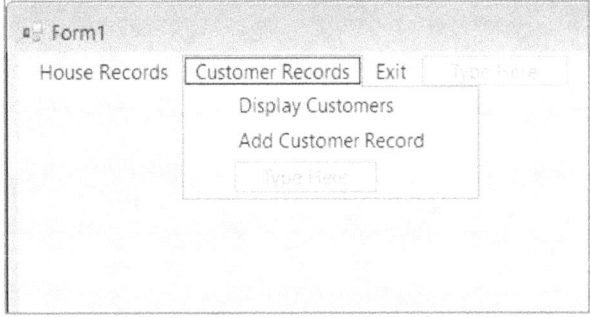

Double click the '*Exit*' menu option. An event handling method will be created. Add the line of code which will close the program.

```
namespace estateAgent
{
    public partial class Form1 : Form
    {
        public Form1()
        {
            InitializeComponent();
        }

        private void exitToolStripMenuItem_Click(object sender, EventArgs e)
        {
            this.Close();
        }
    }
}
```

Go to the **Solution Explorer** window and right click the '*estateAgent*' icon. Select '*Add / New item*'. Choose '*Windows Form*', and set the name to '*DisplayHouses*'.

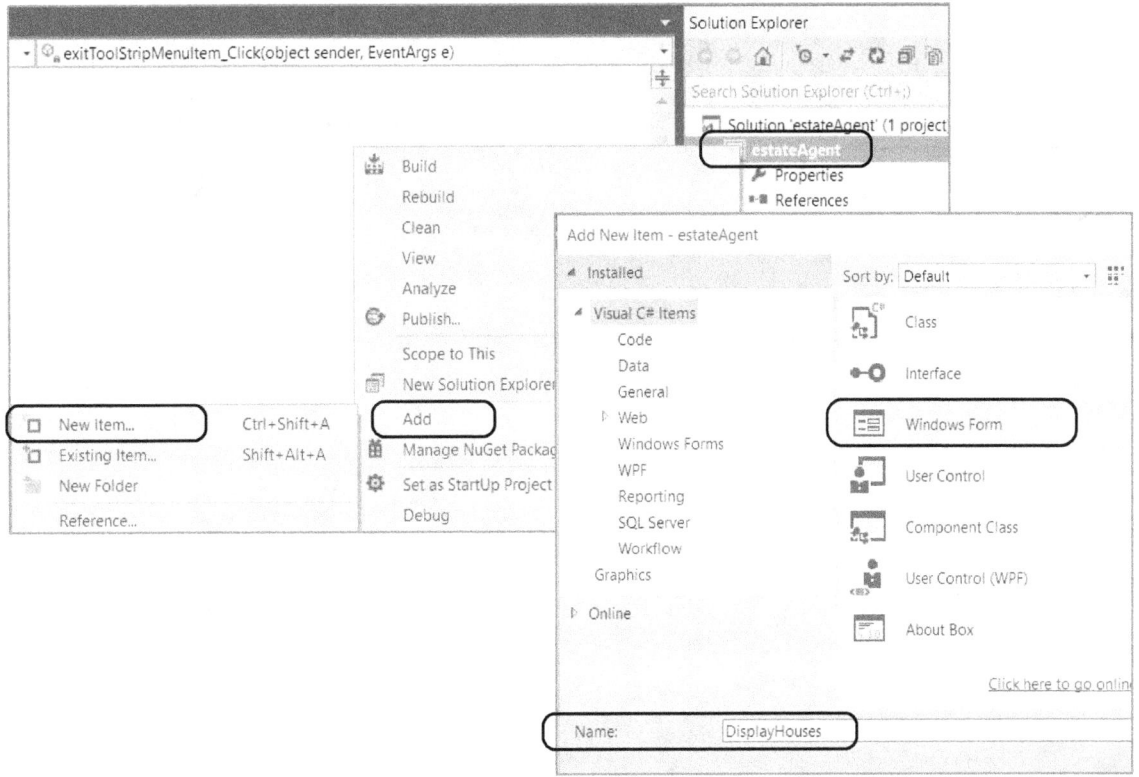

We will link this form to the menu. Double click the '**Display Houses**' option to create an event handling method:

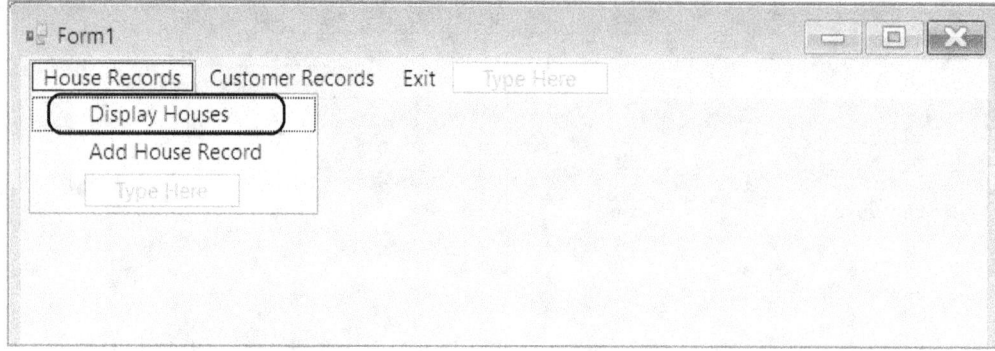

Add lines of code to open the **DisplayHouses** form:

```csharp
private void exitToolStripMenuItem_Click(object sender, EventArgs e)
{
    this.Close();
}

private void displayHousesToolStripMenuItem_Click(object sender, EventArgs e)
{
    DisplayHouses frmDisplayHouses = new DisplayHouses();
    frmDisplayHouses.ShowDialog();
}
```

Run the program and check that the '**Display Houses**' and '**Exit**' menu options operate correctly.

We can now start to work on the **DisplayHouses form**. This will show a list of houses for sale. Add a **listBox** component to the form, and set the **font size** of the listBox to **10pt**. Also add a '**Close**' button and rename this a **btnClose**.

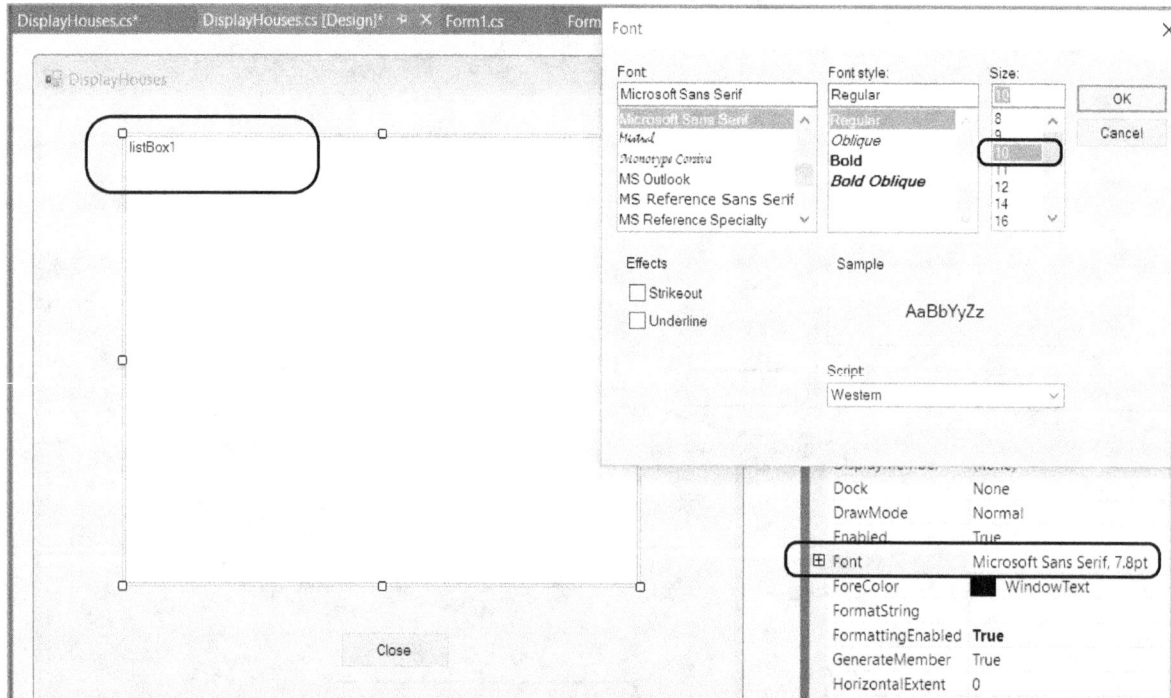

Double click the *Close* button, then add a line of code to event handling method:

```
namespace estateAgent
{
    public partial class DisplayHouses : Form
    {

        public DisplayHouses()
        {
            InitializeComponent();
        }

        private void btnClose_Click(object sender, EventArgs e)
        {
            this.Close();
        }
    }
}
```

We can now set up a method to load details of houses for sale. Using similar code to previous programs, we will:

- Add a '*using SqlClient*' directive.
- Specify the database location.
- Set up an empty *loadAddresses( )* method. This will contain the program code to load house records from the database.
- Create a *dataSet* to receive the house data when it is loaded.
- Call the *loadAddresses( )* method from *DisplayHouses( )*, so that house records are loaded when the form opens.

```
using System.Text;
using System.Windows.Forms;
using System.Data.SqlClient;

namespace estateAgent
{
    public partial class DisplayHouses : Form
    {
        string databaseLocation = "C:\\C#\\estateAgent.mdf;";

        public DisplayHouses()
        {
            InitializeComponent();
            loadAddresses();
        }

        DataSet dsHouses = new DataSet();

        public void loadAddresses()
        {

        }

        private void btnClose_Click(object sender, EventArgs e)
        {
            this.Close();
        }
```

We will add code to load the house records, again closely following the pattern of previous programs. Remember that the line beginning:

SqlConnection con = new SqlConnection(...

must be entered as a single line of code with no line breaks.

```csharp
public void loadAddresses()
{
    SqlConnection con = new SqlConnection(@"Data Source=.\SQLEXPRESS;
        AttachDbFilename=" + databaseLocation + "Integrated Security=True;
        Connect Timeout=30; User Instance=True");

    try
    {
        con.Open();
        SqlCommand cmHouses = new SqlCommand();
        cmHouses.Connection = con;
        cmHouses.CommandType = CommandType.Text;
        cmHouses.CommandText = "SELECT * FROM house";

        SqlDataAdapter daHouses = new SqlDataAdapter(cmHouses);
        daHouses.Fill(dsHouses);
        con.Close();
    }
    catch
    {
        MessageBox.Show("File error");
    }
}
```

Once the house data has been transferred to the *dataSet*, we will use a loop to access each record, picking out the address fields for display in the *list box*:

```csharp
        SqlDataAdapter daHouses = new SqlDataAdapter(cmHouses);
        daHouses.Fill(dsHouses);
        con.Close();

        int countRecords = dsHouses.Tables[0].Rows.Count;

        for (int i = 0; i < countRecords; i++)
        {
            DataRow drHouse = dsHouses.Tables[0].Rows[i];
            string houseAddress = drHouse[1] + ", " + drHouse[2];
            listBox1.Items.Add(houseAddress);
        }
```

Before testing the program, it will be necessary to enter sample house data. Go to the Server Explorer, double click the '*house*' table icon, then select '*Show Table Data*'.

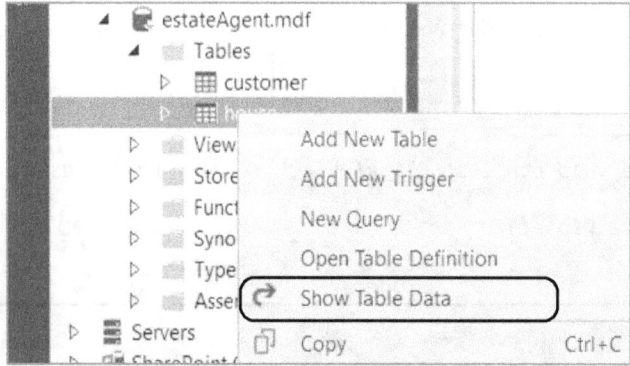

Add example test data to the table. The values for *propertyType*, *location* and *land* are code numbers which will be explained shortly.

houseID	address1	address2	price	bedrooms	propertyType	location	land
1	Sea View	Fairbourne	138000	2	3	2	1
2	37 High Street	Porthmadog	142000	3	4	1	1
3	Pant Mawr Farmhouse	Bala	464000	4	1	3	3
4	The Old Chapel	Tanygrisiau	258000	4	1	2	2
5	4 Barmouth Road	Dolgellau	380000	5	2	1	2
NULL	NULL	NULL	NULL	NULL	NULL	NULL	NULL

Close the *house* table. Select *'estateAgent.mdf'* in the **Server Explorer** window, right-click and use the *Delete* option to delete the data connection. This must be done before the program is run.

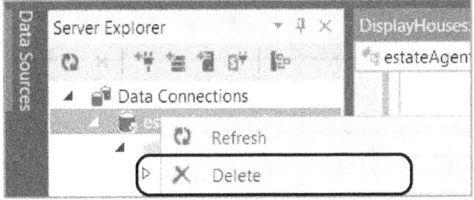

Run the program. Select the menu option to display houses. The house addresses should appear in the listBox on the DisplayHouses form:

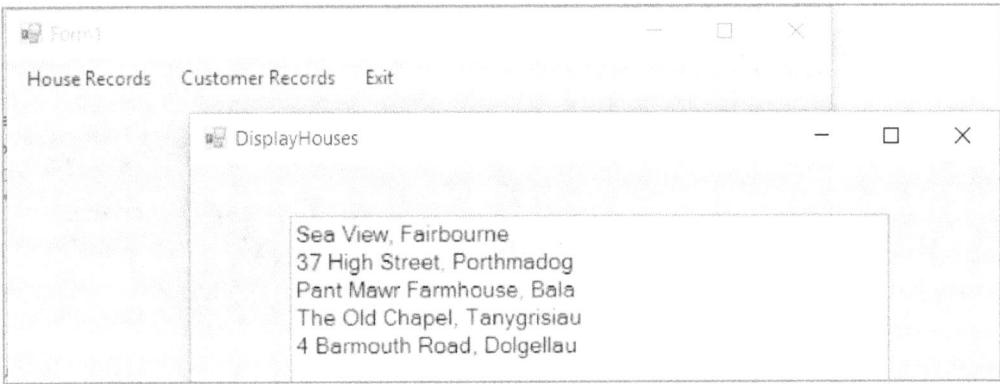

When a user clicks on one of the house addresses, we will arrange for full details of the property to be displayed.

Go to the **Solution Explorer** window, right-click the *'estateAgent'* program icon, and select '**Add / New item**'. Set up a **Windows Form** with the name '*HouseDetails*'.

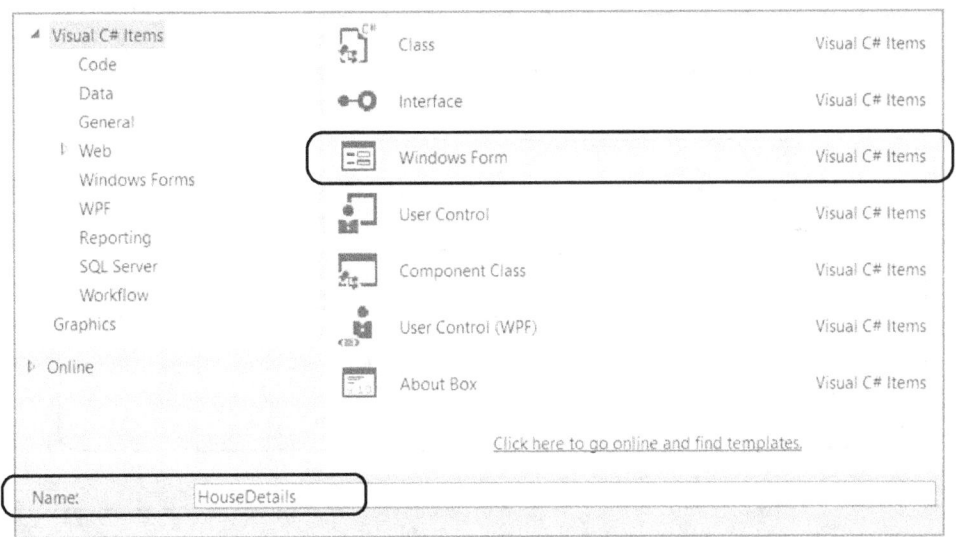

The new *HouseDetails* form will open. Right-click on the form and select '*View code*'. Add an empty method called *getHouseDetails( )*. This will be used to collect and display full information about a selected house.

```
namespace estateAgent
{
    public partial class HouseDetails : Form
    {
        public HouseDetails()
        {
            InitializeComponent();
        }

        public void getHouseDetails(DataRow drHouse)
        {

        }
    }
}
```

Return to *DisplayHouses* form and select the *Design* view. Click to select the *listBox* on the form. Go to the Properties window and click the *Events* icon. Identify the *MouseClick* event in the list, then double click to create an event handler:

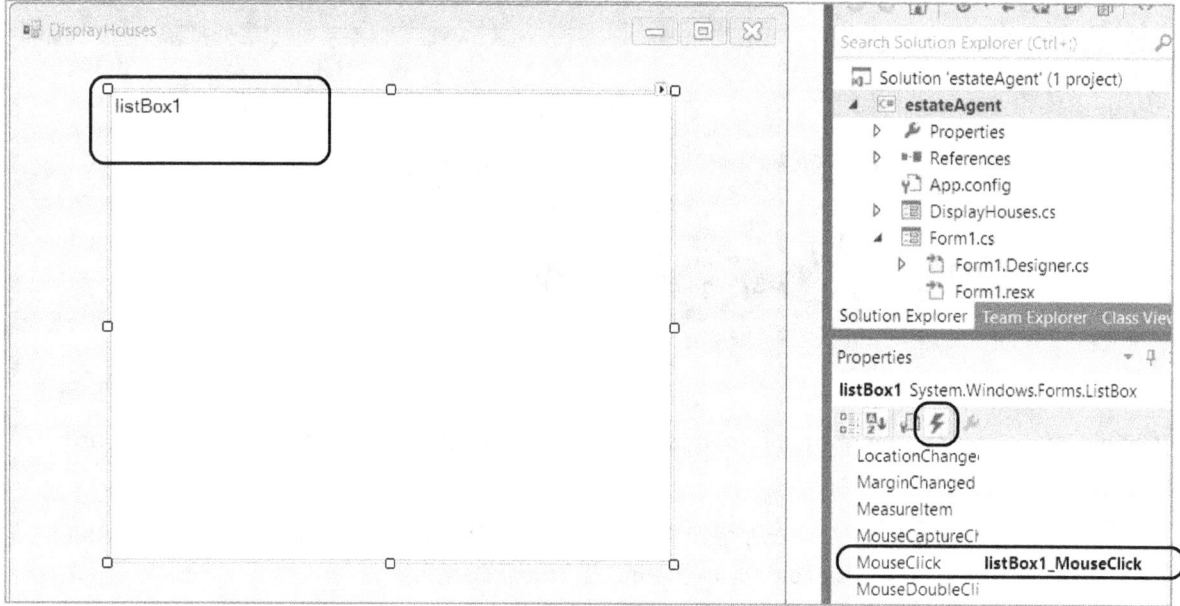

Add lines of code to the *listBox1_mouseClick( )* method

```
private void listBox1_MouseClick(object sender, MouseEventArgs e)
{
    HouseDetails frmHouseDetails = new HouseDetails();
    int houseSelected = listBox1.SelectedIndex;
    DataRow drHouseWanted = dsHouses.Tables[0].Rows[houseSelected];

    frmHouseDetails.getHouseDetails(drHouseWanted);
    frmHouseDetails.ShowDialog();
    this.Close();
}
```

When a house address is clicked in the listBox, this method will carry out a series of tasks:

- It will find the position in the list of the selected house.
- It will collect the corresponding *house record* from the *dataSet*.
- It will then transfer the house record to the *HouseDetails form* where it can be displayed.

Run the program and check that the *HouseDetails* window opens correctly when a house address is clicked in the listBox. The actual details of the house are not yet displayed.

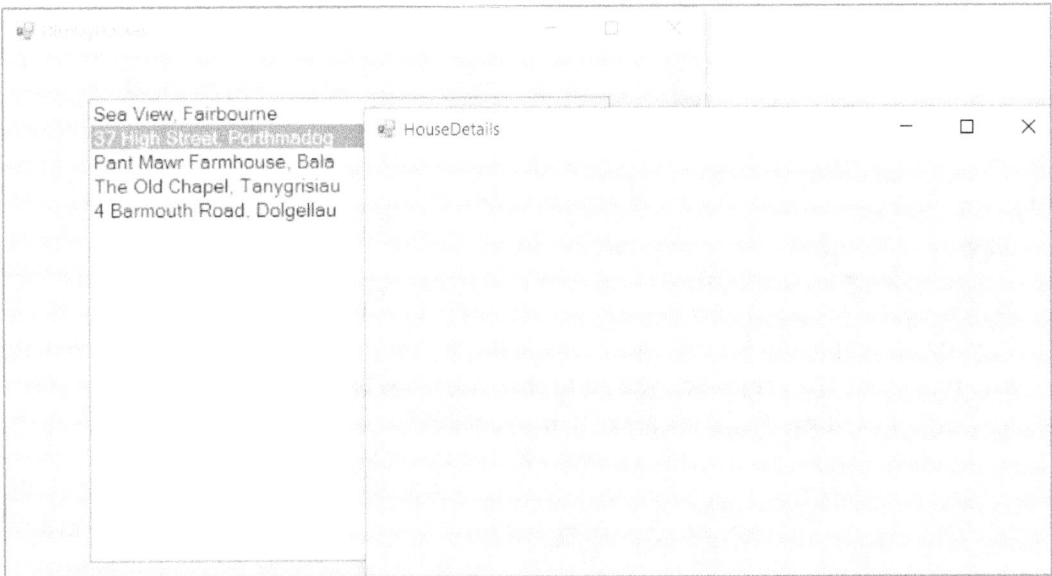

Close the program and open the *HouseDetails form*, where we will display the house data.

The first item to show is the *HouseID*. Unlike other details of the house, this field should not be editable. We will therefore display it with a *Label* component. Give this the name '*lblHouseID*'.

Add the text '*X*' for the label at this stage. This will be replaced by the actual houseID when the program runs.

Continue to build the display screen by adding labels and textBoxes. The textBoxes should be renamed as: **txtAddress1**, **txtAddress2**, **txtPrice**, **txtBedrooms**:

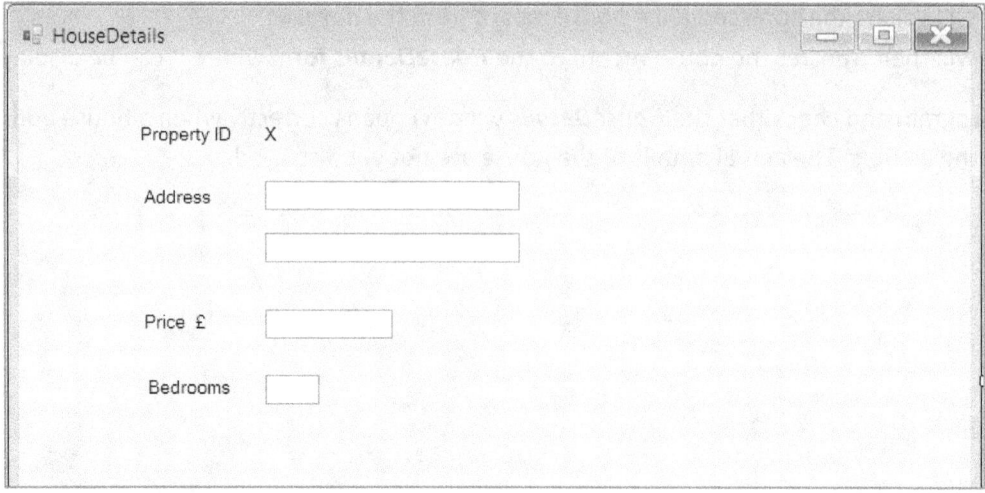

Insert a **ComboBox** component for the **houseType** field. We will provide a drop down list of house types. To do this, select the comboBox and go to the Properties window. Find '**Items**' and click to open a String Editor window. Enter the list of house types as shown, then click the OK button.

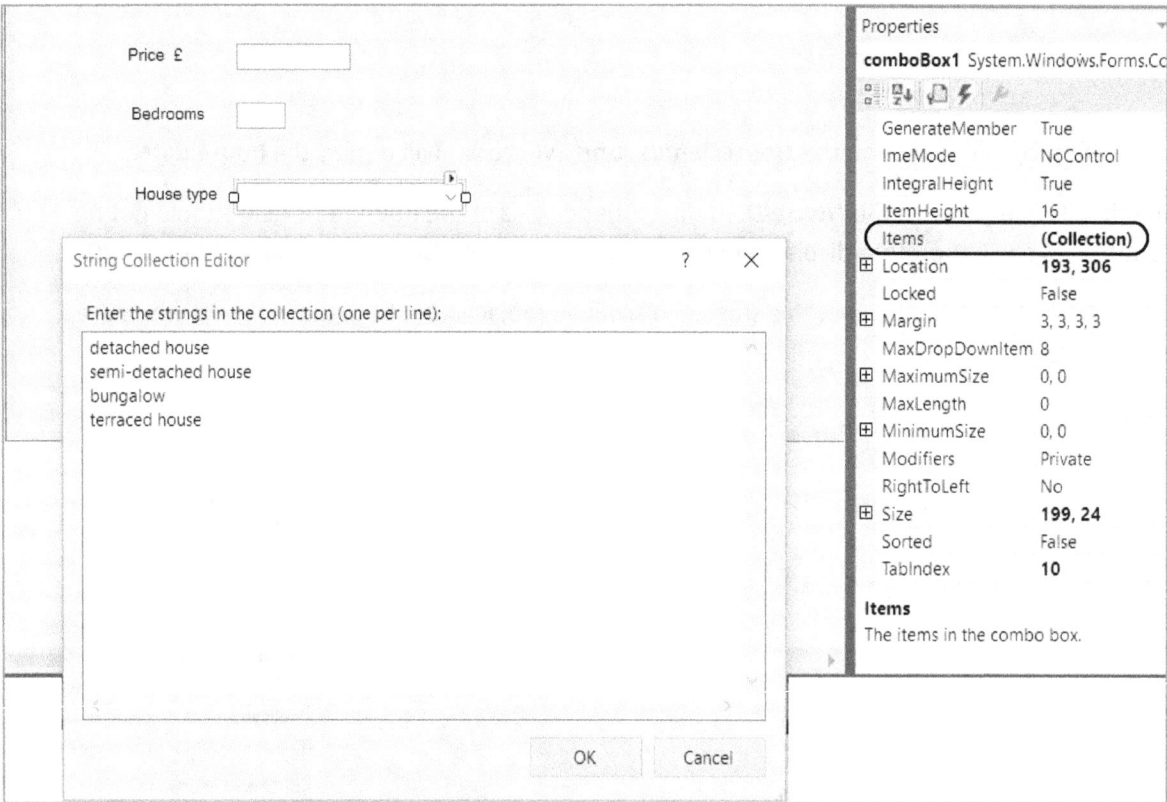

Add a comboBox for *Location*, and enter the list of location options:

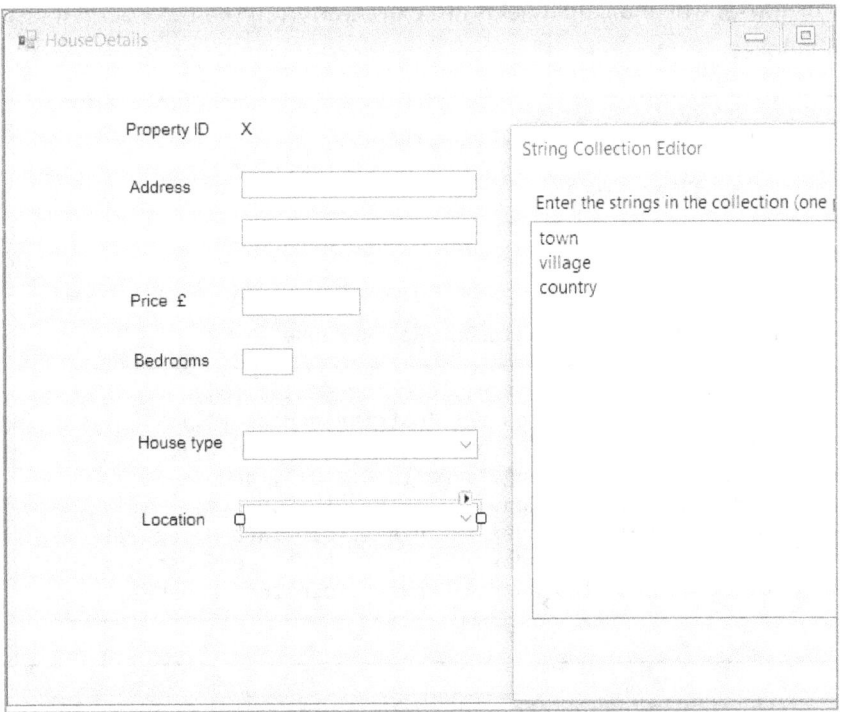

Add a comboBox for the '*Land included*' field and enter the options for the drop down list

Complete the form by adding three buttons for the options '*close*', '*save changes*' and '*delete record*'. Name the buttons as **btnClose**, **btnUpdate** and **btnDelete**.

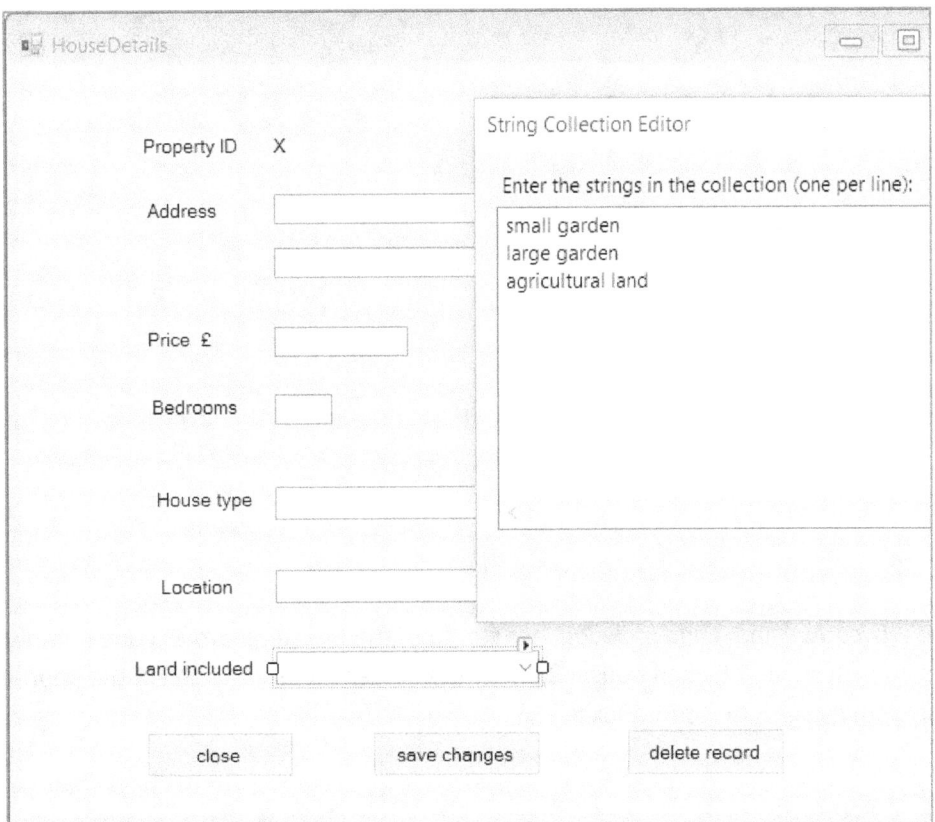

Return to the program listing for the *HouseDetails* form and add lines of code to the *getHouseDetails( )* method. This method receives the selected house record from the previous form as the parameter *drHouse*. The individual fields are extracted from the record, then displayed in the textBoxes or comboBoxes:

```
public partial class HouseDetails : Form
{
    public HouseDetails()
    {
        InitializeComponent();
    }

    public void getHouseDetails(DataRow drHouse)
    {
        lblHouseID.Text = Convert.ToString(drHouse[0]);
        txtAddress1.Text = Convert.ToString(drHouse[1]);
        txtAddress2.Text = Convert.ToString(drHouse[2]);
        txtPrice.Text = String.Format("{0:0,0}", drHouse[3]);
        txtBedrooms.Text = Convert.ToString(drHouse[4]);
        comboBox1.SelectedIndex = Convert.ToInt16(drHouse[5]) - 1;
        comboBox2.SelectedIndex = Convert.ToInt16(drHouse[6]) - 1;
        comboBox3.SelectedIndex = Convert.ToInt16(drHouse[7]) - 1;
    }
}
```

Run the program. Go to the '*Display Houses*' menu option, then select a house. The House Details form should open to display the full set of fields for the house record:

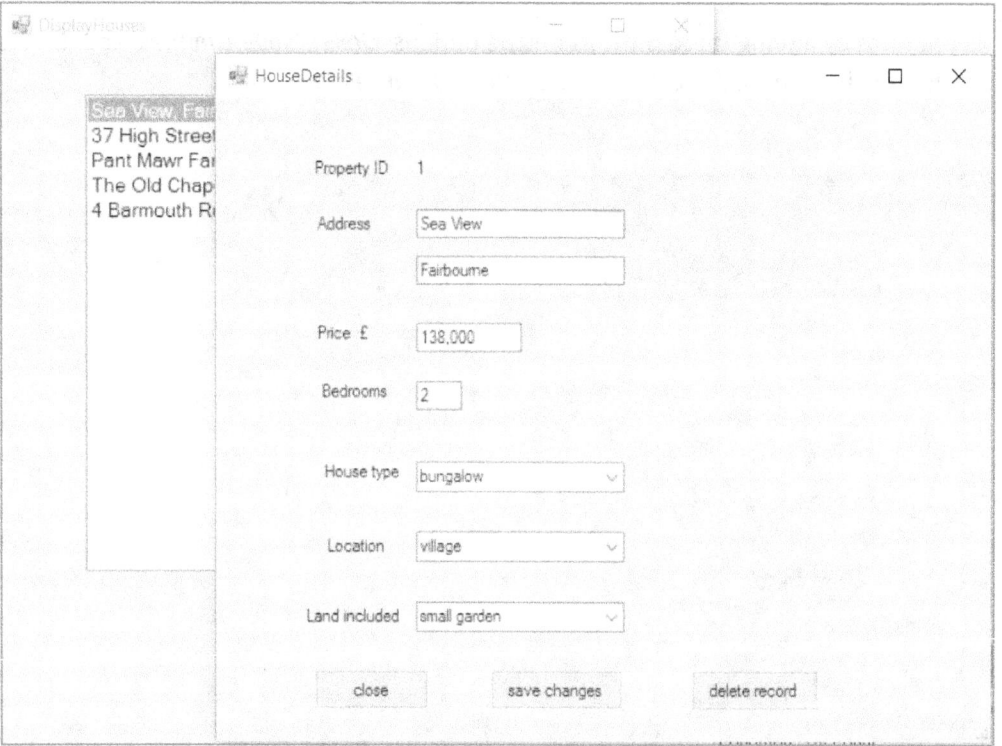

'*House Type*', '*Location*' and '*Land included*' are stored in the house record as code numbers, e.g. detached house = 1, semi-detached house=2, ... These values are used to select the appropriate list item for display in each of the comboBoxes.

Close the program windows and return to the program listing for the *HouseDetails* page. We will now turn our attention to updating the house record if the user wishes to change any of the details.

Add a '*using SqlClient*' directive at the start of the program, and specify the location of the database:

```csharp
using System.Text;
using System.Windows.Forms;
using System.Data.SqlClient;

namespace estateAgent
{
    public partial class HouseDetails : Form
    {
        string databaseLocation = "C:\\C#\\estateAgent.mdf;";

        public HouseDetails()
        {
            InitializeComponent();
        }
```

Double click the '*save changes*' button to create a *btnUpdate_Click( )* method.

Add lines of program code which will take the values from the textBoxes and comboBoxes and store them temporarily as variables of the correct data type, ready for updating the house record. We will also add the lines of code for connection to the database:

```csharp
private void btnUpdate_Click(object sender, EventArgs e)
{
    int HouseID = Convert.ToInt16(lblHouseID.Text);
    string Address1 = txtAddress1.Text;
    string Address2 = txtAddress2.Text;
    double Price = Convert.ToDouble(txtPrice.Text);
    int Bedrooms = Convert.ToInt16(txtBedrooms.Text);
    int Housetype = comboBox1.SelectedIndex + 1;
    int Location = comboBox2.SelectedIndex + 1;
    int Land = comboBox3.SelectedIndex + 1;

    SqlConnection con = new SqlConnection(@"Data Source=.\SQLEXPRESS;
      AttachDbFilename=" +databaseLocation + "Integrated Security=True;
      Connect Timeout=30; User Instance=True");
```

The addition of 1 to the comboBox index values comes about because items in a comboBox are numbered from zero, whereas it is more sensible for our code numbers to begin at 1. For example, in the 'Location' field:

town = code 1   *town = listBox item 0*

village = code 2   *village = listBox item 1*

etc...

We can now add the code to open the database and update the house record. This is similar to the code which we have written previously to load data, but this time makes use of an **UPDATE** command in SQL.

```
SqlConnection con = new SqlConnection(@"Data Source=.\SQLEXPRESS;
    AttachDbFilename=" +databaseLocation + "Integrated Security=True;
    Connect Timeout=30; User Instance=True");
try
{
    con.Open();
    SqlCommand cmHouses = new SqlCommand();
    cmHouses.Connection = con;
    cmHouses.CommandType = CommandType.Text;
    cmHouses.CommandText = "UPDATE house SET address1='"+ Address1
        + "', address2='"+ Address2 + "', price='" + Price + "', bedrooms='"
        + Bedrooms + "', propertyType='" + Housetype + "', location='"
        + Location + "', land='" + Land + "' WHERE houseID='" + HouseID + "'";
    cmHouses.ExecuteNonQuery();
    con.Close();
    this.Close();
}
catch
{
    MessageBox.Show("File error");
}
}
```

Run the program. Select a house and make some changes to the details, such as the address, price or land included. Click '*save changes*'.

Return to the list of properties for sale. Click the house address to reopen the **HouseDetails** form. Check that your changes were made correctly. Close the program windows and return to the program listing for the **HouseDetails** page.

If all is well, we can now program the '*delete record*' option. It is important to give the user an option to cancel if they have clicked the '*delete record*' button by accident. We will do this by making a message box appear before the record is actually deleted from the database.

Double click the '*delete record*' button to create an event method, then add code to open a message box:

```
private void btnDelete_Click(object sender, EventArgs e)
{
    if (MessageBox.Show("Really delete?", "Confirm delete",
                MessageBoxButtons.YesNo) == DialogResult.Yes)
    {

    }
}
```

Run the program. Select a house, then click the '*delete record*' button. Check that the confirm message appears. Close the program and return to the program listing for the *HouseDetails* page.

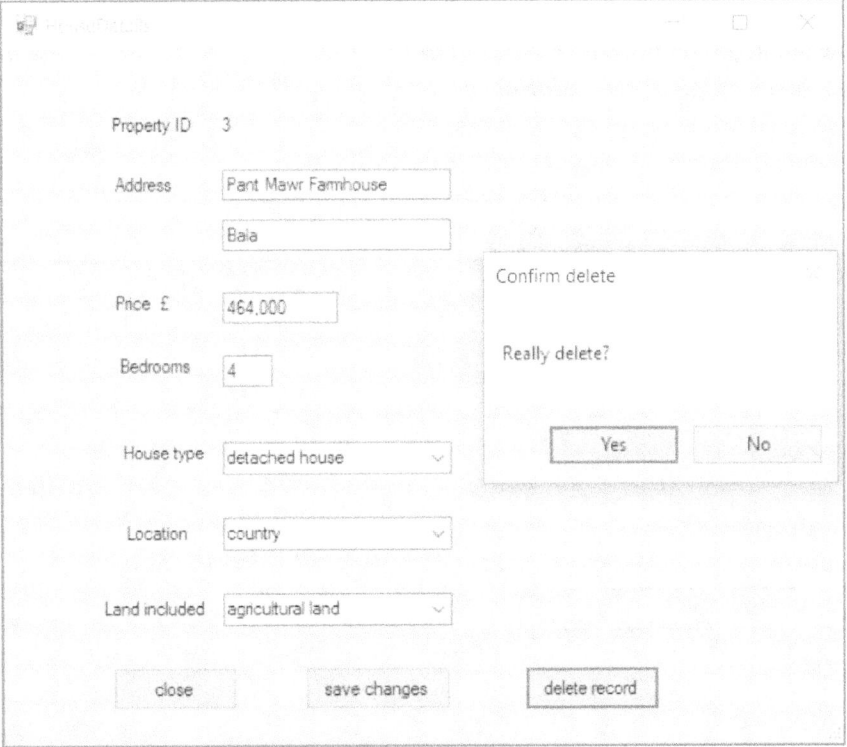

We will now add the code which will actually delete the record from the database if the user answers '*Yes*'. This is again very similar to previous database code we have written, but this time uses the *DELETE* command in SQL. The correct record for deletion is selected by means of the *houseID* value.

```
private void btnDelete_Click(object sender, EventArgs e)
{
    if (MessageBox.Show("Really delete?", "Confirm delete",
                    MessageBoxButtons.YesNo) == DialogResult.Yes)
    {
        int HouseID = Convert.ToInt16(lblHouseID.Text);

        SqlConnection con = new SqlConnection(@"Data Source=.\SQLEXPRESS;
           AttachDbFilename=" + databaseLocation + "Integrated Security=True;
           Connect Timeout=30; User Instance=True");

        try
        {
            con.Open();
            SqlCommand cmHouses = new SqlCommand();
            cmHouses.Connection = con;
            cmHouses.CommandType = CommandType.Text;
            cmHouses.CommandText = "DELETE house WHERE houseID='" + HouseID + "'";
            cmHouses.ExecuteNonQuery();
            con.Close();
            this.Close();
        }
        catch
        {
            MessageBox.Show("File error");
        }
    }
}
```

The final operation we need to carry out on the '*house*' table is to **add new records**. We will postpone testing the '*delete record*' option until this '**add record**' function has been completed.

We will require another **Windows Form** where house details can be entered. Go to the **Solution Explorer** window and right-click on the *estateAgent* program icon. Select '**Add / New item**'. Choose '**Windows Form**', and give the name '**AddHouse**':

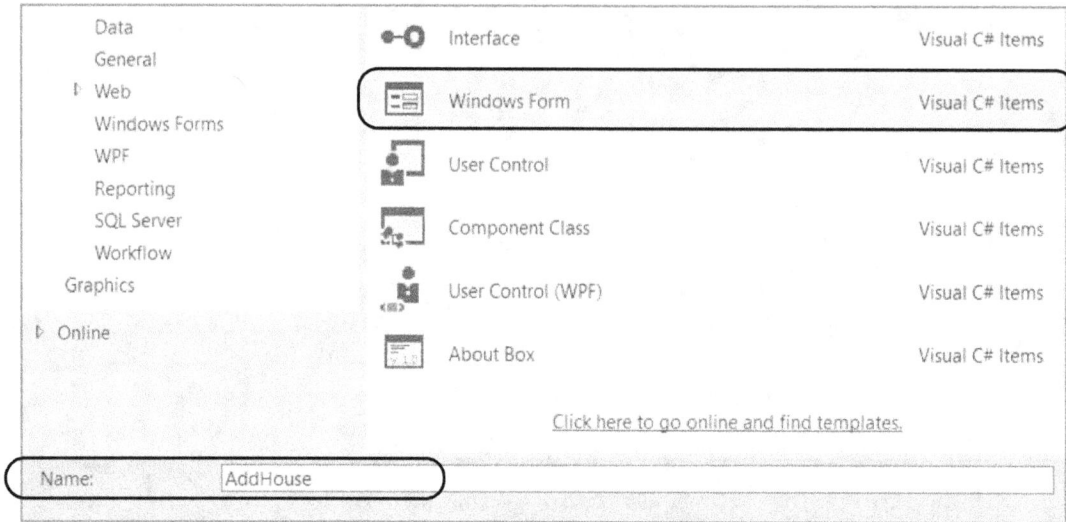

Open the **AddHouse** form and add labels, textBoxes and comboBoxes to create a data entry form. You may find it easiest to copy and paste the required group of components from the **HouseDetails** form which you set up earlier. **Buttons** will be required to *cancel* or *save* the house record:

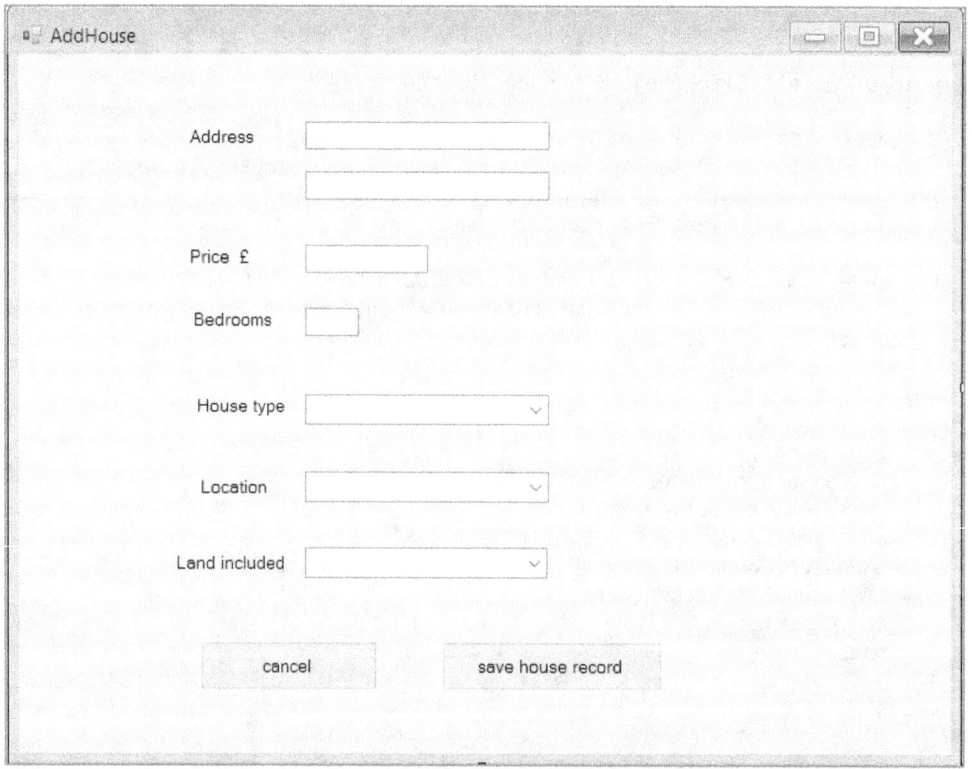

Name the buttons as **btnCancel** and **btnSave**.

Return to **Form1** and link the **AddHouse** form to the menu system by double clicking the '**Add House Record**' menu option:

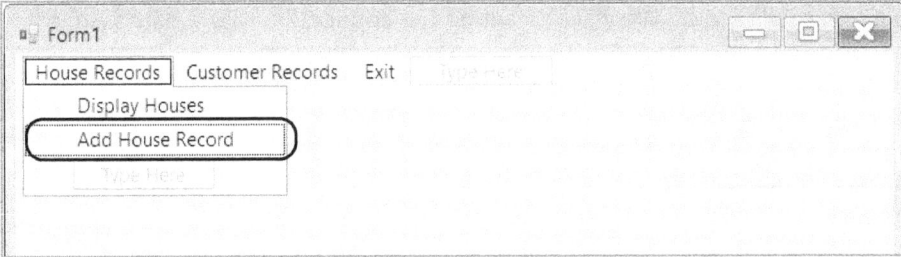

Add lines of code to open the AddHouse form:

```csharp
private void displayHousesToolStripMenuItem_Click(object sender, EventArgs e)
{
    DisplayHouses frmDisplayHouses = new DisplayHouses();
    frmDisplayHouses.ShowDialog();
}

private void addHouseRecordToolStripMenuItem_Click(object sender, EventArgs e)
{
    AddHouse frmAddHouse = new AddHouse();
    frmAddHouse.ShowDialog();
}
```

Return to the '**AddHouse**' form. Double click the '**cancel**' button to create an event procedure and add the **Close( )** command.

Go to the start of the program listing and insert the '**using SqlClient**' directive and the database location.

```csharp
using System.Text;
using System.Windows.Forms;
using System.Data.SqlClient;

namespace estateAgent
{
    public partial class AddHouse : Form
    {
        string databaseLocation = "C:\\C#\\estateAgent.mdf;";

        public AddHouse()
        {
            InitializeComponent();
        }

        private void btnCancel_Click(object sender, EventArgs e)
        {
            this.Close();
        }
    }
}
```

Double click the '*save house record*' button to produce an event method.

Add code which will collect the required data from the textBoxes and comboBoxes, ready for transfer to a database record. We will also set up the connection to the database.

```csharp
private void btnCancel_Click(object sender, EventArgs e)
{
    this.Close();
}
private void btnSave_Click(object sender, EventArgs e)
{
    string Address1 = txtAddress1.Text;
    string Address2 = txtAddress2.Text;
    double Price = Convert.ToDouble(txtPrice.Text);
    int Bedrooms = Convert.ToInt16(txtBedrooms.Text);
    int Housetype = comboBox1.SelectedIndex + 1;
    int Location = comboBox2.SelectedIndex + 1;
    int Land = comboBox3.SelectedIndex + 1;
    SqlConnection con = new SqlConnection(@"Data Source=.\SQLEXPRESS;
       AttachDbFilename=" + databaseLocation + "Integrated Security=True;
       Connect Timeout=30; User Instance=True");
}
```

We then add the code to save the new record into the database. This uses the **INSERT** command in SQL. Notice that no value is included for the *houseID* field. We specified this as an auto-number field, so the value will be allocated automatically by the database.

```csharp
SqlConnection con = new SqlConnection(@"Data Source=.\SQLEXPRESS;
  AttachDbFilename=" + databaseLocation + "Integrated Security=True;
  Connect Timeout=30; User Instance=True");
try
{
    con.Open();
    SqlCommand cmHouses = new SqlCommand();
    cmHouses.Connection = con;
    cmHouses.CommandType = CommandType.Text;
    cmHouses.CommandText = "INSERT INTO house(address1, address2, price,
        bedrooms, propertyType, location, land)
        VALUES ('" + Address1 + "','" + Address2 + "','" + Price + "','"
        + Bedrooms + "','" + Housetype + "','" + Location + "','"
        + Land + "')";
    cmHouses.ExecuteNonQuery();
    con.Close();
    Close();
}
catch
{
    MessageBox.Show("File error");
}
```

Please note that the lines beginning

> *SqlConnection con = new SqlConnection(...*
> *cmHouses.CommandText = "INSERT INTO...*

should each be entered as a single line of code with no line breaks.

Run the program and check that a new house record can be added correctly to the '*house*' table. Click the house list to display the record details. Check that the new record can then be deleted by clicking the '*delete record*' button.

We have now completed the **houses** section of the database program, and can turn our attention to the **customers** of the Estate Agent.

When registering with the company, potential buyers will be asked to specify the *maximum price* they are willing to pay for a property, the *minimum number of bedrooms* which they require, and any preferences concerning the *type of property*, *location* or *land included*. This information can be used by the Estate Agent to select suitable properties which might be of interest to the customer.

Add a **Windows Form** and give this the name '*AddCustomer*'. It will be used for entering details to create new customer records.

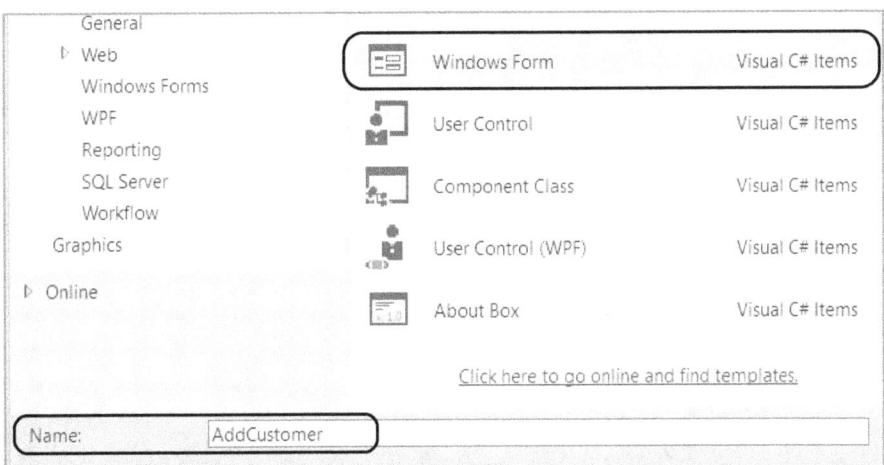

Add textBoxes as shown below, naming these as *txtSurname*, *txtForename*, *txtMaxprice* and *txtMinbeds*.
Add comboBoxes for '*House type wanted*', '*Location wanted*', and '*Land wanted*'. Buttons will be needed for '*cancel*' and '*save customer record*' options. Name these as *btnCancel* and *btnSave*.

We need to enter options for the comboBox drop down lists. These will list the property types, locations and land descriptions in a similar way to the house records, but we will also include a NO PREFERENCE option at the start of each list. If the customer specifies 'no preference', for example in house type, then this field will be ignored when searching for suitable properties.

Select each of the comboBoxes in turn, then go to the *Properties* window and click to the right of *Items* to open the *String Collection Editor*. Enter the option lists as shown below

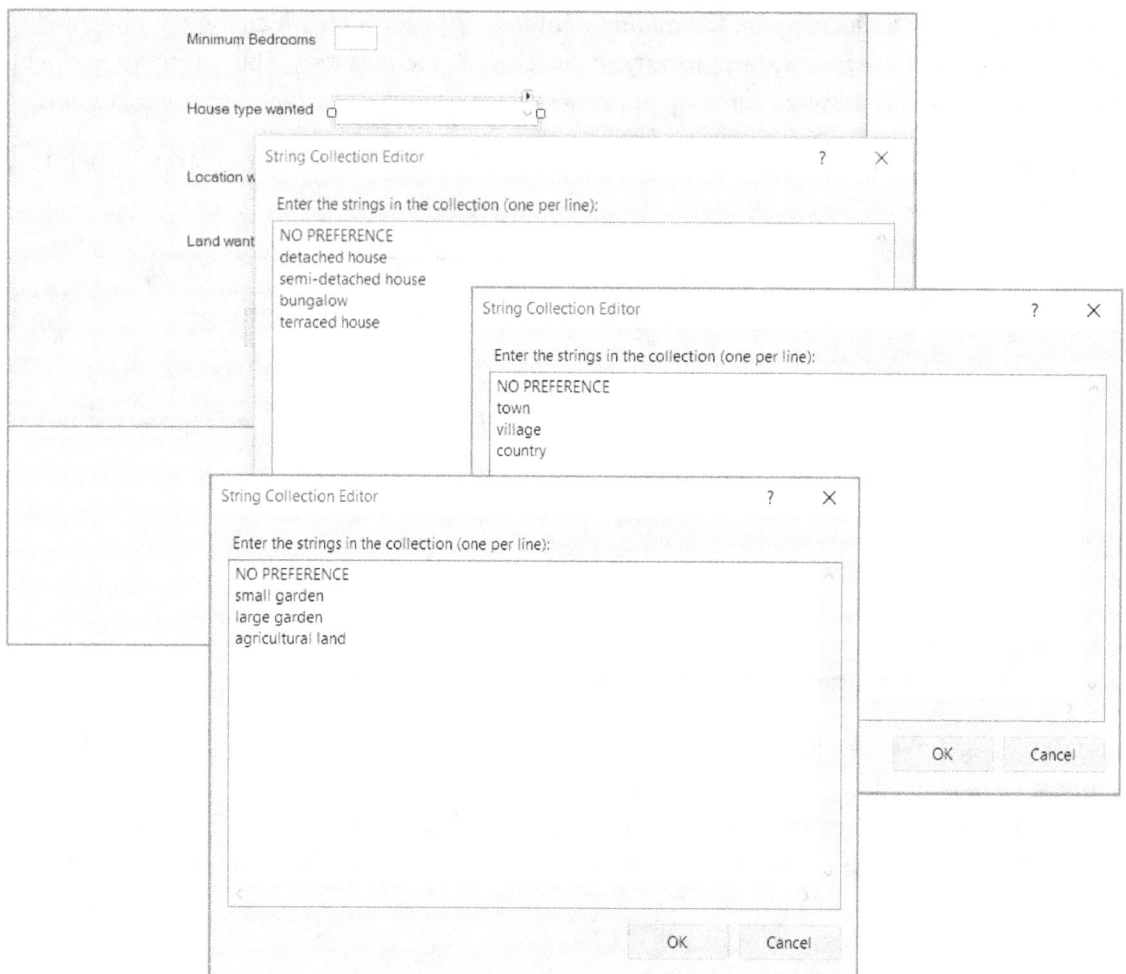

Return to *Form1*. Link the '*AddCustomer*' form to the menu system by double clicking the '*Add Customer Record*' menu option and adding lines of code to the event method:

```csharp
private void addHouseRecordToolStripMenuItem_Click(object sender, EventArgs e)
{
    AddHouse frmAddHouse = new AddHouse();
    frmAddHouse.ShowDialog();
}

private void addCustomerRecordToolStripMenuItem_Click(object sender, EventArgs e)
{
    AddCustomer frmAddCustomer = new AddCustomer();
    frmAddCustomer.ShowDialog();
}
```

Double click the '**save customer record**' button to create an event method. Add code to transfer data from the textBoxes and comboBoxes into variables, ready for saving to the database. Go to the top of the progam listing, and add the '**using SqlClient**' directive and the database location.

```csharp
using System.Text;
using System.Windows.Forms;

using System.Data.SqlClient;

namespace estateAgent
{
    public partial class AddCustomer : Form
    {
        string databaseLocation = "C:\\C#\\estateAgent.mdf;";

        public AddCustomer()
        {
            InitializeComponent();
        }

        private void btnSave_Click(object sender, EventArgs e)
        {
            string Surname = txtSurname.Text;
            string Forename = txtForename.Text;
            double Maxprice = Convert.ToDouble(txtMaxprice.Text);
            int Minbedrooms = Convert.ToInt16(txtMinbeds.Text);
            int Typewanted = comboBox1.SelectedIndex;
            int Locationwanted = comboBox2.SelectedIndex;
            int Landwanted = comboBox3.SelectedIndex;

            SqlConnection con = new SqlConnection(@"Data Source=.\SQLEXPRESS;
              AttachDbFilename=" +databaseLocation + "Integrated Security=True;
              Connect Timeout=30; User Instance=True");
        }
```

The final step is to save the record to the database. Add code to carry out the **INSERT** command in SQL. Notice again that the **auto-number** field **CustomerID** is not included in the list of values:

```csharp
            SqlConnection con = new SqlConnection(@"Data Source=.\SQLEXPRESS;
              AttachDbFilename=" +databaseLocation + "Integrated Security=True;
              Connect Timeout=30; User Instance=True");

            try
            {
                con.Open();
                SqlCommand cmCustomers = new SqlCommand();
                cmCustomers.Connection = con;
                cmCustomers.CommandType = CommandType.Text;
                cmCustomers.CommandText =
                    "INSERT INTO customer(surname, forename, maxprice, minbeds, typeWanted,
                      locationWanted, landWanted) VALUES ('" + Surname + "','" + Forename
                      + "','" + Maxprice + "','" + Minbedrooms + "','" + Typewanted
                      + "','" + Locationwanted + "','" + Landwanted + "')";
                cmCustomers.ExecuteNonQuery();
                con.Close();
                this.Close();
            }
            catch
            {
                MessageBox.Show("File error");
            }
        }
    }
}
```

Run the program. Enter test data for customers:

Surname	Forename	Max price	Min beds	House type	Location	Land
Jenkins	Aled	180,000	3	No preference	No preference	No preference
Humphries	Stuart	400,000	2	No preference	Village	Large garden
Andrews	Ian	600,000	3	No preference	No preference	Agricultural
Edwards	Elisabeth	500,000	2	Detached	No preference	No preference
Pritchard	Tom	550,000	2	Bungalow	Village	No preference

Go to the Server Explorer and check that the records have been inserted into the '*customer*' table. Notice that the preferences for *house type*, *location* and *land* will be shown as code numbers, with zero representing 'NO PREFERENCE'. The *customerID* values have been allocated automatically. Correct any errors in the table, then right-click on the '*Data Connections*' icon and delete the connection.

customerID	surname	forename	maxprice	minbeds	typeWanted	locationWanted	landWanted
1	Jenkins	Aled	180000	3	0	0	0
2	Humphries	Stuart	400000	2	0	2	2
4	Andrews	Ian	600000	3	0	0	3
5	Edwards	Elisabeth	500000	2	1	0	0
6	Pritchard	Tom	550000	2	3	2	0

We will now produce a customer display option. Add a new **Windows Form** and give this the name '*DisplayCustomers*'. Go to **Form1** and link the new form to the '*Display Customers*' menu option:

```
private void addCustomerRecordToolStripMenuItem_Click(object sender, EventArgs e)
{
    AddCustomer frmAddCustomer = new AddCustomer();
    frmAddCustomer.ShowDialog();
}

private void displayCustomersToolStripMenuItem_Click(object sender, EventArgs e)
{
    DisplayCustomers frmDisplayCustomers = new DisplayCustomers();
    frmDisplayCustomers.ShowDialog();
}
```

Add a list box to the *DisplayCustomers* form, and set the *font size* to *10 point*. Add a '*Close*' button.

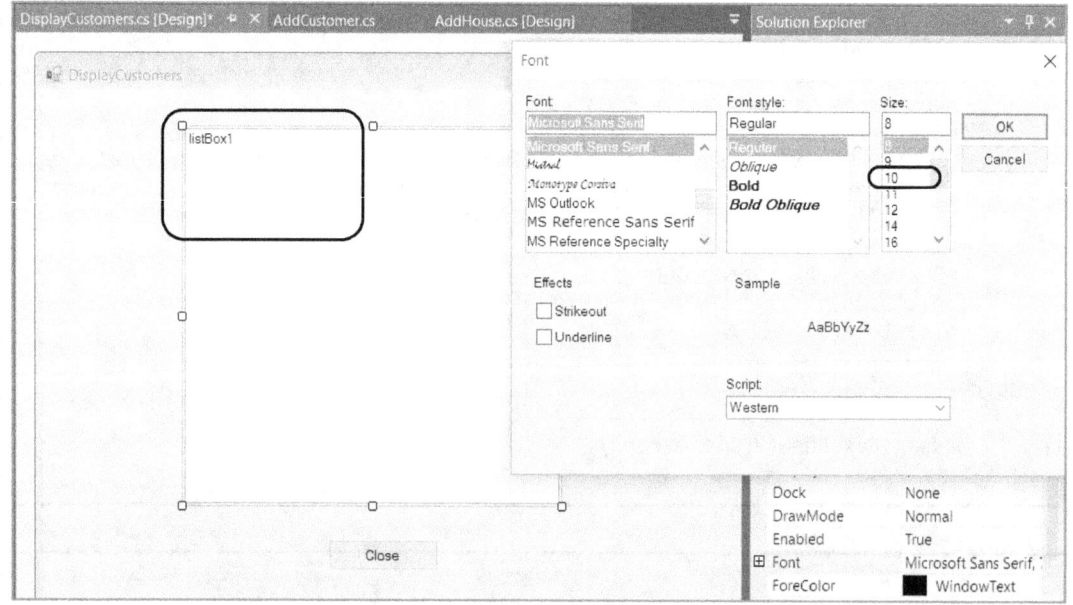

We will add code to the **DisplayCustomers** form to include the *'using SqlClient'* directive and specify the database location. Create an empty **loadCustomerNames( )** method, and call this from the **DisplayCustomers( )** method. Produce a **dataSet** to hold the customer records when they are loaded.

```
using System.Text;
using System.Windows.Forms;
using System.Data.SqlClient;

namespace estateAgent
{
    public partial class DisplayCustomers : Form
    {
        string databaseLocation = "C:\\C#\\estateAgent.mdf;";

        public DisplayCustomers()
        {
            InitializeComponent();
            loadCustomerNames();
        }

        DataSet dsCustomers = new DataSet();

        public void loadCustomerNames()
        {
        }
    }
}
```

The code to load customer records from the database can now be added.

```
public void loadCustomerNames()
{
    SqlConnection con = new SqlConnection(@"Data Source=.\SQLEXPRESS;
      AttachDbFilename=" +databaseLocation + "Integrated Security=True;
      Connect Timeout=30; User Instance=True");
    try
    {
        con.Open();
        SqlCommand cmCustomers = new SqlCommand();
        cmCustomers.Connection = con;
        cmCustomers.CommandType = CommandType.Text;
        cmCustomers.CommandText = "SELECT * FROM customer";
        SqlDataAdapter daCustomers = new SqlDataAdapter(cmCustomers);
        daCustomers.Fill(dsCustomers);
        con.Close();

        int countRecords = dsCustomers.Tables[0].Rows.Count;

        for (int i = 0; i < countRecords; i++)
        {
            DataRow drCustomer = dsCustomers.Tables[0].Rows[i];
            string customerName = drCustomer[1] + ", " + drCustomer[2];
            listBox1.Items.Add(customerName);
        }
    }
    catch
    {
        MessageBox.Show("File error");
    }
}
```

Notice how the loop takes each **data row** in turn from the whole **data set**, then extracts the **surname** and **forename** fields. These are assembled together, separated by a comma, for display in the list box.

Run the program and check that the customer names are displayed correctly.

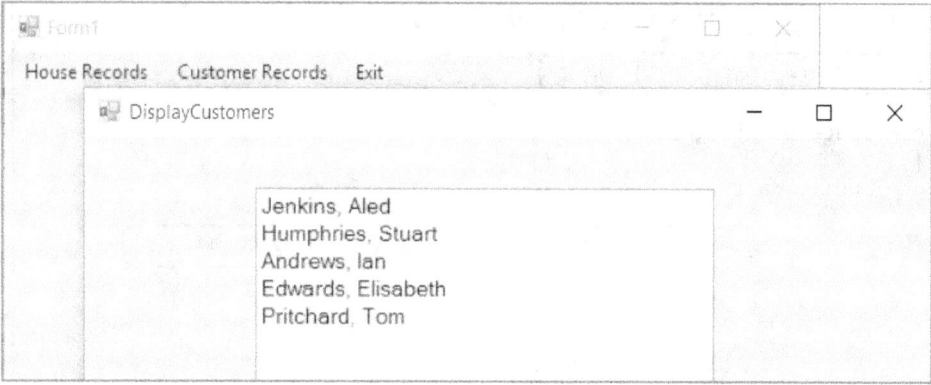

As with the houses earlier, we will create another form to display the full customer record when a name is selected from the list box.

Add a new **Windows Form** and name this '**CustomerDetails**'. Add labels, textBoxes and comboBoxes to the form as shown below. To save time, copy and paste the required components from the **AddCustomer** form which you created earlier, keeping the component names unaltered.

Include a label for display of the **customerID**. Give this the name '**lblCustomerID**', and set the text initially to '**X**'. Add buttons to **close** the form, **save changes** to the record, **delete** the record, and to **search for suitable properties** for this customer, naming these as **btnClose**, **btnSave**, **btnDelete** and **btnSearch**.

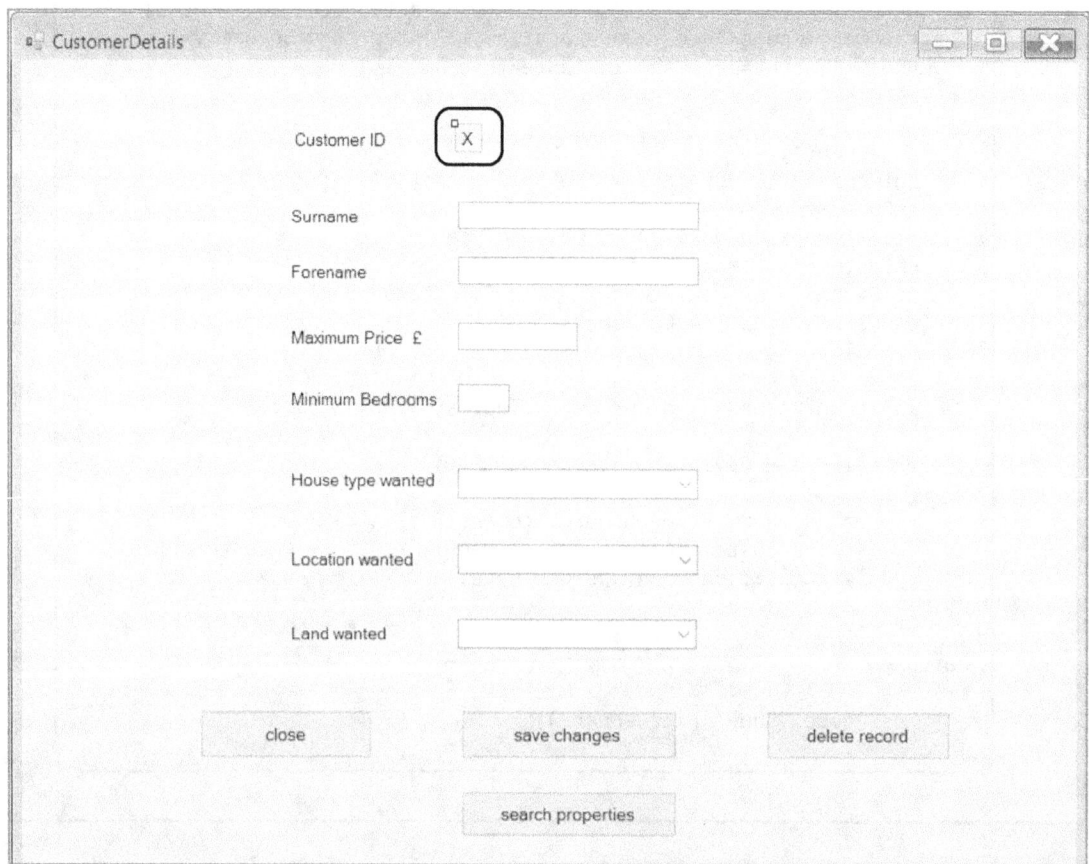

Go to the '*CustomerDetails*' program page and add lines of code to include the '*using SqlClient*' directive, and to specify the database location. Create a *getCustomerDetails( )* method which will accept a customer record, set up variables from each of the fields, then display the data using the screen components.

```csharp
using System.Text;
using System.Windows.Forms;
using System.Data.SqlClient;

namespace estateAgent
{
    public partial class CustomerDetails : Form
    {
        string databaseLocation = "C:\\C#\\estateAgent.mdf;";

        public CustomerDetails()
        {
            InitializeComponent();
        }

        public void getCustomerDetails(DataRow drCustomer)
        {
            lblCustomerID.Text = Convert.ToString(drCustomer[0]);
            txtSurname.Text = Convert.ToString(drCustomer[1]);
            txtForename.Text = Convert.ToString(drCustomer[2]);
            txtMaxprice.Text = String.Format("{0:0,0}", drCustomer[3]);
            txtMinbeds.Text = Convert.ToString(drCustomer[4]);
            comboBox1.SelectedIndex = Convert.ToInt16(drCustomer[5]);
            comboBox2.SelectedIndex = Convert.ToInt16(drCustomer[6]);
            comboBox3.SelectedIndex = Convert.ToInt16(drCustomer[7]);
        }
    }
}
```

Return to the *DisplayCustomers* form and select the *listBox*. Go to the Properties window and click the *Events* icon. Locate the *MouseClick* event, and double click to create an event method.

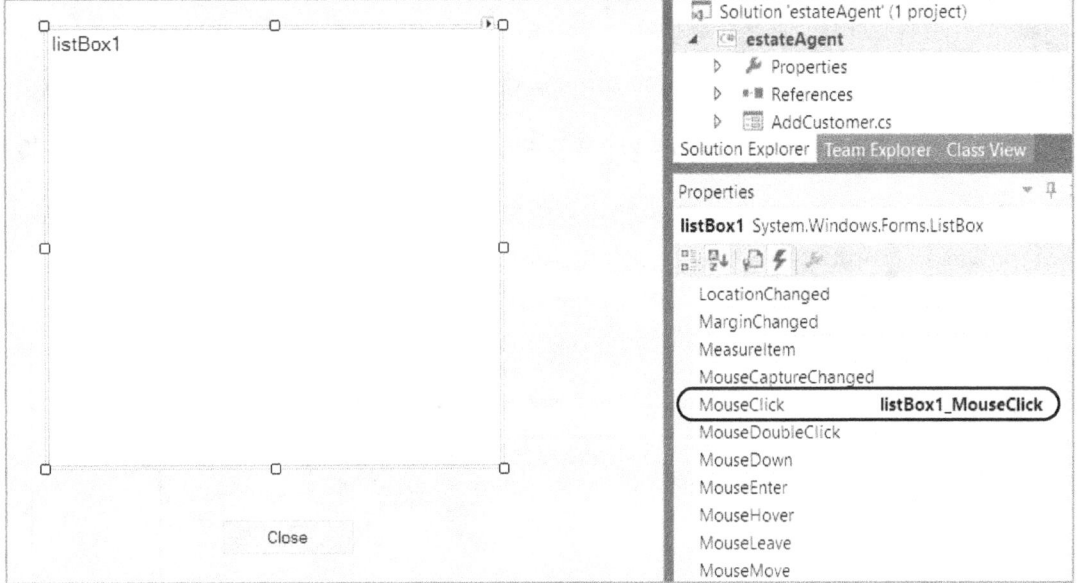

Add code to the *mouseClick( )* method:

```csharp
private void listBox1_MouseClick(object sender, MouseEventArgs e)
{
    CustomerDetails frmCustomerDetails = new CustomerDetails();
    int customerSelected = listBox1.SelectedIndex;

    DataRow drCustomerWanted = dsCustomers.Tables[0].Rows[customerSelected];

    frmCustomerDetails.getCustomerDetails(drCustomerWanted);
    frmCustomerDetails.ShowDialog();

    this.Close();
}
```

Run the program. Check that customers can be selected and their details are displayed correctly.

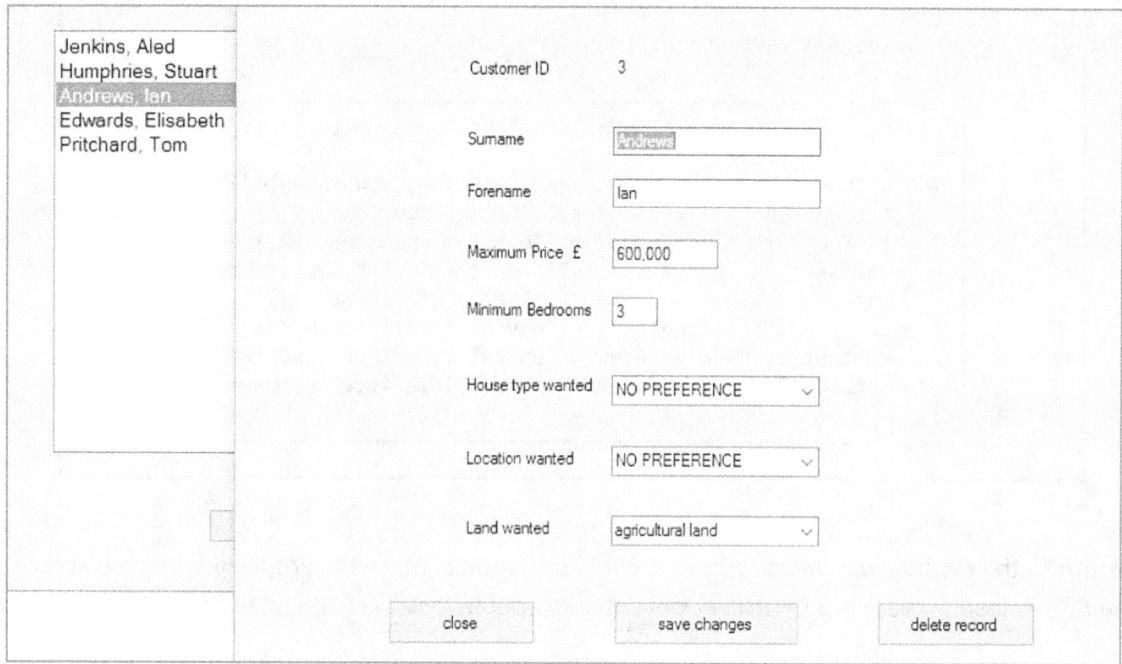

Double click the '*close*' button and add the command **Close( )** to close the form.

Double click the '*delete record*' button, and add code to display a confirm message for the user.

```csharp
private void btnClose_Click(object sender, EventArgs e)
{
    this.Close();
}

private void btnDelete_Click(object sender, EventArgs e)
{
    if (MessageBox.Show("Really delete?", "Confirm delete",
            MessageBoxButtons.YesNo) == DialogResult.Yes)
    {

    }
}
```

Add lines of code to delete the database record if the user clicks to confirm deletion.

```csharp
private void btnDelete_Click(object sender, EventArgs e)
{
    if (MessageBox.Show("Really delete?", "Confirm delete",
                MessageBoxButtons.YesNo) == DialogResult.Yes)
    {
        int CustomerID = Convert.ToInt16(lblCustomerID.Text);
        SqlConnection con = new SqlConnection(@"Data Source=.\SQLEXPRESS;
          AttachDbFilename="+databaseLocation + "Integrated Security=True;
          Connect Timeout=30; User Instance=True");
        try
        {
            con.Open();
            SqlCommand cmCustomers = new SqlCommand();
            cmCustomers.Connection = con;
            cmCustomers.CommandType = CommandType.Text;
            cmCustomers.CommandText =
                    "DELETE customer WHERE customerID='" + CustomerID + "'";
            cmCustomers.ExecuteNonQuery();
            con.Close();
            this.Close();
        }
        catch
        {
            MessageBox.Show("File error");
        }
    }
}
```

Double click the '*save changes*' button to create an event method. Add code to collect data from the textBoxes and comboBoxes and store it as variables, ready for updating the database record.

```csharp
private void btnSave_Click(object sender, EventArgs e)
{
    int CustomerID = Convert.ToInt16(lblCustomerID.Text);
    string Surname = txtSurname.Text;
    string Forename = txtForename.Text;
    double Maxprice = Convert.ToDouble(txtMaxprice.Text);
    int Minbedrooms = Convert.ToInt16(txtMinbeds.Text);
    int Typewanted = comboBox1.SelectedIndex;
    int Locationwanted = comboBox2.SelectedIndex;
    int Landwanted = comboBox3.SelectedIndex;

    SqlConnection con = new SqlConnection(@"Data Source=.\SQLEXPRESS;
      AttachDbFilename=" +databaseLocation + "Integrated Security=True;
      Connect Timeout=30; User Instance=True");
}
```

We will complete the **btnSave_Click( )** method by adding code for an **UPDATE** command in SQL.

```
SqlConnection con = new SqlConnection(@"Data Source=.\SQLEXPRESS;
   AttachDbFilename="+ databaseLocation + "Integrated Security=True;
   Connect Timeout=30; User Instance=True");

try
{
    con.Open();
    SqlCommand cmCustomer = new SqlCommand();
    cmCustomer.Connection = con;
    cmCustomer.CommandType = CommandType.Text;
    cmCustomer.CommandText = "UPDATE customer SET surname='" + Surname
         + "', forename='" + Forename + "', maxprice='" + Maxprice
         + "', Minbeds='" + Minbedrooms + "', typeWanted='" + Typewanted
         + "', locationWanted='" + Locationwanted + "', landWanted='"
         + Landwanted + "' WHERE customerID='" + CustomerID + "'";
    cmCustomer.ExecuteNonQuery();
    con.Close();
    this.Close();
}
catch
{
    MessageBox.Show("File error");
}
}
```

One final option provided by our program is to search for suitable properties for each customer. Begin by adding a new **Windows Form** and give this the name '**SearchProperties**'.

Add labels and textBoxes to the form to display the **customer's name**, **maximum price** they wish to pay, **minimum number of bedrooms** required, and any particular requirements for **house type**, **location** or **land**. Name the text boxes as **txtCustomer**, **txtMaxprice**, **txtMinbeds**, **txtTypewanted**, **txtLocationwanted** and **txtLandwanted**.

Below the text boxes, insert a **DataGridView** component. At present, this will appear as an empty grey rectangle.

Change to the **SearchProperties** program code screen. Add the '*using SqlClient*' directive, and the database location. Create an empty method called **propertySearch( )**.

```csharp
using System.Text;
using System.Windows.Forms;
using System.Data.SqlClient;

namespace estateAgent
{
    public partial class SearchProperties : Form
    {
        string databaseLocation = "C:\\C#\\estateAgent.mdf;";

        public SearchProperties()
        {
            InitializeComponent();
        }

        public void propertySearch(string customerName, double maxprice,
            int minbeds, int typewanted, int locationwanted, int landwanted)
        {

        }
    }
}
```

Return to the **CustomerDetails** form and double click the '*search properties*' button to create an event method. Add code which will collect the necessary information about the customer's requirements, then transfer this to the **SearchProperties** form.

```csharp
private void btnSearch_Click(object sender, EventArgs e)
{
    string CustomerName = txtForename.Text + " " + txtSurname.Text;
    double Maxprice = Convert.ToDouble(txtMaxprice.Text);
    int Minbedrooms = Convert.ToInt16(txtMinbeds.Text);
    int Typewanted = comboBox1.SelectedIndex;
    int Locationwanted = comboBox2.SelectedIndex;
    int Landwanted = comboBox3.SelectedIndex;

    SearchProperties frmSearchProperties = new SearchProperties();

    frmSearchProperties.propertySearch(CustomerName, Maxprice, Minbedrooms,
        Typewanted, Locationwanted, Landwanted);
    frmSearchProperties.ShowDialog();

    this.Close();
}
```

Go to the **SearchProperties** form and find the **propertySeach( )** method. Add code to display the customer requirements in the textBoxes.

```
public void propertySearch(string customerName, double maxprice,
    int minbeds, int typewanted, int locationwanted, int landwanted)
{
    txtCustomer.Text = customerName;
    txtMaxprice.Text = String.Format("{0:0,0}", maxprice);
    txtMinbeds.Text = Convert.ToString(minbeds);
    string s = "";
    switch (typewanted)
    {
        case 0: s = "NO PREFERENCE"; break;
        case 1: s = "Detached house (1)"; break;
        case 2: s = "Semi-detached house (2)"; break;
        case 3: s = "Bungalow (3)"; break;
        case 4: s = "Terraced house (4)"; break;
    }
    txtTypewanted.Text = s;
    switch (locationwanted)
    {
        case 0: s = "NO PREFERENCE"; break;
        case 1: s = "Town (1)"; break;
        case 2: s = "Village (2)"; break;
        case 3: s = "Country (3)"; break;
    }
    txtLocationwanted.Text = s;
    switch (landwanted)
    {
        case 0: s = "NO PREFERENCE"; break;
        case 1: s = "Small garden (1)"; break;
        case 2: s = "Large garden (2)"; break;
        case 3: s = "Agricultural land (3)"; break;
    }
    txtLandwanted.Text = s;
}
```

Run the program, select a customer, then click to search for suitable properties. The SearchProperties form should open, and the customer's requirements should be displayed:

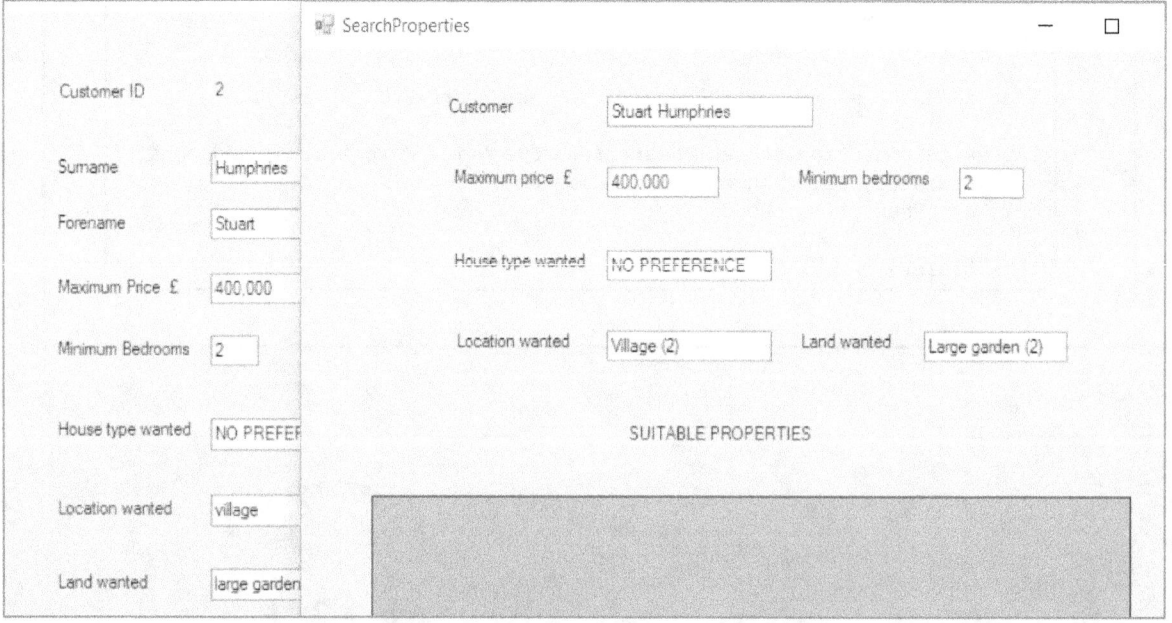

Chapter 7: Estate Agent Database   115

We will now set up an *SQL query* to identify suitable properties for the customer.

Continue the *propertySeach( )* method by creating a *dataSet* to hold the results of the query. Add a connection to the database, and set up the structure for a *TRY ... CATCH* block.

```
        switch (landwanted)
        {
            case 0: s = "NO PREFERENCE"; break;
            case 1: s = "Small garden (1)"; break;
            case 2: s = "Large garden (2)"; break;
            case 3: s = "Agricultural land (3)"; break;
        }
        txtLandwanted.Text = s;

        DataSet dsProperty = new DataSet();

        SqlConnection con = new SqlConnection(@"Data Source=.\SQLEXPRESS;
            AttachDbFilename="+databaseLocation + "Integrated Security=True;
            Connect Timeout=30; User Instance=True");
        try
        {

        }
        catch
        {
            MessageBox.Show("File error");
        }
    }
```

Code can then be added to create the query:

```
    try
    {
        con.Open();
        SqlCommand cmProperty = new SqlCommand();
        cmProperty.Connection = con;
        cmProperty.CommandType = CommandType.Text;
        string query = "SELECT * FROM house WHERE price<=" + maxprice
            + " AND bedrooms>=" + minbeds;
        if (typewanted > 0)
        {
            query = query + " AND propertyType =" + typewanted;
        }
        if (locationwanted > 0)
        {
            query = query + " AND location =" + locationwanted;
        }
        if (landwanted > 0)
        {
            query = query + " AND land =" + landwanted;
        }
        cmProperty.CommandText = query;

        SqlDataAdapter daProperty = new SqlDataAdapter(cmProperty);
        daProperty.Fill(dsProperty);
        con.Close();
    }
    catch
    {
        MessageBox.Show("File error");
```

Look carefully at the way in which the query is built up.

- We begin by asking the computer to select only the records for which the *house price* is less than or equal to the *maximum price* the customer wishes to pay.
- We add a condition that the number of *bedrooms* must be greater than or equal to the *minimum number of bedrooms* required.
- If the customer has indicated a requirement for a particular type of house then we will select only the records for this house type. If the customer has expressed 'NO PREFERENCE' by entering a *typewanted* code of zero, then we will not add this extra requirement to the query.
- Similarly, we will add extra requirements for the house location and land included, unless the customer has expressed 'NO PREFERENCE' for these factors.

Once the query has been constructed and run by the program, suitable house records will be selected from the database and transferred to the *dsProperty* dataset.

The final step is to display the results of the query in the dataGrid:

```
        daProperty.Fill(dsProperty);
        con.Close();

        dataGridView1.DataSource = dsProperty.Tables[0];

        DataGridViewColumn column = dataGridView1.Columns[1];
        column.Width = 160;
    }
    catch
    {
        MessageBox.Show("File error");
    }
```

Run the complete program, and check that suitable properties are selected to meet the customer's requirements:

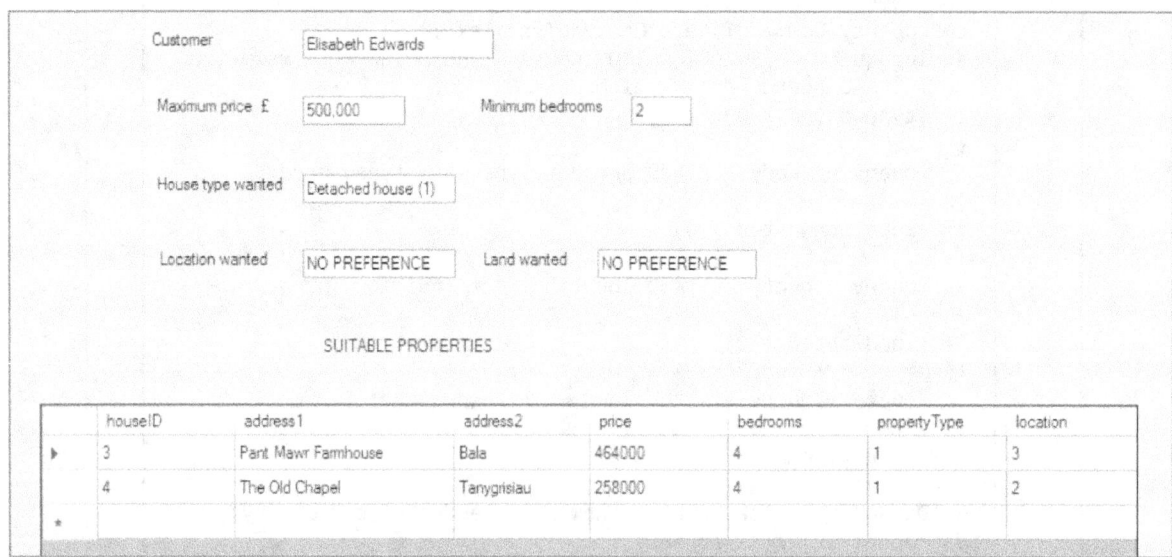

Carry out final testing of all the program options, including options to edit and delete customer records. Add *Close( )* commands to 'Close' buttons where necessary.

8 College Courses

In this program we will introduce **classes** of **objects** as a means of representing entities in a data model. We will design a record keeping system for a college to enter and store details of **courses**, **students**, and **enrolments** of students on particular courses. Three classes of objects will be needed to operate the system:

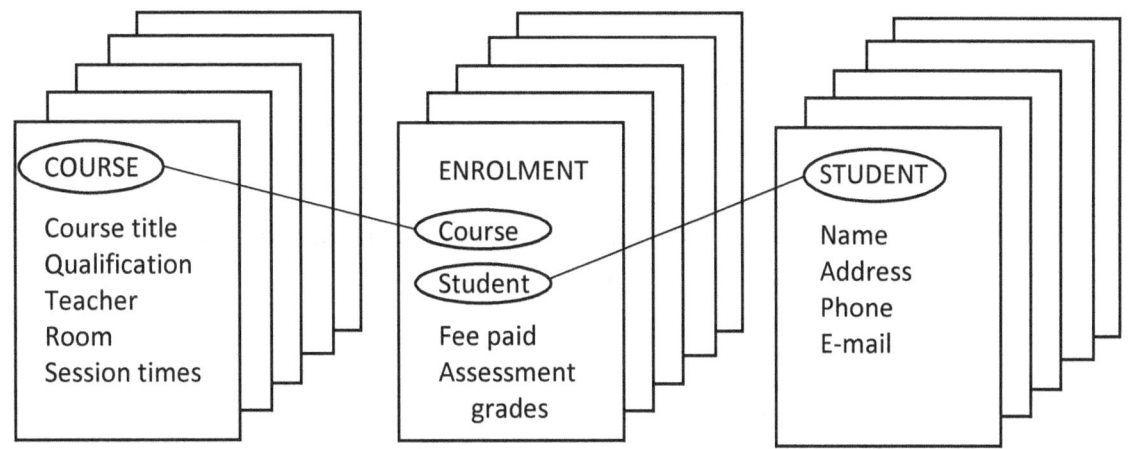

We will begin by setting up a database containing three tables to hold data for courses, students and enrolments.

Open *Visual Studio*, but do not start a new project yet.

On the menu line, select '*View / Server Explorer*'

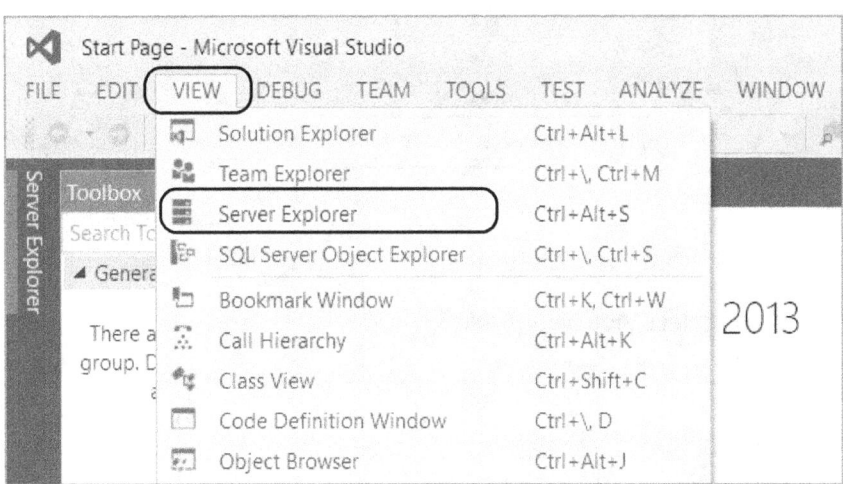

Right-click on '*Data Connections*', then select '*Add Connection*'. If you are asked to choose a Data Source, select:

Microsoft SQL Server Database File

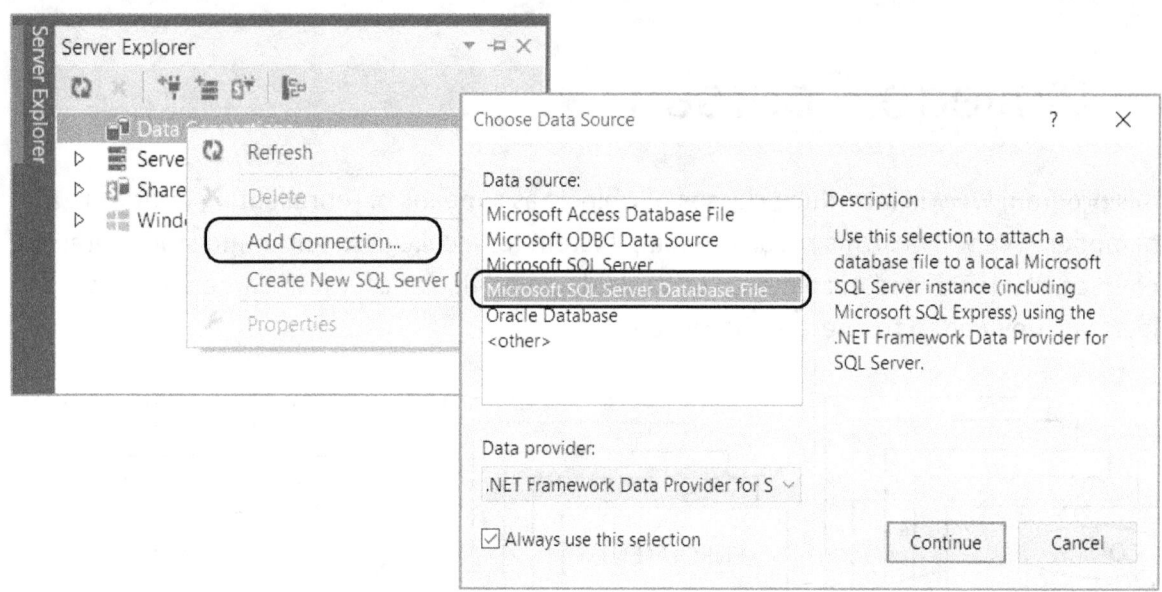

Use the '*Browse*' option to navigate to the location where your C# programs are stored. Give the file name '*collegeCourses*' for the database which will be created.

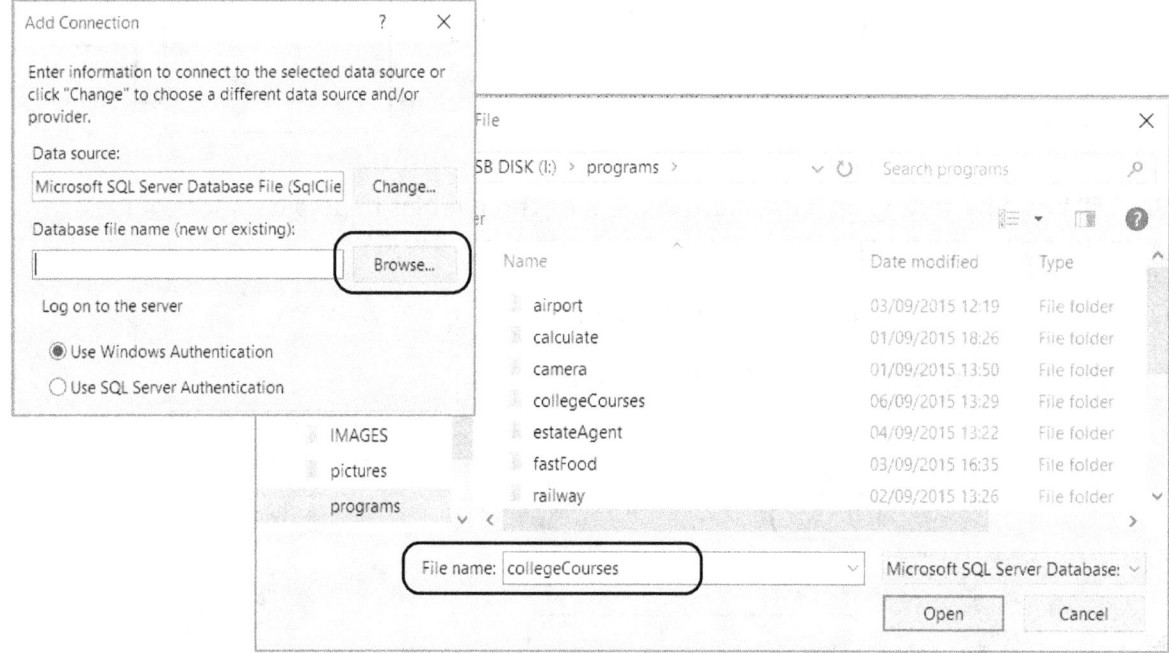

Click '*OK*', then answer '*Yes*' that you wish to create the database file.

Right-click on '*Tables*' and select '*Add New Table*':

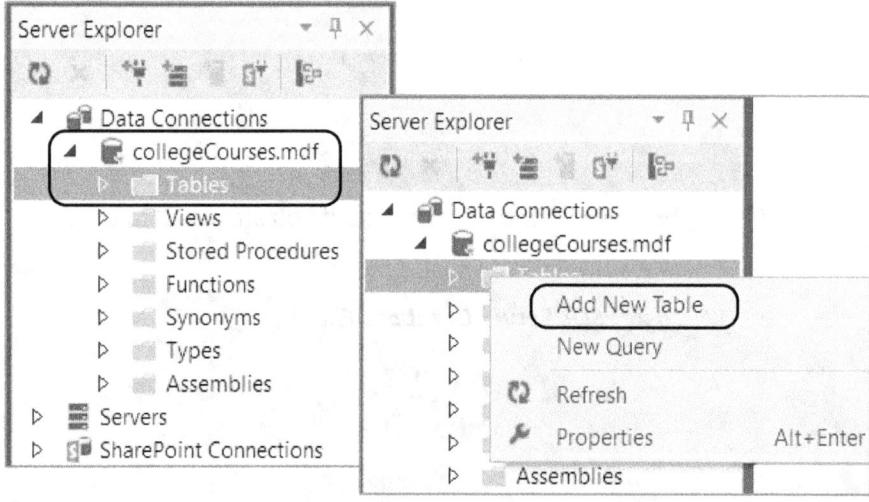

We will begin by setting up a table to store records of the college *courses*. To keep the program simple we will just store the *course title*, although in a real system the database would store further information about each course such as: the tutor, room, days and times of the classes.

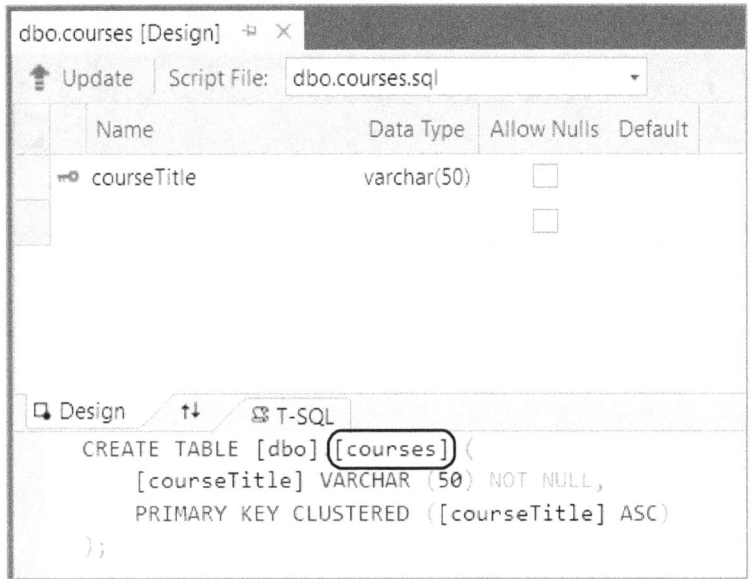

Go to the **CREATE TABLE** line and change the name of the table to '*courses*'.

Click the '*Update*' button above the list of fields. When the **Database Update** window appears, click the '*Update Database*' button.

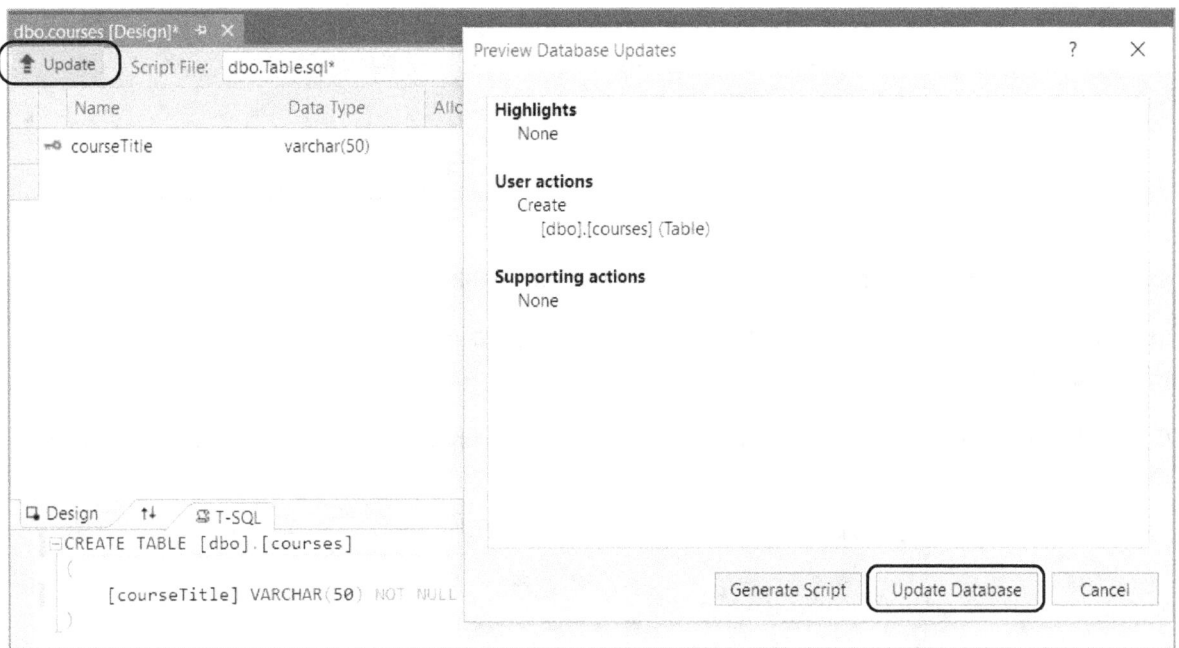

Close the *courses* table design page and re-open the **Server Explorer** window. Right-click on **collegeCourses.mdf** and select '**Refresh**'.

Click the small arrow to the left of the **Tables** icon. The *courses* table which you created should now be shown.

Repeat the steps above to create a *students* table. For simplicity, we will only add three fields: *surname*, *forename* and *dateOfBirth*. In a real system, this table would include the student's address and other contact details.

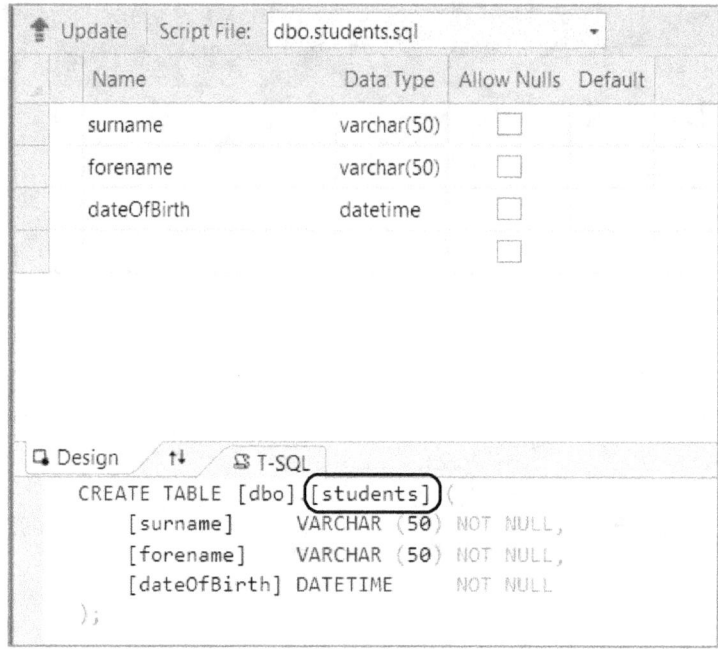

Delete the *Primary Key* by right-clicking on the key icon alongside the first field of the table, then select '*Remove Primary Key*' for the drop down list.

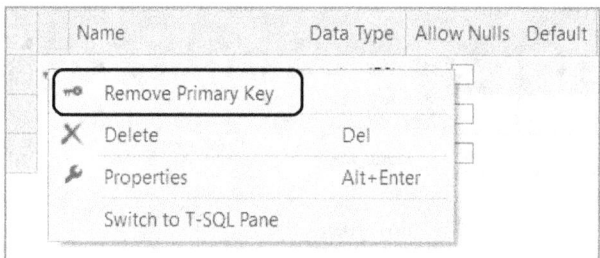

Go to the **CREATE TABLE** line and change the name of the table to '*students*'.

Click the '*Update*' button above the list of fields. When the *Database Update* window appears, click the '*Update Database*' button.

Complete the database structure by adding a third table for *enrolments*. Again delete the *Primary Key* from the table.

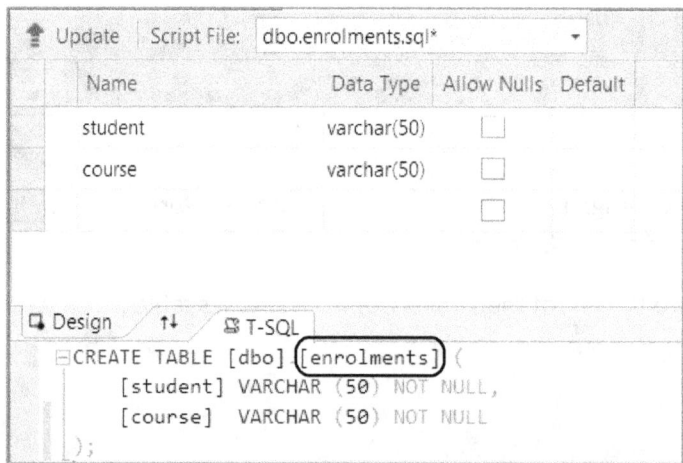

Close the conection to the *collegeCourses* database by right-clicking *collegeCourses.mdf* then selecting *Delete*, ready to begin work on the program.

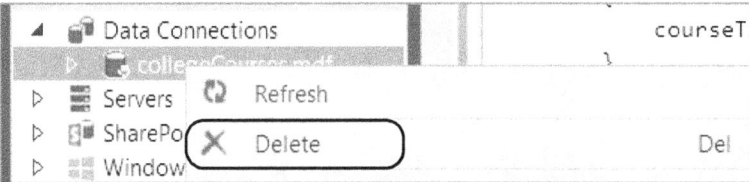

Start a *new C# project*. Select '*Windows Forms Application*', and call the project '*collegeCourses*'.

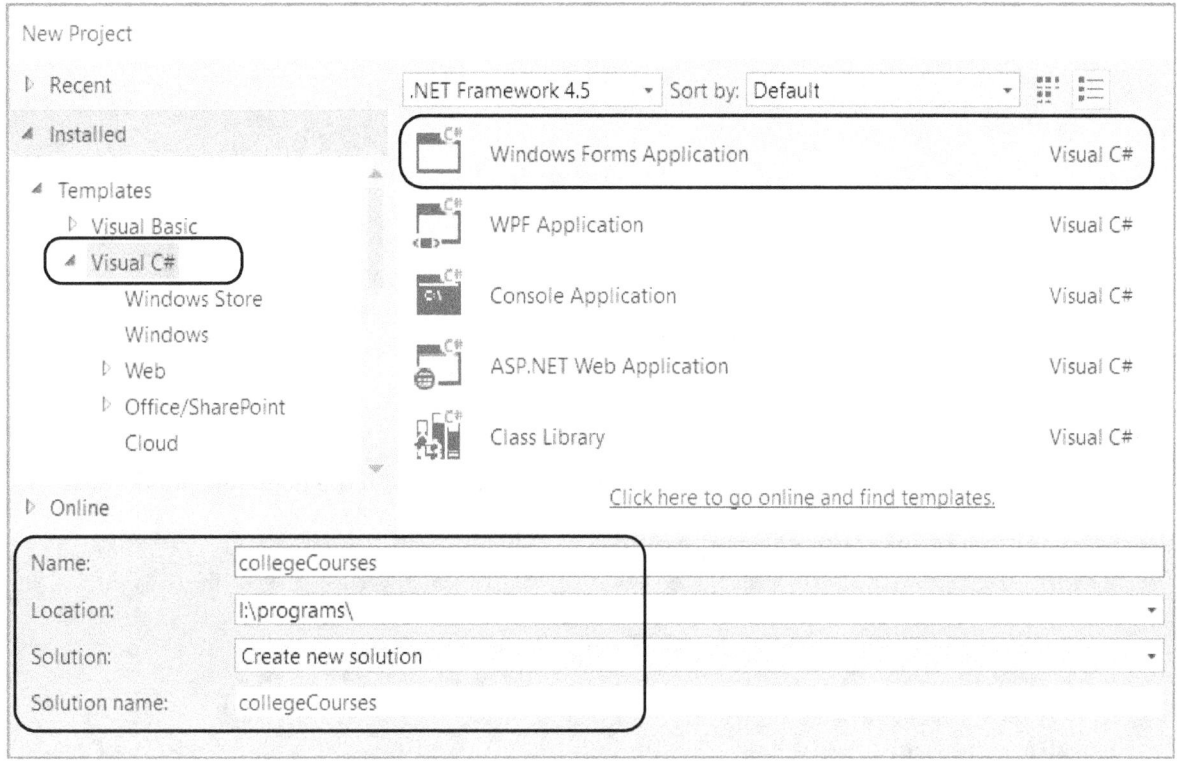

Set up a *menuStrip* on *Form1*, in a similar way to the Estate Agent Database program in Chapter 7. Create options for *adding* and *displaying courses*, *students* and *enrolments*:

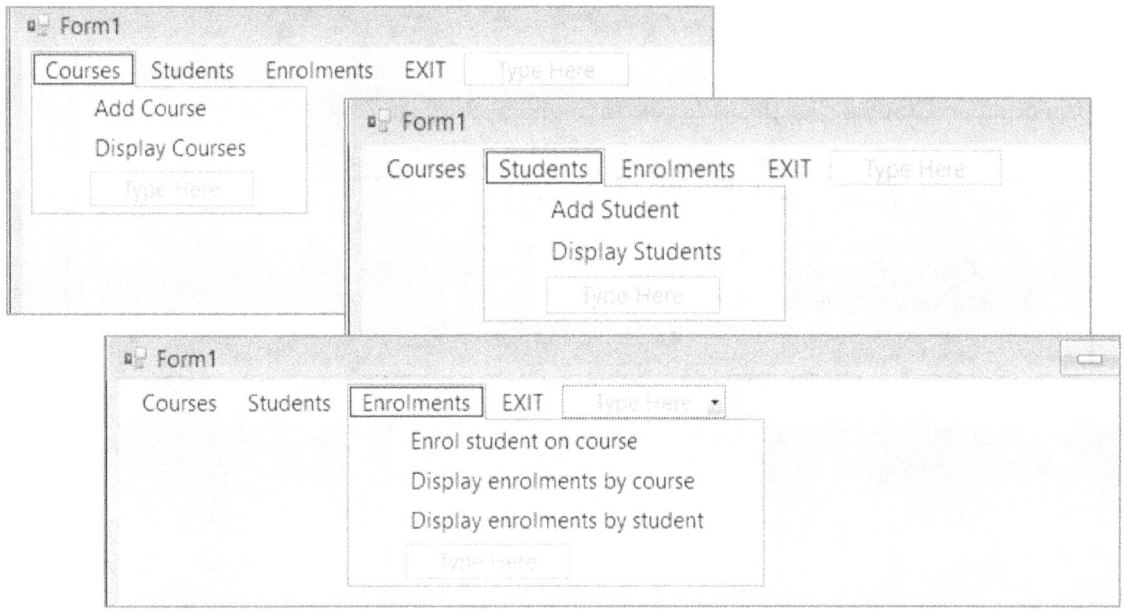

We will create a form for adding courses. Go to the **Solution Explorer** window, right-click on the **collegeCourses** program icon, then select '**Add / New Item**'. Choose **Windows Form** and give the name '**AddCourse**'.

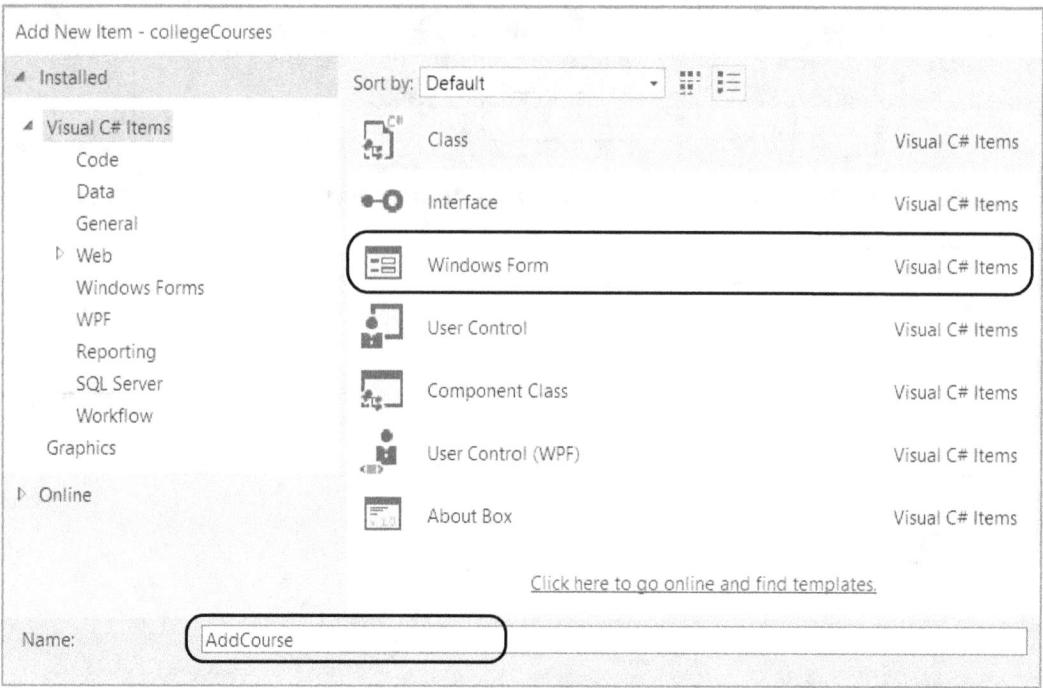

Add a *label*, a *textBox* with the name **txtCourseTitle**, and a *button* with the name **btnAddCourse**.

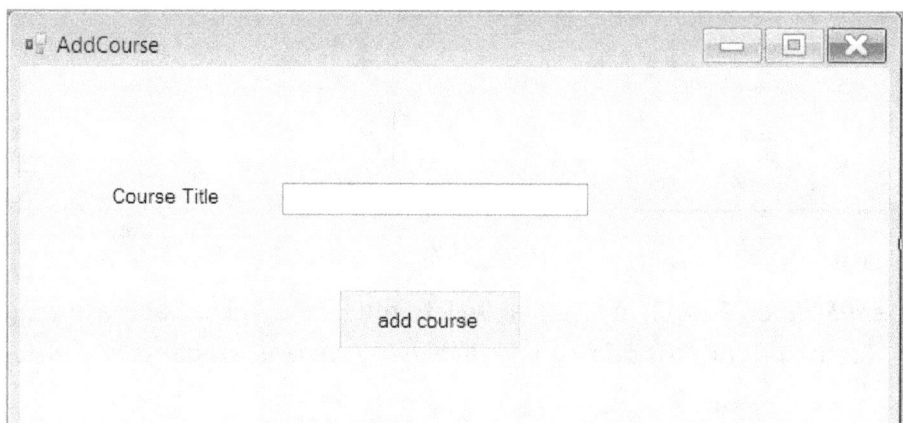

Return to **Form1** and double click the '**Add course**' menu option. Add code to open the AddCourse form.

```
private void addCourseToolStripMenuItem_Click(object sender, EventArgs e)
{
    AddCourse frmAddCourse = new AddCourse();
    frmAddCourse.ShowDialog();
}
```

Run the program and check that the **AddCourse** form opens correctly.

The object oriented way of handling data in this program will be rather different to the procedural approach of previous programs. Each time that a course is entered, a separate *course* object will be created and the *course title* will be assigned to it as a *property* of the object.

We must begin by defining the *course* class. Go to the **Solution Explorer** window, right-click on the *collegeCourses* program, and select '**Add / New Item**'. From the item list, choose '**Class**' and give this the name '*course*'.

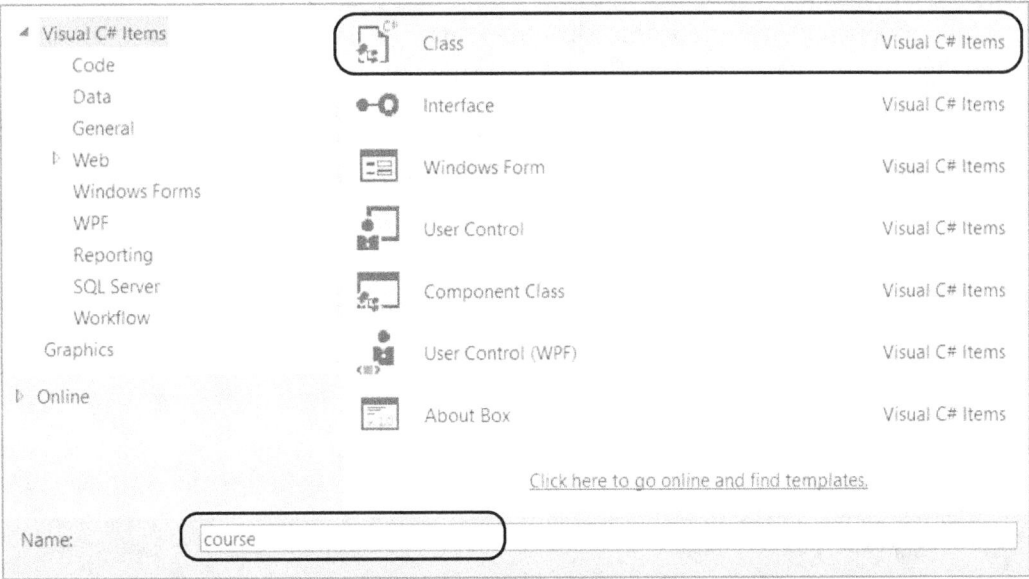

The file that you have created has no Form associated with it. Only its code window can be opened.

We will add some useful functions:

- *courseCount* is an integer which will record the number of courses entered.
- *course[ ]* defines an array of course objects. We are allowing for six courses to be entered, but the array size could be set to any maximum required. No memory space is actually used in the computer until we choose to create course objects when the program is running.
- *courseTitle* is a *property* of the object. In a real system, other properties would be included, such as the name of the course tutor, and the location and times of classes.

```
class course
{
    public static int courseCount;
    public static course[] courseObject = new course[6];
    private string courseTitle;

    public void setTitle(string t)
    {
        courseTitle = t;
    }
    public string getTitle()
    {
        return courseTitle;
    }
}
```

Two methods have been created:

- **setTitle( )** allows the course title to be transferred into the *course* object.
- **getTitle( )** allows the course title to be transferred back from the *course* object to the outside program.

These two methods are the only means by which the value of *courseTitle* can be accessed or changed. This approach makes object oriented programming more secure and less liable to errors. In a procedural program, data is often accessible from different parts of the program, leading to unexpected logical errors which can be difficult to identify and correct.

When a new **course** object is created, it should be added to the database table so that it is available on future occasions that the program is run. We will add a *saveCourse( )* method to do this:

```csharp
using System.Linq;
using System.Text;

using System.Data;
using System.Data.SqlClient;

namespace collegeCourses
{
    class course
    {
        string databaseLocation = "C:\\C#\\collegeCourses.mdf;";

        public static int courseCount;
        public static course[] courseObject = new course[6];
        private string courseTitle;

        public void setTitle(string t)
        {
            courseTitle = t;
        }
        public string getTitle()
        {
            return courseTitle;
        }

        public void saveCourse()
        {
            SqlConnection con = new SqlConnection(@"Data Source=.\SQLEXPRESS;
              AttachDbFilename=" +databaseLocation + "Integrated Security=True;
              Connect Timeout=30; User Instance=True");
            con.Open();
            SqlCommand cmCourse = new SqlCommand();
            cmCourse.Connection = con;
            cmCourse.CommandType = CommandType.Text;
            cmCourse.CommandText ="INSERT INTO courses(courseTitle)
                    VALUES ('" + courseTitle + "')";
            cmCourse.ExecuteNonQuery();
            con.Close();
        }
```

The lines beginning:

> *SqlConnection con = new SqlConnection(...*
> *cmCourse.CommandText ="INSERT INTO...*

should each be entered as a single line of code with no line breaks.

It is necessary to add '*using Data*' and '*using SqlClient*' directives, and to give the location of the database.

Return to the **AddCourse** form. Double click the '**add course**' button and add code to the **btnAddCourse_Click( )** method.

```
public partial class AddCourse : Form
{
    public AddCourse()
    {
        InitializeComponent();
    }

    private void btnAddCourse_Click(object sender, EventArgs e)
    {
        string title = txtCourseTitle.Text;
        course.courseObject[course.courseCount] = new course();
        course.courseObject[course.courseCount].setTitle(title);
        course.courseObject[course.courseCount].saveCourse();
        course.courseCount++;
        this.Close();
    }
}
```

This method carries out a series of actions:
- The course title entered in the textBox is collected.
- A new course object is created. This is assigned a location in the **courseObject[ ]** array according to the current value of **courseCount**.
- The course title is transferred to the new object using the **setTitle( )** method.
- The new course object has its **property** details saved into the database table – in this case, just the course title needs to be saved.
- Finally, **courseCount** is increased by one.

Return to **Form1**. We will initialise the number of courses to zero when the program first starts by adding a line of code to the **Form1( )** method:

```
public partial class Form1 : Form
{
    public Form1()
    {
        InitializeComponent();
        course.courseCount = 0;
    }
```

Run the program and enter test data for courses. Connect to the database and check that the course titles appear correctly in the database table, then delete the database connection.

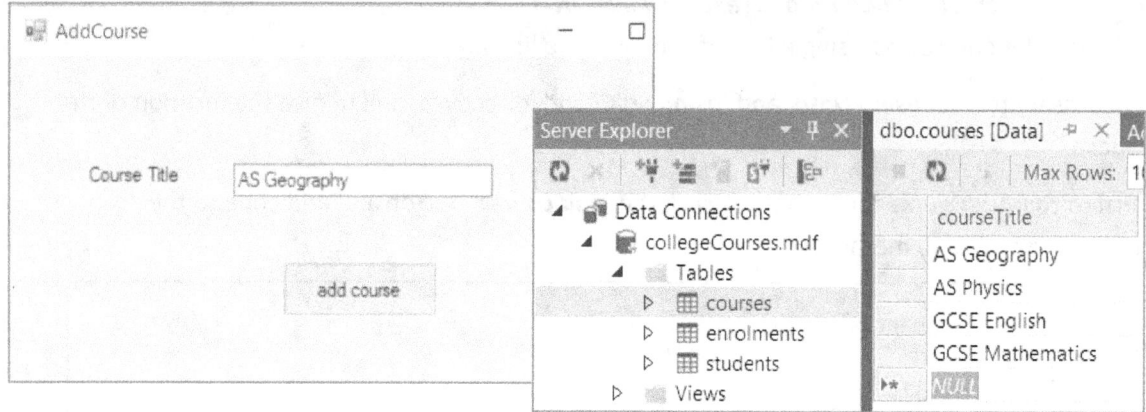

We can now produce a form to display the list of courses. Right click the *collegeCourses* program icon in the *Solution Explorer* window and select '*Add / New item*'. Create a *Windows Form*, and name this '*DisplayCourses*':

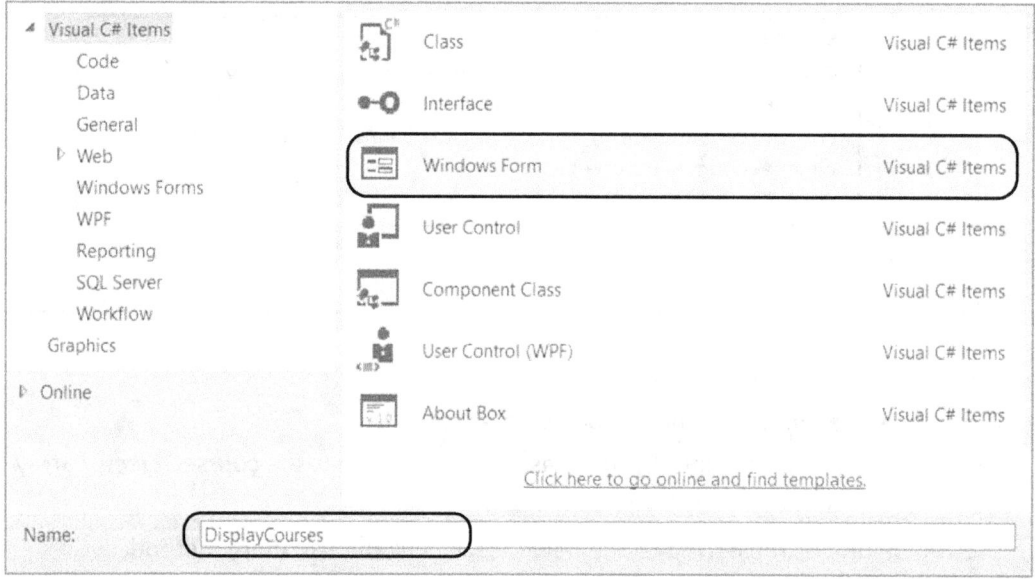

Add a *ListBox* and *Button* to the form.

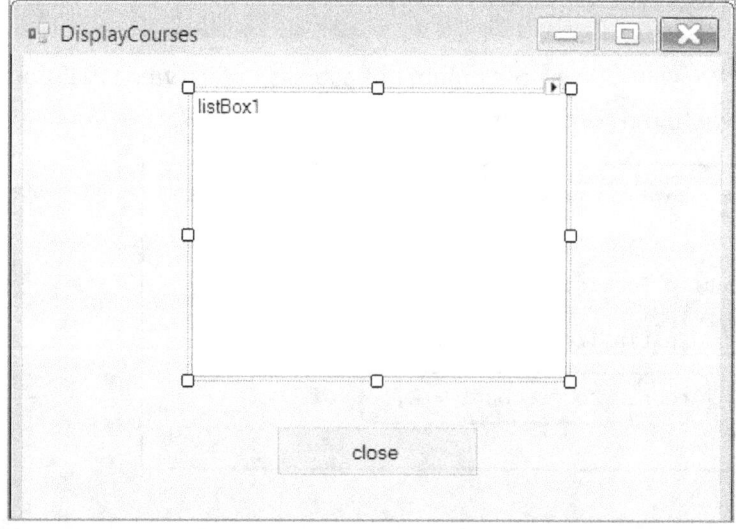

Rename the button as **btnClose**. Double click the button and add a line of code to close the form.

```
public partial class DisplayCourses : Form
{
    public DisplayCourses()
    {
        InitializeComponent();
    }

    private void btnClose_Click(object sender, EventArgs e)
    {
        this.Close();
    }
}
```

Add a **courseList( )** method, and call this from the **DisplayCourses( )** method.

```
public partial class DisplayCourses : Form
{
    public DisplayCourses()
    {
        InitializeComponent();
        courseList();
    }

    private void courseList()
    {
        int courseCount = course.courseCount;
        string title;

        listBox1.Items.Clear();
        for (int i = 0; i < courseCount; i++)
        {
            title = course.courseObject[i].getTitle();
            listBox1.Items.Add(title);
        }
    }
}
```

Notice how the **courseList( )** method collects **courseCount** from the **course** class. It then uses this variable to operate a loop which loads the title of each course and displays it in the list box. Each course title is obtained from the array of **course** objects using the **getTitle( )** method.

Return to **Form1**. Double click the '**Display Courses**' menu option and add code to open the **displayCourses** form:

```
private void displayCoursesToolStripMenuItem_Click(object sender, EventArgs e)
{
    DisplayCourses frmDisplayCourses = new DisplayCourses();
    frmDisplayCourses.ShowDialog();
}
```

We have one more task to complete before courses can be displayed by the program. It is necessary to add a method to **Form1** which will load the course information from the database table and create *course* objects when the program first runs.

Begin by adding the *'using SqlClient'* directive and the database location:

```
using System.Windows.Forms;
using System.Data.SqlClient;

namespace collegeCourses
{
    public partial class Form1 : Form
    {
        string databaseLocation = "C:\\C#\\collegeCourses.mdf;";
```

Create a *loadCourses( )* method to load the records from the database table. Call this from the *Form1( )* method:

```
public Form1()
{
    InitializeComponent();
    course.courseCount = 0;
    loadCourses();
}

private void loadCourses()
{
    DataSet dsCourses = new DataSet();

    SqlConnection con = new SqlConnection(@"Data Source=.\SQLEXPRESS;
       AttachDbFilename=" + databaseLocation + "Integrated Security=True;
       Connect Timeout=30; User Instance=True");
    try
    {
        con.Open();
        SqlCommand cmCourses = new SqlCommand();
        cmCourses.Connection = con;
        cmCourses.CommandType = CommandType.Text;
        cmCourses.CommandText = "SELECT * FROM courses";
        SqlDataAdapter daCourses = new SqlDataAdapter(cmCourses);
        daCourses.Fill(dsCourses);
        con.Close();
    }
    catch
    {
        MessageBox.Show("File error");
    }
}
```

Remember that the line beginning:

SqlConnection con = new SqlConnection(...

should be entered as a single line of code with no line breaks.

Add code to find the number of courses loaded, then use a loop to create the correct number of course objects and set the *courseTitle* for each object.

```
        SqlDataAdapter daCourses = new SqlDataAdapter(cmCourses);
        daCourses.Fill(dsCourses);
        con.Close();

        int countRecords = dsCourses.Tables[0].Rows.Count;

        for (int i = 0; i < countRecords; i++)
        {
            DataRow drCourse = dsCourses.Tables[0].Rows[i];
            string courseTitle = Convert.ToString(drCourse[0]);

            course.courseObject[course.courseCount] = new course();
            course.courseObject[course.courseCount].setTitle(courseTitle);

            course.courseCount++;
        }
    }
    catch
    {
```

Run the program and select the '*Display courses*' menu option. The course titles which you entered earlier should be displayed.

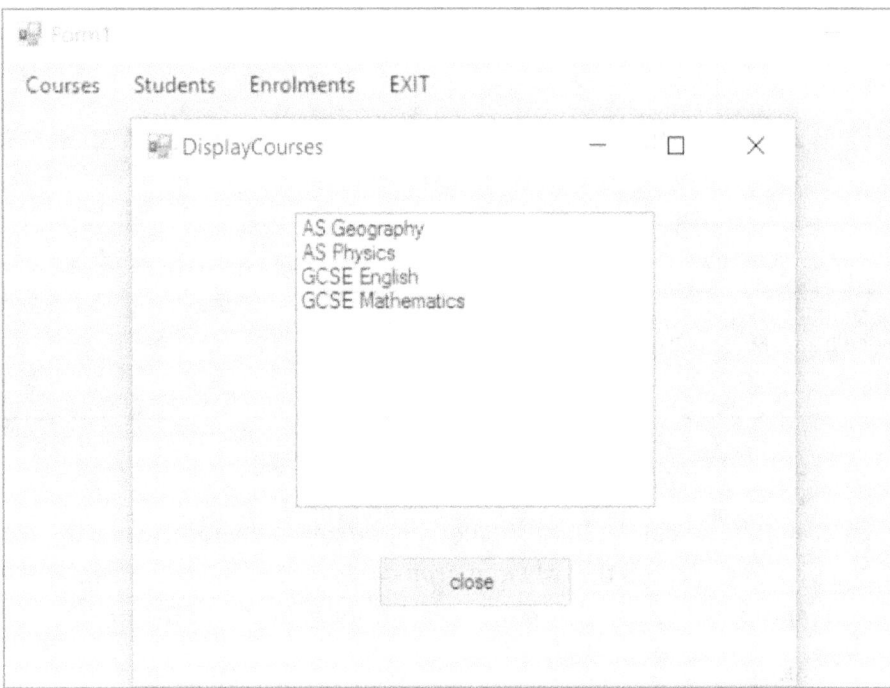

This completes the *courses* section of the program.

We can now work on the *students* section which will be structured in a very similar way. Begin by creating a *Windows Form* with the name '*AddStudent*'.

- Insert two *textBoxes* and two *labels* for '*Surname*' and '*Forename*'. Name the textBoxes as *txtSurname* and *txtForename*.
- Add a *DateTimePicker* component which will be used to enter the student's date of birth. This should also have a *label*.
- Complete the form with a *button*. Give this the name *btnAddStudent*.

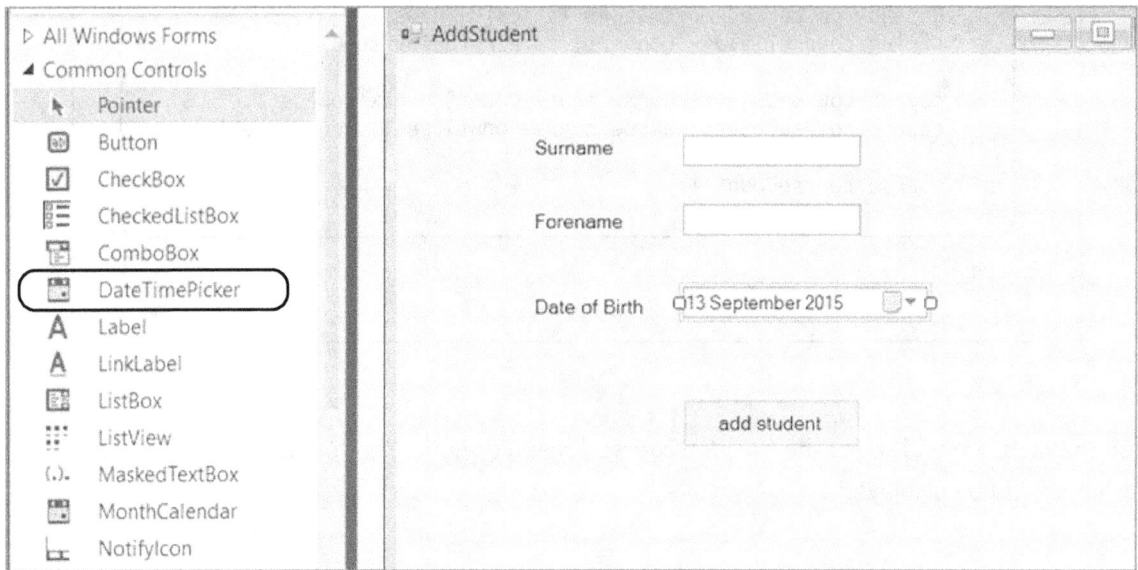

Go to **Form1** and add code to the '*Add student*' menu option to open the *AddStudent* form.

```
private void addStudentToolStripMenuItem_Click(object sender, EventArgs e)
{
    AddStudent frmAddStudent = new AddStudent();
    frmAddStudent.ShowDialog();
}
```

Run the program and check that the '*Add student*' option opens the form correctly. *Date of birth* can be selected by clicking first on the *calendar drop down arrow*, then on the *month heading*, and finally on the *year heading* to reach the scrolling year display, as shown below.

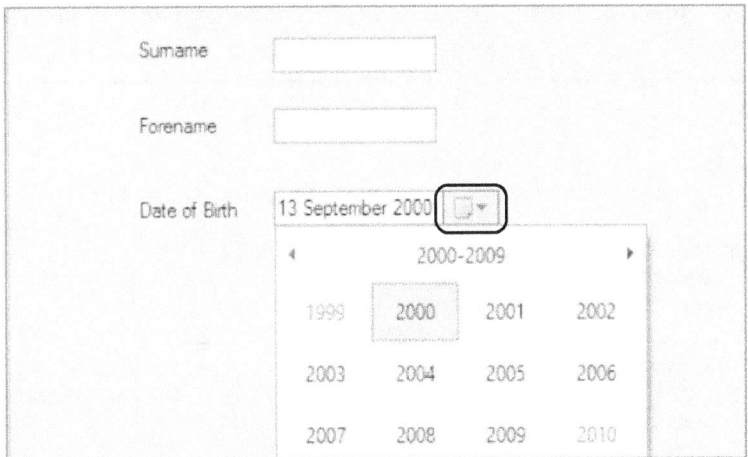

It is now necessary to create a **student** class file. Go to the **Solution Explorer** window, right-click the *collegeCourses* program icon, and select '**Add / New Item**'.
Choose '**Class**', and give the name '*student*':

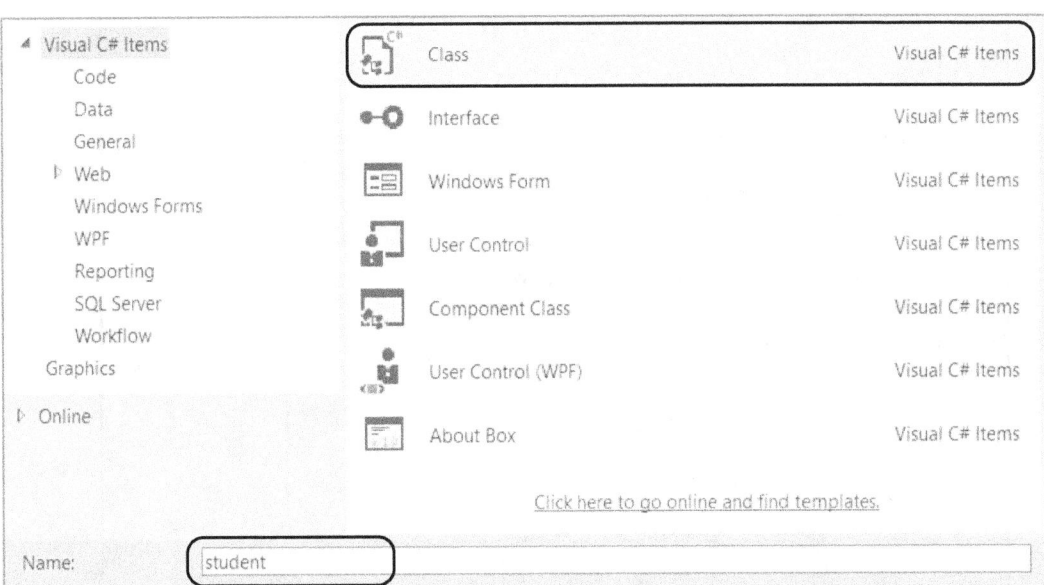

We will first set up a class property to record the total number of students input, and an array to hold up to 12 **student** objects. We can then add the **surname**, **forename** and **date of birth** properties needed for a student object.

```
class student
{
    public static int studentCount;
    public static student[] studentObject = new student[12];

    private string surname;
    private string forename;
    private DateTime dateOfBirth;
}
```

Methods can then be added to transfer the *surname*, *forename* and *date of birth* into and out of the *student* object:

```csharp
class student
{
    public static int studentCount;
    public static student[] studentObject = new student[12];

    private string surname;
    private string forename;
    private DateTime dateOfBirth;

    public void setSurname(string s)
    {
        surname = s;
    }
    public string getSurname()
    {
        return surname;
    }
    public void setForename(string f)
    {
        forename = f;
    }
    public string getForename()
    {
        return forename;
    }
    public void setDateOfBirth(DateTime d)
    {
        dateOfBirth = d;
    }
    public DateTime getDateOfBirth()
    {
        return dateOfBirth;
    }
}
```

We will complete the student class with a *saveStudent( )* method, to transfer a student record into the database table. Add '*using Data*' and '*using SqlClient*' directives, and give the database location:

```csharp
using System.Linq;
using System.Text;
using System.Data;
using System.Data.SqlClient;

namespace collegeCourses
{
    class student
    {
        string databaseLocation = "C:\\C#\\collegeCourses.mdf;";

        public static int studentCount;
        public static student[] studentObject = new student[12];
```

Insert the **saveStudent( )** method into the class file after the list of properties:

```
private string surname;
private string forename;
private DateTime dateOfBirth;

public void saveStudent()
{
    SqlConnection con = new SqlConnection(@"Data Source=.\SQLEXPRESS;
      AttachDbFilename=" +databaseLocation + "Integrated Security=True;
      Connect Timeout=30;User Instance=True");

    con.Open();
    SqlCommand cmStudent = new SqlCommand();
    cmStudent.Connection = con;
    cmStudent.CommandType = CommandType.Text;
    cmStudent.CommandText = "INSERT INTO students(surname, forename, dateOfBirth)
        VALUES ('" + surname + "','" + forename + "','" +
        dateOfBirth.ToString("MM/dd/yyyy") + "')";
    cmStudent.ExecuteNonQuery();
    con.Close();
}
```

Return to **Form1** and add a line of code to the **Form1( )** method to initialise the number of students to zero when the program first runs:

```
public Form1()
{
    InitializeComponent();
    course.courseCount = 0;
    student.studentCount = 0;
    loadCourses();
}
```

Go to the **AddStudent** form and double click the '**Add student**' button. Insert code into the **btnAddStudent_Click( )** method to create a new **student** object:

```
private void btnAddStudent_Click(object sender, EventArgs e)
{
    string surname = txtSurname.Text;
    string forename = txtForename.Text;
    string d = Convert.ToString(dateTimePicker1.Value);
    DateTime dateOfBirth = Convert.ToDateTime(d);

    student.studentObject[student.studentCount] = new student();
    student.studentObject[student.studentCount].setSurname(surname);
    student.studentObject[student.studentCount].setForename(forename);
    student.studentObject[student.studentCount].setDateOfBirth(dateOfBirth);
    student.studentObject[student.studentCount].saveStudent();

    student.studentCount++;

    this.Close();
}
```

Run the program and enter test data for several students:

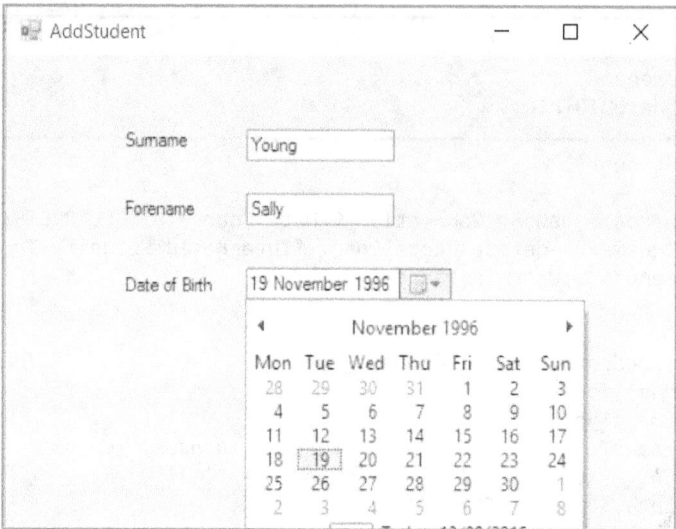

Exit from the program and use the **Server Explorer** to open the **students** table in the database. Check that the student data has been saved correctly, then close the connection to the database.

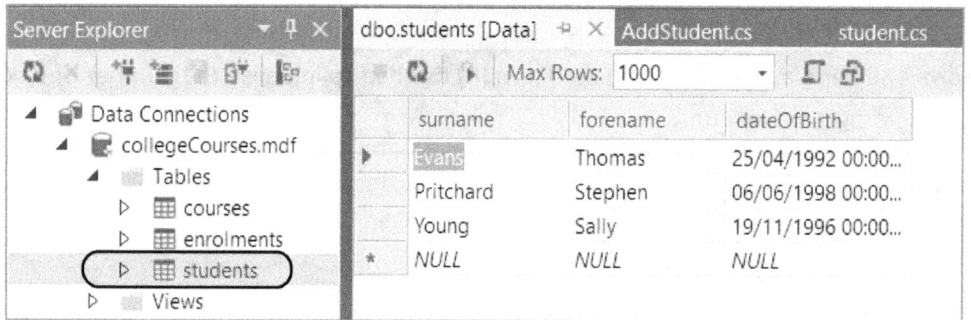

With the student input form now working, we can move on to create a **DisplayStudents** form. Go to the Solution Explorer window and select **Add / New item**. Select **Windows Form** and give the name '**DisplayStudents**'.

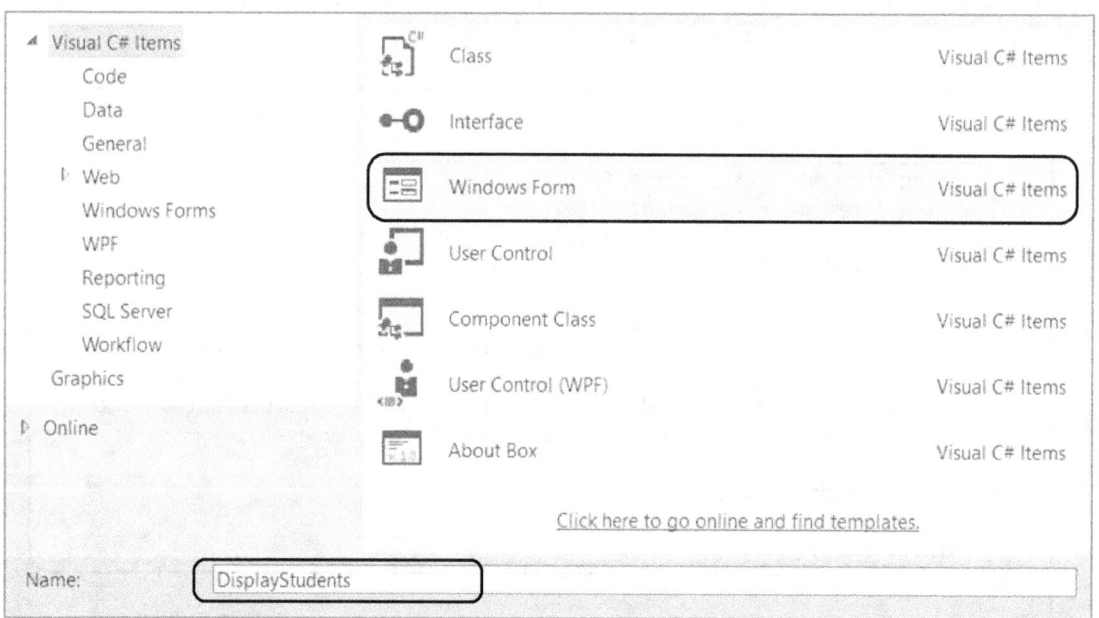

Add a *listBox* and *button* to the form.

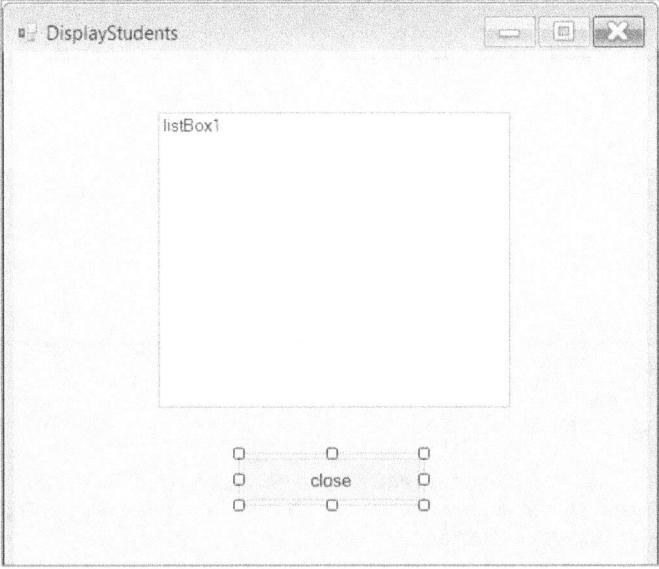

Right-click on the form and select the program code view.

We will display students' details in the list box in the format: *date of birth*, *surname*, *forename*. For example: *19/11/1996   Young, Sally*

Create a *studentList( )* method, and call this from the *DisplayStudents( )* method:

```
public partial class DisplayStudents : Form
{
    public DisplayStudents()
    {
        InitializeComponent();
        studentList();
    }

    private void studentList()
    {
        int studentCount = student.studentCount;
        string surname;
        string forename;
        DateTime dateOfBirth;

        listBox1.Items.Clear();
        for (int i = 0; i < studentCount; i++)
        {
            surname = student.studentObject[i].getSurname();
            forename = student.studentObject[i].getForename();
            dateOfBirth = student.studentObject[i].getDateOfBirth();

            listBox1.Items.Add(dateOfBirth.ToString("dd/MM/yyyy")
                + " " + surname + ", " + forename);
        }
    }
}
```

Notice how the number of students is obtained from the *student* class, then a loop is used to access the *surname*, *forename* and *date of birth* from each of the objects in the *studentObject* array.

To complete the display of student details, return to **Form1** and add a **loadStudents( )** method. Call this from the **Form1( )** method:

```
public Form1()
{
    InitializeComponent();
    course.courseCount = 0;
    student.studentCount = 0;
    loadCourses();
    loadStudents();
}

private void loadStudents()
{
    DataSet dsStudents = new DataSet();

    SqlConnection con = new SqlConnection(@"Data Source=.\SQLEXPRESS;
        AttachDbFilename=" + databaseLocation + "Integrated Security=True;
        Connect Timeout=30; User Instance=True");
    try
    {
        con.Open();
        SqlCommand cmStudents = new SqlCommand();
        cmStudents.Connection = con;
        cmStudents.CommandType = CommandType.Text;
        cmStudents.CommandText = "SELECT * FROM students";
        SqlDataAdapter daStudents = new SqlDataAdapter(cmStudents);
        daStudents.Fill(dsStudents);
        con.Close();

        int countRecords = dsStudents.Tables[0].Rows.Count;

        for (int i = 0; i < countRecords; i++)
        {
            DataRow drStudent = dsStudents.Tables[0].Rows[i];
            string surname = Convert.ToString(drStudent[0]);
            string forename = Convert.ToString(drStudent[1]);
            DateTime dateOfBirth = Convert.ToDateTime(drStudent[2]);

            student.studentObject[student.studentCount] = new student();
            student.studentObject[student.studentCount].setSurname(surname);
            student.studentObject[student.studentCount].setForename(forename);
            student.studentObject[student.studentCount].setDateOfBirth(dateOfBirth);

            student.studentCount++;
        }
    }
    catch
    {
        MessageBox.Show("File error");
    }
}
```

This method works in a similar way to **loadCourses( )** which you wrote earlier. A loop is used to collect the **surname**, **forename** and **date of birth** from each student record in the data set. A new **studentObject** is created, and we set its properties using this data.

Double click the '**Display students**' menu option and add code to open the **DisplayStudents** form:

```
private void displayStudentsToolStripMenuItem_Click(object sender, EventArgs e)
{
    DisplayStudents frmDisplayStudents = new DisplayStudents();
    frmDisplayStudents.ShowDialog();
}
```

Run the program. Select the '**Display students**' option, and check that your student test data is shown correctly.

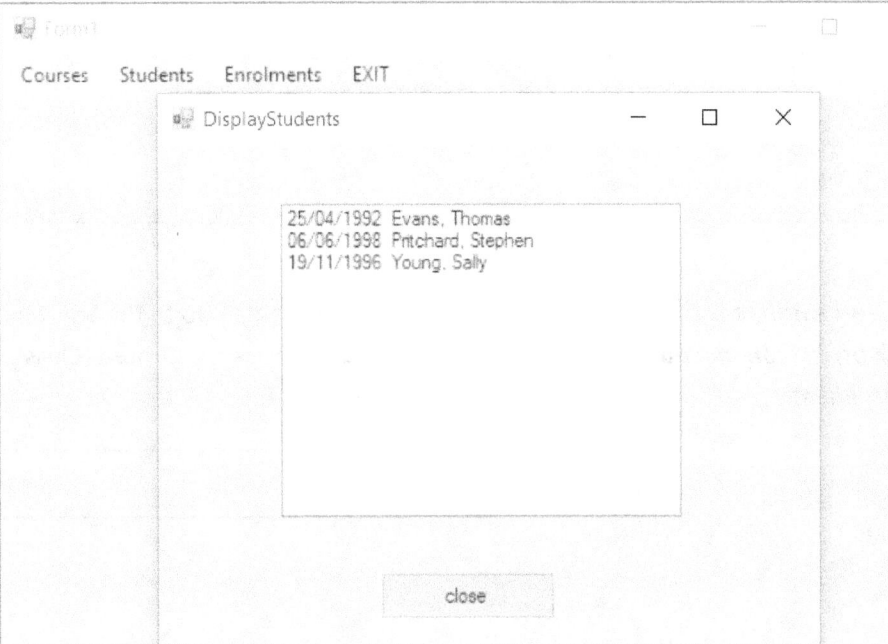

The final stage of the progam is to handle the enrolment of students on courses. Create a new **Windows Form** and give this the name '**AddEnrolment**'.

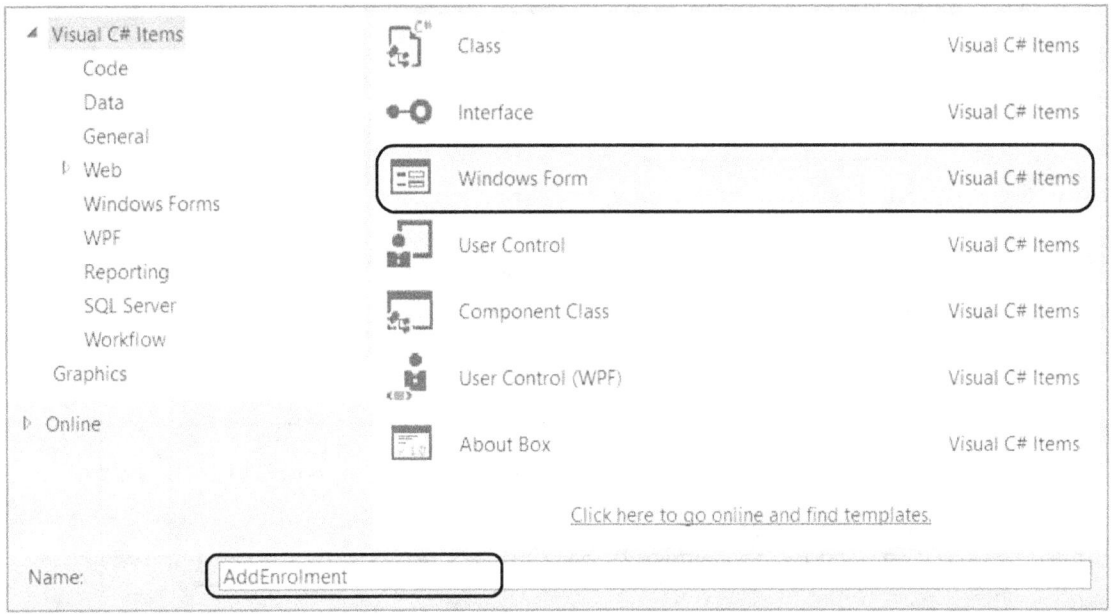

Add two **ComboBoxes** to the form, along with **labels**. Complete the form with a **button** to enrol a student on a course. Name the button as **btnAddEnrolment**.

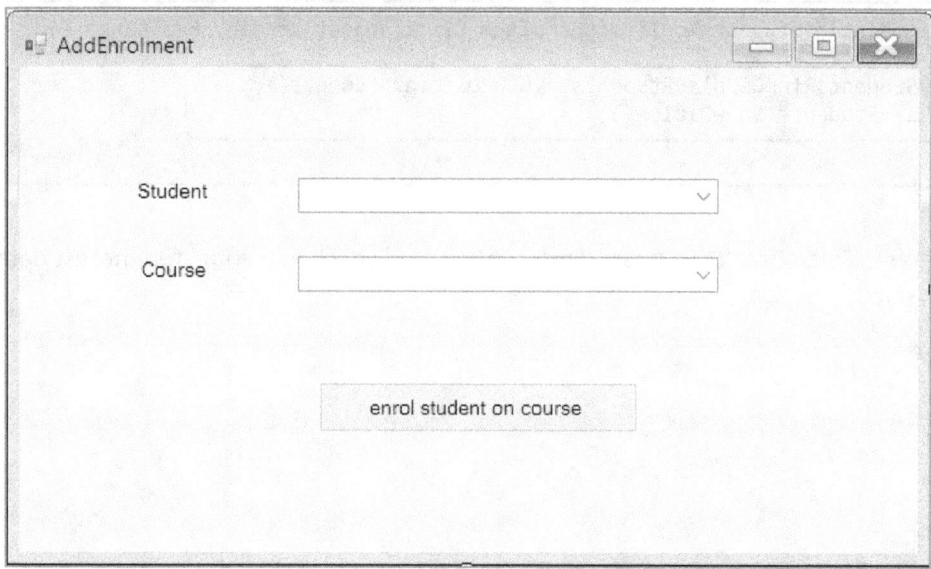

We will create an **enrolment** class, as we did for courses and students. Go to the **Solution Explorer** and right-click on the **collegeCourses** program to select '**Add /New item**'. Choose '**Class**', and give the name '**enrolment**'.

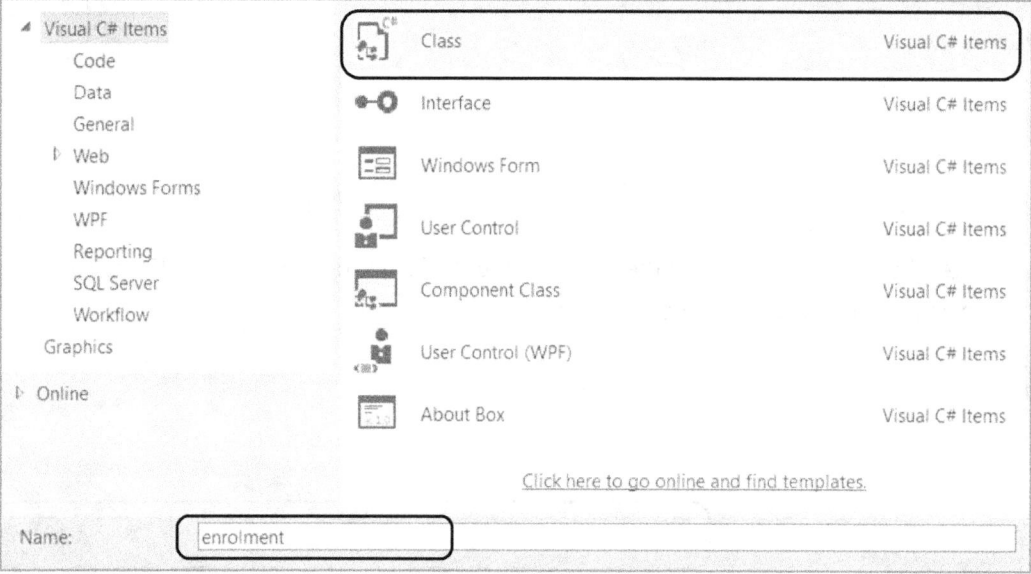

Add a property to store the **total number of enrolments**, an array for **enrolment objects**, and **course title** and **student name** properties for each enrolment recorded:

```
class enrolment
    {
        public static int enrolCount;
        public static enrolment[] enrolObject = new enrolment[16];

        private string course;
        private string student;
    }
```

Add methods to the *enrolment* class for transfering the *course title* and *student name* into and out of an enrolment object:

```
class enrolment
{
    public static int enrolCount;
    public static enrolment[] enrolObject = new enrolment[16];

    private string course;
    private string student;

    public void setCourse(string c)
    {
        course = c;
    }

    public string getCourse()
    {
        return course;
    }

    public void setStudent(string s)
    {
        student = s;
    }

    public string getStudent()
    {
        return student;
    }
```

The final requirement for the *enrolment* class is a method to store enrolment records in the database. Begin by adding '*using Data*' and '*using SqlClient*' directives, and giving the database location:

```
using System.Linq;
using System.Text;
using System.Data;
using System.Data.SqlClient;

namespace collegeCourses
{
    class enrolment
    {
        string databaseLocation = "C:\\C#\\collegeCourses.mdf;";

        public static int enrolCount;
        public static enrolment[] enrolObject = new enrolment[16];
```

The *saveEnrolment( )* method can now be written:

```
private string course;
private string student;

public void saveEnrolment()
{
    SqlConnection con = new SqlConnection(@"Data Source=.\SQLEXPRESS;
      AttachDbFilename=" + databaseLocation + "Integrated Security=True;
      Connect Timeout=30; User Instance=True");

    con.Open();
    SqlCommand cmEnrol = new SqlCommand();
    cmEnrol.Connection = con;
    cmEnrol.CommandType = CommandType.Text;
    cmEnrol.CommandText = "INSERT INTO enrolments(student, course)
      VALUES ('" + student + "','" + course + "')";
    cmEnrol.ExecuteNonQuery();
    con.Close();
}

public void setCourse(string c)
{
    course = c;
}
```

Go to *Form1* and add a line of code to the *Form1( )* method to initialise the number of enrolments to zero when the program begins:

```
public Form1()
{
    InitializeComponent();
    course.courseCount = 0;
    student.studentCount = 0;

    enrolment.enrolCount = 0;

    loadCourses();
    loadStudents();
}
```

Double click the '*Enrol student on course*' menu option, then add code to open the *addEnrolment* form.

```
private void enrolStudentToolStripMenuItem_Click(object sender, EventArgs e)
{
    AddEnrolment frmAddEnrolment = new AddEnrolment();
    frmAddEnrolment.ShowDialog();
}
```

Open the program code view for the *addEnrolment* form. This form has two *comboBoxes* which should provide drop-down lists of student names and course titles. It will then be possible to make an enrolment by selecting the relevant *student* and *course* from the lists, as in the design below:

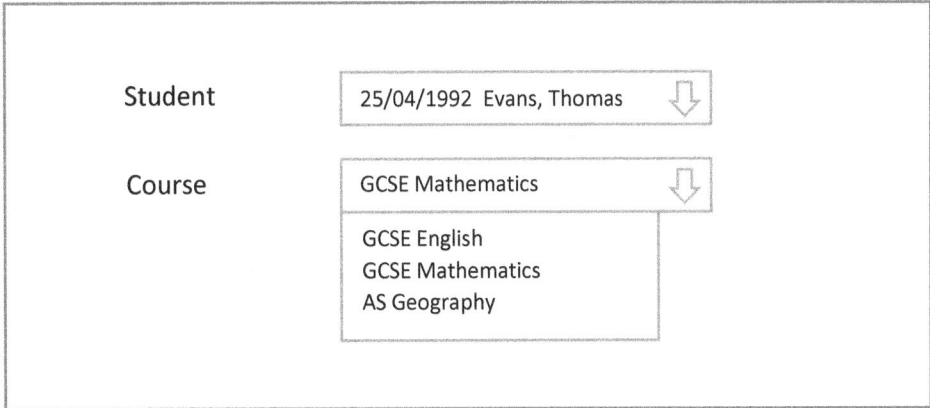

Begin by producing a *loadData( )* method. This uses loops to obtain the student and course data from the arrays of objects, and then inserts this data into the *comboBox* drop-down lists.
Add a line of code to call the *loadData( )* method from the *AddEnrolment( )* method when the form is opened.

```
public AddEnrolment()
{
    InitializeComponent();
    loadData();
}

private void loadData()
{
    int studentCount = student.studentCount;
    string surname;
    string forename;
    DateTime dateOfBirth;

    comboBox1.Items.Clear();
    for (int i = 0; i < studentCount; i++)
    {
        surname = student.studentObject[i].getSurname();
        forename = student.studentObject[i].getForename();
        dateOfBirth = student.studentObject[i].getDateOfBirth();

        comboBox1.Items.Add(dateOfBirth.ToString("dd/MM/yyyy")
            + " " + surname + ", " + forename);
    }

    int courseCount = course.courseCount;
    string title;

    comboBox2.Items.Clear();
    for (int i = 0; i < courseCount; i++)
    {
        title = course.courseObject[i].getTitle();
        comboBox2.Items.Add(title);
    }
}
```

Move to the form design view and double click the '*enrol student on course*' button. Add code to the **btnAddEnrolment_Click( )** method to collect the selected *student* and *course* names from the *comboBoxes*, create a new *enrolment* object, set the properties of the object, then save the data into the database file.

```
private void btnAddEnrolment_Click(object sender, EventArgs e)
{
    string student = comboBox1.Text;
    string course = comboBox2.Text;

    enrolment.enrolObject[enrolment.enrolCount] = new enrolment();
    enrolment.enrolObject[enrolment.enrolCount].setStudent(student);
    enrolment.enrolObject[enrolment.enrolCount].setCourse(course);
    enrolment.enrolObject[enrolment.enrolCount].saveEnrolment();

    enrolment.enrolCount++;

    this.Close();
}
```

Run the program. Go to the **Add enrolment** form and select combinations of *students* and *courses*, then click the button to enter each enrolment.

Exit from the program and use the Server Explorer to open the collegeCourses database. Check that the enrolments have been recorded correctly in the enrolments table, then close the database connection.

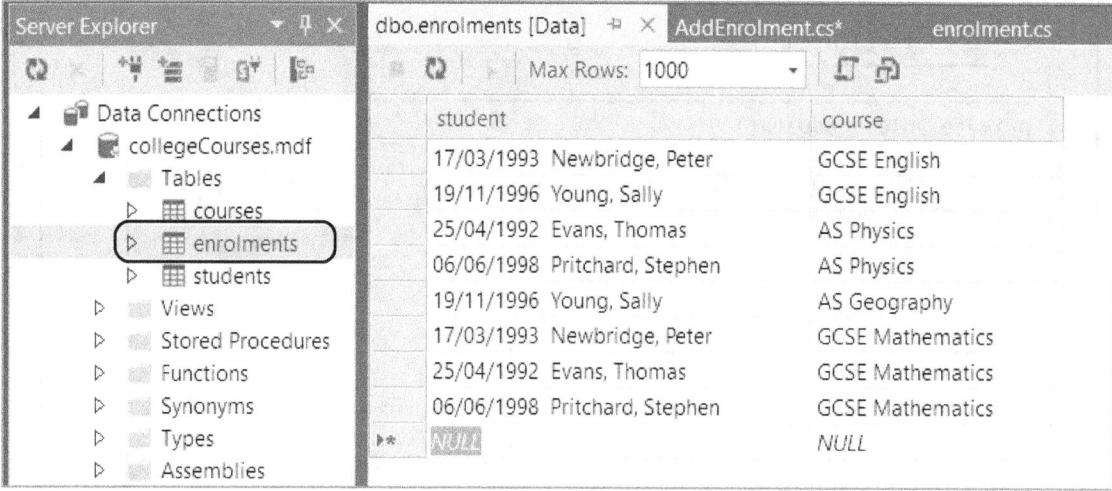

We can now consider how the enrolments can be displayed by the program. It will be useful for the staff of the college if this can be done in two different ways:

- As a *list of the courses*, showing the students enrolled on each course.
- As a *list of students*, showing the courses for which each student is enrolled.

We will provide these options as two separate forms.

Return to **Form1** and add a **loadEnrolments( )** method. This will work in a very similar way to the methods which you wrote earlier to load course and student records.

Call the **loadEnrolments( )** method from the **Form1( )** method.

```
public Form1()
{
    InitializeComponent();
    course.courseCount = 0;
    student.studentCount = 0;
    enrolment.enrolCount = 0;
    loadCourses();
    loadStudents();
    loadEnrolments();
}

private void loadEnrolments()
{
    DataSet dsEnrol = new DataSet();

    SqlConnection con = new SqlConnection(@"Data Source=.\SQLEXPRESS;
       AttachDbFilename=" +databaseLocation + "Integrated Security=True;
       Connect Timeout=30; User Instance=True");
    try
    {
        con.Open();
        SqlCommand cmEnrol = new SqlCommand();
        cmEnrol.Connection = con;
        cmEnrol.CommandType = CommandType.Text;
        cmEnrol.CommandText = "SELECT * FROM enrolments";
        SqlDataAdapter daEnrol = new SqlDataAdapter(cmEnrol);
        daEnrol.Fill(dsEnrol);
        con.Close();

        int countRecords = dsEnrol.Tables[0].Rows.Count;

        for (int i = 0; i < countRecords; i++)
        {
            DataRow drEnrol = dsEnrol.Tables[0].Rows[i];
            string student = Convert.ToString(drEnrol[0]);
            string course = Convert.ToString(drEnrol[1]);

            enrolment.enrolObject[enrolment.enrolCount] = new enrolment();
            enrolment.enrolObject[enrolment.enrolCount].setStudent(student);
            enrolment.enrolObject[enrolment.enrolCount].setCourse(course);

            enrolment.enrolCount++;

        }
    }
    catch
    {
        MessageBox.Show("File error");
    }
}
```

Create a new **Windows Form** and give this the name '**EnrolByCourse**'.

Add a **listBox** and **button** to the form:

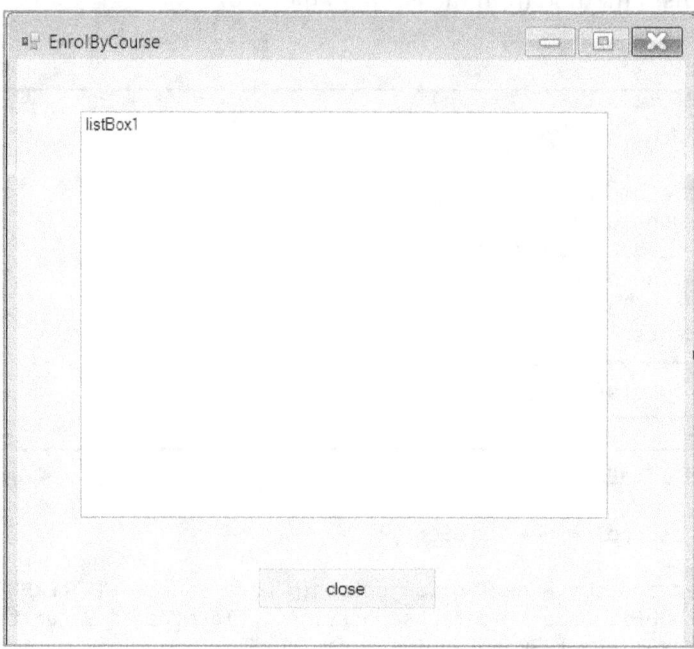

Go to **Form1**, double click the '**Display enrolments by course**' menu option and add lines of code to open the form:

```
private void displayEnrolmentsByCourseToolStripMenuItem_Click
                                    (object sender, EventArgs e)
{
    EnrolByCourse frmEnrolByCourse = new EnrolByCourse();
    frmEnrolByCourse.ShowDialog();
}
```

Change to the program code view for the **EnrolByCourse** form. Create a **courseList( )** method and call this from the **EnrolByCourse( )** method. Add variables to hold the **student** and **course** properties when they are accessed from the object classes.

```
public EnrolByCourse()
{
    InitializeComponent();

    courseList();
}

private void courseList()
{
    int courseCount = course.courseCount;
    string title;

    int enrolCount = enrolment.enrolCount;
    string student;
    string courseName;
}
```

The strategy we will use to display the courses, showing the students enrolled on each course, is:

1. LOOP for each *course*
   Display the title of *this course*
   2. LOOP for each *enrolment*
      3. IF the enrolment is for *this course* THEN
         Display the *student name*

Add lines of code to the *courseList( )* method to operate the loops and IF condition:

```
private void courseList()
{
    int courseCount = course.courseCount;
    string title;

    int enrolCount = enrolment.enrolCount;
    string student;
    string courseName;

    listBox1.Items.Clear();
    for (int i = 0; i < courseCount; i++)
    {
        title = course.courseObject[i].getTitle();
        listBox1.Items.Add(title);
        for (int j = 0; j < enrolCount; j++)
        {
            student = enrolment.enrolObject[j].getStudent();
            courseName = enrolment.enrolObject[j].getCourse();
            if (courseName == title)
            {
                listBox1.Items.Add("     "+student);
            }
        }
        listBox1.Items.Add("");
    }
}
```

Run the program and select the '*Display enrolments by course*' menu option.

The *EnrolByCourse* form should open, with your test data displayed in the listBox in a similar way to the example below.

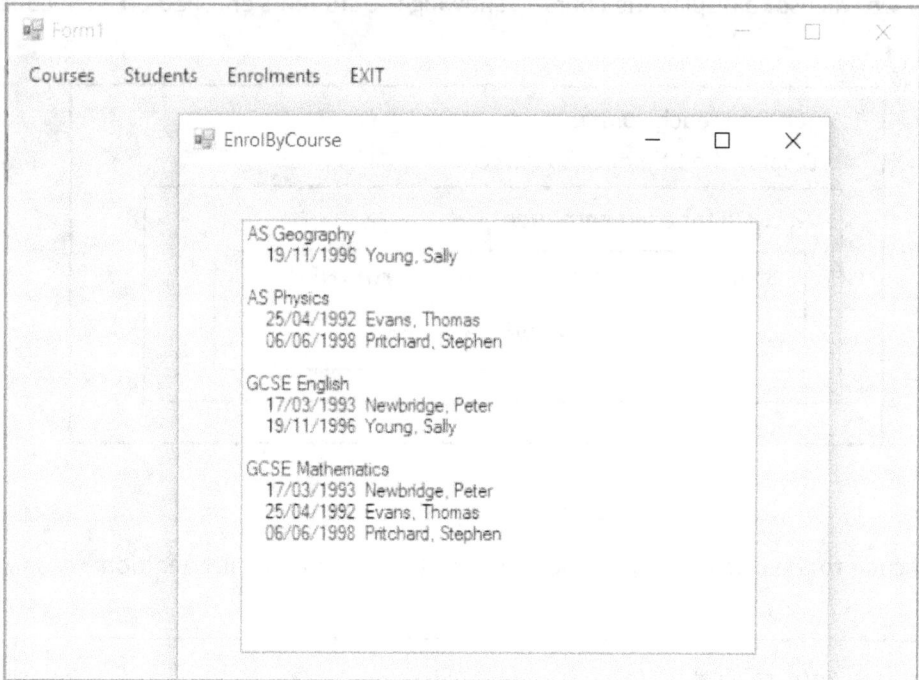

The final task in this program is to display a list of students, showing the courses for which each student is enrolled.

Create another **Windows Form** and name this '**EnrolByStudent**'. Add a list box and button as before:

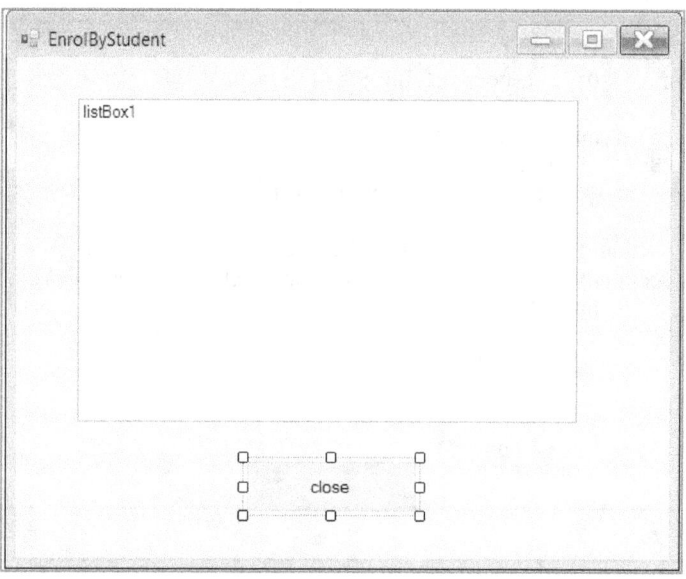

The strategy we will use to display the students, showing the courses for which they are enrolled, is:

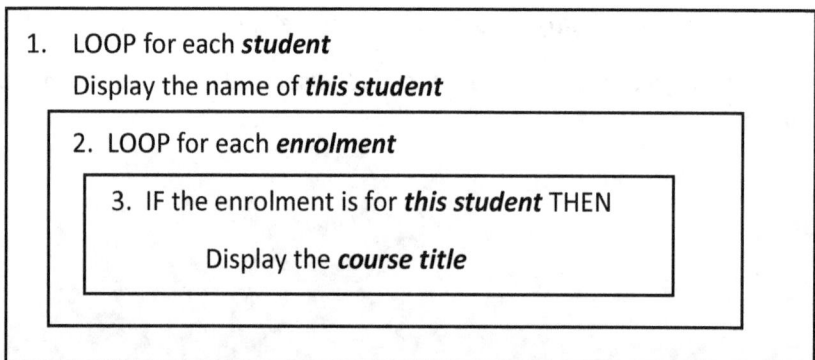

1. LOOP for each **student**
   Display the name of **this student**
   2. LOOP for each **enrolment**
      3. IF the enrolment is for **this student** THEN
         Display the **course title**

Right-click on the *EnrolByStudent* form to change to the Code view. Create a *studentList( )* method to implement the algorithm. Call the *studentList( )* method from the *EnrolByStudent( )* method.

```csharp
public EnrolByStudent()
{
    InitializeComponent();
    studentList();
}

private void studentList()
{
    int studentCount = student.studentCount;
    string surname;
    string forename;
    DateTime dateOfBirth;

    int enrolCount = enrolment.enrolCount;
    string studentName;
    string courseName;

    listBox1.Items.Clear();
    for (int i = 0; i < studentCount; i++)
    {
        surname = student.studentObject[i].getSurname();
        forename = student.studentObject[i].getForename();
        dateOfBirth = student.studentObject[i].getDateOfBirth();
        string s = dateOfBirth.ToString("dd/MM/yyyy") + "  "
            + surname + ", " + forename;
        listBox1.Items.Add(s);
        for (int j = 0; j < enrolCount; j++)
        {
            studentName = enrolment.enrolObject[j].getStudent();
            courseName = enrolment.enrolObject[j].getCourse();
            if (studentName == s)
            {
                listBox1.Items.Add("     " + courseName);
            }
        }
        listBox1.Items.Add("");
    }
}
```

Go to *Form1*, double click the '*Display enrolments by student*' menu option and add lines of code to open the form:

```csharp
private void displayEnrolmentsByStudentToolStripMenuItem_Click
                                    (object sender, EventArgs e)
{
    EnrolByStudent frmEnrolByStudent = new EnrolByStudent();
    frmEnrolByStudent.ShowDialog();
}
```

Run the program and check that a correct list of students is produced from your enrolment data:

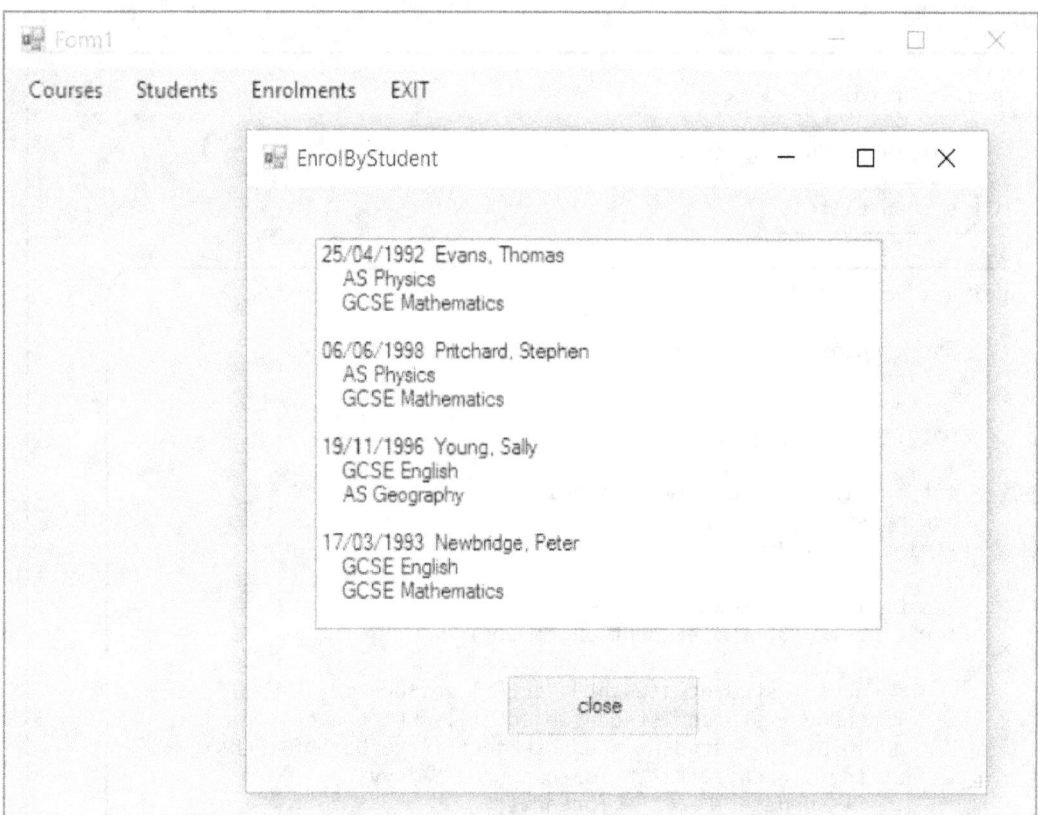

9 Fast Food

This program introduces the technique for uploading picture images to a C# program and storing them in a database table, in a similar way to text or numeric data. This can be very useful, for example, in a shop database where images of the products can accompany the written descriptions.

For this example, we will set up a small program to display a picture menu for a fast food take-away shop.

Use the Internet to collect some example photographs of fast food, for example: pizza, burgers, kebabs or tacos. Store these pictures as .JPG images in a folder on your computer.

We begin by setting up a database for the fast food shop, with a table to store details of the food items.

Open *Visual Studio*, but do not start a new project yet.

On the menu line, select '*View / Server Explorer*'

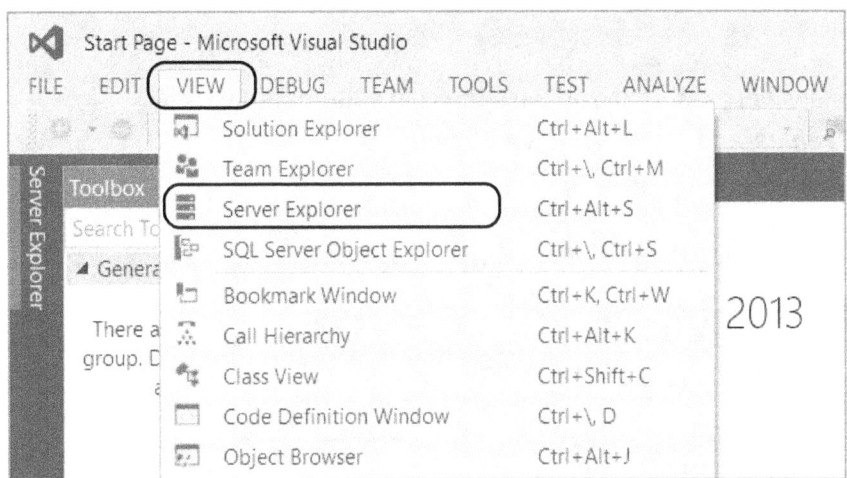

Right-click on '**Data Connections**', then select '**Add Connection**'. If you are asked to choose a Data Source, select:

Microsoft SQL Server Database File

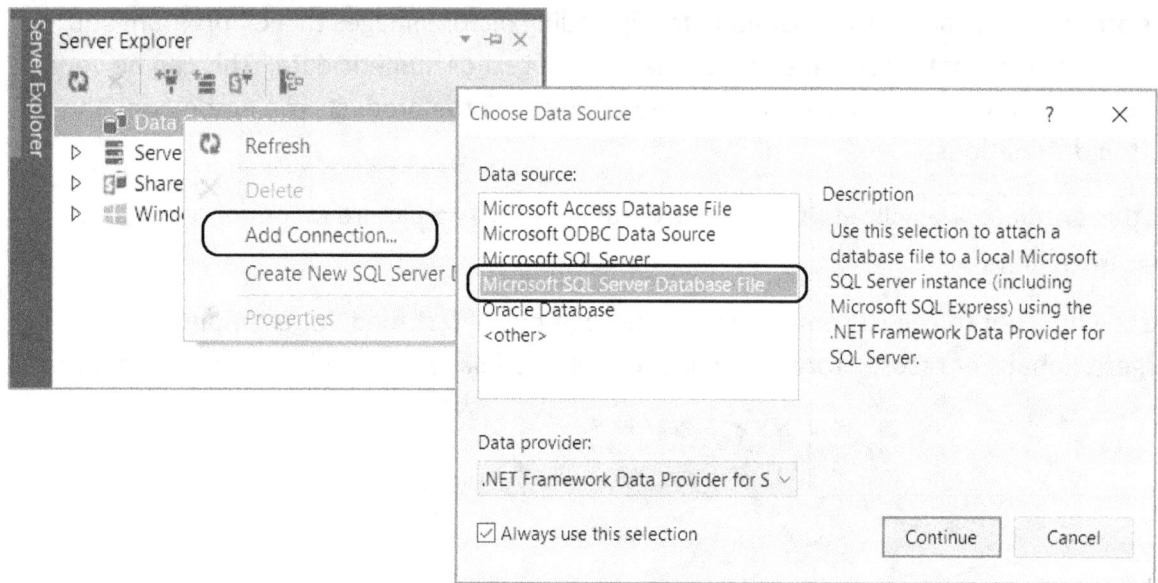

Use the '**Browse**' option to navigate to the location where your C# programs are stored. Give the file name '**fastFood**' for the database which will be created.

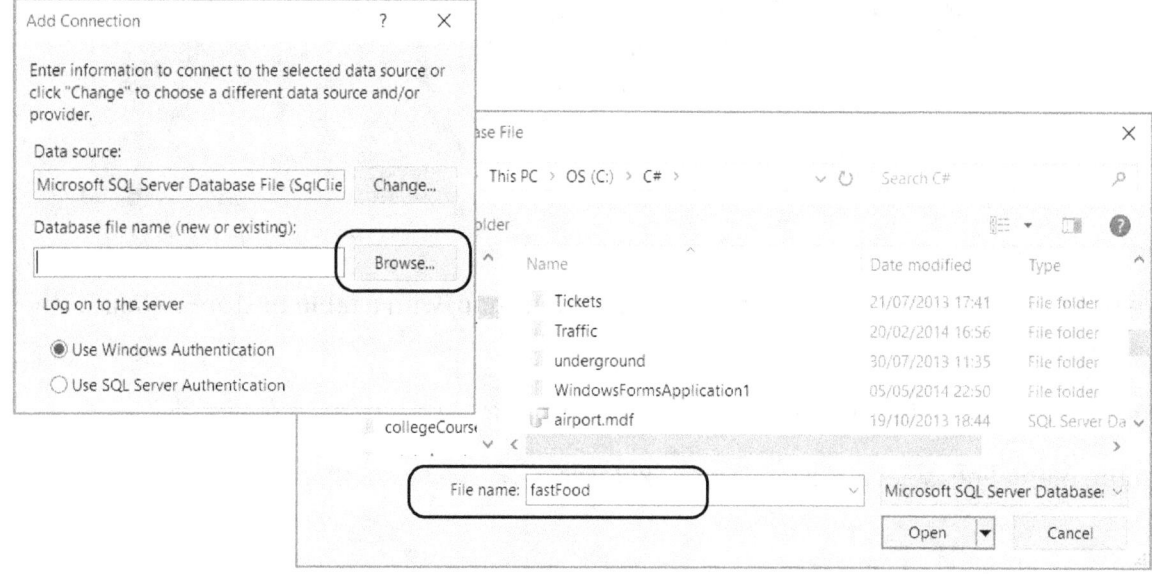

Click '**OK**', then answer '**Yes**' that you wish to create the database file.
Right-click on '**Tables**' and select '**Add New Table**':

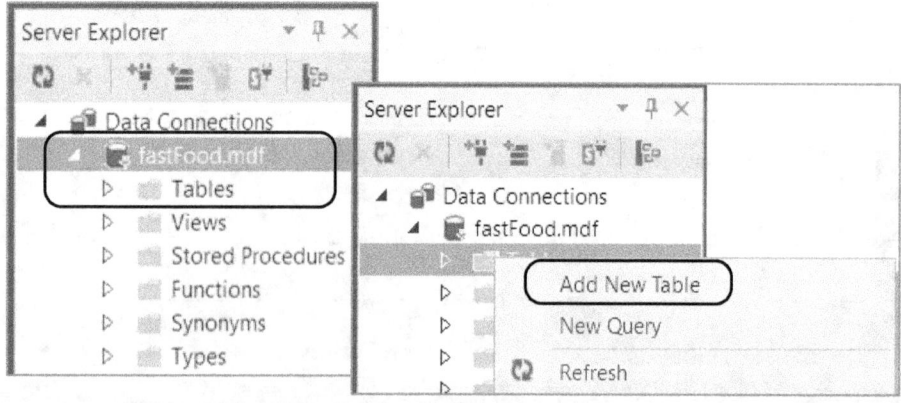

Add two fields to the table: *description* which will be a text field, and *picture* which has the data type '*image*'.

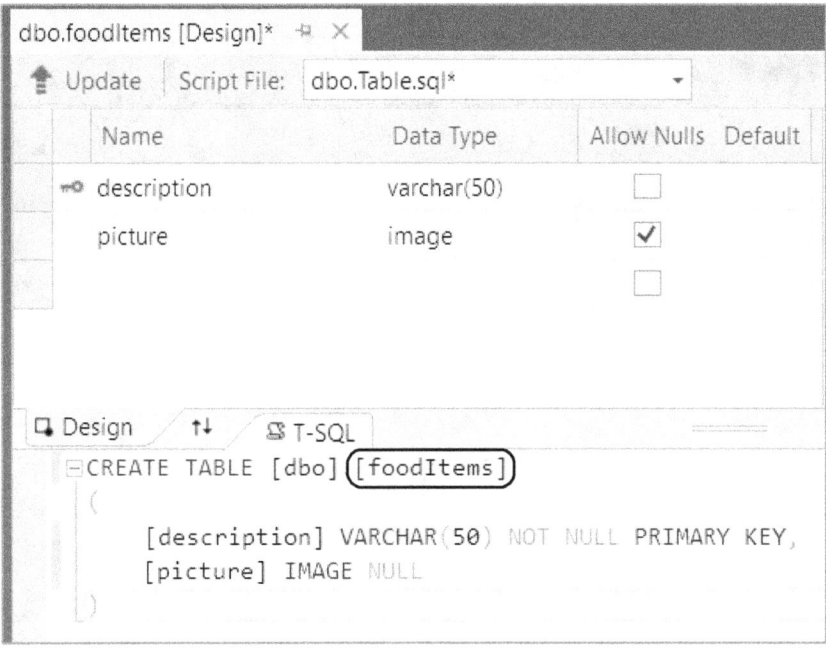

Go to the **CREATE TABLE** line and change the name of the table to '*foodItems*'.
Click the '*Update*' button above the list of fields. When the **Database Update** window appears, click the '*Update Database*' button.

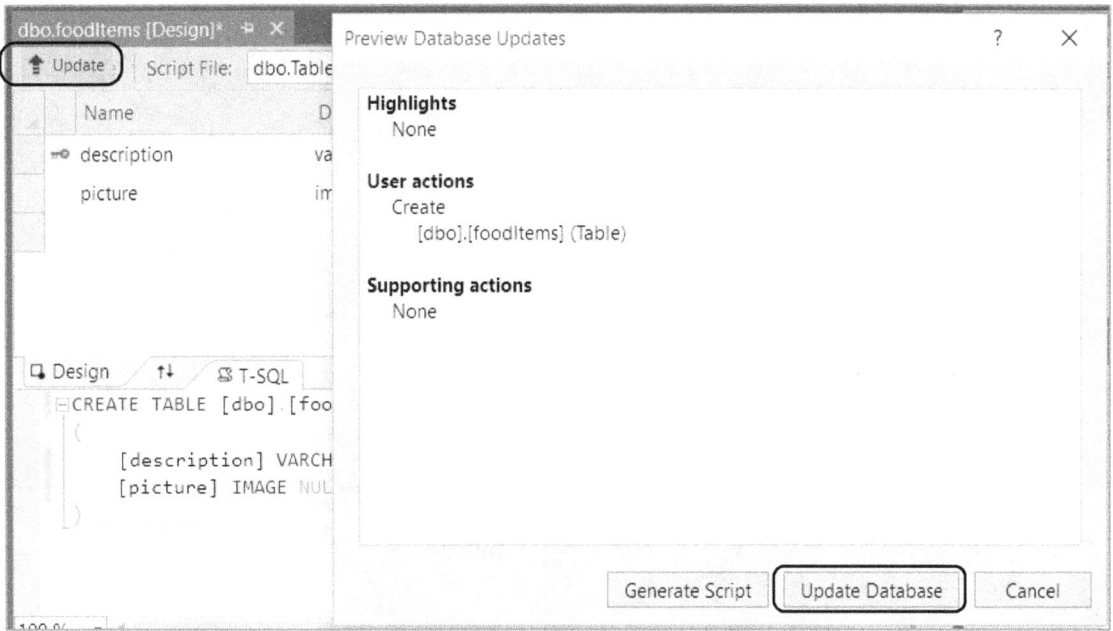

Close the *foodItems* table design page and re-open the **Server Explorer** window. Right-click on *fastFood.mdf* and select '**Refresh**'. Click the small arrow to the left of the **Tables** icon. The table which you created should now be shown.

Right-click on *fastFood.mdf* and select the '**Delete**' option to close the connection to the database.

We can now begin work on the program to load and display the images. Start a new project, select **Windows Forms Application**, and give this the name '*fastFood*'.

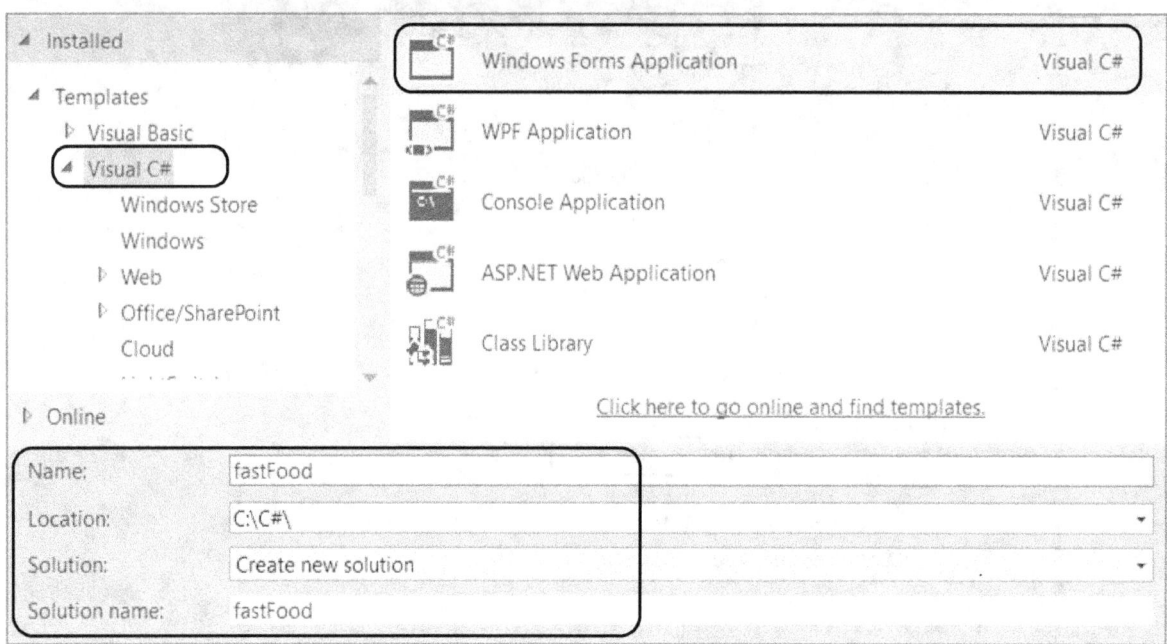

In the **Form1** design window, add the components shown:

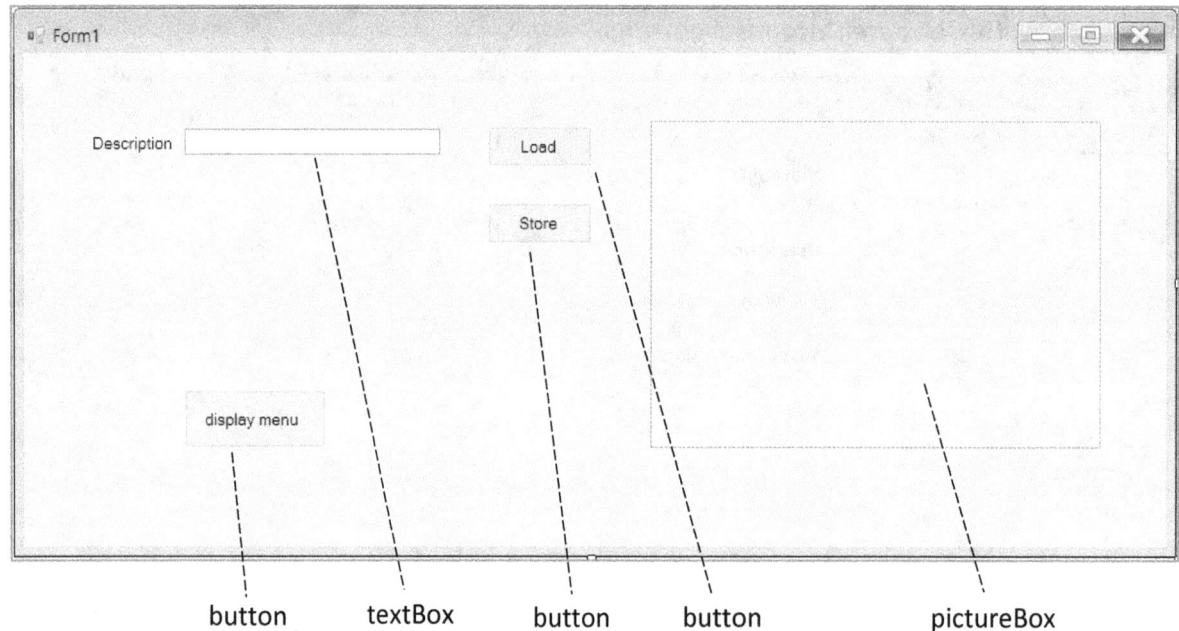

Rename the components:

textBox	**txtDescription**
'*Store*' button	**btnStore**
'*Load*' button	**btnLoad**
'*display menu*' button	**btnDisplay**

The first step is to set up a **btnLoad_click( )** method which will display a file selection window. The user will then be able to select the picture that they wish to upload to the database.

Double click the '**Load**' button and add the necessary code. Notice the filter line, which displays only files which are in graphics format. When the picture is selected, it will be displayed in the pictureBox on the form.

A **TRY..CATCH** structure is used, to prevent the program stopping if the selected file cannot be loaded for some reason.

A variable '**imagename**' is also required, to temporarily store the file name and path of the chosen picture.

```csharp
public partial class Form1 : Form
{
    string imagename;

    public Form1()
    {
        InitializeComponent();
    }

    private void btnLoad_Click(object sender, EventArgs e)
    {
        try
        {
            FileDialog fileDialog = new OpenFileDialog();
            fileDialog.Filter="Image File (*.jpg;*.bmp;*.gif)|*.jpg;*.bmp;*.gif";

            if (fileDialog.ShowDialog() == DialogResult.OK)
            {
                imagename = fileDialog.FileName;
                Bitmap newimg = new Bitmap(imagename);
                pictureBox1.SizeMode = PictureBoxSizeMode.StretchImage;
                pictureBox1.Image = (Image)newimg;
            }

            fileDialog = null;
        }
        catch
        {
            MessageBox.Show("Error");
        }
    }
}
```

Run the program to test the image loading. Click the '**Load**' button and navigate to the folder where your images are stored.

Select an image.

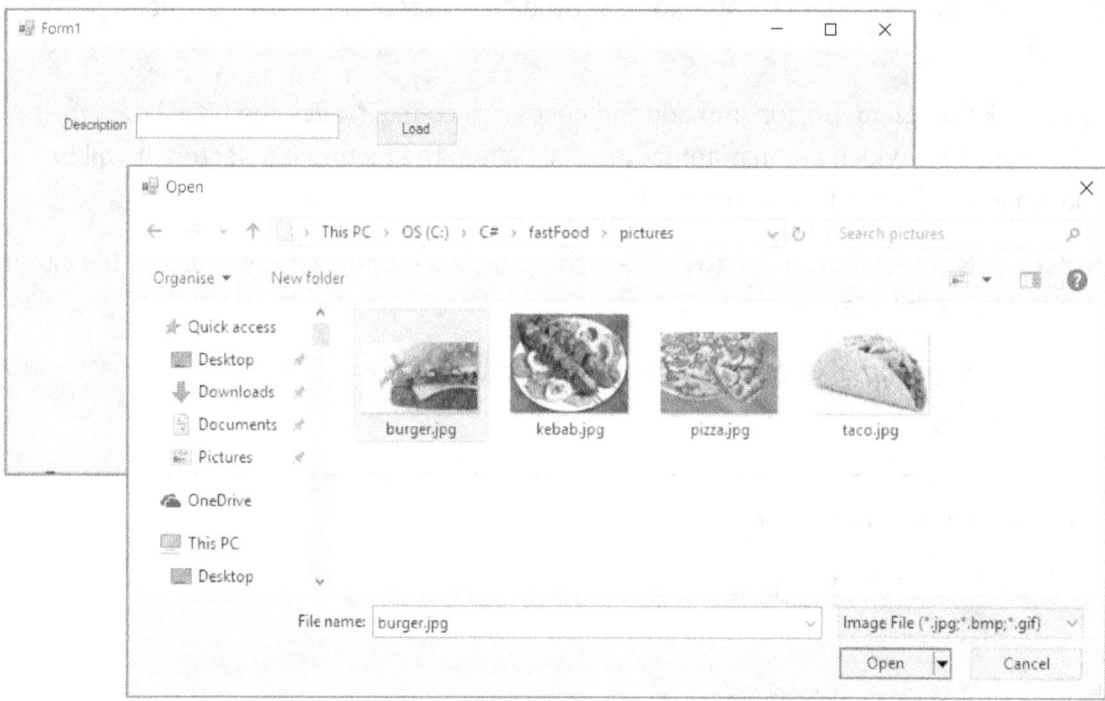

Click the '*Open*' button, and the image should appear in the pictureBox on the form:

The user will enter a description of the food item in the textBox.

The next step is to save the image and description into the database table. Begin by double clicking the '*Store*' button and adding a line of code to call an *addRecord( )* method:

```
private void btnStore_Click(object sender, EventArgs e)
{
    addRecord();
}
```

Go to the start of the program listing and add '*using IO*' and '*using SqlClient*' directives. We also need to specify the database location.

```
using System.Text;
using System.Windows.Forms;

using System.IO;
using System.Data.SqlClient;

namespace fastFood
{
    public partial class Form1 : Form
    {
        string databaseLocation = "C:\\C#\\fastFood.mdf;";

        string imagename;
```

We will now write the *addRecord( )* method. Add this after *btnStore_Click( )*.

The method uses a *TRY..CATCH* structure to prevent the program stopping in the event of an error during the file handling operation.

We include an *IF...* condition to check that an image has been selected, before going any further.

The program opens the graphics file and transfers it into a storage array as bytes of binary data. This type of data is known as a '*binary large object*', or '*blob*'.

```
private void addRecord()
{
    try
    {
        if (imagename != "")
        {
            FileStream fs;
            fs = new FileStream(@imagename, FileMode.Open, FileAccess.Read);

            byte[] picbyte = new byte[fs.Length];
            fs.Read(picbyte, 0, System.Convert.ToInt32(fs.Length));
            fs.Close();
        }
    }
    catch
    {
        MessageBox.Show("File error");
    }
}
```

We now save the '**description**' field and the '**picture**' data into the database table. This requires a similar SQL command to those used in previous programs, but the '**picture**' data is identifed by a parameter '**@pic**' which tells the program where to find the binary large object array.

Add code to the **addRecord( )** method to save the record. Notice the messageBox line, which gives confirmation that the record has been saved successfully.   Please note that the lines beginning:
  '**SqlConnection con =**' and ' **string query = "INSERT INTO...**'
should be entered as single lines of code with no line breaks.

```
try
{
    if (imagename != "")
    {
        FileStream fs;
        fs = new FileStream(@imagename, FileMode.Open, FileAccess.Read);

        byte[] picbyte = new byte[fs.Length];
        fs.Read(picbyte, 0, System.Convert.ToInt32(fs.Length));
        fs.Close();

        SqlConnection con = new SqlConnection(@"Data Source=.\SQLEXPRESS;
            AttachDbFilename="+ databaseLocation + "Integrated Security=True;
            Connect Timeout=30; User Instance=True");
        con.Open();

        string query = "INSERT INTO foodItems(description,picture)
            VALUES('" + txtDescription.Text + "'," + " @pic)";

        SqlParameter picparameter = new SqlParameter();
        picparameter.SqlDbType = SqlDbType.Image;
        picparameter.ParameterName = "pic";
        picparameter.Value = picbyte;

        SqlCommand cmd = new SqlCommand(query, con);

        cmd.Parameters.Add(picparameter);
        cmd.ExecuteNonQuery();
        MessageBox.Show("Image Added");
        con.Close();
    }
}
catch
{
    MessageBox.Show("File error");
}
```

Run the program. Select a picture, add a description for the food item, then click the '**Store**' button. A message should appear to confirm that the record has been saved.

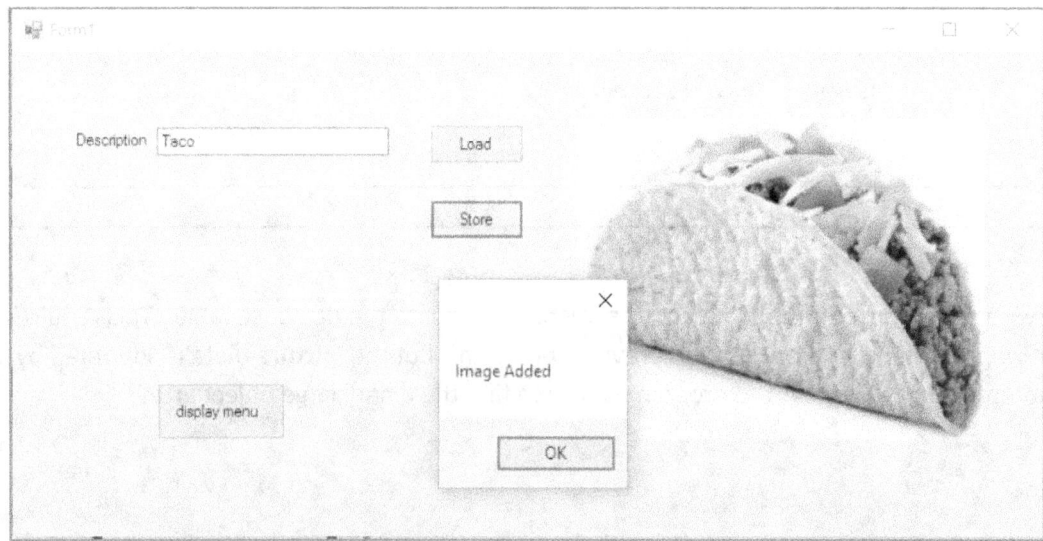

Go to the **Server Explorer** and add a connection to the **fastFood.mdf** database. Right-click on the **foodItems** table and select '**Show Table Data**'. Check that the records have been saved correctly. The picture fields will appear as **<Binary data>**

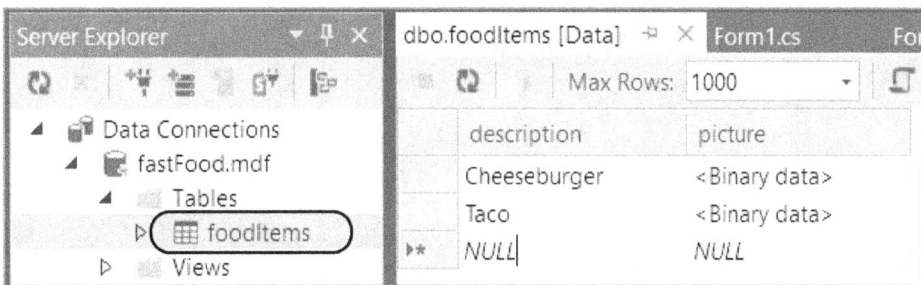

Right-click on **fastFood.mdf** and select '**Delete**' to close the connection to the database.

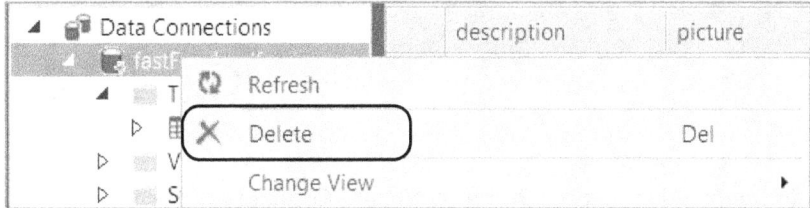

We will now set up another form which will display the images and descriptions of the food items as a Menu for the fast food shop.

Go to the **Solution Explorer** and create another **Windows Form**. You can leave the name as '**Form2**'.

Double click the '**display menu**' button on **Form1** and add lines of code to the **btnDisplay_Click( )** method to open **Form2**.

```
private void btnDisplay_Click(object sender, EventArgs e)
{
    Form2 frmForm2 = new Form2();
    frmForm2.ShowDialog();
}
```

Place a **panel** on **Form2**. Click the panel once to select it, then change the height to **2,000 pixels** by altering the second number value of the '**Size**' entry in the **Properties** window:

Select **Form2** by clicking outside the panel. Set the '**AutoScroll**' property to '**True**'. Notice that a vertical scroll bar now appears on the edge of the form.

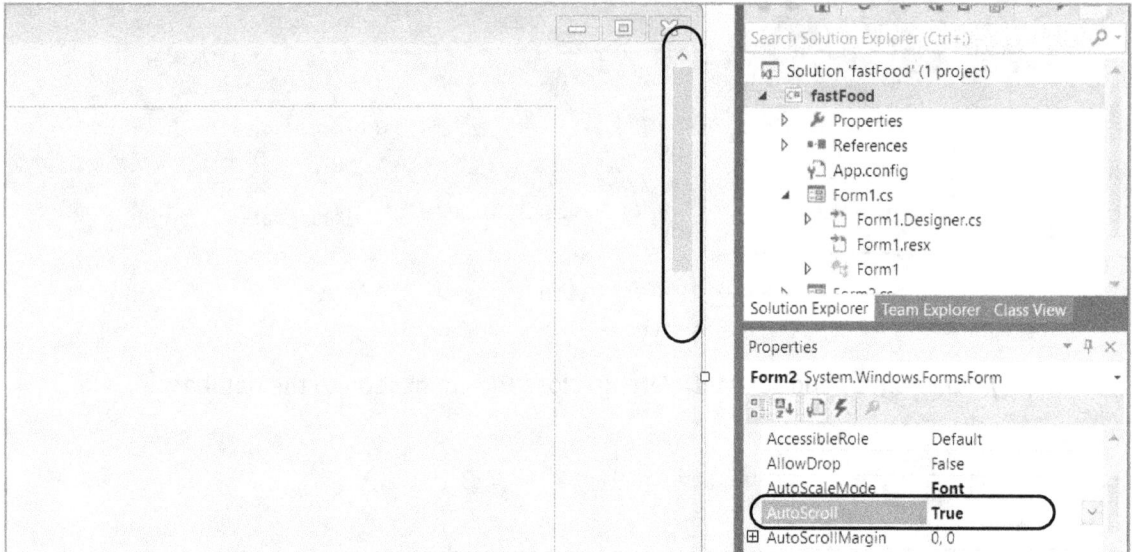

Adjust the width of the panel to just reach the scroll bar. Complete the screen layout by adding a label '**Fast Food Menu**'.

We can now write methods to load and diplay the descriptions and pictures of the food items.

Go to the program code window for **Form2**. Add '**using IO**' and '**using SqlClient**' directives, give the database location, and add the variables '**dAdapt**' and '**dSet**':

```
using System.Text;
using System.Windows.Forms;

using System.IO;
using System.Data.SqlClient;

namespace fastFood
{
    public partial class Form2 : Form
    {
        string databaseLocation = "C:\\C#\\fastFood.mdf;";
        SqlDataAdapter dAdapt;
        DataSet dSet;
```

Add a **Connection( )** method which will access the database table and transfer the records into the storage area called '**dTable**'. Call the **Connection( )** method from the **Form2( )** method.

```
    public Form2()
    {
        InitializeComponent();
        Connection();
    }

    private void Connection()
    {
        try
        {
            SqlConnection con = new SqlConnection(@"Data Source=.\SQLEXPRESS;
                AttachDbFilename="+ databaseLocation+ "Integrated Security=True;
                Connect Timeout=30; User Instance=True");
            con.Open();
            dAdapt = new SqlDataAdapter();
            dAdapt.SelectCommand = new SqlCommand("SELECT * FROM foodItems", con);
            dSet = new DataSet("dSet");
            dAdapt.Fill(dSet);
            con.Close();
            DataTable dTable;
            dTable = dSet.Tables[0];
        }
        catch (Exception ex)
        {
            MessageBox.Show(ex.Message);
        }
    }
```

Run the program. Click the '**display menu**' button and check that **Form2** opens without any error message. The **panel** on Form2 should scroll vertically, but no images are displayed yet. We will deal with the display method next.

Set up a **displayPictures( )** method, and call this from the **Form2( )** method. We will create arrays for up to eight pictures and labels to be added when the program runs.

```
    public Form2()
    {
        InitializeComponent();
        Connection();
        displayPictures();
    }

    private void displayPictures()
    {
        DataTable dataTable = dSet.Tables[0];
        int countRecords = dataTable.Rows.Count;
        PictureBox[] pictureBox = new PictureBox[8];
        Label[] label = new Label[8];
    }
```

Create a loop which will repeat for each record in the database table. Within the loop, the program collects the *binary large object* from the data record and converts it back into an *image file*.

```
private void displayPictures()
{
    DataTable dataTable = dSet.Tables[0];
    int countRecords = dataTable.Rows.Count;
    PictureBox[] pictureBox = new PictureBox[8];
    Label[] label = new Label[8];

    Random r = new Random();
    for (int i = 0; i < countRecords; i++)
    {
        DataRow dataRow = dataTable.Rows[i];
        int random = r.Next(1,1000);
        string finalString = "pic" + Convert.ToString(random);
        FileStream FS1 = new FileStream(finalString + ".jpg", FileMode.Create);
        byte[] blob = (byte[])dataRow[1];
        FS1.Write(blob, 0, blob.Length);
        FS1.Close();
        FS1 = null;
    }
}
```

The final step is to display the description of the food item and its picture image on the panel. The vertical position is moved down by 300 pixels as each record is displayed.

```
for (int i = 0; i < countRecords; i++)
{
    DataRow dataRow = dataTable.Rows[i];
    int random = r.Next(1,1000);
    string finalString = "pic" + Convert.ToString(random);
    FileStream FS1 = new FileStream(finalString + ".jpg", FileMode.Create);
    byte[] blob = (byte[])dataRow[1];
    FS1.Write(blob, 0, blob.Length);
    FS1.Close();
    FS1 = null;

    pictureBox[i] = new PictureBox();
    pictureBox[i].Image = Image.FromFile(finalString + ".jpg");
    pictureBox[i].Size = new System.Drawing.Size(314, 238);
    pictureBox[i].Location = new System.Drawing.Point(244, 134 + 300 * i);
    pictureBox[i].SizeMode = PictureBoxSizeMode.StretchImage;
    panel1.Controls.Add(pictureBox[i]);
    pictureBox[i].Refresh();

    label[i] = new Label();
    label[i].Size = new System.Drawing.Size(200, 60);
    label[i].Text = Convert.ToString(dataRow[0]);
    label[i].Font = new System.Drawing.Font("Microsoft Sans Serif", 14F,
                    System.Drawing.FontStyle.Regular,
                    System.Drawing.GraphicsUnit.Point, ((byte)(0)));
    label[i].Location = new System.Drawing.Point(20, 134 + 300 * i);

    panel1.Controls.Add(label[i]);
}
```

Run the program and click the '***display menu***' button. Form2 should open and display the food items in a scrolling list.

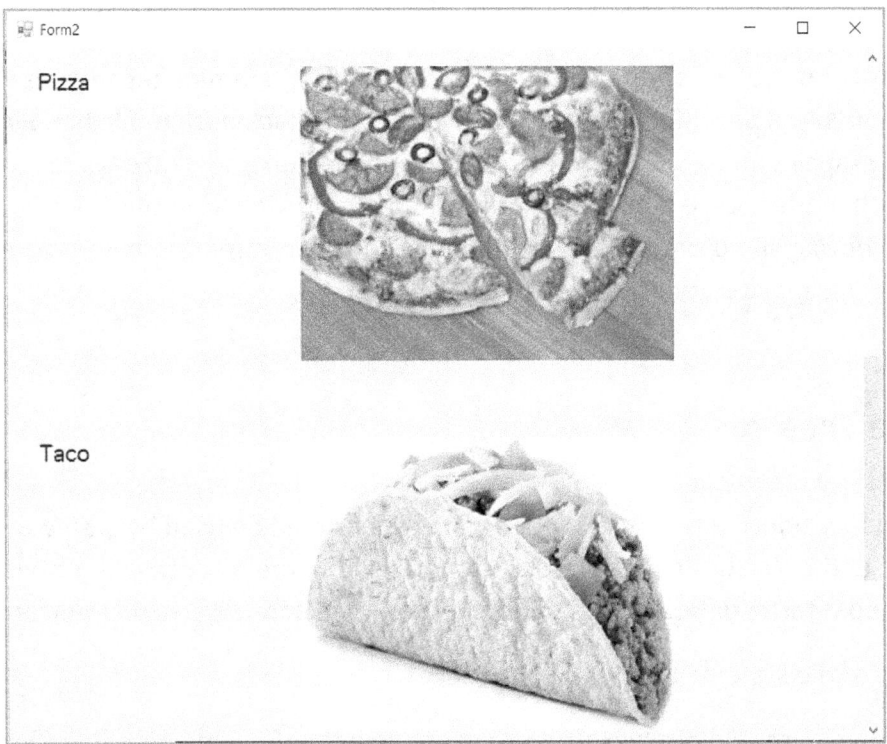

10 Theatre Bookings

In this final program, we will bring together many of the programming techniques which you have met earlier in the book, including interactive user interface design, file handling, and the display of graphics images. The project is large and may take several days to complete. However, much of the code is similar to work carried out previously in this book. You may save time by copying and pasting methods from previous programs you have written, then making any necessary alterations.

Newbridge Theatre

You are asked to produce a seat booking program which could be used by staff working in the box office of the Newbridge Theatre. Customers phone the box office to obtain information about forthcoming events, then may book seats for a particular performance.

Requirements of the system:

- The program should display information and images of events, to help office staff in answering customer enquiries. The dates and times of performances for a particular event should be shown.
- When a performance is selected, a plan of the theatre will be displayed to indicate available seats. The theatre plan is:

				1	2	3	4	5	6	7	8	9	10	11	A	12	13	14			
			1	2	3	4	5	6	7	8	9	10	11	12	B	13	14	15	16		
		1	2	3	4	5	6	7	8	9	10	11	12	13	C	14	15	16	17		
	1	2	3	4	5	6	7	8	9	10	11	12	13	14	D	15	16	17	18	19	
1	2	3	4	5	6	7	8	9	10	11	12	13	14	15	E	16	17	18	19	20	
1	2	3	4	5	6	7	8	9	10	11	12	13	14	15	F	16	17	18	19	20	
	1	2	3	4	5	6	7	8	9	10	11	12	13	14	G	15	16	17	18	19	
	1	2	3	4	5	6	7	8	9	10	11	12	13	14	H	15	16	17	18	19	
	1	2	3	4	5	6	7	8	9	10	11	12	13	14	J	15	16	17	18	19	
1	2	3	4	5	6	7	8	9	10	11	12	13	14	15	K	16	17	18	19	20	
1	2	3	4	5	6	7	8	9	10	11	12	13	14	15	L	16	17	18	19		

- As seats are selected, the total price of tickets will be displayed. The theatre has a policy of charging the same price for all seats at a performance, although seat prices may differ between performances.
- If the customer wishes to proceed with a booking, their name, address, e-mail and telephone details will be required. For existing customers, these details can be selected from a database. For new customers, the details must be entered into the system.

- The customer will confirm their booking by providing credit card details. (Note: obtaining payment from the customer's bank and delivering tickets to the customer are outside the scope of the system which you are asked to produce.)
- Theatre staff should be able to review the bookings received and the total value of ticket sales for any performance.
- Staff should be able to add new events and performances to the system.

Design

As for the *College Courses* program in Chapter 8, we will separate the code into two categories:

- A set of **Windows Forms** will be used for on-screen *input* by the user and for the *output* of data using text or graphics as required.
- A set of **Object Classes** will be used to handle all *database operations*, including the loading, saving and updating of records.

A good starting point for a complex project is to identify classes of objects for the data model. We will use the following structure:

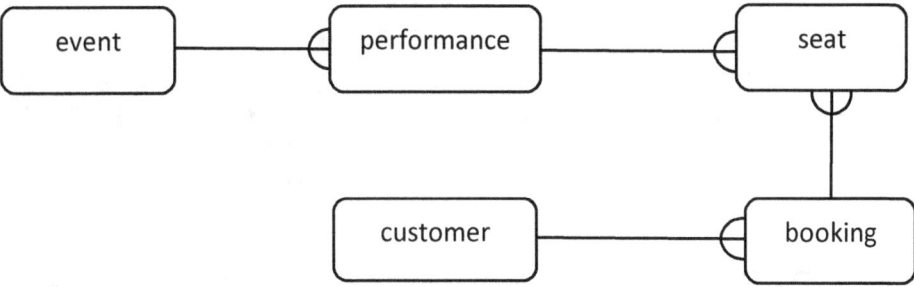

- An **event** may have a number of **performances** on different days or at different times.
- Each **performance** will have a complete set of **seats** available in the theatre.
- A **customer** may make one or more **bookings**.
- Each **booking** will be for a particular **performance**, and may be for a number of **seats**.

Begin the project by creating a '*theatreBookings*' database

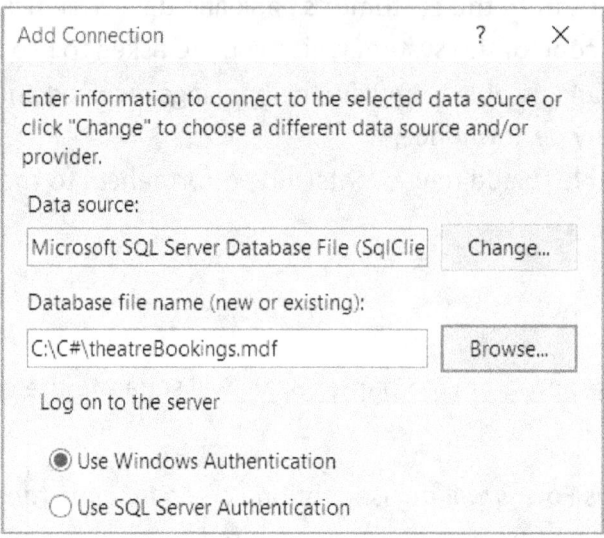

Set up a table for storing data for each of the object classes. Begin with an *Event* table:

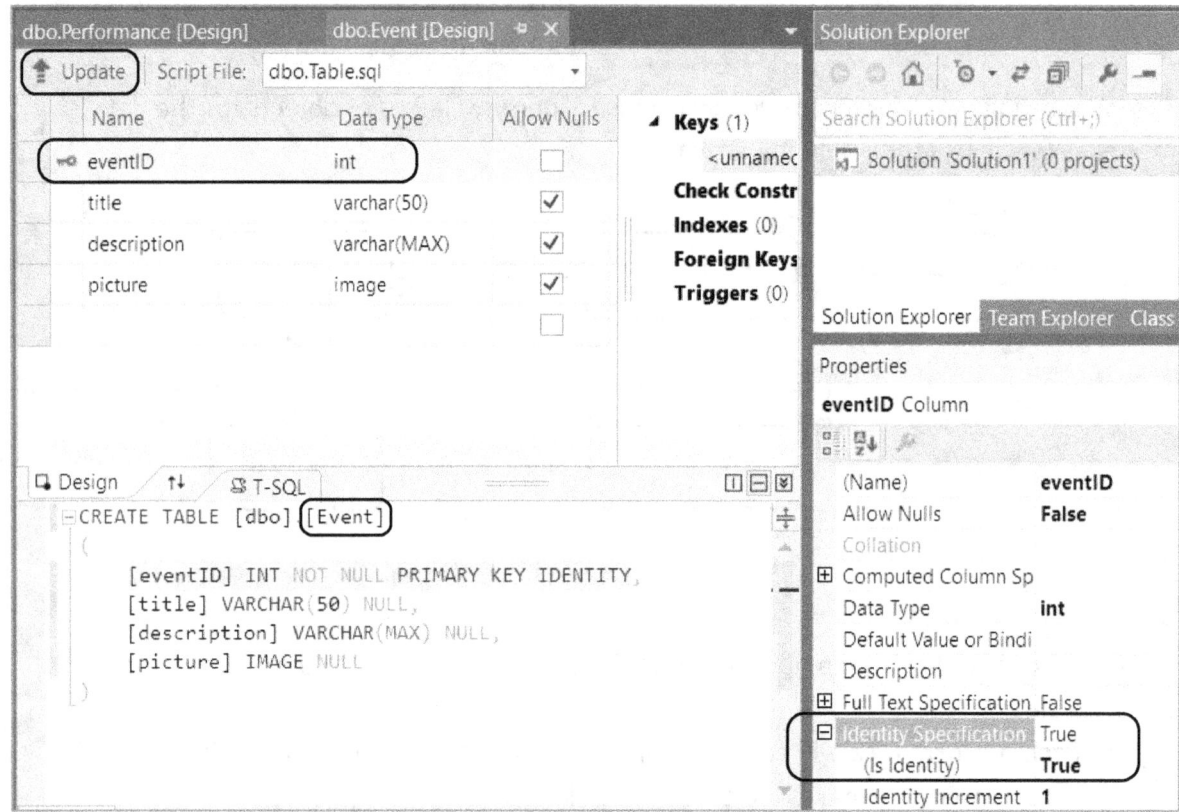

Make the *eventID* field an auto-number by selecting '*Identity Specification*' and setting the '*(Is Identity)*' property to '*True*'.

When the table design is completed, click the '*Update*' button to add the table to the database.

Add a *Performance* table. Set the *performanceID* field to be an auto-number.

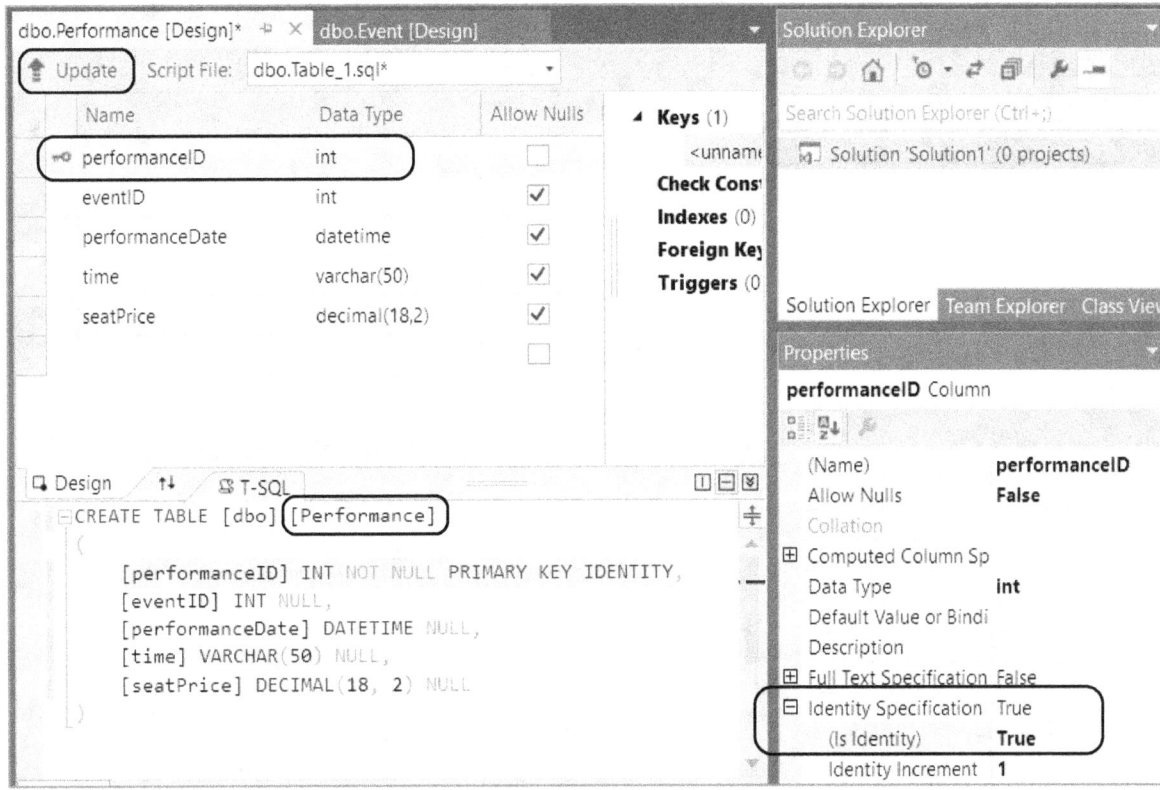

Add a *Seat* table. A primary key does not need to be set, so delete the key from the first line of the table by right-clicking on the '*key*' icon:

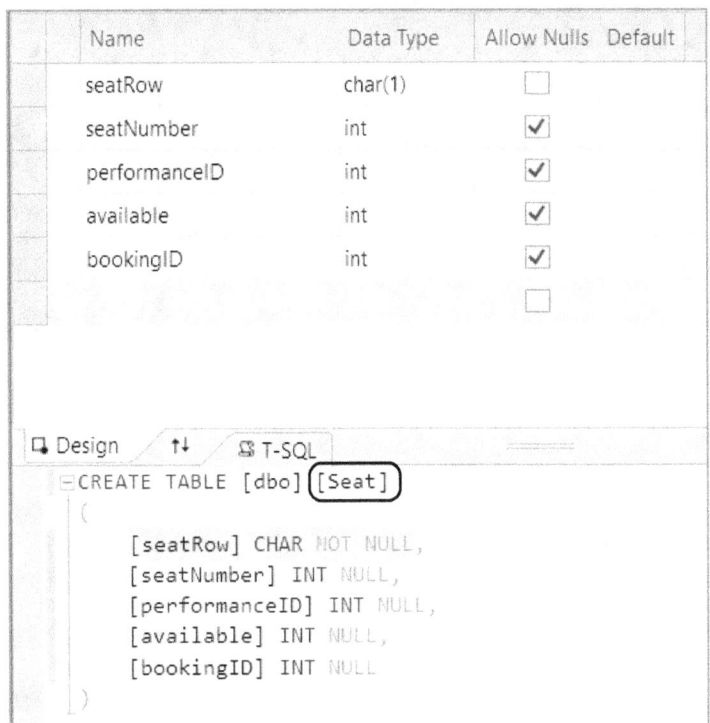

Add a *Customer* table, making the *customerID* field an auto-number:

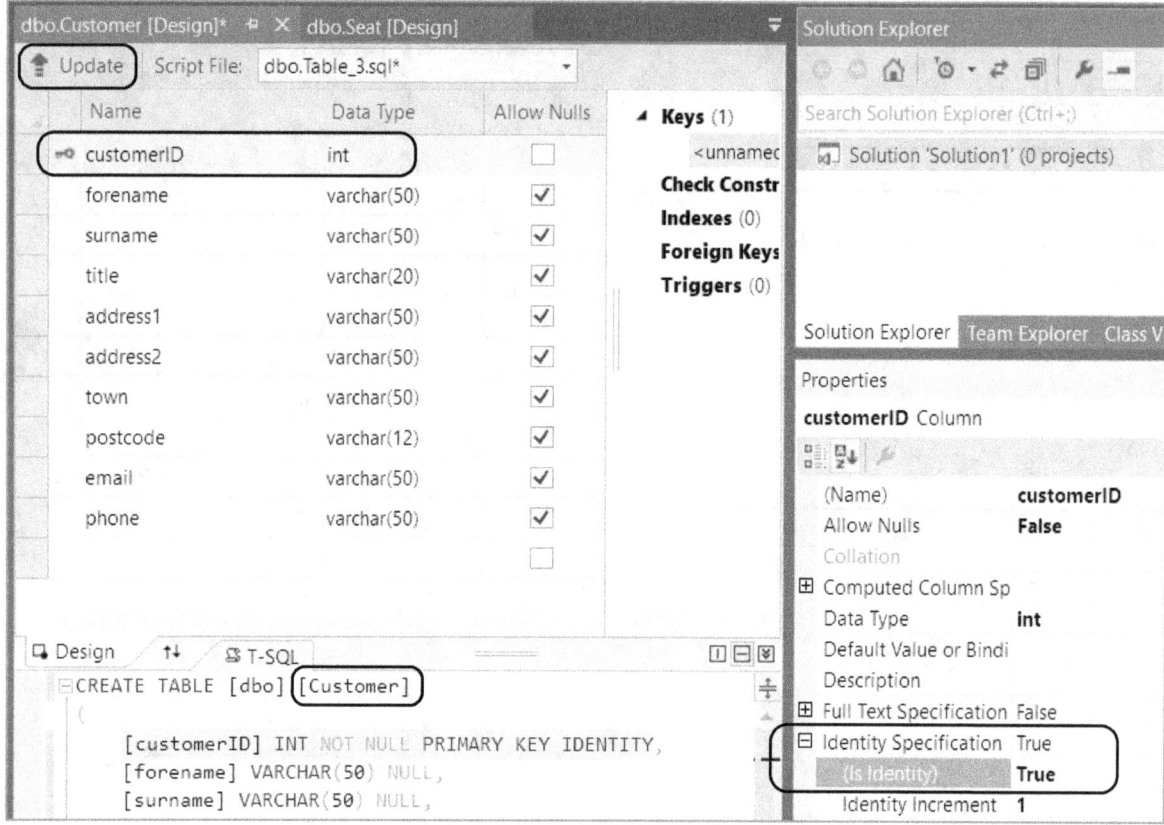

We finally require a *Booking* table. Make the *bookingID* field an auto-number:

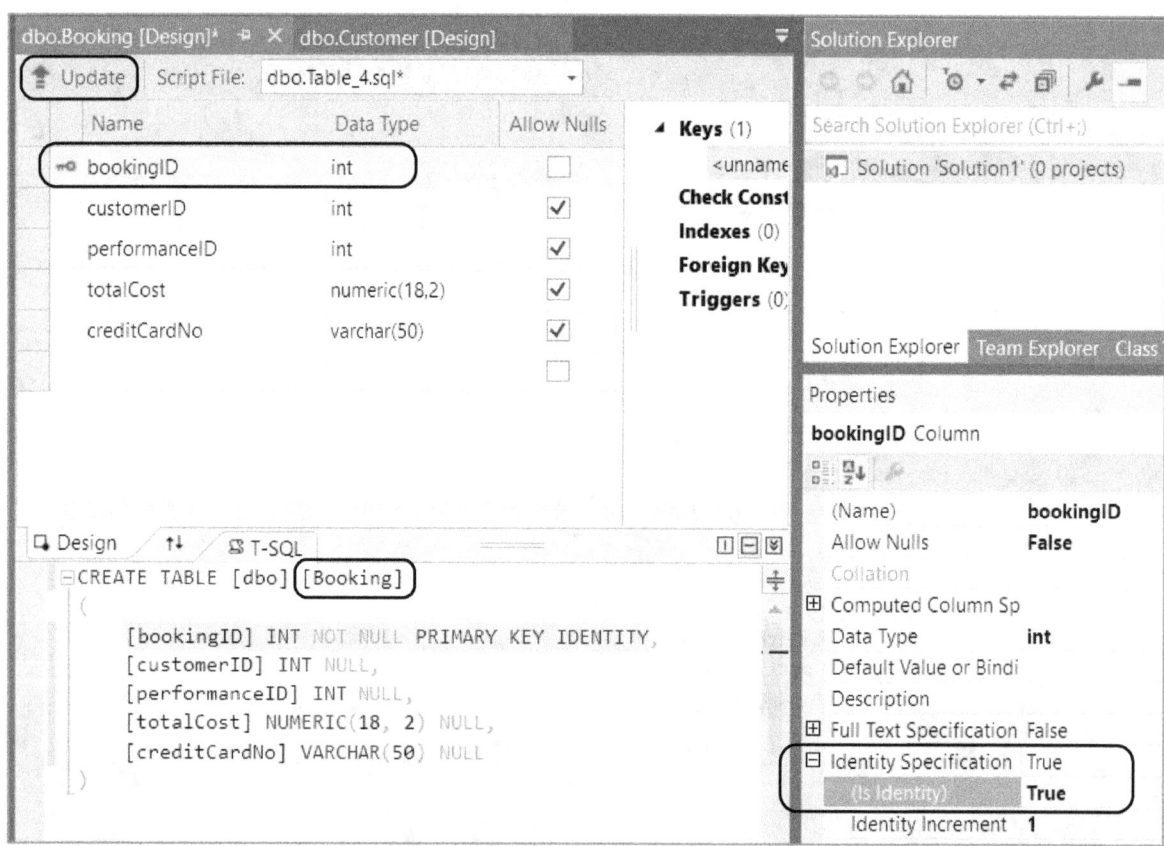

Click the 'Refresh' icon in the Server Explorer window, then check that all the tables have been created correctly:

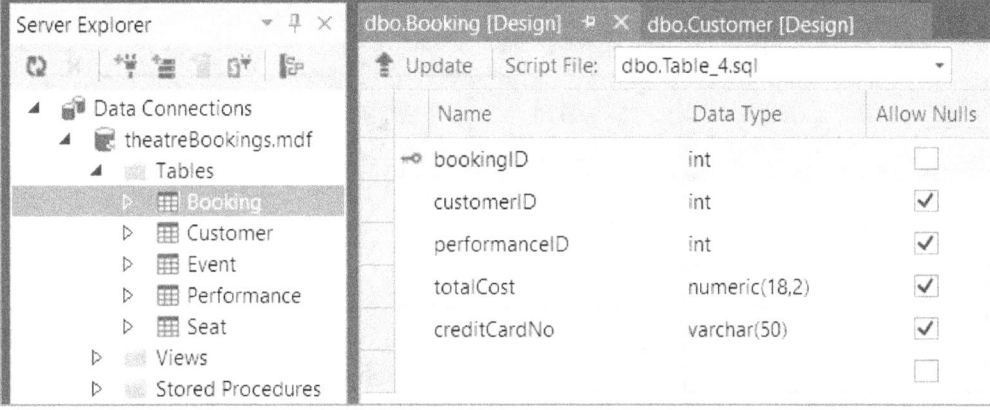

Right-click on *theatreBookings.mdf* and delete the connection to the database.

We can now plan how the Windows forms of the project will be related. From the specification it seems that we will need four program sections: to handle the input of new *event and performance details*, to *process a booking* by a customer, to *display customer records* for the theatre staff, and to display the *seat bookings and ticket sales* for each performance.

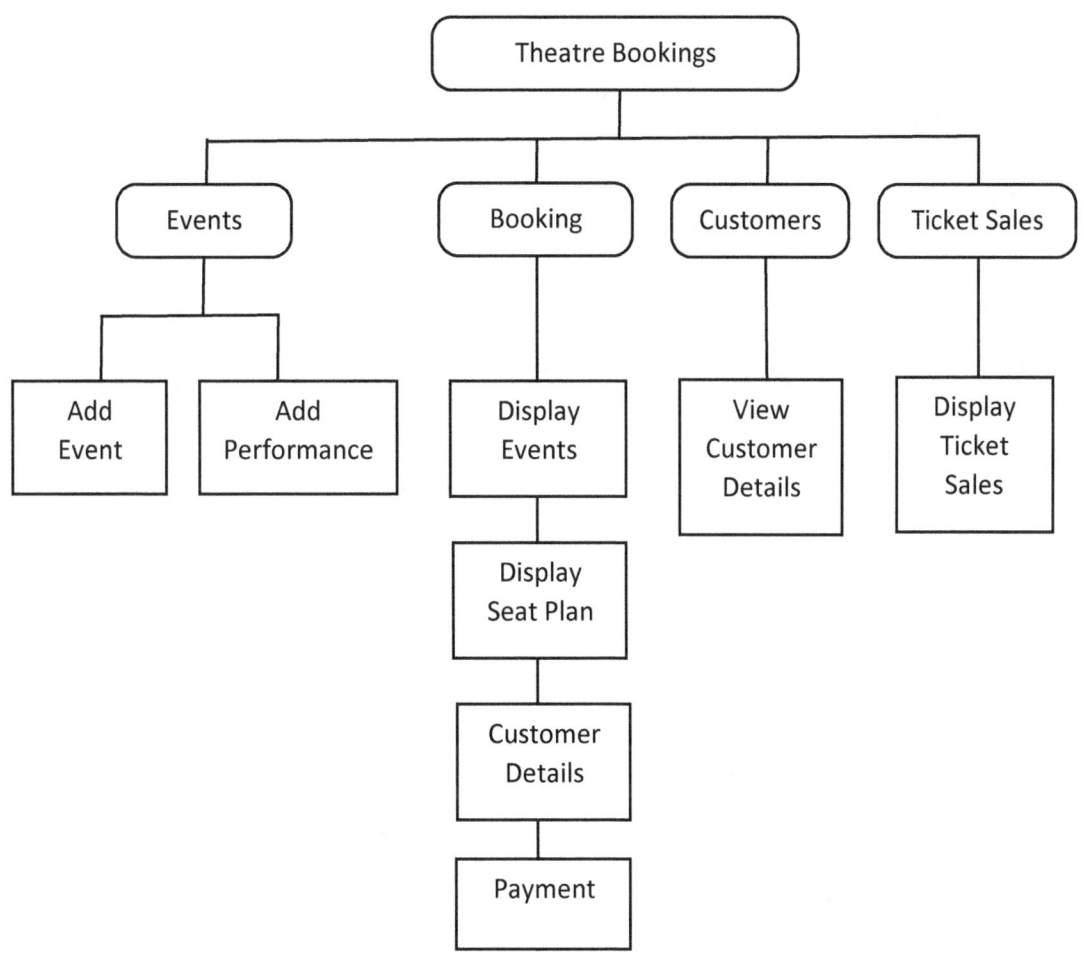

Start a new Visual C# project. Select **Windows Forms Application** and give the name *theatreBookings*.

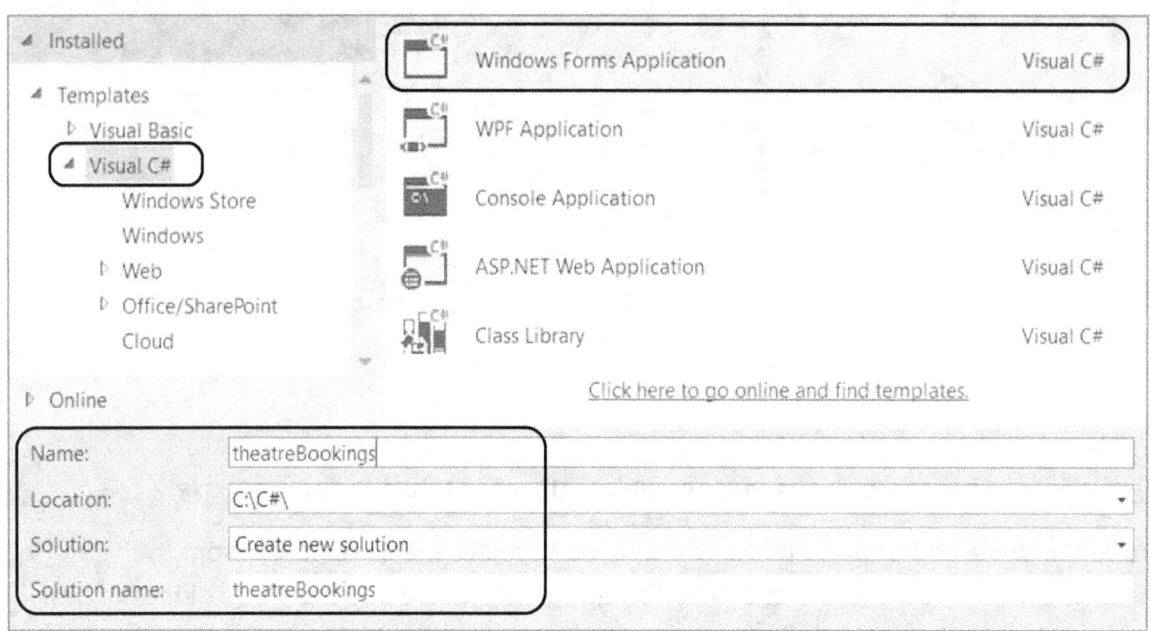

Rename Form1 as *DisplayEvents*. Add a *menuStrip* component, and configure the menu options as shown:

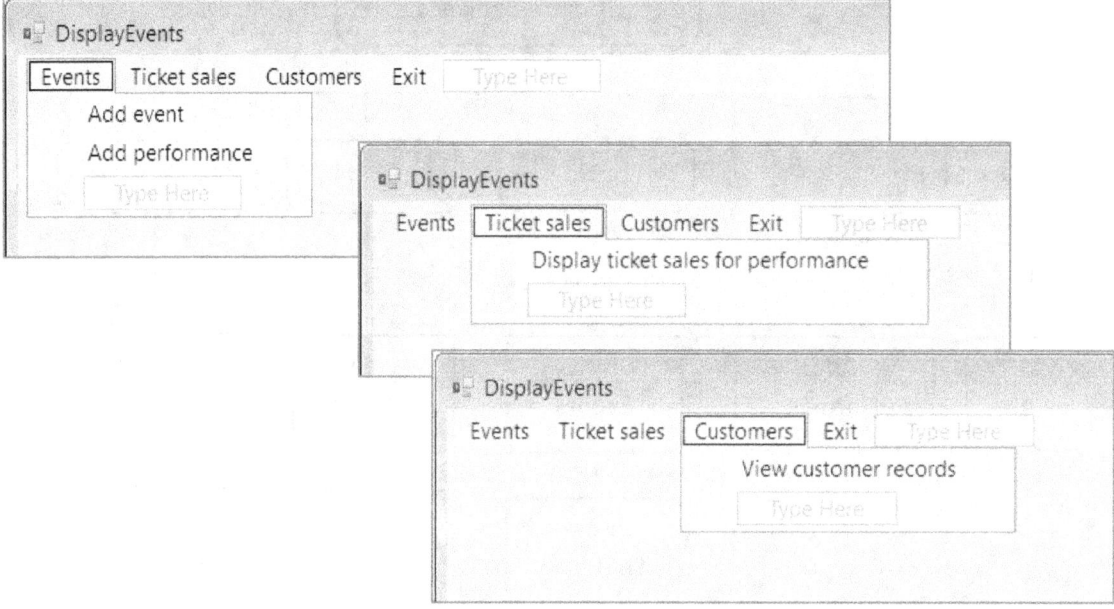

Add a Windows Form and give this the name '*AddEvent*'. Link the *AddEvent* form to the menu system by adding code to the '**Add event**' menu option:

```
private void addEventToolStripMenuItem_Click(object sender, EventArgs e)
{
    AddEvent frmAddEvent = new AddEvent();
    frmAddEvent.ShowDialog();
}
```

Chapter 10: Theatre Bookings

Add components to the **AddEvent** form. For the **txtDescription** text box, set the **Multiline** property to **True**.

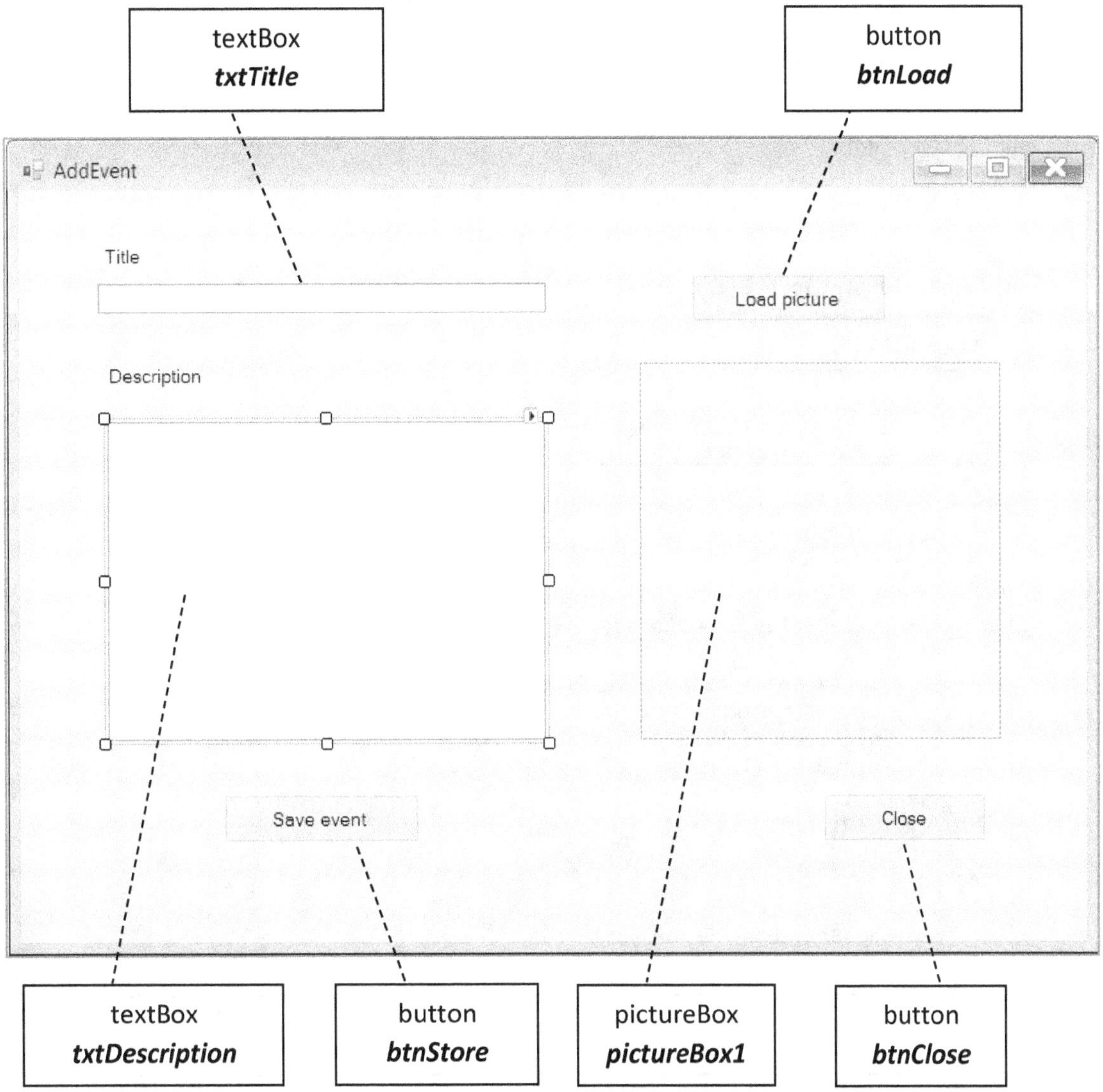

- textBox **txtTitle**
- button **btnLoad**
- textBox **txtDescription**
- button **btnStore**
- pictureBox **pictureBox1**
- button **btnClose**

The AddEvent form contains: Title label with text box, Load picture button, Description label with multiline text box, picture box, Save event button, and Close button.

For each theatre event, it would be good to provide a picture image and a written description of the event. Go to the Internet and find suitable images and text for some events that the theatre might host:

West Side Story is set in the East 40s and West 50s of the Upper West Side neighborhood in New York City in the mid-1950s, an ethnic, blue-collar neighborhood. The musical explores the rivalry between the Jets and the Sharks, two teenage street gangs of different ethnic backgrounds. The members of the Sharks from Puerto Rico are taunted by the Jets, a Polish-American working-class group. Tony, one of the Jets, falls in love with Maria, the sister of Bernardo, the leader of the Sharks.

Add code for the *Load* and *Close* buttons on the *AddEvent* form. A variable called *imagename* is also required:

```csharp
public partial class AddEvent : Form
{
    string imagename;

    public AddEvent()
    {
        InitializeComponent();
    }

    private void btnClose_Click(object sender, EventArgs e)
    {
        this.Close();
    }

    private void btnLoad_Click(object sender, EventArgs e)
    {
        try
        {
            FileDialog fileDialog = new OpenFileDialog();
            fileDialog.Filter = "Image File (*.jpg;*.bmp;*.gif)|*.jpg;*.bmp;*.gif";

            if (fileDialog.ShowDialog() == DialogResult.OK)
            {
                imagename = fileDialog.FileName;
                Bitmap newimg = new Bitmap(imagename);
                pictureBox1.SizeMode = PictureBoxSizeMode.StretchImage;
                pictureBox1.Image = (Image)newimg;
            }
            fileDialog = null;
        }
        catch
        {
            MessageBox.Show("Error");
        }
    }
}
```

Run the program. Select the '*Add event*' menu option to open the *AddEvent* form. Click the '*Load picture*' button, and check that a picture image can be selected and displayed.

Create a class file called '***theatreEvent***'. (Note: It is not possible to create a class called '***event***', as the word 'event' has a special meaning in the C# language.)

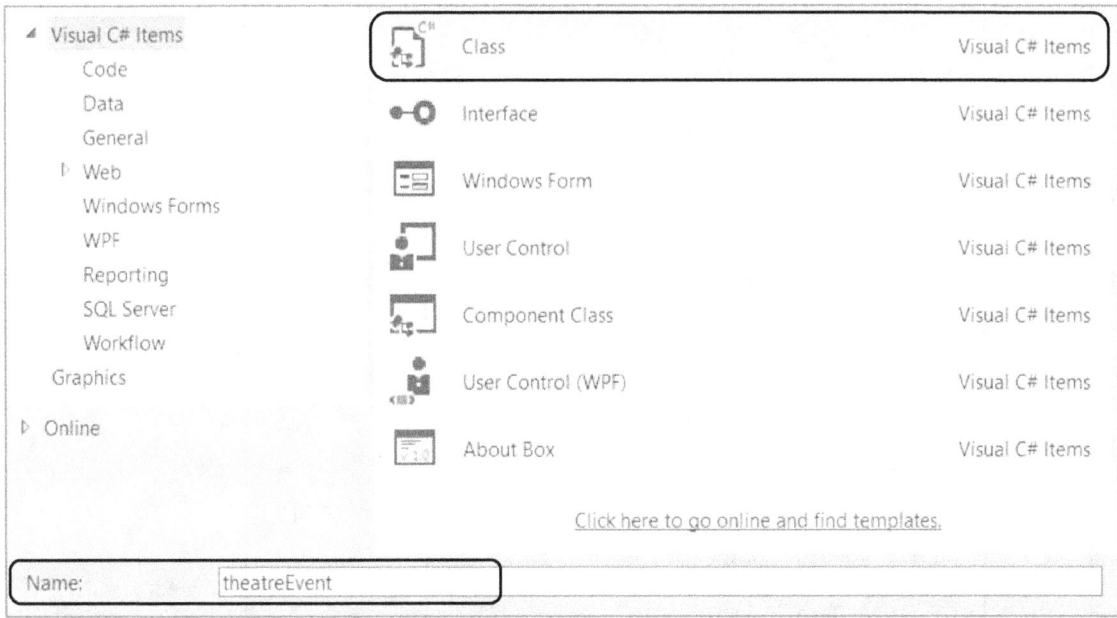

Open the ***theatreEvent*** class file and add the properties for a ***theatreEvent*** object. Since we are using picture images, it is necessary to include a '***using Drawing***' directive:

```csharp
using System.Linq;
using System.Text;
using System.Drawing;

namespace theatreBookings
{
    class theatreEvent
    {
        private int eventID;
        private string title;
        private string description;
        private Image imageData;
    }
}
```

We will now add the series of methods required to move data values into or out of each property field of the ***theatreEvent*** objects.

```csharp
        private string description;
        private Image imageData;

        public void setEventID(int e)
        {
            eventID = e;
        }

        public int getEventID()
        {
            return eventID;
        }
```

```csharp
        public void setTitle(string t)
        {
            title = t;
        }

        public string getTitle()
        {
            return title;
        }

        public void setDescription(string d)
        {
            description = d;
        }

        public string getDescription()
        {
            return description;
        }

        public void setImage(Image im)
        {
            imageData = im;
        }

        public Image getImage()
        {
            return imageData;
        }
    }
}
```

We need to create a method to save *theatreEvent* records into the database. Before doing that, a few more '*using*' directives will be needed, and the database location must be specified. You should also set up a variable to keep a *count* of the number of *theatreEvent objects* in the system, and an *array* to link to these *theatreEvent objects*.

```csharp
using System.Text;
using System.Drawing;
using System.IO;
using System.Data.SqlClient;
using System.Data;

namespace theatreBookings
{
    class theatreEvent
    {
        private static string databaseLocation ="C:\\C#\\theatreBookings.mdf;";
        public static int eventCount;
        public static theatreEvent[] eventObject = new theatreEvent[12];

        private int eventID;
        private string title;
        private string description;
        private Image imageData;
```

Notice that the variables '*eventCount*' and '*eventObject*' have been marked as '*static*'. This means that they occur only once and are used by the whole class.

By contrast, the properties *eventID*, *title*, *description* and *imageData* are '*dynamic*': a set of these variables is created for each new object added whilst the program is running.

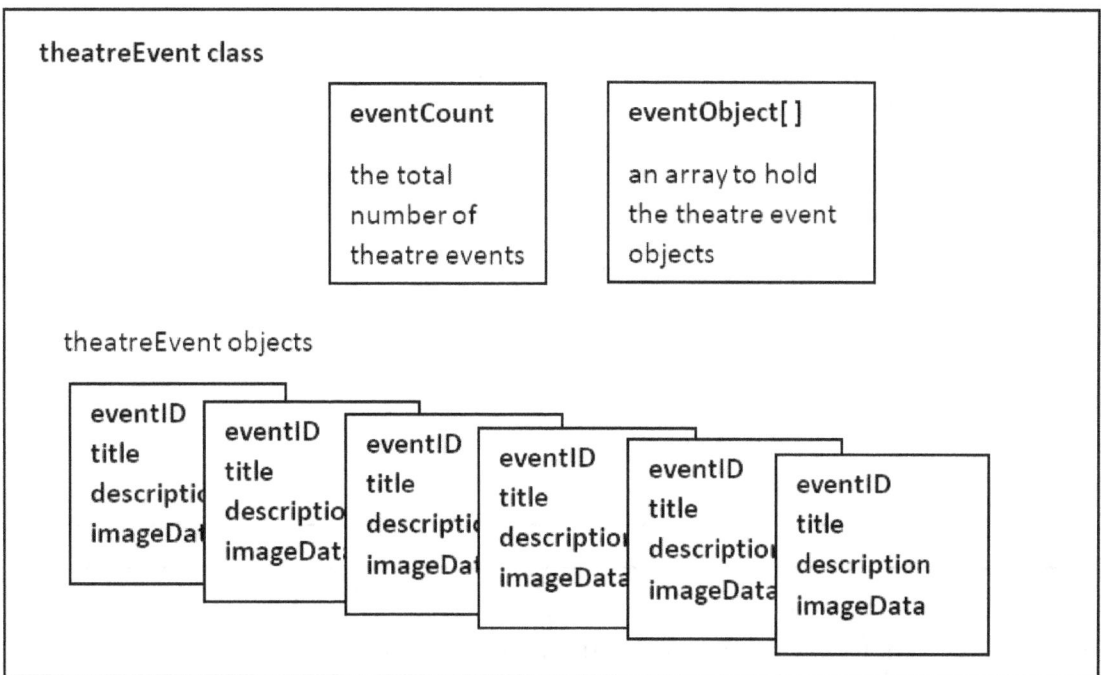

We will now add an **AddEvent( )** method to the **theatreEvent** class. This will convert the picture image into an array of binary data, then save it into a database record, along with the event title and description. The same technique was used to store the **Fast Food** images in Chapter 9. Insert the new method below the list of **theatreEvent** properties.

```
public static void AddEvent(string im, string t, string d)
{
    FileStream fs;
    fs = new FileStream(im, FileMode.Open, FileAccess.Read);
    byte[] picbyte = new byte[fs.Length];
    fs.Read(picbyte, 0, System.Convert.ToInt32(fs.Length));
    fs.Close();

    SqlConnection con = new SqlConnection(@"Data Source=.\SQLEXPRESS;
        AttachDbFilename="+ databaseLocation + "Integrated Security=True;
        Connect Timeout=30; User Instance=True");
    con.Open();
    string query = "INSERT INTO Event(title,description,picture) "+
        "VALUES('" + t + "','" + d + "," + " @pic)";
    SqlParameter picparameter = new SqlParameter();
    picparameter.SqlDbType = SqlDbType.Image;
    picparameter.ParameterName = "pic";
    picparameter.Value = picbyte;
    SqlCommand cmd = new SqlCommand(query, con);
    cmd.Parameters.Add(picparameter);
    cmd.ExecuteNonQuery();
    con.Close();
}
```

Return to the **AddEvent** form and double click the '*Save event*' button. Include a line of code in the button click method to call an **AddRecord( )** method, then add this method:

```
    private void btnStore_Click(object sender, EventArgs e)
    {
        addRecord();
    }
    private void addRecord()
    {
        try
        {
            if (imagename != "")
            {
                theatreEvent.AddEvent(imagename, txtTitle.Text, txtDescription.Text);
                MessageBox.Show("Event Added");
            }
        }
        catch
        {
            MessageBox.Show("File error");
        }
    }
```

Notice how this method calls **AddEvent( )** in the **theatreEvent** class to save the event. We simply pass the necessary data to the **AddEvent( )** method as a series of parameters.

A problem might occur when entering titles or descriptions of events if *apostrophe* characters (') are present in the text, for example:

"The songs include 'Sherry', 'Walk Like A Man' and 'Big Girls Don't Cry'."

The apostrophe is used as a special control character by the C# language, and can cause an error when data is being uploaded to the database. Fortunately there is a simple solution. The computer has an alternative symbol which looks similar to an apostrophe, but is not recognised as a C# control character. This is located in the upper left hand corner of the keyboard.

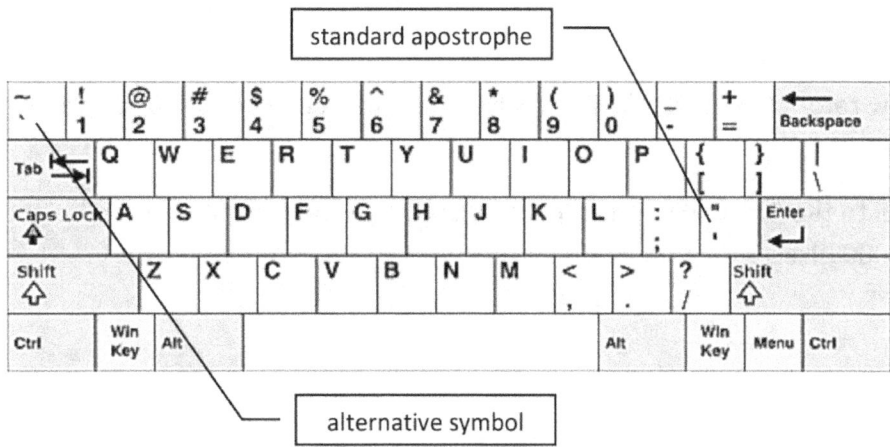

Return to the *addRecord( )* method in the **AddEvent** form, and insert lines of code to make the replacements from the standard apostrophe to the alternative symbol:

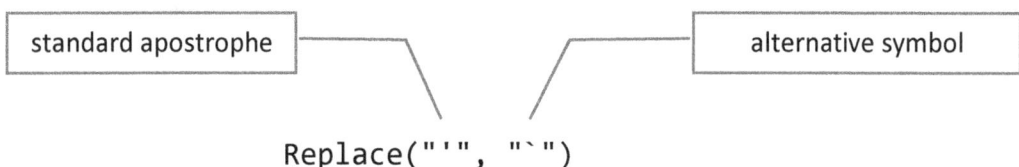

```
private void addRecord()
{
    try
    {
        txtTitle.Text = txtTitle.Text.Replace("'", "`");
        txtDescription.Text = txtDescription.Text.Replace("'", "`");

        if (imagename != "")
        {
            theatreEvent.AddEvent(imagename, txtTitle.Text, txtDescription.Text);
            MessageBox.Show("Event Added");
        }
    }
    catch
    {
        MessageBox.Show("File error");
    }
}
```

Add a series of event records and check that these are being stored correctly in the database *Event* table:

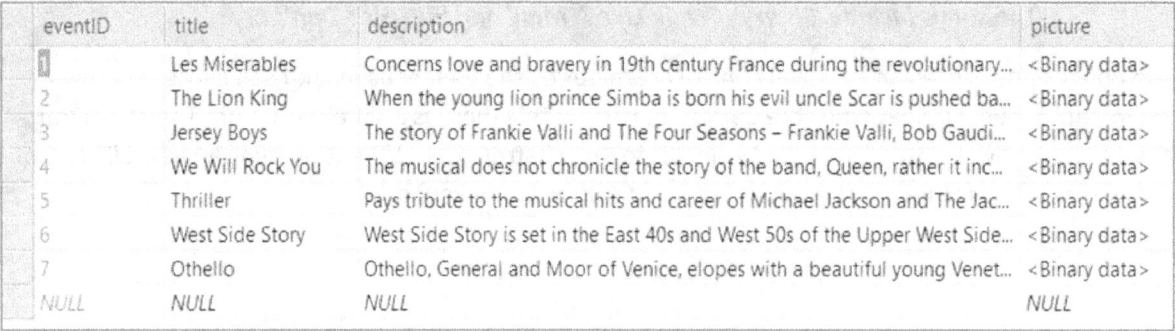

We can now return to the *DisplayEvents* form and work on the task of displaying the event text and pictures.

Add a panel to the *DisplayEvents* form and name this '*pnlEvents*'. Set the height of the panel to 3,000 pixels.

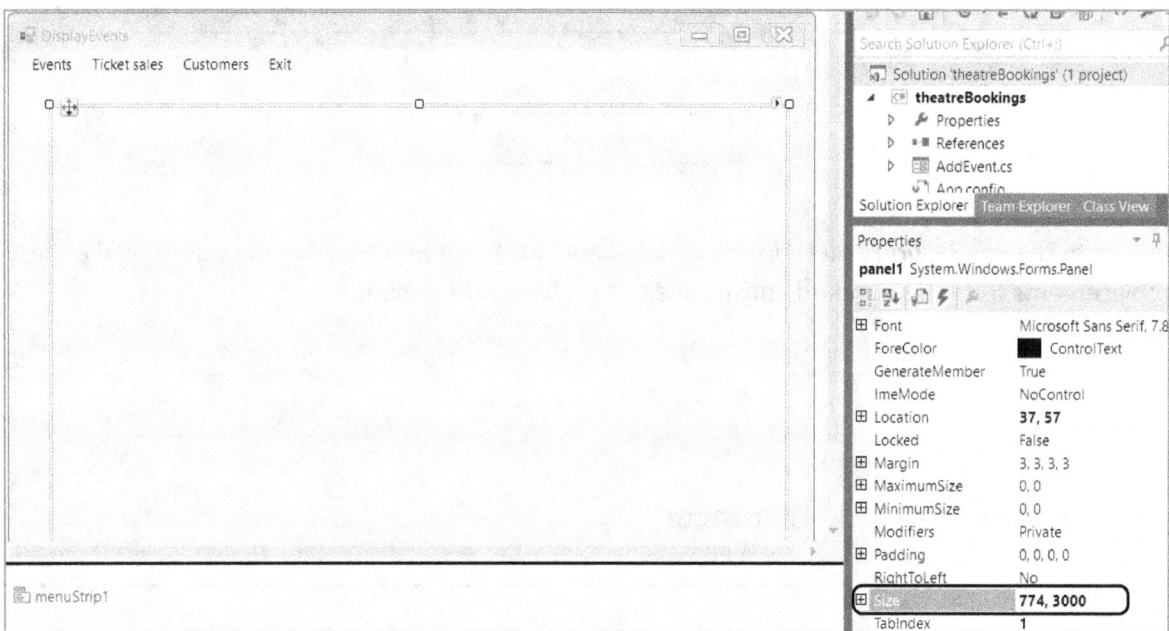

Click once on the *DisplayEvents* form beyond the edge of the panel to select it, then set the '*AutoScroll*' property to '*True*'. Run the program to check that a scrolling window has been produced on the *DisplayEvents* form.

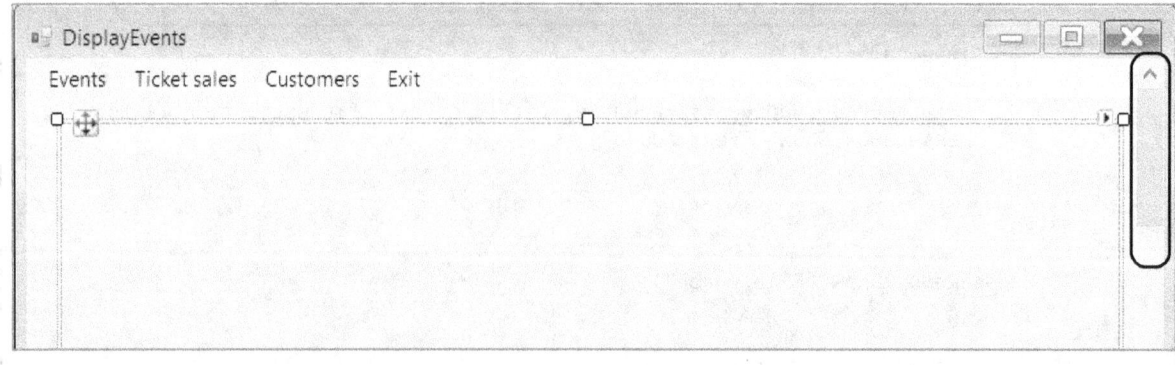

We must now return to the *theatreEvent* class file to add a method to load the event records from the database. Insert the *loadEvents( )* method below the list of properties:

```csharp
private int eventID;
private string title;
private string description;
private Image imageData;

public static void loadEvents()
{
    SqlDataAdapter dAdapt;
    DataSet dSet;

    SqlConnection con = new SqlConnection(@"Data Source=.\SQLEXPRESS;
        AttachDbFilename="+ databaseLocation+ "Integrated Security=True;
        Connect Timeout=30; User Instance=True");
    con.Open();
    dAdapt = new SqlDataAdapter();
    dAdapt.SelectCommand = new SqlCommand("SELECT * FROM Event", con);
    dSet = new DataSet("dSet");
    dAdapt.Fill(dSet);
    con.Close();
    DataTable dTable;
    dTable = dSet.Tables[0];

    DataTable dataTable = dSet.Tables[0];
    eventCount = dataTable.Rows.Count;

    for (int i = 0; i < eventCount; i++)
    {
        eventObject[i] = new theatreEvent();
        DataRow dataRow = dataTable.Rows[i];
        string finalString = "pic" + Convert.ToString(i);
        FileStream FS1 = new FileStream(finalString + "jpg", FileMode.Create);
        byte[] blob = (byte[])dataRow[3];
        FS1.Write(blob, 0, blob.Length);
        FS1.Close();
        FS1 = null;

        eventObject[i].setImage(Image.FromFile(finalString + "jpg"));
        eventObject[i].setEventID((int)dataRow[0]);
        eventObject[i].setTitle(Convert.ToString(dataRow[1]));
        eventObject[i].setDescription(Convert.ToString(dataRow[2]));
    }
}
```

This method accesses the database, then uses a *loop* to create an *eventObject* from each event *record* in the database. The picture data is converted into *.JPG image* format so that it can be easily displayed.

Go to the *DisplayEvents* form and add code to the *DisplayEvents( )* method. This calls the *loadEvents( )* method in the *theatreEvent* class, to load the data from the database and set up an *eventObject* for each theatre event.

```csharp
public DisplayEvents()
{
    InitializeComponent();

    theatreEvent.eventCount = 0;
    try
    {
        theatreEvent.loadEvents();
    }
    catch (Exception ex)
    {
        MessageBox.Show(ex.Message);
    }
}
```

Run the program and check that no error message is displayed. If all is well, we can now display the events on the panel. Write a *displayPictures( )* method, and call this from the *DisplayEvents( )* method.

```csharp
    catch (Exception ex)
    {
        MessageBox.Show(ex.Message);
    }
    displayPictures();
}

private void displayPictures()
{
    PictureBox[] pictureBox = new PictureBox[8];
    Label[] label = new Label[8];
    TextBox[] textBox = new TextBox[8];
    Button[] button = new Button[8];

    for (int i = 0; i < theatreEvent.eventCount; i++)
    {
        pictureBox[i] = new PictureBox();
        pictureBox[i].Image = theatreEvent.eventObject[i].getImage();
        pictureBox[i].Size = new System.Drawing.Size(240, 240);
        pictureBox[i].Location = new System.Drawing.Point(60, 60 + 300 * i);
        pictureBox[i].SizeMode = PictureBoxSizeMode.StretchImage;
        pnlEvents.Controls.Add(pictureBox[i]);
        pictureBox[i].Refresh();

        label[i] = new Label();
        label[i].Size = new System.Drawing.Size(200, 30);
        label[i].Text = theatreEvent.eventObject[i].getTitle();
        label[i].Font = new System.Drawing.Font("Microsoft Sans Serif", 14F,
                System.Drawing.FontStyle.Regular, System.Drawing.GraphicsUnit.Point,
                ((byte)(0)));
        label[i].Location = new System.Drawing.Point(320, 60 + 300 * i);
        pnlEvents.Controls.Add(label[i]);
    }
}
```

Run the program. The titles and images for your theatre events should be displayed in the scrolling window.

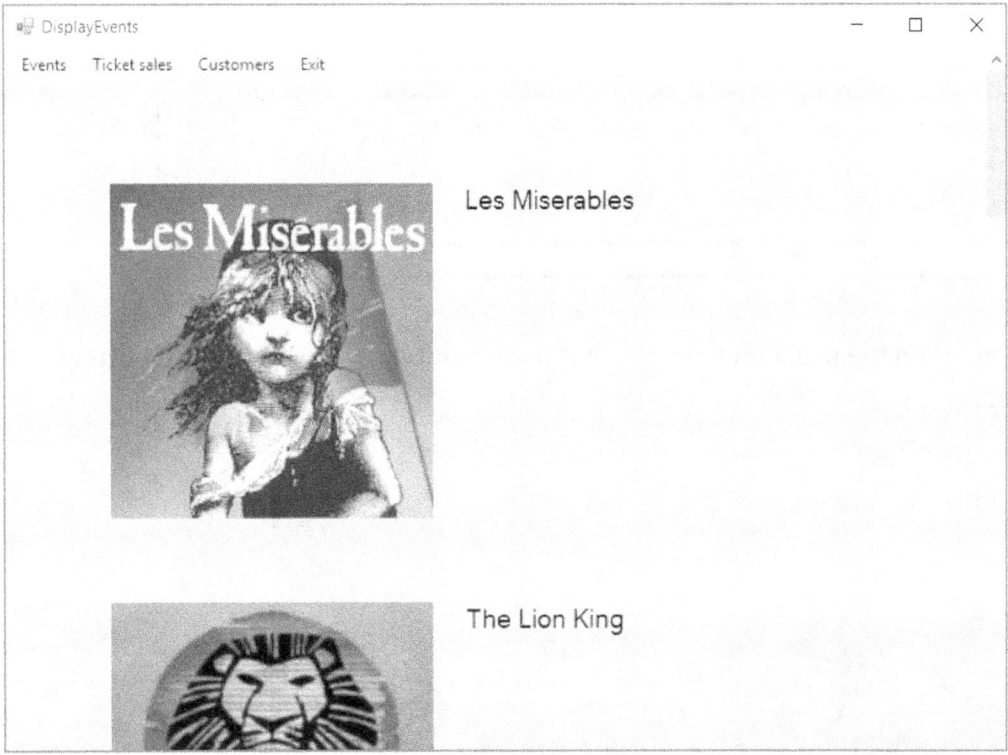

Return to the *displayPictures( )* method and add two more sections of code. These will produce a textBox to display the description of the event, and a button which can be clicked to go to the bookings screen.

```
        label[i].Location = new System.Drawing.Point(320, 60 + 300 * i);
        pnlEvents.Controls.Add(label[i]);

        textBox[i] = new TextBox();
        textBox[i].TabStop = false;
        textBox[i].BorderStyle = System.Windows.Forms.BorderStyle.None;
        textBox[i].Location = new System.Drawing.Point(320, 100 + 300 * i);
        textBox[i].Multiline = true;
        textBox[i].Size = new System.Drawing.Size(500, 200);
        textBox[i].Text = theatreEvent.eventObject[i].getDescription();
        textBox[i].ReadOnly = true;
        textBox[i].Font = new System.Drawing.Font("Microsoft Sans Serif", 10F,
            System.Drawing.FontStyle.Regular, System.Drawing.GraphicsUnit.Point,
            ((byte)(0)));
        pnlEvents.Controls.Add(textBox[i]);

        button[i] = new Button();
        button[i].Location = new System.Drawing.Point(700, 60 + 300 * i);
        button[i].Size = new System.Drawing.Size(112, 28);
        button[i].Text = "Book seats";
        String buttonName = "btn" + i;
        button[i].Name = buttonName;
        button[i].Click += new EventHandler(loadPlan);
        pnlEvents.Controls.Add(button[i]);
    }
}
```

When the '**Book seats**' button is clicked, this will call a **loadPlan( )** method, to display a seating plan of the theatre. For now, just create an empty **loadPlan( )** method immediately after the **displayPictures( )** method. We will come back to complete this later.

```
private void loadPlan(object sender, EventArgs e)
{

}
```

We can now run the program to check that the event text and '**Book seats**' buttons are displayed.

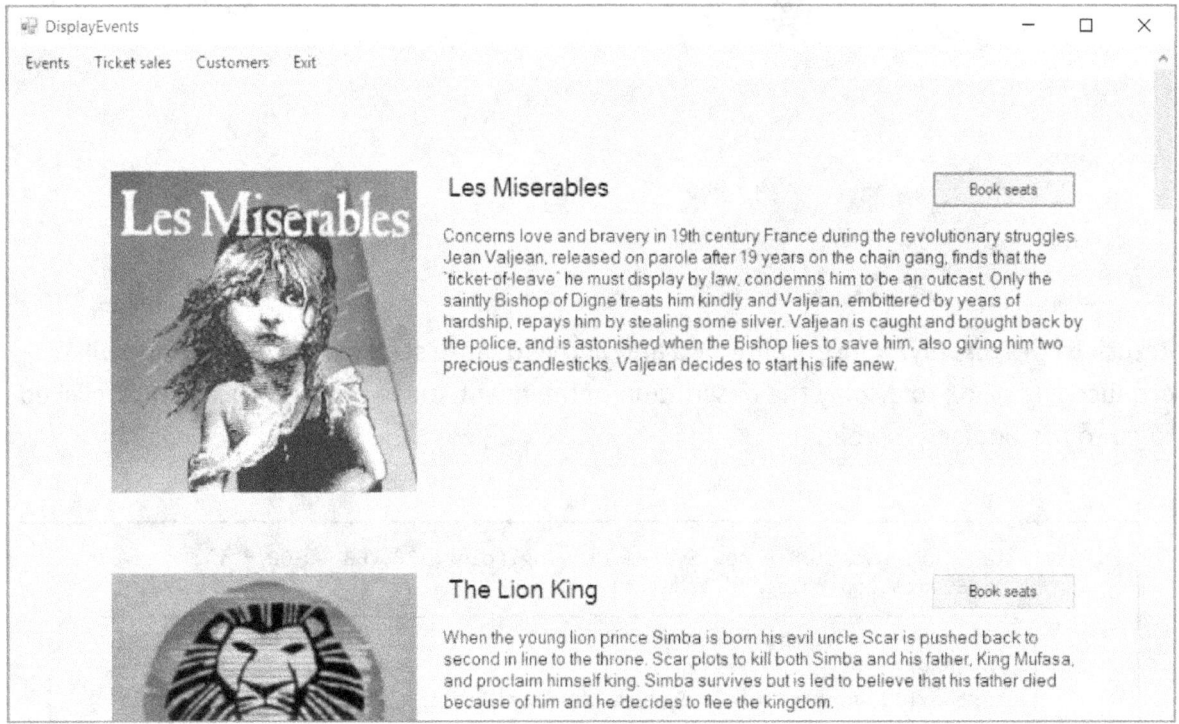

Before working on the theatre bookings, we must produce a form for entering the seat prices, dates and times of performances.

Add a **Windows Form** to the project. Give this the name '**AddPerformance**'.

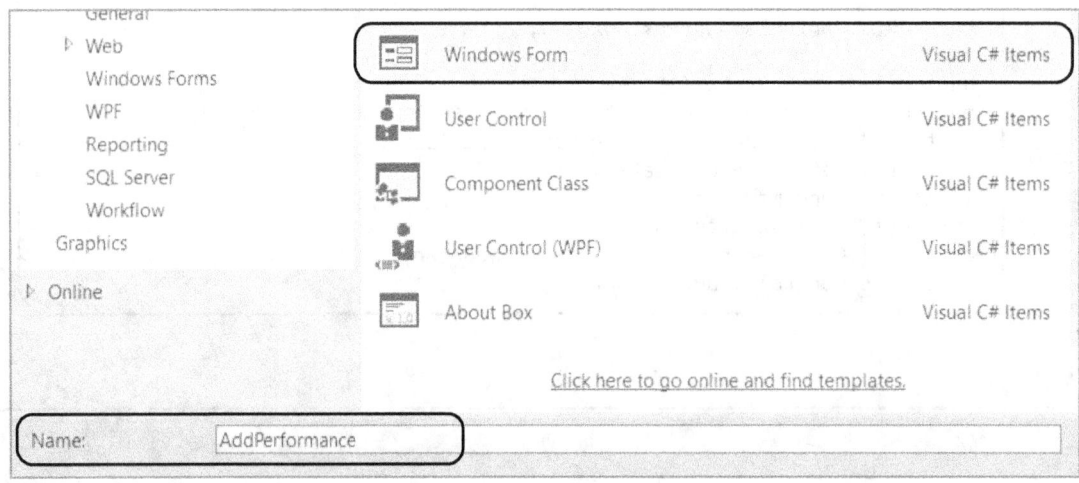

Set up components on the form as shown:

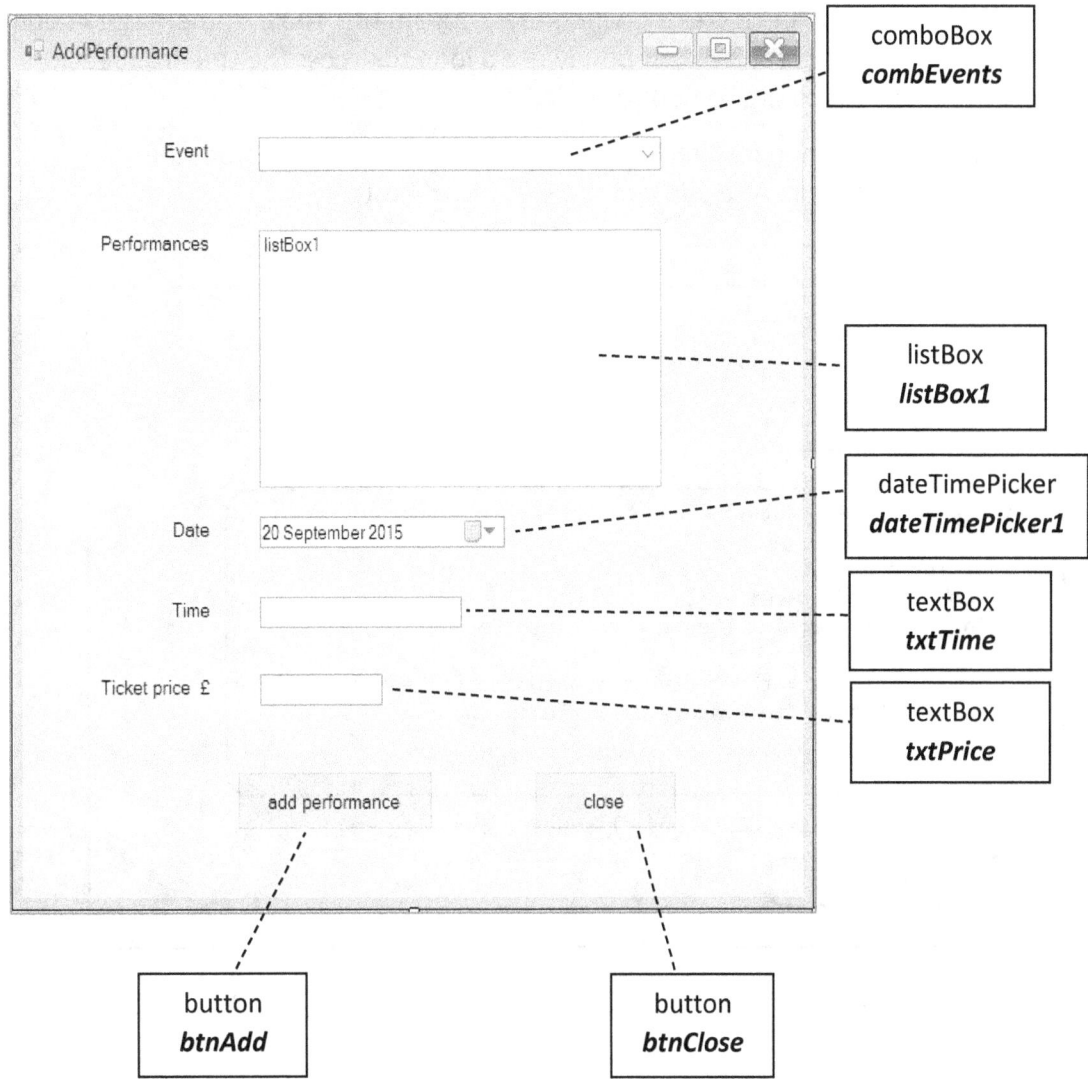

Link the **AddPerformance** form to the menu system by double clicking the 'Add performance' menu option on the **DisplayEvents** form, then add lines of code:

```
private void addPreformanceToolStripMenuItem_Click(object sender, EventArgs e)
{
    AddPerformance frmAddPerformance = new AddPerformance();
    frmAddPerformance.ShowDialog();
}
```

The first requirement for the **AddPerformance** form is to load a list of the theatre events into the drop down combo box.

Event objects have already been created when the program first runs, so there is no need to reload data from the database. We can simply use a loop to access the title from each eventObject and add this to the comboBox list.

Write a **loadEvents( )** method for the **AddPerformance** form. Call this from the **AddPerformance( )** method. Also add code to the '*close*' button.

```
public AddPerformance()
{
    InitializeComponent();
    loadEvents();
}
private void loadEvents()
{
    string eventTitle;
    combEvents.Items.Clear();
    for (int i = 0; i < theatreEvent.eventCount; i++)
    {
        eventTitle = theatreEvent.eventObject[i].getTitle();
        combEvents.Items.Add(eventTitle);
    }
}

private void btnClose_Click(object sender, EventArgs e)
{
    this.Close();
}
```

Run the program and check that the list of events is shown correctly in the comboBox list.

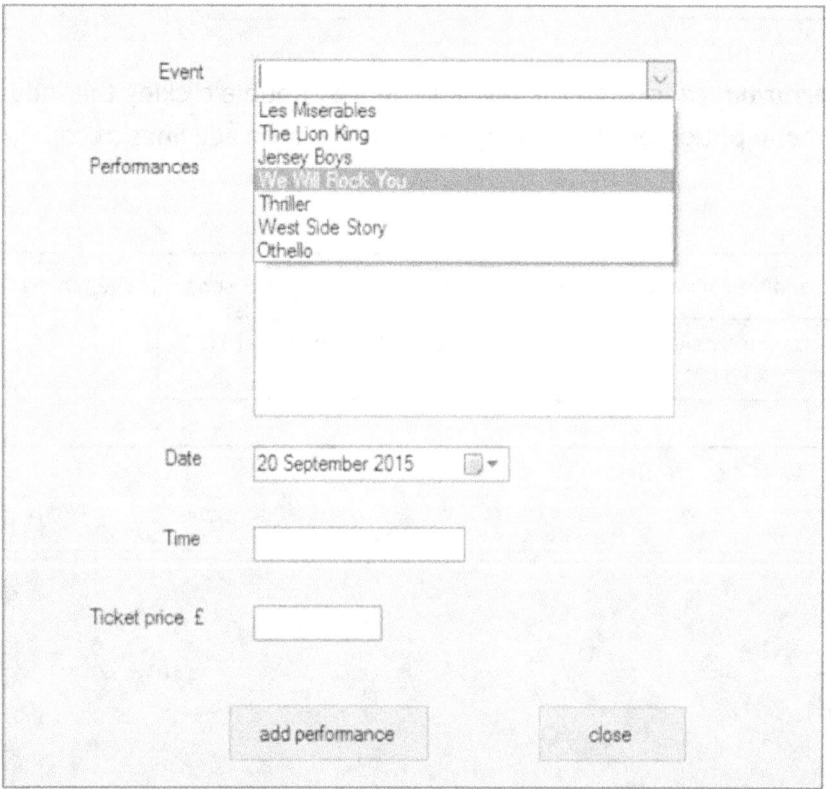

When the user clicks the '*add performance*' button, we want two things to happen:

- The *eventID*, *performance date*, *time* and *ticket price* should be saved into the **Performance** table of the database.
- A set of *seat* records will be created for the performance, all initially set as '*available for booking*'.

In preparation for these tasks, we will set up a class file called '*performance*'.

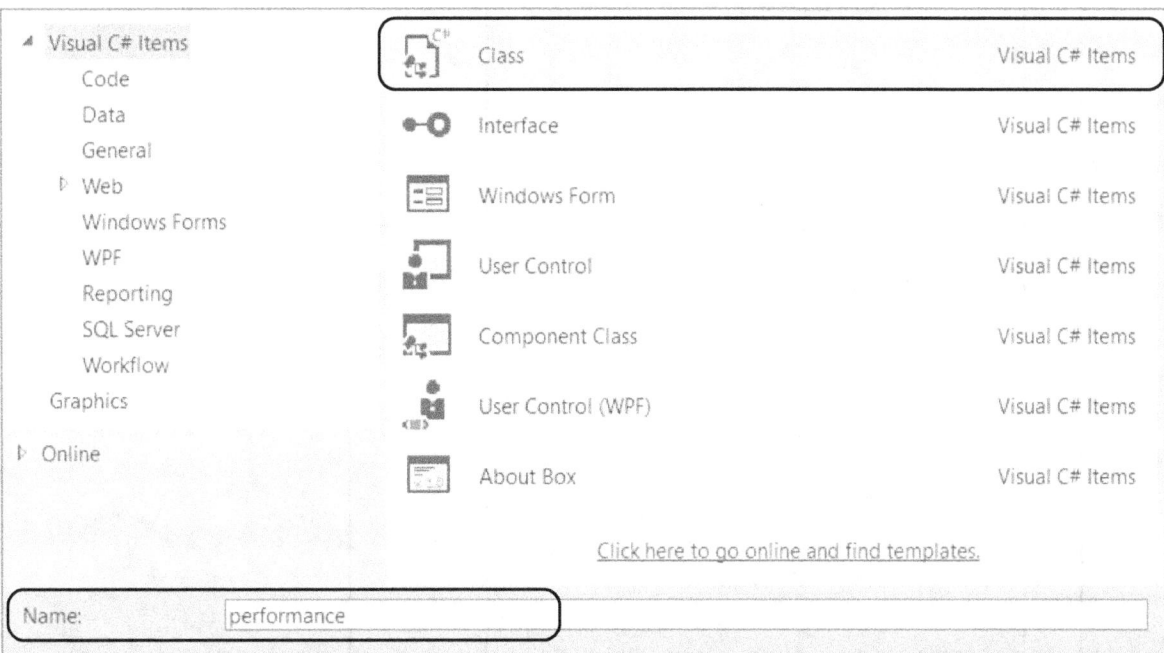

Add the properties for *performance* objects, and a set of methods for transfering data into and out of the property fields.

```
class performance
{
    private int performanceID;
    private int eventID;
    private DateTime performanceDate;
    private string time;
    private double seatPrice;

    public void setPerformanceID(int pID)
    {
        performanceID = pID;
    }

    public int getPerformanceID()
    {
        return performanceID;
    }

    public void setEventID(int e)
    {
        eventID = e;
    }
```

```
        public int getEventID()
        {
            return eventID;
        }

        public void setDate(DateTime d)
        {
            performanceDate = d;
        }

        public DateTime getDate()
        {
            return performanceDate;
        }

        public void setTime(string t)
        {
            time = t;
        }

        public string getTime()
        {
            return time;
        }

        public void setPrice(double p)
        {
            seatPrice = p;
        }

        public double getPrice()
        {
            return seatPrice;
        }
```

We will now create a method to save a performance record into the database. It will be necessary to add '**using SqlClient**' and '**using Data**' directives, and to give the database location.

```
using System.Linq;
using System.Text;

using System.Data.SqlClient;
using System.Data;

namespace theatreBookings
{
    class performance
    {
        private static string databaseLocation = "C:\\C#\\theatreBookings.mdf;";
```

Write the **AddPerformance( )** method. Remember that **performanceID** is an auto-number generated by the computer. We will need to know this value, as it forms a property of the **seat** objects which will be created for the performance. We can obtain the **performanceID** for the record which has just been saved by using the '**SELECT SCOPE_IDENTITY( )**' command.

```
private int performanceID;
private int eventID;
private DateTime performanceDate;
private string time;
private double seatPrice;
```

```
public static void AddPerformance(int ID, DateTime d, string t, double p)
{
    SqlConnection con = new SqlConnection(@"Data Source=.\SQLEXPRESS;
      AttachDbFilename=" +databaseLocation + "Integrated Security=True;
      Connect Timeout=30; User Instance=True");
    con.Open();
    SqlCommand cmPerformance = new SqlCommand();
    cmPerformance.Connection = con;
    cmPerformance.CommandType = CommandType.Text;
    cmPerformance.CommandText = "INSERT INTO Performance(eventID, performanceDate,"
      + "time, seatPrice) VALUES ('" + ID + "','" + d.ToString("MM/dd/yyyy") + "','"
      + t + "','" + p + "')";
    cmPerformance.ExecuteNonQuery();

    cmPerformance.CommandText = "SELECT SCOPE_IDENTITY()";
    int identity = Convert.ToInt32(cmPerformance.ExecuteScalar());
    con.Close();
    assignSeats(identity);
}
```

Add the **assignSeats( )** method to create the set of seat objects for the performance.

```
public static void assignSeats(int performanceID)
{
    SqlConnection con = new SqlConnection(@"Data Source=.\SQLEXPRESS;
       AttachDbFilename=" +databaseLocation + "Integrated Security=True;
       Connect Timeout=30; User Instance=True");
    con.Open();
    SqlCommand cmSeat = new SqlCommand();
    cmSeat.Connection = con;
    cmSeat.CommandType = CommandType.Text;
    for (int r = 1; r <= 11; r++)
    {
        char rowLetter = Convert.ToChar(64 + r);
        if (r > 8)
            rowLetter = Convert.ToChar(65 + r);
        for (int s = 1; s <= 20; s++)
        {
            cmSeat.CommandText = "INSERT INTO Seat(seatRow,seatNumber,"
              + "performanceID,available,bookingID) VALUES ('" + rowLetter + "','"
              + s + "','" + performanceID + "','" + "0" + "','" + "0" + "')";
            cmSeat.ExecuteNonQuery();
        }
    }
    con.Close();
}
```

This method creates a block of 11 rows of 20 seats. Some rows in the theatre have fewer than 20 seats, but the additional records can just be ignored and will not be accessed by the booking system.

Notice how the row number is converted to a letter using ASCII code: letter 'A' has ASCII value 65, 'B' is 66, etc. One slight complication is that the theatre does not use a row letter 'I', going instead from row 'H' to row 'J'. This is common practice, to avoid confusion between the letter 'I' the number 1. We compensate for the missing letter by altering the ASCII code calculation for row numbers above 8.

Return to the **AddPerformance** form and double click the '**add performance**' button. Add code to the button click method which will gather the necessary information for a new performance, then send this to the **AddPerformance( )** method of the **performance** class.

```
private void btnAdd_Click(object sender, EventArgs e)
{
    DateTime performanceDate = Convert.ToDateTime(dateTimePicker1.Value);
    string performanceTime = txtTime.Text;
    double seatPrice = Convert.ToDouble(txtPrice.Text);
    int i = combEvents.SelectedIndex;
    int eventID = theatreEvent.eventObject[i].getEventID();
    performance.AddPerformance(eventID, performanceDate, performanceTime,
                                                        seatPrice);
    this.Close();
}
```

Run the program and enter test data for performances of different events. When each entry is complete, click the '**add performance**' button.

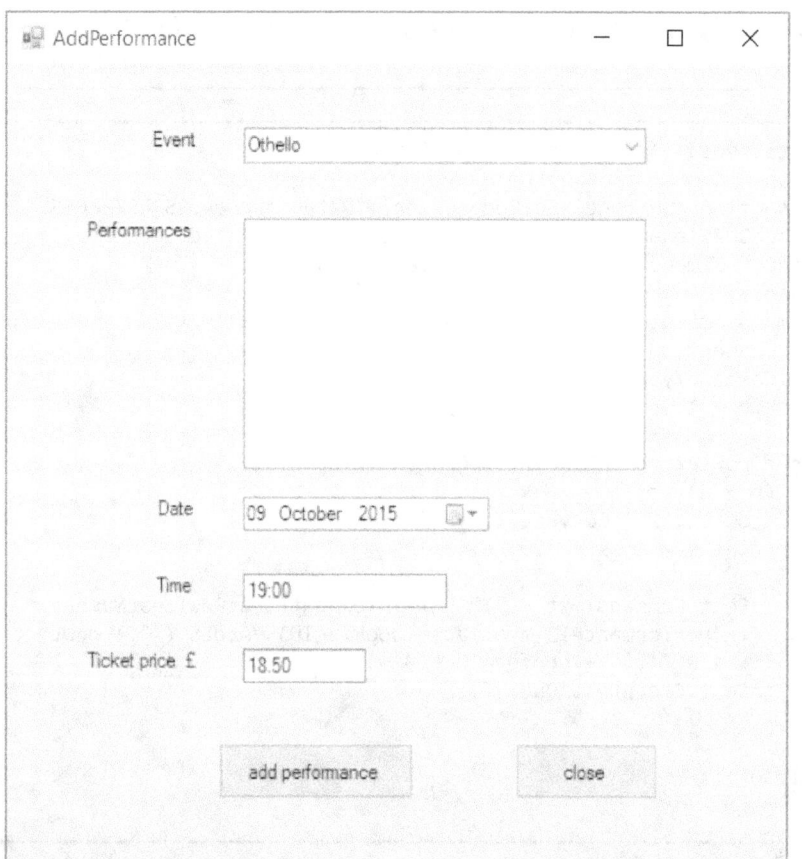

Exit from the program and go to the Server Explorer. Check that the performances you have entered are stored correctly in the **Performance** table. Check that the **eventID** corresponds with the correct theatre event.

performan...	eventID	performanceDate	time	seatPrice
1	7	09/10/2015 00:00:00	19:00	18.50
2	7	10/10/2015 00:00:00	19:00	21.50
3	5	25/09/2015 00:00:00	18:30	19.00
4	4	24/10/2015 00:00:00	18:30	17.50
5	2	17/10/2015 00:00:00	19:00	32.50
6	2	18/10/2015 00:00:00	19:00	32.50
7	3	27/10/2015 00:00:00	18:30	26.80
NULL	NULL	NULL	NULL	NULL

Go now to the **Seat** table. A set of 11 rows (A-L) of 20 seats should have been created for each performance. The '**available**' field of each seat record will be set to 0, indicating that the seat has not yet been booked.

seatRow	seatNumber	performanceID	available	bookingID
L	13	1	0	0
L	14	1	0	0
L	15	1	0	0
L	16	1	0	0
L	17	1	0	0
L	18	1	0	0
L	19	1	0	0
L	20	1	0	0
A	1	2	0	0
A	2	2	0	0
A	3	2	0	0
A	4	2	0	0
A	5	2	0	0
A	6	2	0	0
A	7	2	0	0
A	8	2	0	0
A	9	2	0	0
A	10	2	0	0
A	11	2	0	0
A	12	2	0	0
A	13	2	0	0
A	14	2	0	0
A	15	2	0	0
A	16	2	0	0
A	17	2	0	0
A	18	2	0	0
A	19	2	0	0
A	20	2	0	0
B	1	2	0	0
B	2	2	0	0
B	3	2	0	0

One additional feature which we will include on the **AddPerformance** form is a list of the performances which have already been entered for each event. This information will be displayed in the *listBox*.

Begin by going to the *performance* class file and adding a *loadPerformances( )* method. This takes as a parameter the *eventID* of the required theatre event, then searches the *performance* table in the database for any performances of this event.

When performance records have been found, these are used to create a set of *performance objects*.

We must also add variables to record the number of performance objects created, and an array to hold these objects.

```csharp
private int performanceID;
private int eventID;
private DateTime performanceDate;
private string time;
private double seatPrice;

public static int performanceCount;
public static performance[] performanceObject = new performance[12];

public static void loadPerformances(int e)
{
    performanceCount = 0;
    DataSet dsPerformances = new DataSet();

    SqlConnection con = new SqlConnection(@"Data Source=.\SQLEXPRESS;
      AttachDbFilename=" +databaseLocation + "Integrated Security=True;
      Connect Timeout=30; User Instance=True");
    con.Open();
    SqlCommand cmPerformances = new SqlCommand();
    cmPerformances.Connection = con;
    cmPerformances.CommandType = CommandType.Text;
    cmPerformances.CommandText = "SELECT * FROM Performance WHERE eventID='"
        + e + "'";
    SqlDataAdapter daPerformances = new SqlDataAdapter(cmPerformances);
    daPerformances.Fill(dsPerformances);
    con.Close();

    performanceCount = dsPerformances.Tables[0].Rows.Count;
    for (int i = 0; i < performanceCount; i++)
    {
        performanceObject[i] = new performance();
        DataRow dataRow = dsPerformances.Tables[0].Rows[i];
        performanceObject[i].setPerformanceID((int)dataRow[0]);
        performanceObject[i].setEventID((int)dataRow[1]);
        performanceObject[i].setDate(Convert.ToDateTime(dataRow[2]));
        performanceObject[i].setTime(Convert.ToString(dataRow[3]));
        performanceObject[i].setPrice(Convert.ToDouble(dataRow[4]));
    }
}
```

Return to the **AddPerformance** form. Double click the events comboBox to create an *indexchanged( )* method. This will operate whenever the user selects a different option from the drop down list.

Add code to the method. This calls the **loadPerformances( )** method in the **performance** class file, using **eventID** to specify which theatre event has been selected. Objects are created for all performances of the required event. We then use a loop to access each **performance object** and display the information in the listBox.

```
private void combEvents_SelectedIndexChanged(object sender, EventArgs e)
{
    listBox1.Items.Clear();
    int i=combEvents.SelectedIndex;
    int eventID = theatreEvent.eventObject[i].getEventID();
    try
    {
        performance.loadPerformances(eventID);
    }
    catch
    {
        MessageBox.Show("File error");
    }
    for (i = 0; i < performance.performanceCount; i++)
    {
        DateTime performanceDate = performance.performanceObject[i].getDate();
        string format = " ddd d MMM yyyy";
        string performanceDateString = performanceDate.ToString(format);
        listBox1.Items.Add("Date: " + performanceDateString);
        string performanceTime = performance.performanceObject[i].getTime();
        listBox1.Items.Add("Time: " + performanceTime);
        double seatPrice = performance.performanceObject[i].getPrice();
        string seatPriceString = seatPrice.ToString("f2");
        listBox1.Items.Add("Seat price: £" + seatPriceString);
        listBox1.Items.Add("");
    }
}
```

Run the program. Select an event, and details of all previously entered performances for that event should be displayed.

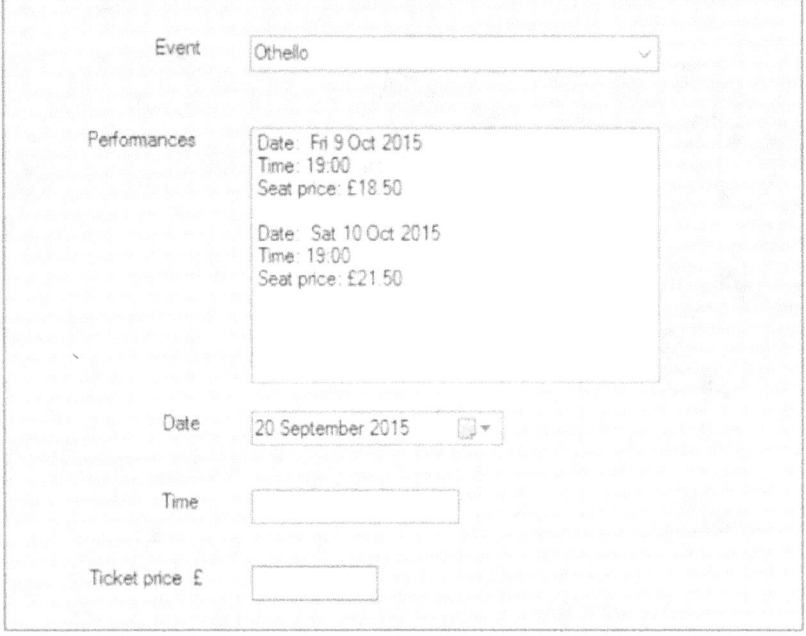

We are now ready to start work on the theatre plan screen which will allow the user to select the seats for a booking.

Set up a new Windows Form with the name '*TheatrePlan*'. Return to the *DisplayEvents* form and add code to the empty *loadPlan( )* method which you created earlier on page 177.

```
private void loadPlan(object sender, EventArgs e)
{
    Button clickedButton = (Button)sender;
    string s = clickedButton.Name;
    int i = Convert.ToInt16(s.Substring(3, 1));
    TheatrePlan frmTheatrePlan = new TheatrePlan();
    frmTheatrePlan.showTheatre(i);
    frmTheatrePlan.ShowDialog();
}
```

Go to the *TheatrePlan* form and add an empty *showTheatre( )* method. This will bring in a parameter '*i*' to indicate which theatre event had been selected from the scrolling list on the *DisplayEvents* page.

```
public TheatrePlan()
{
    InitializeComponent();
}

public void showTheatre(int i)
{

}
```

Run the program. Click one of the '*Book seats*' buttons and check that the *TheatrePlan* form opens correctly.

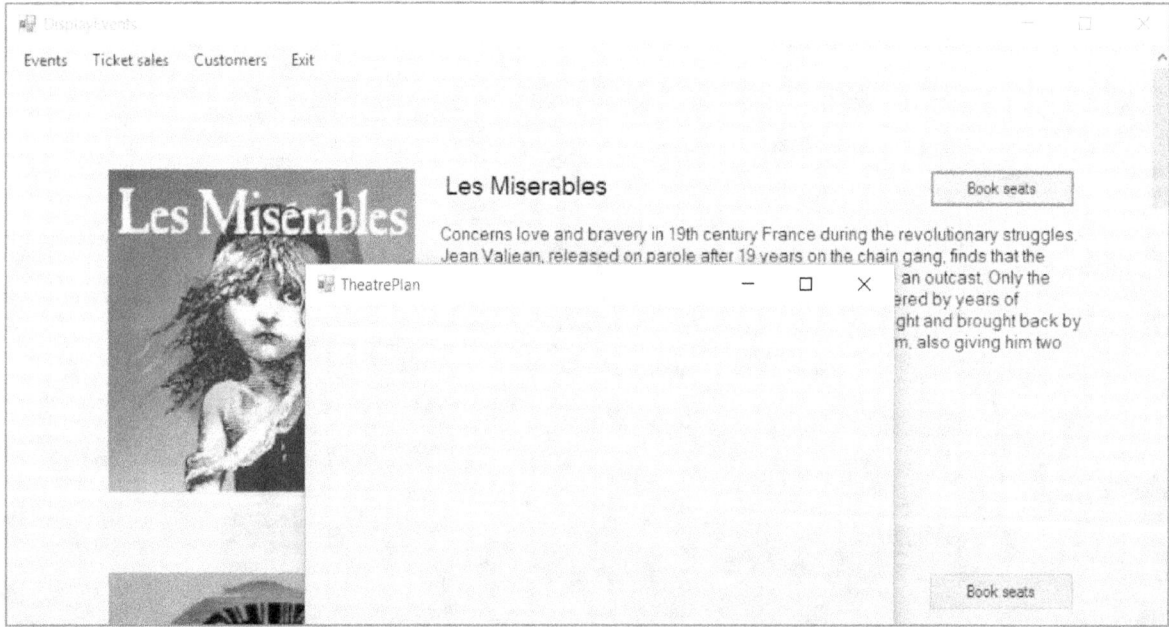

Set up components on the TheatrePlan form as show below:

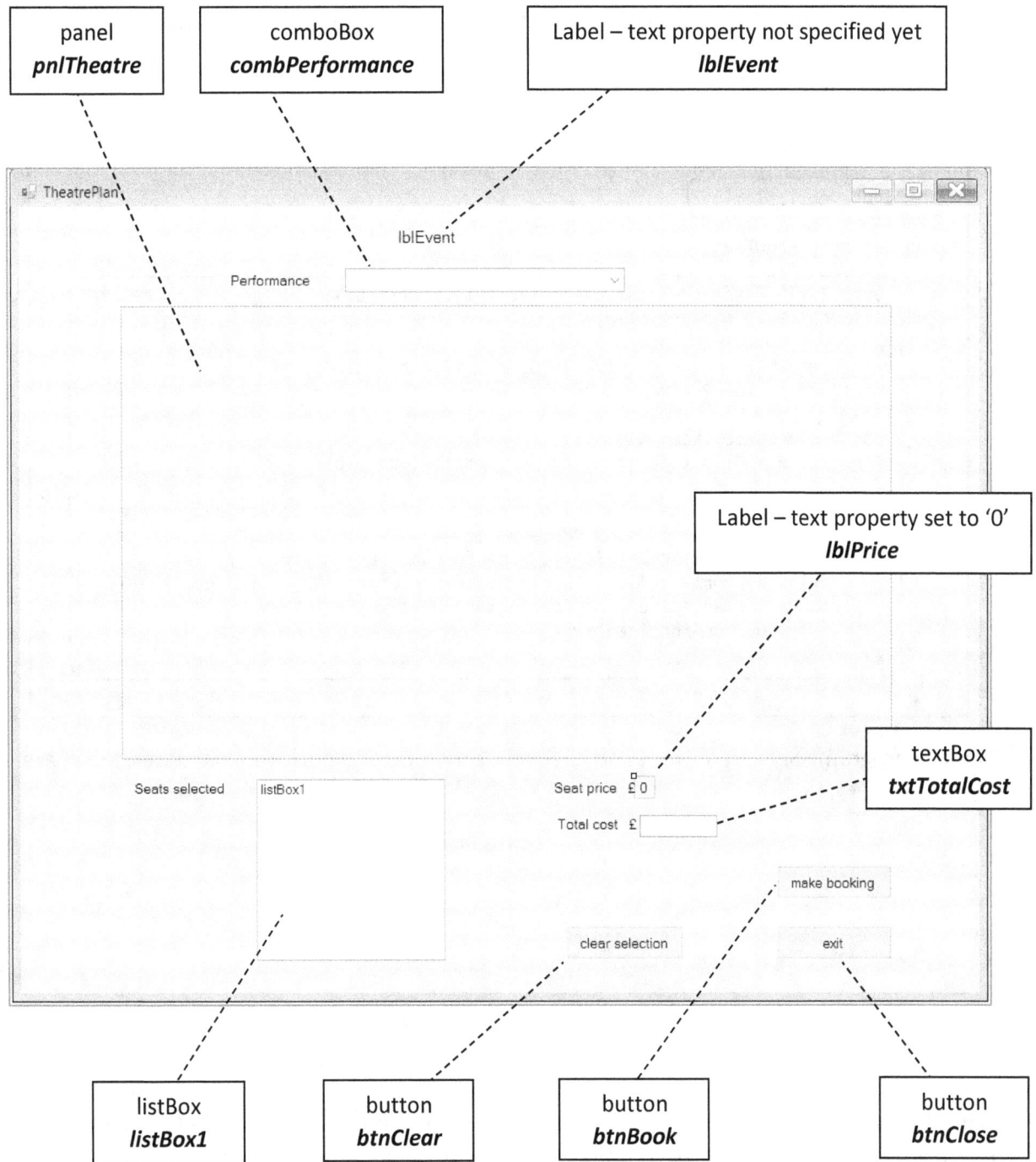

Add code to the 'exit' button:

```
private void btnClose_Click(object sender, EventArgs e)
{
    this.Close();
}
```

The first requirement of the booking screen is to display the title of the selected theatre event, and provide a drop down list of the performance dates and times in the comboBox. Add code to the *showTheatre( )* method to do this. Notice how this reuses the *loadPerformances( )* method which we wrote earlier in the *performance* class. Add a definition for the *eventTitle* variable above the method heading.

```
string eventTitle;

public void showTheatre(int i)
{
    eventTitle = theatreEvent.eventObject[i].getTitle();
    lblEvent.Text = eventTitle;

    int eventID = theatreEvent.eventObject[i].getEventID();
    performance.loadPerformances(eventID);

    combPerformance.Items.Clear();
    for (int p = 0; p < performance.performanceCount; p++)
    {
        DateTime performanceDate = performance.performanceObject[p].getDate();
        string format = " ddd d MMM yyyy";
        string performanceDateString = performanceDate.ToString(format);
        string performanceTime = performance.performanceObject[p].getTime();
        combPerformance.Items.Add(performanceDateString + " at "
            + performanceTime);
    }
}
```

Run the program. Select an event and check that the title and performance dates/times are displayed correctly.

We can now start to construct the seating plan diagram for the theatre. It is first necessary to make a small graphics image to represent a theatre seat on the plan. This should be about 20 pixels square, and can be saved in .PNG format with the name '*seat1.png*'

Go to the SolutionExplorer window and right click on the *theatreBookings* program icon. Load the seat image into the C# project by selecting '*Add / Existing item*', then locating the *seat1.png* graphics file in the file selection window.

We will build up the theatre plan from buttons displaying the seat image, using a similar technique to the **Solitaire** board display in chapter 4. Add an array at the start of the **TheatrePlan** form to hold these buttons.

```
public partial class TheatrePlan : Form
{
    Button[,] btnSeat = new Button[22, 12];

    public TheatrePlan()
    {
        InitializeComponent();
    }
```

You may recall from the program specification that the theatre has quite a complicated arrangement of seats:

				1	2	3	4	5	6	7	8	9	10	11	A	12	13	14			
			1	2	3	4	5	6	7	8	9	10	11	12	B	13	14	15	16		
		1	2	3	4	5	6	7	8	9	10	11	12	13	C	14	15	16	17		
	1	2	3	4	5	6	7	8	9	10	11	12	13	14	D	15	16	17	18	19	
1	2	3	4	5	6	7	8	9	10	11	12	13	14	15	E	16	17	18	19	20	
1	2	3	4	5	6	7	8	9	10	11	12	13	14	15	F	16	17	18	19	20	
	1	2	3	4	5	6	7	8	9	10	11	12	13	14	G	15	16	17	18	19	
	1	2	3	4	5	6	7	8	9	10	11	12	13	14	H	15	16	17	18	19	
	1	2	3	4	5	6	7	8	9	10	11	12	13	14	J	15	16	17	18	19	
1	2	3	4	5	6	7	8	9	10	11	12	13	14	15	K	16	17	18	19	20	
1	2	3	4	5	6	7	8	9	10	11	12	13	14	15	L	16	17	18	19		

We will construct this plan in several stages. The first will be to display the correct number of seats in each row. Create a **drawPlan( )** method in the **TheatrePlan** form.

```
private void drawPlan()
{
    int seatMax;
    for (int j = 1; j <= 11; j++)
    {
        seatMax = 20;
        if (j == 1) seatMax = 14;
        if (j == 2) seatMax = 16;
        if (j == 3) seatMax = 17;
        if (j == 4) seatMax = 19;
        if (j >= 7 && j <= 9) seatMax = 19;
        if (j == 11) seatMax = 19;
        for (int i = 1; i <= seatMax; i++)
        {
            btnSeat[i, j] = new Button();
            btnSeat[i, j].Width = 28;
            btnSeat[i, j].Height = 28;
            btnSeat[i, j].Left = (28 * i);
            btnSeat[i, j].Top = (28 * j);
            btnSeat[i, j].Image = Image.FromFile("../../seat1.png");
            pnlTheatre.Controls.Add(btnSeat[i, j]);
        }
    }
}
```

This method uses an outer loop to repeat for each of the 11 rows of seats, and an inner loop to repeat for the seats along each row. Before running the inner loop, the maximum number of seats is specified according to the theatre plan – this may vary between 14 and 20, depending on the row. The inner loop then creates button objects displaying the seat image.

Double click the comboBox component, and add a line of code to call the *drawPlan( )* method when a performance date is selected.

```
private void combPerformance_SelectedIndexChanged(object sender, EventArgs e)
{
    drawPlan();
}
```

Run the program. Select an event and click the 'Book seats' button, then choose a performance date/time from the comboBox on the **TheatrePlan** form. The array of seats should be displayed. Check that the correct number of seats are present in each row.

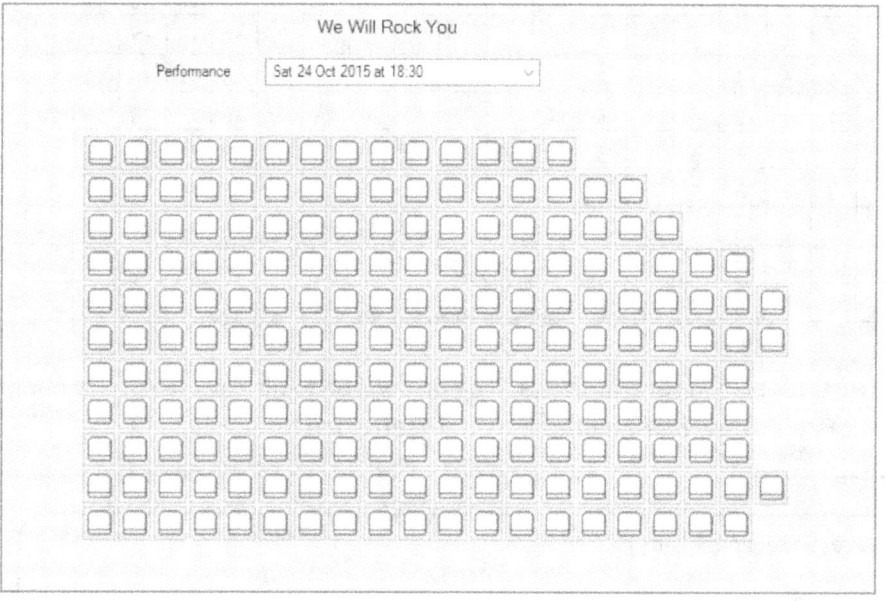

We are making progress, but you will notice from the seating plan that rows start at different distances from the left wall of the theatre. We must allow for this if our seating plan is to be realistic.

We can allocate a variable called '**offset**' which records the number of seat positions by which each row is indented:

offset = 4					1	2	3	4	5	6	7	8	9	10	11	A	12
offset = 3				1	2	3	4	5	6	7	8	9	10	11	12	B	13
offset = 2			1	2	3	4	5	6	7	8	9	10	11	12	13	C	14
offset = 1		1	2	3	4	5	6	7	8	9	10	11	12	13	14	D	15
offset = 0	1	2	3	4	5	6	7	8	9	10	11	12	13	14	15	E	16
offset = 0	1	2	3	4	5	6	7	8	9	10	11	12	13	14	15	F	16

Return to the *drawPlan( )* method. Add the *offset* variable and the code to set the number of offset positions for each row of seats. Change the left positions of the buttons to allow for the offsets.

```
private void drawPlan()
{
    int offset;

    int seatMax;

    for (int j = 1; j <= 11; j++)
    {
        seatMax = 20;
        if (j == 1) seatMax = 14;
        if (j == 2) seatMax = 16;
        if (j == 3) seatMax = 17;
        if (j == 4) seatMax = 19;
        if (j >= 7 && j <= 9) seatMax = 19;
        if (j == 11) seatMax = 19;

        for (int i = 1; i <= seatMax; i++)
        {
            offset = 0;
            if (j == 1) offset = 4;
            if (j == 2) offset = 3;
            if (j == 3) offset = 2;
            if (j == 4) offset = 1;
            if (j >= 7 && j <= 9) offset = 1;

            btnSeat[i, j] = new Button();
            btnSeat[i, j].Width = 28;
            btnSeat[i, j].Height = 28;

            btnSeat[i, j].Left = ((28 * i) + (28 * offset));    ⇐ change this line

            btnSeat[i, j].Top = (28 * j);
```

Run the program and check that the rows are now indented in the correct pattern.

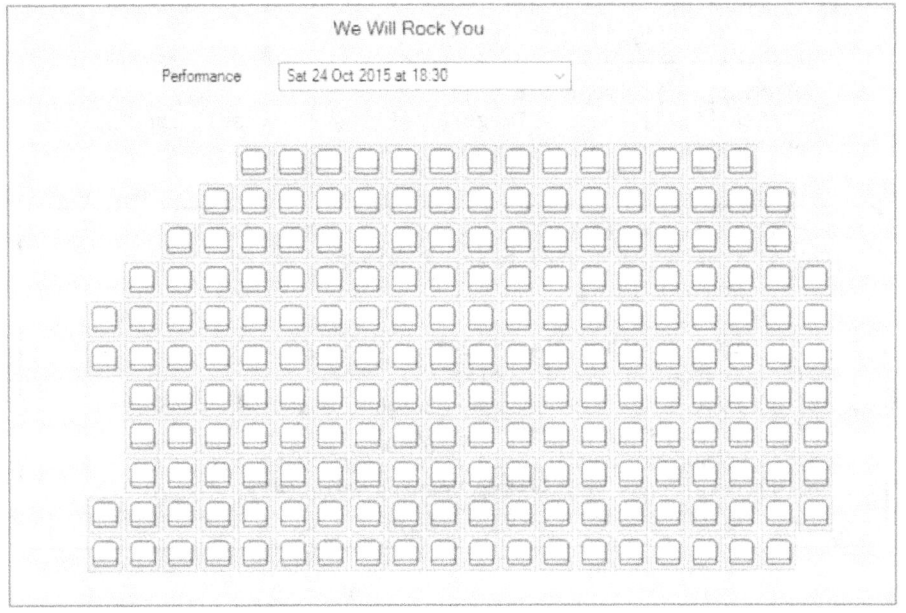

The next slight complication is that the theatre has an aisle between the blocks of seats. On the plan, this can be used to display the row letters.

		1	2	3	4	5	6	7	8	9	10	11	A	12	13	14	
	1	2	3	4	5	6	7	8	9	10	11	12	B	13	14	15	16
1	2	3	4	5	6	7	8	9	10	11	12	13	C	14	15	16	17

We will need an array to hold the label which display the row letters. Add this at the start of **TheatrePlan**.

```
public partial class TheatrePlan : Form
{
    Button[,] btnSeat = new Button[22, 12];

    Label[] label = new Label[12];

    public TheatrePlan()
    {
        InitializeComponent();
    }
```

Add a line of code to the **drawPlan( )** method which will move all seat positions to the right by 28 pixels if they are beyond the position of the aisle. This will create the gap between the seat blocks. We then add code to place labels in this gap to show the row letters.

Notice how the row letters are generated from the row numbers using **ASCII values**, and how the letter is incremented beyond row 8 to allow for the missing letter '*I*'.

```
            btnSeat[i, j] = new Button();
            btnSeat[i, j].Width = 28;
            btnSeat[i, j].Height = 28;
            btnSeat[i, j].Left = ((28 * i) + (28 * offset));

            if ((i + offset) > 15)
                btnSeat[i, j].Left += 28;

            btnSeat[i, j].Top = (28 * j);
            btnSeat[i, j].Image = Image.FromFile("../../seat1.png");
            pnlTheatre.Controls.Add(btnSeat[i, j]);
        }

        label[j] = new Label();
        label[j].Size = new System.Drawing.Size(24, 30);
        char c = Convert.ToChar(64 + j);
        if (j > 8)
            c = Convert.ToChar(65 + j);
        label[j].Text = Convert.ToString(c);
        label[j].Font = new System.Drawing.Font("Microsoft Sans Serif",
            10F, System.Drawing.FontStyle.Regular,
            System.Drawing.GraphicsUnit.Point, ((byte)(0)));
        label[j].Location = new System.Drawing.Point(455, 4 + 28 * j);
        pnlTheatre.Controls.Add(label[j]);
    }
}
```

Run the program and select an event and performance. The theatre plan should now be displayed with an aisle and row letters.

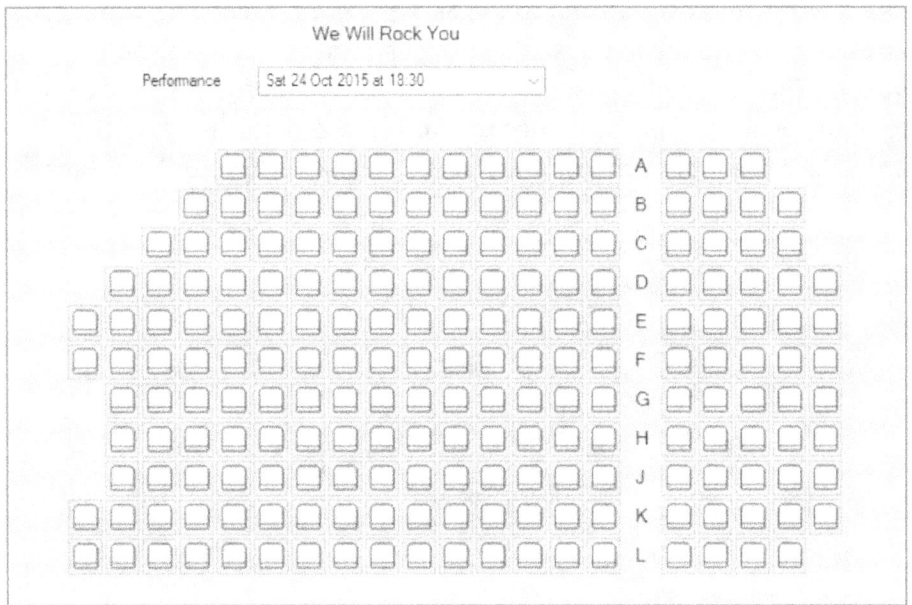

A further small feature that you might like to impliment is a *toolTip* message box. This is a small box which appears when the user hovers the mouse over a component. We can set this up to display the seat row and number:

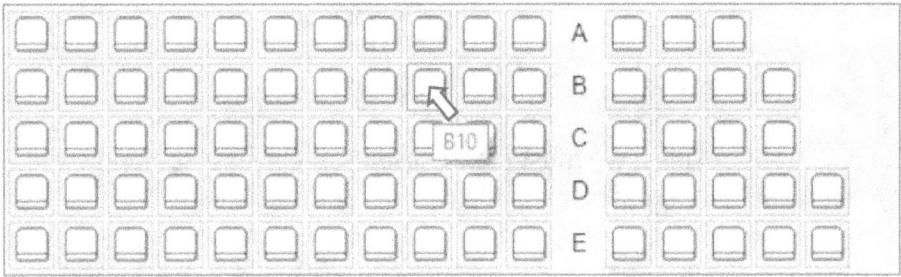

Return to the *drawPlan( )* method and add code to link a *toolTip* message to each seat button. We again make use of ASCII codes in converting the row number to the corresponding row letter.

```
            btnSeat[i, j].Image = Image.FromFile("../../seat1.png");
            pnlTheatre.Controls.Add(btnSeat[i, j]);

            int rowNumber = j;
            if (j > 8)
                rowNumber++;
            string tooltipText = Convert.ToChar(rowNumber + 64).ToString()
                    + (i).ToString();
            ToolTip buttonToolTip = new ToolTip();
            buttonToolTip.SetToolTip(btnSeat[i, j], tooltipText);
        }
        label[j] = new Label();
        label[j].Size = new System.Drawing.Size(24, 30);
        char c = Convert.ToChar(64 + j);
```

Run the program to check that the *toolTip* messages are displayed correctly.

We can now turn our attention to displaying the seat bookings which have been made for performances. To provide test data, go to the **Server Explorer**, connect the database and open the **Seat** table. Locate the set of seats for a performance and set some of the seats in **row A** as **booked**. This is done by changing the value of the '**available**' field from **0** to **1**. Make a note of the event and performance to which these seats are allocated. When you have done this, close the table window and **delete the connection** to the database.

seatRow	seatNumber	performanceID	available	bookingID
A	1	2	0	0
A	2	2	0	0
A	3	2	1	0
A	4	2	1	0
A	5	2	1	0
A	6	2	1	0
A	7	2	0	0
A	8	2	0	0

It will be necessary to create a second version of the seat image, this time in a colour such as red, to represent a booked seat. Call this '*seat2.png*' and load it into the project using the '**Add / Existing item**' option:

seat1.png   seat2.png

Before displaying seat bookings, we must create a *seat* object class to handle the data. Select '**Add / New item**' and create a class file called '*seat*'.

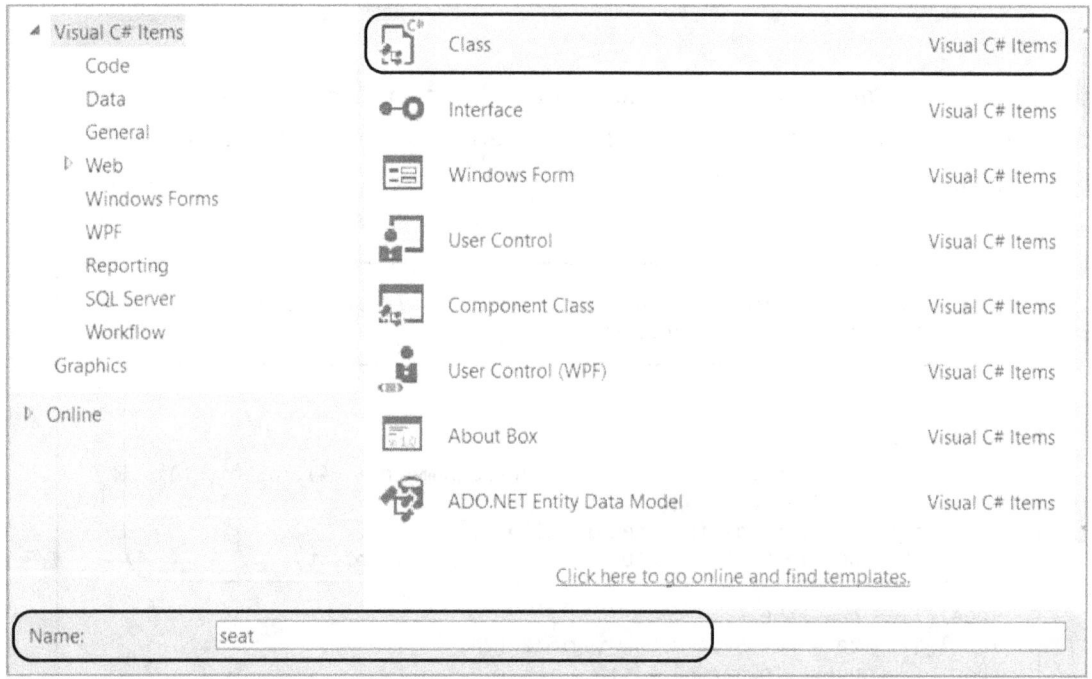

As with previous classes, insert the property fields for seat objects and the methods for transfering data into and out from these properties.

```
class seat
{
    private char seatRow;
    private int seatNumber;
    private int performanceID;
    private int available;
    private int bookingID;

    public void setSeatRow(char r)
    {
        seatRow = r;
    }

    public char getSeatRow()
    {
        return seatRow;
    }

    public void setSeatNumber(int s)
    {
        seatNumber = s;
    }

    public int getSeatNumber()
    {
        return seatNumber;
    }

    public void setPerformanceID(int p)
    {
        performanceID = p;
    }

    public int getPerformanceID()
    {
        return performanceID;
    }

    public void setAvailable(int a)
    {
        available = a;
    }

    public int getAvailable()
    {
        return available;
    }

    public void setBookingID(int b)
    {
        bookingID = b;
    }

    public int getBookingID()
    {
        return bookingID;
    }
}
```

We will now produce a ***loadSeats( )*** method which uses a parameter '***p***' to specify the ***performanceID*** of the performance for which the seat data is required. The set of seat records is loaded from the database table, then used to create a set of seat objects.

It will be necessary to add '***using SqlClient***' and '***using Data***' directives to the start of the seat class file, set up a variable ***seatCount*** to record the number of seat objects created, and to declare an array to link to the seat objects.

```csharp
using System.Linq;
using System.Text;

using System.Data.SqlClient;
using System.Data;

namespace theatreBookings
{
    class seat
    {
        private char seatRow;
        private int seatNumber;
        private int performanceID;
        private int available;
        private int bookingID;

        private static string databaseLocation="C:\\C#\\theatreBookings.mdf;";

        public static int seatCount;
        public static seat[] seatObject = new seat[240];

        public static void loadSeats(int p)
        {
            seatCount = 0;
            DataSet dsSeats = new DataSet();
            SqlConnection con = new SqlConnection(@"Data Source=.\SQLEXPRESS;
               AttachDbFilename=" +databaseLocation + "Integrated Security=True;
               Connect Timeout=30; User Instance=True");
            con.Open();
            SqlCommand cmSeats = new SqlCommand();
            cmSeats.Connection = con;
            cmSeats.CommandType = CommandType.Text;
            cmSeats.CommandText = "SELECT * FROM Seat WHERE performanceID='"
                    + p + "'";
            SqlDataAdapter daSeats = new SqlDataAdapter(cmSeats);
            daSeats.Fill(dsSeats);
            con.Close();

            seatCount = dsSeats.Tables[0].Rows.Count;
            for (int i = 0; i < seatCount; i++)
            {
                seatObject[i] = new seat();
                DataRow dataRow = dsSeats.Tables[0].Rows[i];
                seatObject[i].setSeatRow(Convert.ToChar(dataRow[0]));
                seatObject[i].setSeatNumber((int)dataRow[1]);
                seatObject[i].setPerformanceID((int)dataRow[2]);
                seatObject[i].setAvailable((int)dataRow[3]);
                seatObject[i].setBookingID((int)dataRow[4]);
            }
        }
```

Return to the *TheatrePlan* form.

It will be convenient to use a two dimensional integer array, similar to the array in the Solitaire game, to keep track of the status of each seat as available or booked. Set up the *seatStatus* array at the start of *TheatrePlan*.

```
public partial class TheatrePlan : Form
{
    Button[,] btnSeat = new Button[22, 12];
    Label[] label = new Label[12];

    int[,] seatStatus = new int[21, 12];
```

Double click the comboBox to go to the *IndexChanged( )* method. Add code which carries out several activities:
- The *performanceID* is first obtained from the selected performance date/time in the comboBox.
- The *loadSeats( )* method in the *seat* class is called, which retrieves data from the database table and creates a set of *seat objects* for the required performance.
- A loop accesses each of the *seat* objects. The row letter is converted to a row number by means of its ASCII code.
- The value of the '*available*' property is stored in the *seatStatus* array using the seat and row numbers as the array indices '*s*' and '*r*'. The value of '*available*' will be 0 for an empty seat, and 1 for a booked seat.
- Existing seat buttons are removed from the panel, ready to redisplay the plan.
- Finally, the ticket price for the performance is displayed in the *lblPrice* label.

```
private void combPerformance_SelectedIndexChanged(object sender, EventArgs e)
{
    int p = combPerformance.SelectedIndex;
    int performanceID = performance.performanceObject[p].getPerformanceID();
    seat.loadSeats(performanceID);

    for (int i = 0; i < seat.seatCount; i++)
    {
        char c = seat.seatObject[i].getSeatRow();
        int r = ((int)c) - 64;
        if (r > 8)
            r--;
        int s = seat.seatObject[i].getSeatNumber();
        int available = seat.seatObject[i].getAvailable();
        seatStatus[s, r] = available;
    }

    int totalButtons = pnlTheatre.Controls.Count;
    for (int i = 0; i < totalButtons; i++)
    {
        pnlTheatre.Controls.RemoveAt(0);
    }
    lblPrice.Text = performance.performanceObject[p].getPrice().ToString("f2");

    drawPlan();
}
```

One change is needed to the **drawPlan( )** method to display the coloured **seat2.png** image for booked seats, where **seatStatus** has a value of 1. Add the extra lines of code:

```
btnSeat[i, j] = new Button();
btnSeat[i, j].Width = 28;
btnSeat[i, j].Height = 28;
btnSeat[i, j].Left = ((28 * i) + (28 * offset));
if ((i + offset) > 15)
    btnSeat[i, j].Left += 28;
btnSeat[i, j].Top = (28 * j);
btnSeat[i, j].Image = Image.FromFile("../../seat1.png");

if (seatStatus[i, j] == 1)
    btnSeat[i, j].Image = Image.FromFile("../../seat2.png");

pnlTheatre.Controls.Add(btnSeat[i, j]);
```

Run the program. Select the event and performance for which you altered the '**available**' properties of some seats (page 195). The seats which you set as '**booked**' should appear with colour coding on the seat plan.

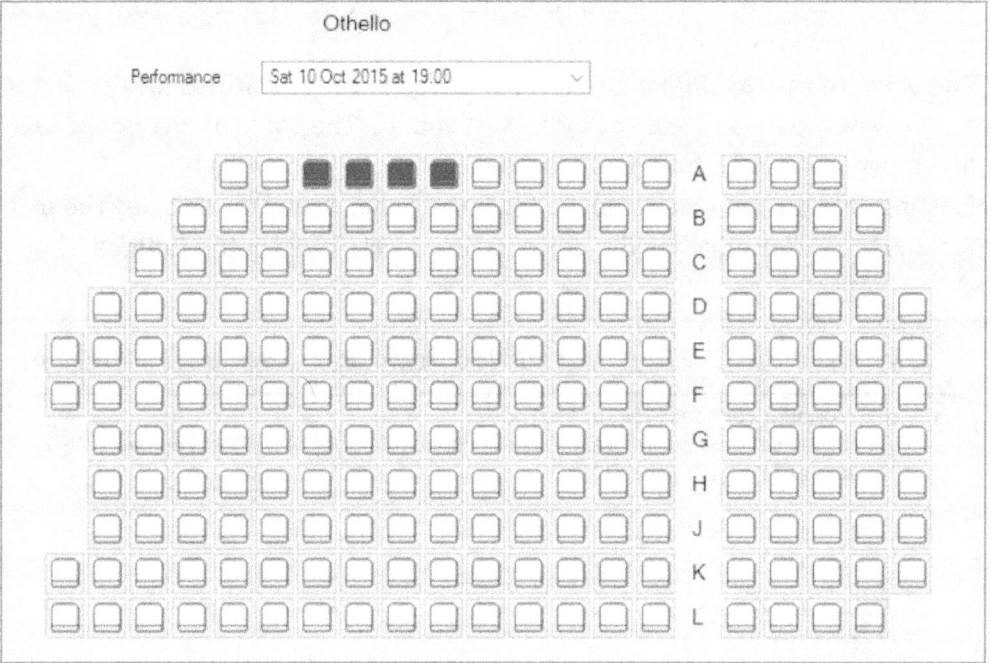

We can now move on to the task of selecting and booking seats. As the user selects seats by clicking on the theatre plan, it will be convenient for these seats to be appear in another colour, for example: green. Make a third seat image, called '**seat3.png**' in this additional colour and load it into the project.

seat1.png   seat2.png   seat3.png

Return to the *drawPlan( )* method and add code which will do two things:
- Each button is allocated a name, made up from the letters '**btn**', followed by the row number and the seat number. To avoid ambiguity, a space is added before a single digit row or seat number.
- A button click procedure called *seat_Click( )* is linked to each button.

```
btnSeat[i, j].Image = Image.FromFile("../../seat1.png");
if (seatStatus[i, j] == 1)
    btnSeat[i, j].Image = Image.FromFile("../../seat2.png");

String buttonName = "btn";
if (j <= 9)
    buttonName += " ";
buttonName += j;
if (i <= 9)
    buttonName += " ";
buttonName += i;

btnSeat[i, j].Name = buttonName;
btnSeat[i, j].Click += new EventHandler(seat_Click);

pnlTheatre.Controls.Add(btnSeat[i, j]);
```

Add the *seatClick( )* method immediately after *drawPlan( )*. This will process the button click by carrying out a series of actions:
- The button name is broken down to obtain the row and seat number.
- The program checks that this seat does not have a *seatStatus* value of 1, which would indicate that it was already booked.
- If the seat is currently available, a *seatStatus* value of 2 is allocated, and the image is changed to *seat3.png*.
- It the seat is already selected, then the selection is cancelled by re-setting *seatStatus* to 0 and changing the image back to *seat1.png*.

```
private void seat_Click(object sender, EventArgs e)
{
    Button clickedButton = (Button)sender;

    string s = clickedButton.Name;
    int j = Convert.ToInt16(s.Substring(3, 2));
    int i = Convert.ToInt16(s.Substring(5, 2));

    if (seatStatus[i, j] != 1)
    {
        if (seatStatus[i, j] == 0)
        {
            seatStatus[i, j] = 2;
            btnSeat[i, j].Image = Image.FromFile("../../seat3.png");
        }
        else
        {
            seatStatus[i, j] = 0;
            btnSeat[i, j].Image = Image.FromFile("../../seat1.png");
        }
    }
}
```

Run the program and select your test event/performance. Check that seats can be selected by clicking on the seat plan, and that seats can be deselected by clicking a second time.

We can display details of the seats selected in the *listBox* at the bottom of the form. Add a *listSelectedSeats( )* method to the *TheatrePlan* page below the *seatClick( )* method.

```csharp
private void listSelectedSeats()
{
    try
    {
        int p = combPerformance.SelectedIndex;
        double seatPrice = performance.performanceObject[p].getPrice();
        totalCost = 0;
        listBox1.Items.Clear();
        for (int j = 1; j <= 11; j++)
        {
            for (int i = 1; i <= 20; i++)
            {
                if (seatStatus[i, j] == 2)
                {
                    char c = Convert.ToChar(64 + j);
                    if (j > 8)
                        c = Convert.ToChar(65 + j);
                    listBox1.Items.Add("Row " + c + "  Seat " + i);
                    totalCost += seatPrice;
                }
            }
        }
        txtTotalCost.Text = totalCost.ToString("f2");
    }
    catch
    {
        MessageBox.Show("A performance must be selected");
    }
}
```

This method uses two loops to check the *seatStatus* array value for each seat. If a value of 2 is found, indicating that the user has selected that seat, then the seat row letter and seat number are added to the list box. We also take the opportunity to calculate the total cost of the seats booked, using the seat price loaded earlier from the *performance* object.

Add a line of code at the end of the *seatClick( )* method to call *listSelectedSeats( )*. We also need to add the *totalCost* variable.

```
        if (seatStatus[i, j] == 0)
        {
            seatStatus[i, j] = 2;
            btnSeat[i, j].Image = Image.FromFile("../../seat3.png");
        }
        else
        {
            seatStatus[i, j] = 0;
            btnSeat[i, j].Image = Image.FromFile("../../seat1.png");
        }
        listSelectedSeats();
    }
}
double totalCost;

private void listSelectedSeats()
{
    try
    {
        int p = combPerformance.SelectedIndex;
        double seatPrice = performance.performanceObject[p].getPrice();
        totalCost = 0;
        listBox1.Items.Clear();
```

Run the program. Check that seats selected are added to the listBox, and that the total cost of the selected seats is calculated correctly.

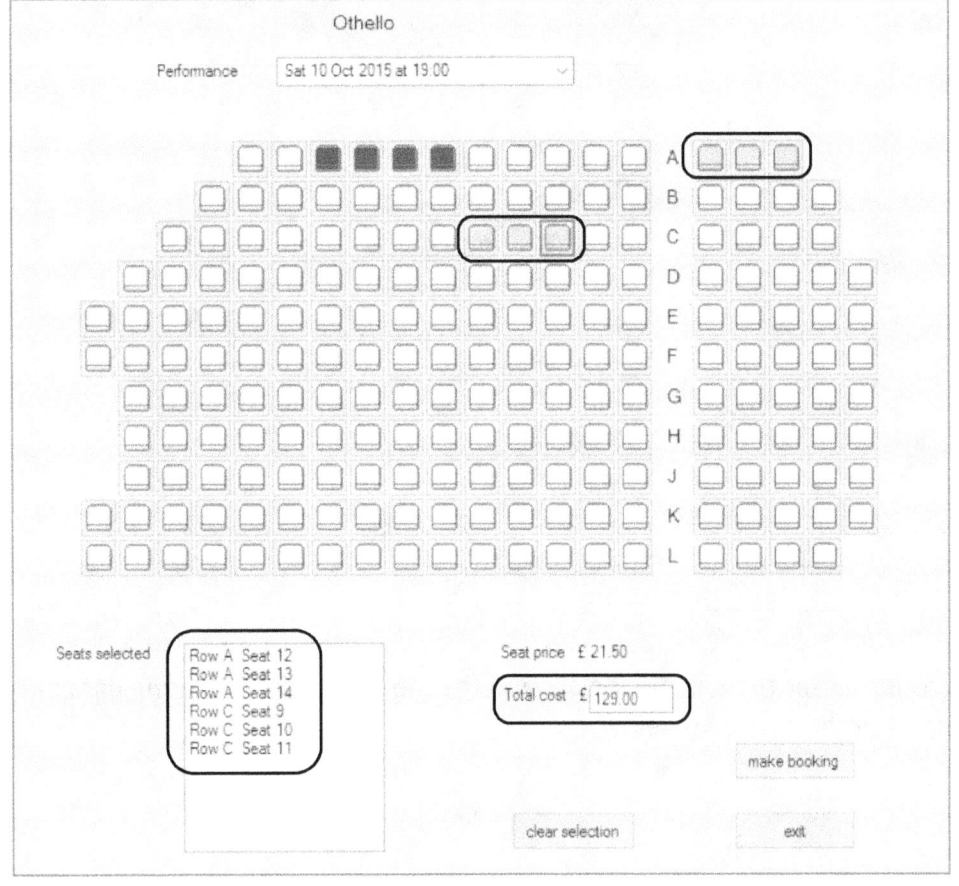

A final feature to complete is the *'clear selection'* button, which will reset all selected seats to the *'available'* state. Double click the button and add code to the **btnClear_Click( )** method. This uses two loops to check the *seatStatus* array. If a value of 2 is found, indicating that the seat is currently selected, then the array value is reset to 0 and the image on the corresponding seat button is changed back to *'seat1.png'*.

```
private void btnClear_Click(object sender, EventArgs e)
{
    listBox1.Items.Clear();
    for (int j = 1; j <= 11; j++)
    {
        for (int i = 1; i <= 20; i++)
        {
            if (seatStatus[i, j] == 2)
            {
                seatStatus[i, j] = 0;
                btnSeat[i, j].Image = Image.FromFile("../../seat1.png");
            }
        }
    }
    txtTotalCost.Clear();
}
```

Run the program and check that seat selections can be cancelled.

Once the required seats have been selected, the user will move to the next form to input contact details for the customer. We will develop this section next, but first we must create a *customer* object class. Go to the **Solution Explorer** window and add a new class file with the name '**customer**'.

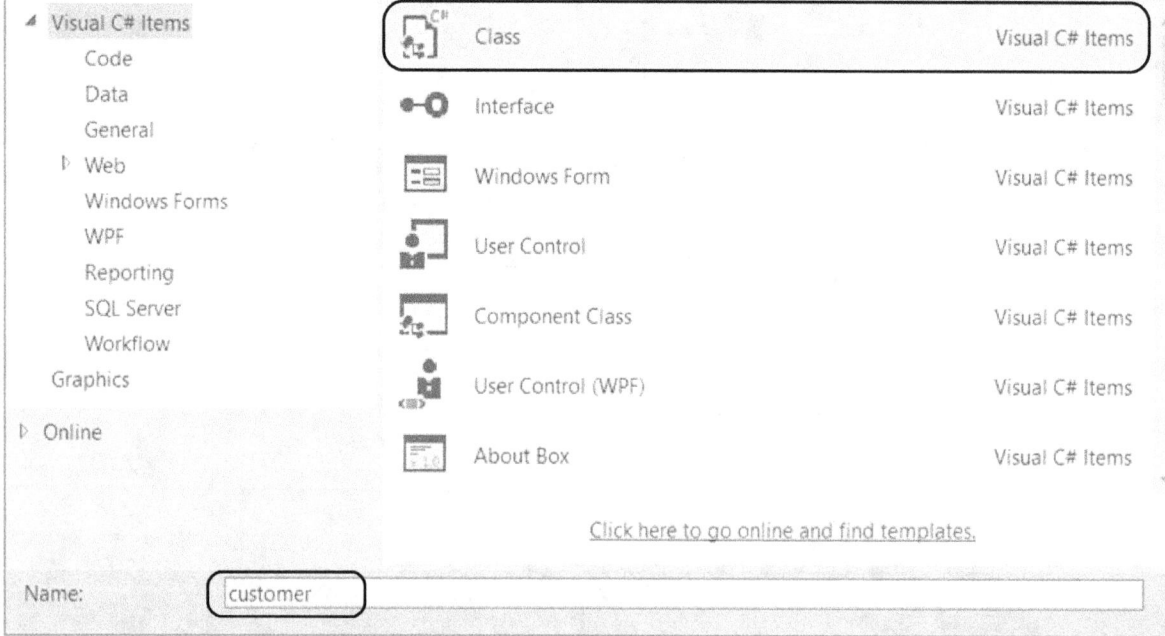

Add the properties for the *customer* class and the methods for transfering data into and out of *customer* objects, as shown below:

```
class customer
{
    private int customerID;
    private string surname;
    private string forename;
    private string title;
    private string address1;
    private string address2;
    private string town;
    private string postcode;
    private string email;
    private string phone;

    public void setCustomerID(int c)
    {
        customerID = c;
    }
    public int getCustomerID()
    {
        return customerID;
    }
    public void setSurname(string s)
    {
        surname = s;
    }
    public string getSurname()
    {
        return surname;
    }
    public void setForename(string f)
    {
        forename = f;
    }
    public string getForename()
    {
        return forename;
    }
    public void setTitle(string t)
    {
        title = t;
    }
    public string getTitle()
    {
        return title;
    }
    public void setAddress1(string a1)
    {
        address1 = a1;
    }
    public string getAddress1()
    {
        return address1;
    }
    public void setAddress2(string a2)
    {
        address2 = a2;
    }
    public string getAddress2()
    {
        return address2;
    }
```

```csharp
        public void setTown(string to)
        {
            town = to;
        }
        public string getTown()
        {
            return town;
        }
        public void setPostcode(string pc)
        {
            postcode = pc;
        }
        public string getPostcode()
        {
            return postcode;
        }
        public void setEmail(string em)
        {
            email = em;
        }
        public string getEmail()
        {
            return email;
        }
        public void setPhone(string ph)
        {
            phone = ph;
        }
        public string getPhone()
        {
            return phone;
        }
```

Return to the Solution Explorer window and add a Windows Form with the name '**CustomerDetails**'.

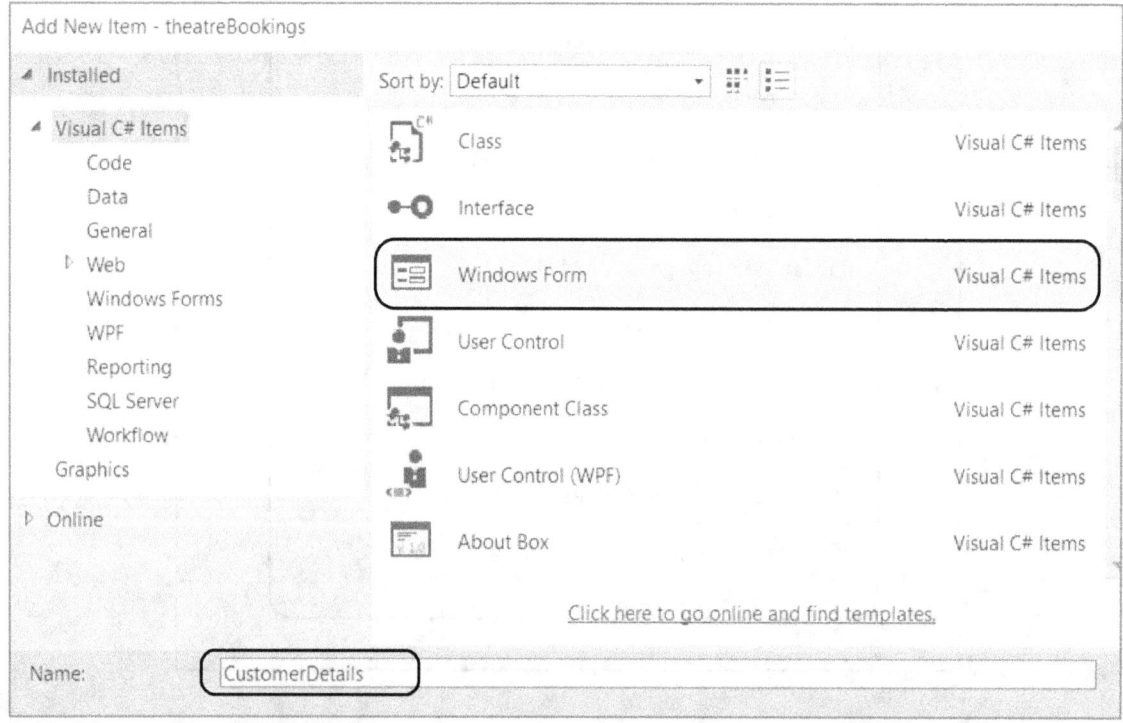

Add components to the *Customer Details* form:

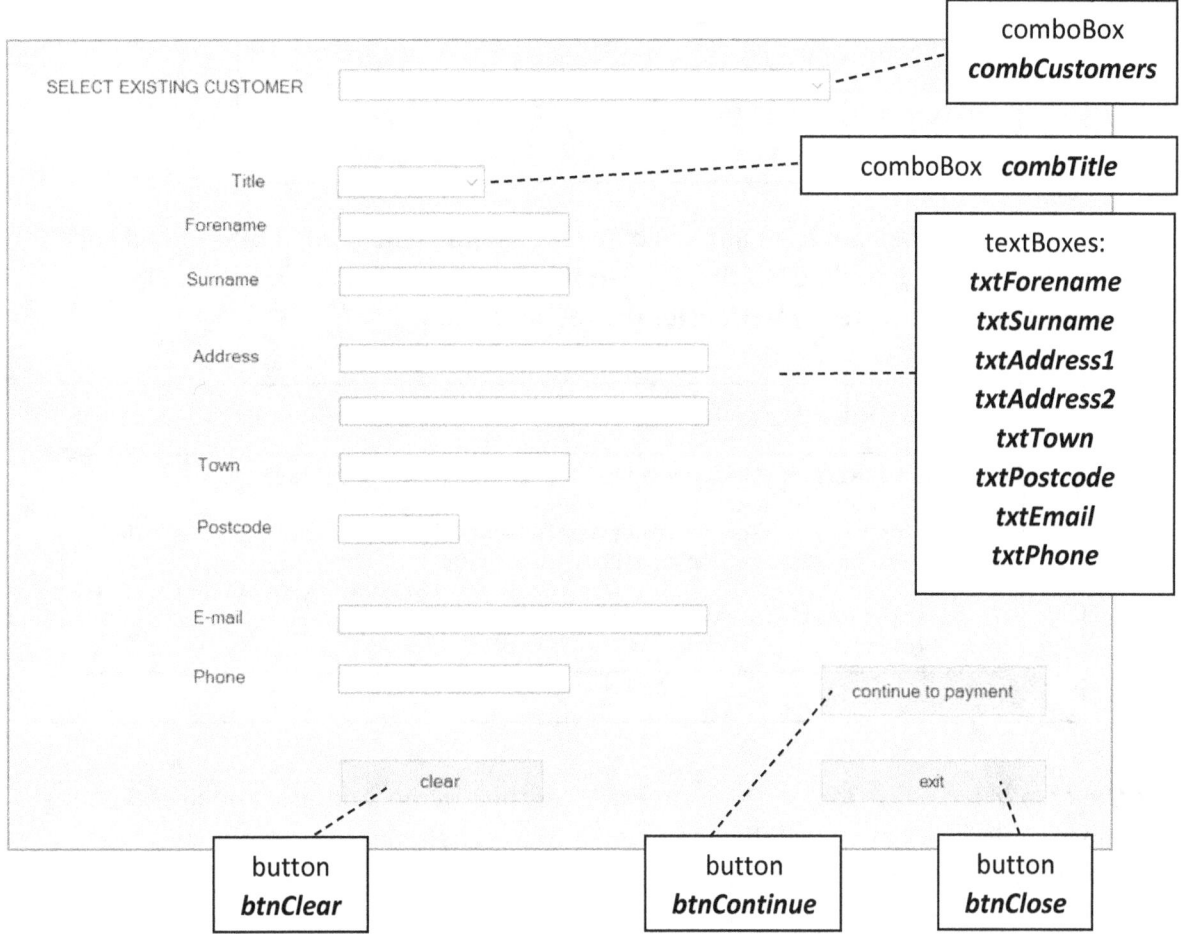

We will need to carry forward various data from the *TheatrePlan* form to the *CustomerDetails* form, ready to record the booking in the database: the title of the theatre event, the performanceID, the seats selected and the total cost of the tickets. Go to the *CustomerDetails* form and add a *getBooking( )* method and variables.

```
public partial class CustomerDetails : Form
{
    int f_performanceID;
    double f_totalCost;
    int[,] f_seatStatus;
    string f_eventTitle;

    public CustomerDetails()
    {
        InitializeComponent();
    }

    public void getBooking(int performanceID, double totalCost,
                           int[,] seatStatus, string eventTitle)
    {
        f_performanceID = performanceID;
        f_totalCost = totalCost;
        f_seatStatus = seatStatus;
        f_eventTitle = eventTitle;
    }
```

Add code to the *'exit'* button.

```
private void btnClose_Click(object sender, EventArgs e)
{
    this.Close();
}
```

Return to the *TheatrePlan* form and double click the *'make booking'* button. Add code to the *btnBook_Click( )* method which will open the *CustomerDetails* form and call the *getBooking( )* method, ready to transfer the required data.

```
private void btnBook_Click(object sender, EventArgs e)
{
    CustomerDetails frmCustomerDetails = new CustomerDetails();
    int p = combPerformance.SelectedIndex;
    int performanceID = performance.performanceObject[p].getPerformanceID();
    frmCustomerDetails.getBooking(performanceID, totalCost,
                                        seatStatus, eventTitle);
    frmCustomerDetails.ShowDialog();
    this.Close();
}
```

In the case of a *new customer*, the user will enter their name, address, e-mail and phone number. This information will then be saved into the *customer* table of the database. We will now write the method to save this record.

Go to the *customer class* file. Add *'using SqlClient'* and *'using Data'* directives, and insert the database location.

```
using System.Linq;
using System.Text;
using System.Data.SqlClient;
using System.Data;

namespace theatreBookings
{
    class customer
    {
        private static string databaseLocation = "C:\\C#\\theatreBookings.mdf;";
        private int customerID;
        private string surname;
        private string forename;
        private string title;
```

Add the *saveCustomer( )* method to the *customer* class file. This takes as parameters the fields of the customer record, then uses the SQL *INSERT* command to save the record into the *customer* table of the database.

We will need to know the *customerID* value for the new record, so that this can be linked to the particular seat booking which is made. The computer will allocate a *customerID* automatically as an auto-number field. We can find the allocated value using the *SELECT SCOPE_IDENTITY( )* command and return it from the *saveCustomer( )* method.

```
public static int saveCustomer(string forename, string surname,string title,
   string address1, string address2,string town, string postcode, string email,
   string phone)
{
    SqlConnection con = new SqlConnection(@"Data Source=.\SQLEXPRESS;
       AttachDbFilename=" +databaseLocation + "Integrated Security=True;
       Connect Timeout=30; User Instance=True");
    con.Open();
    SqlCommand cmCustomer = new SqlCommand();
    cmCustomer.Connection = con;
    cmCustomer.CommandType = CommandType.Text;
    cmCustomer.CommandText = "INSERT INTO Customer(forename,surname, title,"
       +"address1, address2, town, postcode, email, phone)"
       + "VALUES ('" + forename + "','" + surname + "','" + title + "','"
       + address1 + "','" + address2 + "','" + town + "','" + postcode + "','"
       + email + "','" + phone + "')";
    cmCustomer.ExecuteNonQuery();

    cmCustomer.CommandText = "SELECT SCOPE_IDENTITY()";
    int identity = Convert.ToInt32(cmCustomer.ExecuteScalar());
    con.Close();
    return identity;
}
```

Return to the *CustomerDetails* form. Select the comboBox for customer title. Go to the Properties window and select 'Items' to open the String Collection Editor window. Enter a choice of titles: Mr, Ms, Miss, Mrs, Dr...

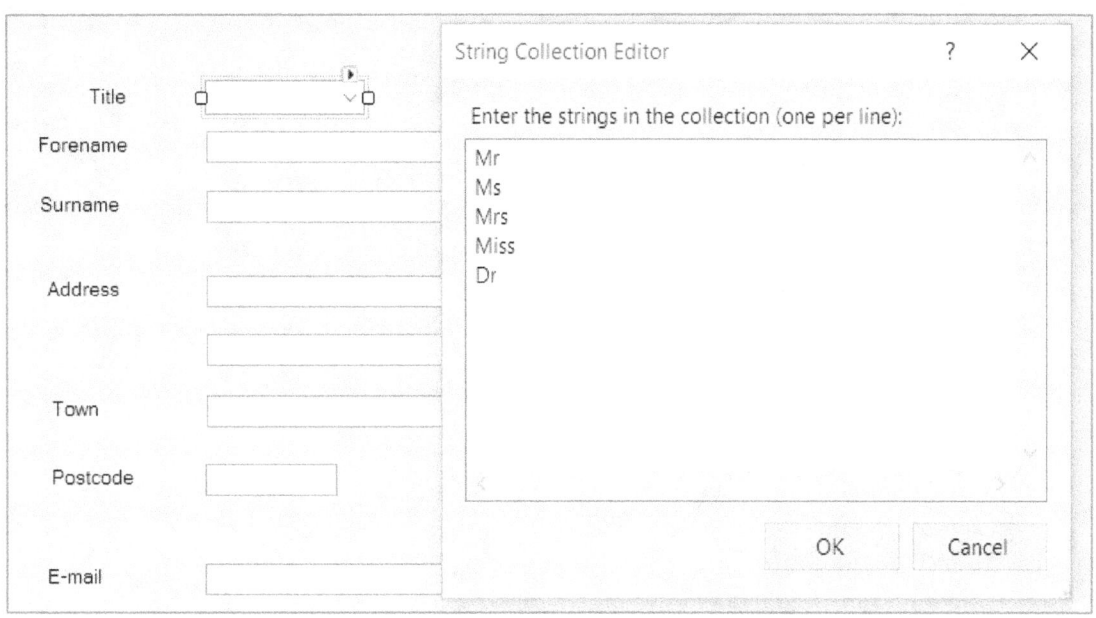

Double click the '*continue to payment*' button and add code to the **btnContinue_Click( )** method. Also add a *customerID* variable immediately before the method.

The button click method first checks that data has been entered in the required fields: *surname, forename, address1* and *postcode*. If data is present, then all data fields are passed as parameters to the *saveCustomer( )* method in the *customer* class, which saves the record to the database table.

```csharp
int customerID;

private void btnContinue_Click(object sender, EventArgs e)
{
    customerID = 0;
    if (txtSurname.Text.Length > 0 && txtForename.Text.Length > 0 &&
            txtAddress1.Text.Length > 0 && txtPostcode.Text.Length > 0)
    {
        customerID = customer.saveCustomer(txtForename.Text, txtSurname.Text,
        combTitle.Text, txtAddress1.Text, txtAddress2.Text, txtTown.Text,
        txtPostcode.Text, txtEmail.Text, txtPhone.Text);
    }
    else
    {
        MessageBox.Show(
          "Missing customer information - name, address, postcode are required");
    }
}
```

Run the program. Select an event and performance, then click the '*make booking*' button to open the **CustomerDetails** form.

Enter test data for a customer. Click the '*continue to payment*' button, then '*exit*'.

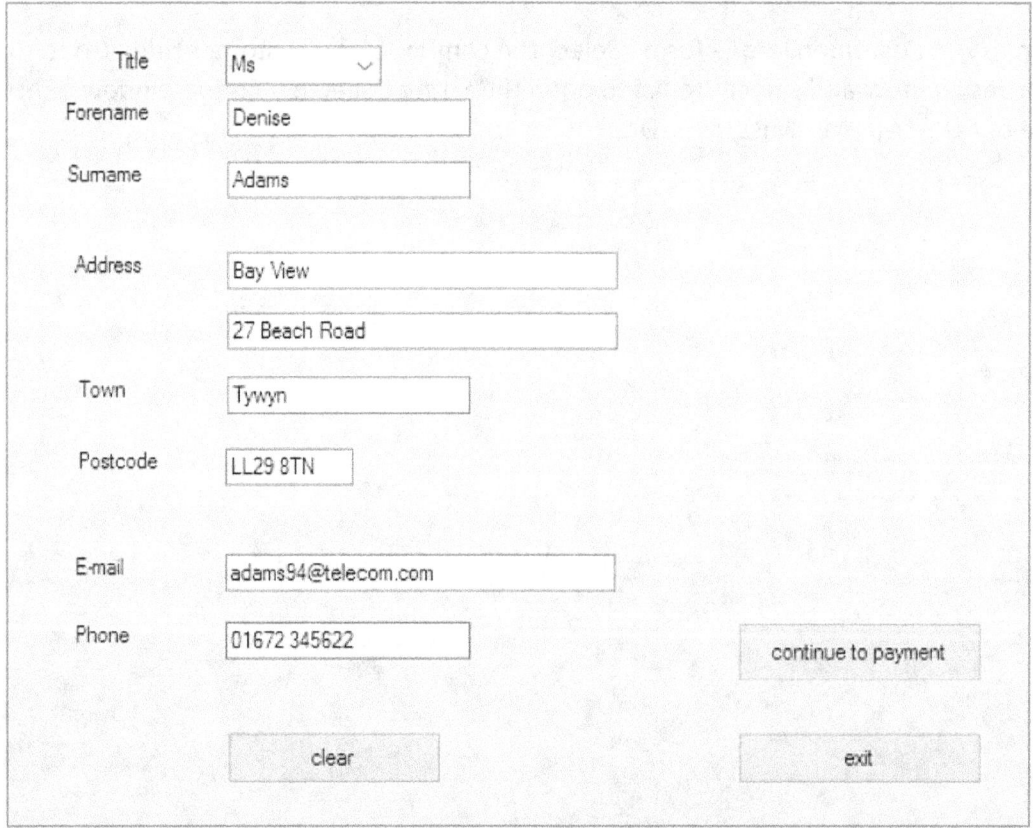

Enter several more customers in a similar way, then close the program windows. Go to the *Server Explorer* window and link to the *theatreBookings.mdf* database. Open the *customer* table and check that your test records have been saved, then delete the data connection.

customerID	forename	surname	title	address1	address2	town	postcode	email	phone
1	Denise	Adams	Ms	Bay View	27 Beach Road	Tywyn	LL29 8TN	adams94@telecom.com	01672 345622
2	Stuart	Andrews	Mr	Ty Gwyn	Harlech Road	Barmouth	LL39 7TR	andrews6@telecom.com	01762 345671
3	Ruth	Southhill	Ms	17 West Beach		Fairbourne	LL45 6TW	ruthsouth@btinternet.com	01567 341344
4	Judith	Williams	Mrs	36 Heol Glyndwr		Machynlleth	LL31 5UP	williams56@gmail.com	01678 965477
NULL	NULL	NULL	NULL	NULL	NULL	NULL	NULL	NULL	NULL

Apart from entering new customers, we also want to be able to select details of existing customers from the database. Go to the customer class and add a *loadCustomers( )* method, a *customerCount* variable and an *array* to link to customer objects.

The *loadCustomers( )* method will load all customer records from the database. We ask for these to be sorted alphabetically by surname with the 'ORDER BY...' command in SQL. A *customerObject* is then created from each of the records.

```csharp
private string email;
private string phone;
private static string databaseLocation = "C:\\C#\\theatreBookings.mdf;";

public static int customerCount;
public static customer[] customerObject = new customer[12];

public static void loadCustomers()
{
    customerCount = 0;
    DataSet dsCustomers = new DataSet();
    SqlConnection con = new SqlConnection(@"Data Source=.\SQLEXPRESS;
        AttachDbFilename=" +databaseLocation + "Integrated Security=True;
        Connect Timeout=30; User Instance=True");
    con.Open();
    SqlCommand cmCustomers = new SqlCommand();
    cmCustomers.Connection = con;
    cmCustomers.CommandType = CommandType.Text;
    cmCustomers.CommandText = "SELECT * FROM Customer ORDER BY surname ASC";
    SqlDataAdapter daCustomers = new SqlDataAdapter(cmCustomers);
    daCustomers.Fill(dsCustomers);
    con.Close();

    customerCount = dsCustomers.Tables[0].Rows.Count;
    for (int i = 0; i < customerCount; i++)
    {
        customerObject[i] = new customer();
        DataRow dataRow = dsCustomers.Tables[0].Rows[i];
        customerObject[i].setCustomerID((int)dataRow[0]);
        customerObject[i].setForename(Convert.ToString(dataRow[1]));
        customerObject[i].setSurname(Convert.ToString(dataRow[2]));
        customerObject[i].setTitle(Convert.ToString(dataRow[3]));
        customerObject[i].setAddress1(Convert.ToString(dataRow[4]));
        customerObject[i].setAddress2(Convert.ToString(dataRow[5]));
        customerObject[i].setTown(Convert.ToString(dataRow[6]));
        customerObject[i].setPostcode(Convert.ToString(dataRow[7]));
        customerObject[i].setEmail(Convert.ToString(dataRow[8]));
        customerObject[i].setPhone(Convert.ToString(dataRow[9]));
    }
}
```

Return to the **CustomerDetails** form and add a **loadCustomers( )** method. This will call the method in the **customer** class which loads records from the database and creates a set of **customerObjects**. A loop then accesses each object and adds the customer name to the comboBox list.

Call **loadCustomers( )** from the **CustomerDetails( )** method.

```csharp
public CustomerDetails()
{
    InitializeComponent();
    loadCustomers();
}

private void loadCustomers()
{
    customer.loadCustomers();
    combCustomers.Items.Clear();
    for (int i = 0; i < customer.customerCount; i++)
    {
        string customerName = customer.customerObject[i].getSurname()
            + ", " + customer.customerObject[i].getTitle() + " "
            + customer.customerObject[i].getForename();
        combCustomers.Items.Add(customerName);
    }
}
```

Run the program, move through to the **CustomerDetails** page and check that the comboBox displays a list of your customer test data.

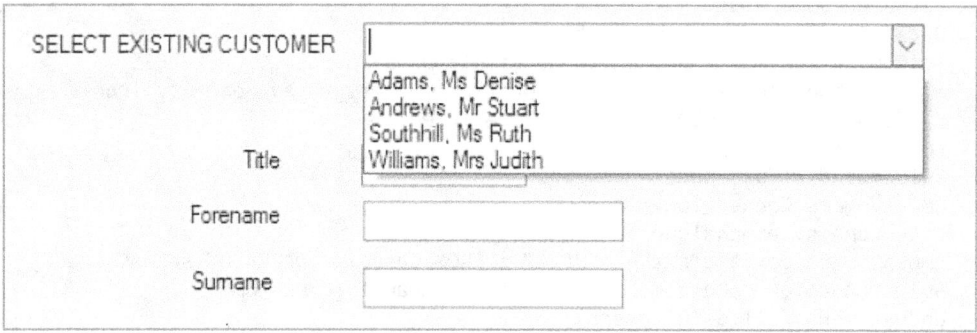

The next step is to transfer data to the textBoxes when an existing customer is selected. Double click the customers **comboBox** and add code to the method.

```csharp
private void combCustomers_SelectedIndexChanged(object sender, EventArgs e)
{
    int i = combCustomers.SelectedIndex;
    combTitle.Text = customer.customerObject[i].getTitle();
    txtForename.Text = customer.customerObject[i].getForename();
    txtSurname.Text = customer.customerObject[i].getSurname();
    txtAddress1.Text = customer.customerObject[i].getAddress1();
    txtAddress2.Text = customer.customerObject[i].getAddress2();
    txtTown.Text = customer.customerObject[i].getTown();
    txtPostcode.Text = customer.customerObject[i].getPostcode();
    txtEmail.Text = customer.customerObject[i].getEmail();
    txtPhone.Text = customer.customerObject[i].getPhone();
}
```

Run the program and check that customer contact information is displayed correctly when a customer name is selected from the comboBox.

Care must be taken to avoid existing customer records being saved for a second time, producing duplicate records in the database. Only records for new customers should be saved. We can control this by means of a boolean '*True/False*' variable to indicate whether we have entered a new customer.

Add the boolean variable at the start of **CustomerDetails**.

```
public partial class CustomerDetails : Form
{
    int f_performanceID;
    double f_totalCost;
    int[,] f_seatStatus;
    string f_eventTitle;

    bool newCustomer = true;

    public CustomerDetails()
    {
        InitializeComponent();

        loadCustomers();
    }
```

We will begin by assuming that a new customer is being entered. If, however, an existing customer is selected from the comboBox list, then **newCustomer** will be set to '*false*'. Add a line to the start of the comboBox click method to do this.

```
private void combCustomers_SelectedIndexChanged(object sender, EventArgs e)
{
    newCustomer = false;

    int i = combCustomers.SelectedIndex;
    combTitle.Text = customer.customerObject[i].getTitle();
```

Modify the '**continue to payment**' button click method so that records are only saved for new customers.

```
private void btnContinue_Click(object sender, EventArgs e)
{
    customerID = 0;
    if (newCustomer == true)
    {
        if (txtSurname.Text.Length > 0 && txtForename.Text.Length > 0 &&
            txtAddress1.Text.Length > 0 && txtPostcode.Text.Length > 0)
        {
            customerID = customer.saveCustomer(txtForename.Text, txtSurname.Text,
                combTitle.Text, txtAddress1.Text, txtAddress2.Text, txtTown.Text,
                txtPostcode.Text, txtEmail.Text, txtPhone.Text);
        }
        else
        {
            MessageBox.Show(
                "Missing customer information - name, address, postcode are required");
        }
    }
    else
    {
        int i = combCustomers.SelectedIndex;
        customerID = customer.customerObject[i].getCustomerID();
    }
}
```

Run the program. Select an exiting customer from the comboBox list, then click the '**continue to payment**' button. Exit from the program, then connect to the database. Check that a duplicate copy of the customer record has NOT been saved into the database table. Delete the connection to the database.

One final function to add to the **CustomerDetails** form is to clear all data from the textBoxes when the '**clear**' button is clicked.

Double click the '**clear**' button and add code to the **btnClear_Click( )** method. Notice that the **newCustomer** variable is reset to '**true**', as the user may now want to enter the details of a new customer, rather than select a customer from the comboBox list.

```
private void btnClear_Click(object sender, EventArgs e)
{
    combCustomers.Text = "";
    combTitle.Text = "";
    txtForename.Clear();
    txtSurname.Clear();
    txtAddress1.Clear();
    txtAddress2.Clear();
    txtTown.Clear();
    txtPostcode.Clear();
    txtEmail.Clear();
    txtPhone.Clear();
    newCustomer = true;
}
```

This completes the collection of customer contact information, and the program can now proceeed to the payment form.

Create a new **Windows Form** with the name '**Payment**', and add components as shown:

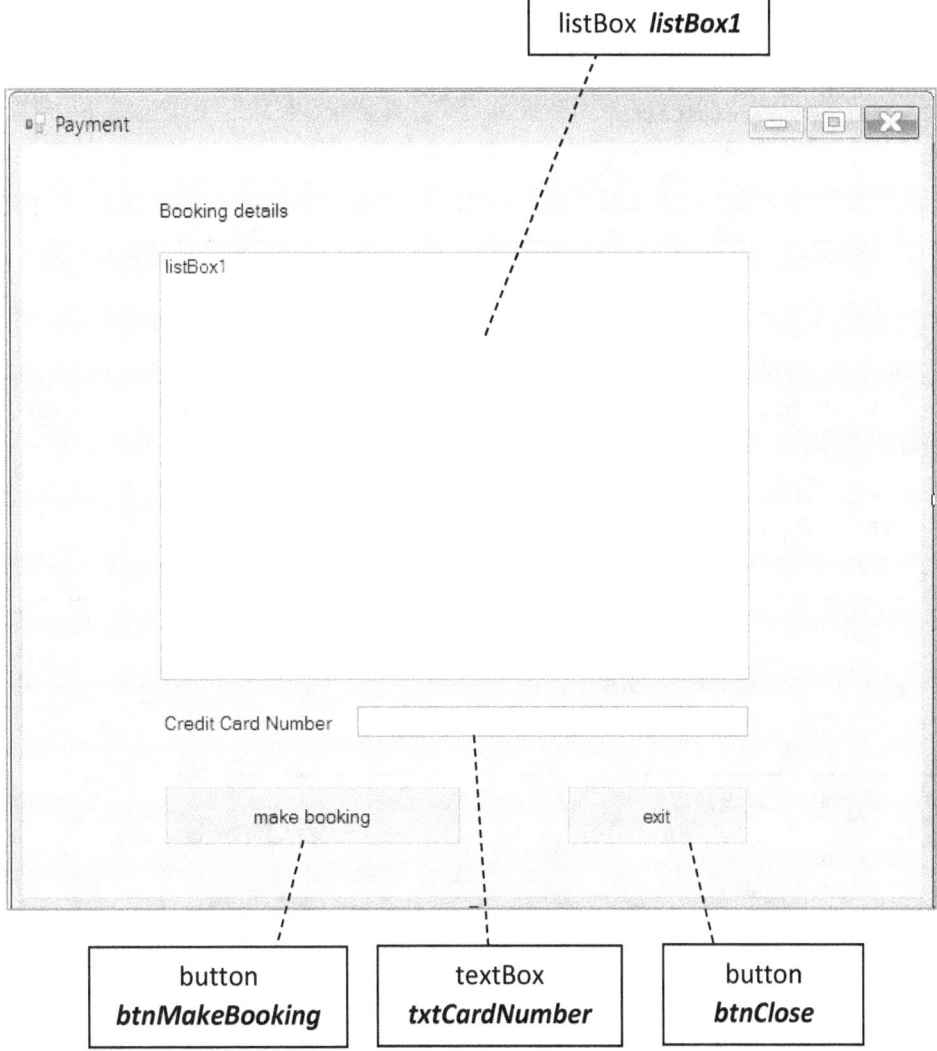

Add a line of code to the '**exit**' button click method.

```
private void btnClose_Click(object sender, EventArgs e)
{
    this.Close();
}
```

We will again transfer data from the **CustomerDetails** form, ready for use in saving the booking into the database. Add a set of variables at the start of the **Payment** form.

```
public partial class Payment : Form
{
    int f_performanceID;
    int f_customerID;
    double f_totalCost;
    int[,] f_seatStatus;
```

Begin a *getBooking( )* method which will import data from the *CustomerDetails* form.

```
public void getBooking(int performanceID, double totalCost,
            int[,] seatStatus, int customerID, string eventTitle)
{
    f_performanceID = performanceID;
    f_customerID = customerID;
    f_totalCost = totalCost;
    f_seatStatus = seatStatus;
}
```

Return to the *CustomerDetails* form and add a block of code to the end of the *btnContinue_Click( )* method. This will only operate if a customer record has been loaded from disc or a new customer record entered in the database, so that a valid *customerID* has been generated.

Booking data is transferred using the *getBooking( )* method of the *Payment* form.

```
    else
    {
        int i = combCustomers.SelectedIndex;
        customerID = customer.customerObject[i].getCustomerID();
    }

    if (customerID > 0)
    {
        Payment frmPayment = new Payment();
        frmPayment.getBooking(f_performanceID, f_totalCost,
                        f_seatStatus, customerID, f_eventTitle);
        frmPayment.ShowDialog();
        this.Close();
    }
}
```

Run the program and work through to the *CustomerDetails* form. Click the '*continue to payment*' button and check that the *Payment* form opens correctly.

The next task is to display details of the booking in the *listBox* on the *Payment* form, so that this can be confirmed as correct by the user before the booking is saved to the database.

Go to the *getBooking( )* method of the *Payment* form and add lines of code as shown below to clear the listBox and then display the title of the selected event.

```
public void getBooking(int performanceID, double totalCost, int[,]
    seatStatus, int customerID, string eventTitle)
{
    f_performanceID = performanceID;
    f_customerID = customerID;
    f_totalCost = totalCost;
    f_seatStatus = seatStatus;

    listBox1.Items.Clear();
    listBox1.Items.Add("Event: "+eventTitle);
    listBox1.Items.Add("");
```

Test the program to make sure the title of the chosen event is displayed:

We will next display details of the chosen performance. To do this, another method will be required in the **performance class** file which will load the details of a performance from the database using the **performanceID** value, then create a **performance** object from this data.

Go to the performance class file and add a **performanceDetails( )** method.
(This is very similar to the **loadPerformances( )** method, so you may save time by copying **loadPerformances( )** and just making changes where necessary.)

```
public static void performanceDetails(int p)
{
    DataSet dsPerformances = new DataSet();

    SqlConnection con = new SqlConnection(@"Data Source=.\SQLEXPRESS;
        AttachDbFilename=" +databaseLocation + "Integrated Security=True;
        Connect Timeout=30; User Instance=True");
    con.Open();
    SqlCommand cmPerformances = new SqlCommand();
    cmPerformances.Connection = con;
    cmPerformances.CommandType = CommandType.Text;
    cmPerformances.CommandText = "SELECT * FROM Performance"
        + " WHERE performanceID='" + p + "'";
    SqlDataAdapter daPerformances = new SqlDataAdapter(cmPerformances);
    daPerformances.Fill(dsPerformances);
    con.Close();

    performanceObject[0] = new performance();
    DataRow dataRow = dsPerformances.Tables[0].Rows[0];
    performanceObject[0].setPerformanceID((int)dataRow[0]);
    performanceObject[0].setEventID((int)dataRow[1]);
    performanceObject[0].setDate(Convert.ToDateTime(dataRow[2]));
    performanceObject[0].setTime(Convert.ToString(dataRow[3]));
    performanceObject[0].setPrice(Convert.ToDouble(dataRow[4]));
}
```

Return to the *Payment* form and add lines of code to the *getBooking( )* method.

```
listBox1.Items.Clear();
listBox1.Items.Add("Event: "+eventTitle);
listBox1.Items.Add("");
performance.performanceDetails(performanceID);
DateTime performanceDate = performance.performanceObject[0].getDate();
string format = " ddd d MMM yyyy";
string performanceDateString = performanceDate.ToString(format);
string performanceTime = performance.performanceObject[0].getTime();
listBox1.Items.Add("Performance Date: "+performanceDateString + " at "
    + performanceTime);
string seatPrice=(performance.performanceObject[0].getPrice()).ToString("f2");
listBox1.Items.Add("Seat prince: " + seatPrice);
```

Run the program and check that performance details are displayed correctly.

```
Booking details

Event: Les Miserables

Performance Date: Wed 18 Nov 2015 at 19:00
Seat prince: 27.80
```

We will now list the rows and numbers of the selected seats. This can be done from data carried over in the *seatStatus* array. Selected seats will have a *seatStatus* value of 2. Add further lines of code to the *getBooking( )* method.

```
listBox1.Items.Add("Performance Date: "+performanceDateString + " at "
    + performanceTime);
string seatPrice=(performance.performanceObject[0].getPrice()).ToString("f2");
listBox1.Items.Add("Seat prince: " + seatPrice);
listBox1.Items.Add("");
for (int j = 1; j <= 11; j++)
{
    for (int i = 1; i <= 20; i++)
    {
        if (seatStatus[i, j] == 2)
        {
            char c = Convert.ToChar(64 + j);
            if (j > 8)
                c = Convert.ToChar(65 + j);
            listBox1.Items.Add("Row " + c + "  Seat " + i);
        }
    }
}
listBox1.Items.Add("");
listBox1.Items.Add("Total cost £ " + totalCost.ToString("f2"));
listBox1.Items.Add(" ");
```

Run the program. Make a booking for several seats, and check that the row and seat numbers are displayed correctly. Check also that the total ticket cost is carried over correctly to the *Payment* form.

```
Booking details

Event: Les Miserables

Performance Date: Wed 18 Nov 2015 at 19:00
Seat prince: 27.80

Row B  Seat 8
Row B  Seat 9
Row B  Seat 10

Total cost £ 83.40
```

The final block of information to be displayed in the list box is the name and address of the customer. Another method will be required in the *customer* class file which will load the details for a customer using their *customerID* value, then create a *customer* object from this data.

Go to the *customer class* file and add a *customerDetails( )* method. (This is very similar to the *loadCustomers( )* method, so you may save time by copying and pasting.)

```
public static void customerDetails(int c)
{
    DataSet dsCustomers = new DataSet();
    SqlConnection con = new SqlConnection(@"Data Source=.\SQLEXPRESS;
        AttachDbFilename=" +databaseLocation + "Integrated Security=True;
        Connect Timeout=30; User Instance=True");
    con.Open();
    SqlCommand cmCustomers = new SqlCommand();
    cmCustomers.Connection = con;
    cmCustomers.CommandType = CommandType.Text;
    cmCustomers.CommandText = "SELECT * FROM Customer"
        +" WHERE customerID ='" + c + "'";
    SqlDataAdapter daCustomers = new SqlDataAdapter(cmCustomers);
    daCustomers.Fill(dsCustomers);
    con.Close();

    customerObject[0] = new customer();
    DataRow dataRow = dsCustomers.Tables[0].Rows[0];
    customerObject[0].setCustomerID((int)dataRow[0]);
    customerObject[0].setForename(Convert.ToString(dataRow[1]));
    customerObject[0].setSurname(Convert.ToString(dataRow[2]));
    customerObject[0].setTitle(Convert.ToString(dataRow[3]));
    customerObject[0].setAddress1(Convert.ToString(dataRow[4]));
    customerObject[0].setAddress2(Convert.ToString(dataRow[5]));
    customerObject[0].setTown(Convert.ToString(dataRow[6]));
    customerObject[0].setPostcode(Convert.ToString(dataRow[7]));
    customerObject[0].setEmail(Convert.ToString(dataRow[8]));
    customerObject[0].setPhone(Convert.ToString(dataRow[9]));
}
```

Return to the *Payment* form and add code to complete the *getBooking( )* method.

```
    listBox1.Items.Add("");
    listBox1.Items.Add("Total cost £ " + totalCost.ToString("f2"));
    listBox1.Items.Add(" ");
    customer.customerDetails(customerID);
    string customerName = customer.customerObject[0].getTitle() + " "
        + customer.customerObject[0].getForename() + " "
        + customer.customerObject[0].getSurname();
    listBox1.Items.Add(customerName);
    string address = customer.customerObject[0].getAddress1() + ", "
        + customer.customerObject[0].getAddress2();
    listBox1.Items.Add(address);
    string town = customer.customerObject[0].getTown() + ", "
        + customer.customerObject[0].getPostcode();
    listBox1.Items.Add(town);
}
```

Run the program and check that customer details are shown correctly.

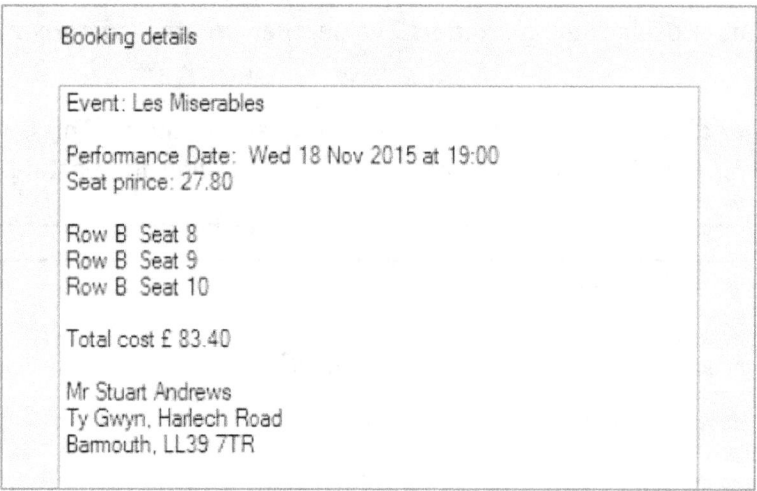

If the customer wishes to go ahead with their booking, they will provide their credit card number and the user will click the '*make booking*' button.

Before going further with the procedure to save the booking, we must create a *booking object class* to handle the data. Create a *booking* class file.

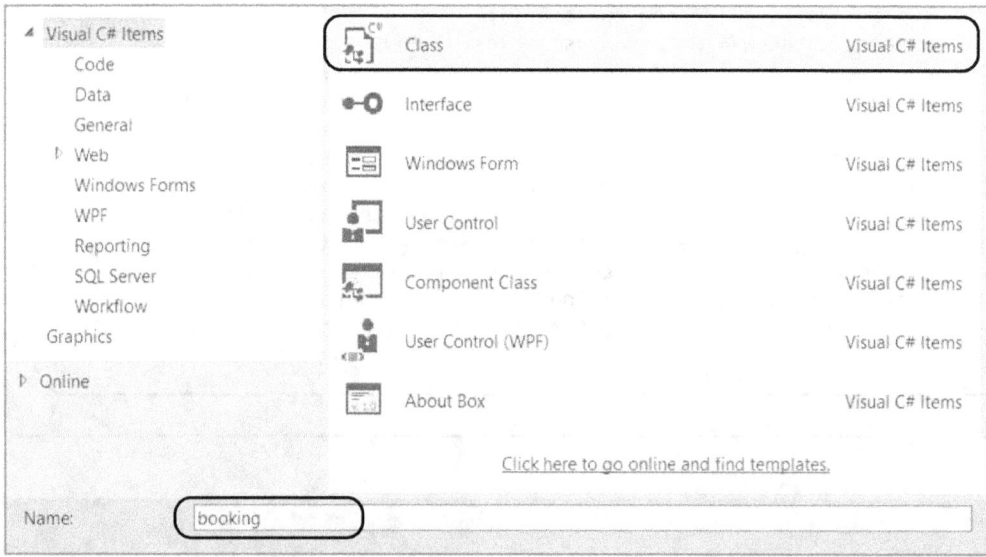

Add the properties for the *booking* class, and the methods for transfering data into and out of the *booking objects.*

```
class booking
{
    private int bookingID;
    private int customerID;
    private int performanceID;
    private double totalCost;
    private string creditCardNumber;

    public void setBookingID(int b)
    {
        bookingID = b;
    }

    public int getBookingID()
    {
        return bookingID;
    }

    public void setCustomerID(int c)
    {
        customerID = c;
    }

    public int getCustomerID()
    {
        return customerID;
    }

    public void setPerformanceID(int p)
    {
        performanceID = p;
    }

    public int getPerformanceID()
    {
        return performanceID;
    }

    public void setTotalCost(double t)
    {
        totalCost = t;
    }

    public double getTotalCost()
    {
        return totalCost;
    }

    public void setCreditCardNumber(string cn)
    {
        creditCardNumber = cn;
    }

    public string getCreditCardNumber()
    {
        return creditCardNumber;
    }
}
```

When a booking is saved, the computer must carry out two tasks:

- Add a record to the *booking* table of the database. This will contain details of the event, performance, seats selected, ticket cost and identification of the customer.
- The *seat* records for the selected seats must be updated to show them as no longer available. The record for each booked seat should include the *bookingID* value, as a link to the details of the booking.

We will begin by writing an *AddBooking( )* method for the *booking class*. It is also necessary to add '*using SqlClient*' and '*using Data*' directives, and to give the database location.

The *AddBooking( )* method uses the *SELECT SCOPE_IDENTITY( )* command to obtain the bookingID value allocated to the new record.

```csharp
using System.Linq;
using System.Text;
using System.Data.SqlClient;
using System.Data;

namespace theatreBookings
{
    class booking
    {
        public static string databaseLocation="C:\\C#\\theatreBookings.mdf;";
        private int bookingID;
        private int customerID;
        private int performanceID;
        private double totalCost;
        private string creditCardNumber;

        public static int AddBooking(int performanceID, int customerID,
            double t, string cn, int[,] seatStatus)
        {
            SqlConnection con = new SqlConnection(@"Data Source=.\SQLEXPRESS;
                AttachDbFilename="+databaseLocation + "Integrated Security=True;
                Connect Timeout=30; User Instance=True");
            con.Open();
            SqlCommand cmBooking = new SqlCommand();
            cmBooking.Connection = con;
            cmBooking.CommandType = CommandType.Text;
            cmBooking.CommandText="INSERT INTO Booking(customerID,performanceID,
                totalCost, creditCardNo)" + "VALUES ('" + customerID + "','"
                + performanceID + "','" + t + "','" + cn + "')";
            cmBooking.ExecuteNonQuery();
            cmBooking.CommandText = "SELECT SCOPE_IDENTITY()";
            int identity = Convert.ToInt32(cmBooking.ExecuteScalar());
            con.Close();
            return identity;
        }
```

Return to the *Payment* form and double click the '*make booking*' button to create a button_Click method. Add code to call the *AddBooking( )* method in the *booking* class, which will save the booking record in the database.

```
private void btnMakeBooking_Click(object sender, EventArgs e)
{
    string creditCardNumber = txtCardNumber.Text;

    try
    {
        int bookingID = booking.AddBooking(f_performanceID, f_customerID,
            f_totalCost, creditCardNumber, f_seatStatus);
    }
    catch
    {
        MessageBox.Show("ERROR");
    }
}
```

Run the program and make a booking, then click the '*make booking*' button. Keep a note of the event, performance and customer selected.

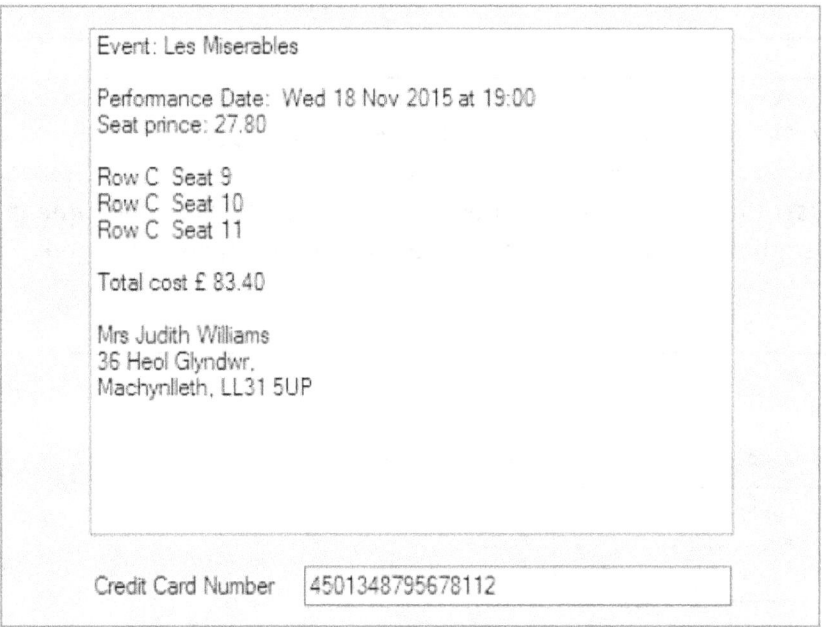

Exit from the program and go to the *Server Explorer* window. Connect the database and open the *Booking* table. Check that the booking has been saved correctly. You may need to use the *performanceID* and *customerID* values to look up details in the *Performance* and *Customer* tables.

bookingID	customerID	performanceID	totalCost	creditCardNo
1	4	9	83.40	4501348795678112
NULL	NULL	NULL	NULL	NULL

After checking the tables, delete the connection to the database.

The final step in recording the booking is to update the seats as no longer available. We will need to add a method to the *seat* class to do this.

Open the seat class file and add an *updateSeat( )* method.

```
public static int seatCount;
public static seat[] seatObject = new seat[240];
public static void updateSeat(int performanceID, char seatRow,
    int seatNumber, int bookingID)
{
    SqlConnection con = new SqlConnection(@"Data Source=.\SQLEXPRESS;
      AttachDbFilename=" +databaseLocation + "Integrated Security=True;
      Connect Timeout=30; User Instance=True");
    con.Open();
    SqlCommand cmSeats = new SqlCommand();
    cmSeats.Connection = con;
    cmSeats.CommandType = CommandType.Text;
    cmSeats.CommandText = "UPDATE Seat SET available='1', bookingID='"
      + bookingID + "' WHERE performanceID='" + performanceID
      + "' AND seatRow='" + seatRow + "' AND seatNumber='" + seatNumber + "'";
    cmSeats.ExecuteNonQuery();
    con.Close();
}
```

Return to the *Payment* form and modify the *btnMakeBooking_Click( )* method to allow seats to be updated. Begin by adding variables to identify a seat, and a message box to confirm to the user that the booking has been saved successfully. The *Payment* form can then be closed, so that the user returns to the *DisplayEvents* page at the end of the booking procedure.

```
private void btnMakeBooking_Click(object sender, EventArgs e)
{
    string creditCardNumber = txtCardNumber.Text;
    char seatRow;
    int seatNumber;
    int rowNumber;
    try
    {
        int bookingID = booking.AddBooking(f_performanceID, f_customerID,
            f_totalCost, creditCardNumber, f_seatStatus);
        MessageBox.Show("Booking completed");
        this.Close();
    }
    catch
    {
        MessageBox.Show("ERROR");
    }
}
```

We can now add the code which updates the seat records. Seat data is first loaded, then a loop accesses each object in the *seat* array. If this seat has a *seatStatus* value of 2, indicating that it has been selected for the booking, then it will be marked as '*booked*' by calling the *updateSeat( )* method in the *seat* class.

```
try
{
    int bookingID = booking.AddBooking(f_performanceID, f_customerID,
        f_totalCost, creditCardNumber, f_seatStatus);

    seat.loadSeats(f_performanceID);
    for (int i = 0; i < seat.seatCount; i++)
    {
        seatRow = seat.seatObject[i].getSeatRow();
        seatNumber = seat.seatObject[i].getSeatNumber();

        rowNumber = (int)seatRow - 64;
        if (rowNumber > 8)
            rowNumber--;

        if (f_seatStatus[seatNumber, rowNumber] == 2)
        {
            seat.updateSeat(f_performanceID, seatRow, seatNumber, bookingID);
        }
    }

    MessageBox.Show("Booking completed");
    this.Close();
}
```

Run the program and make a booking for several seats. Keep a record of the performance and seats selected.

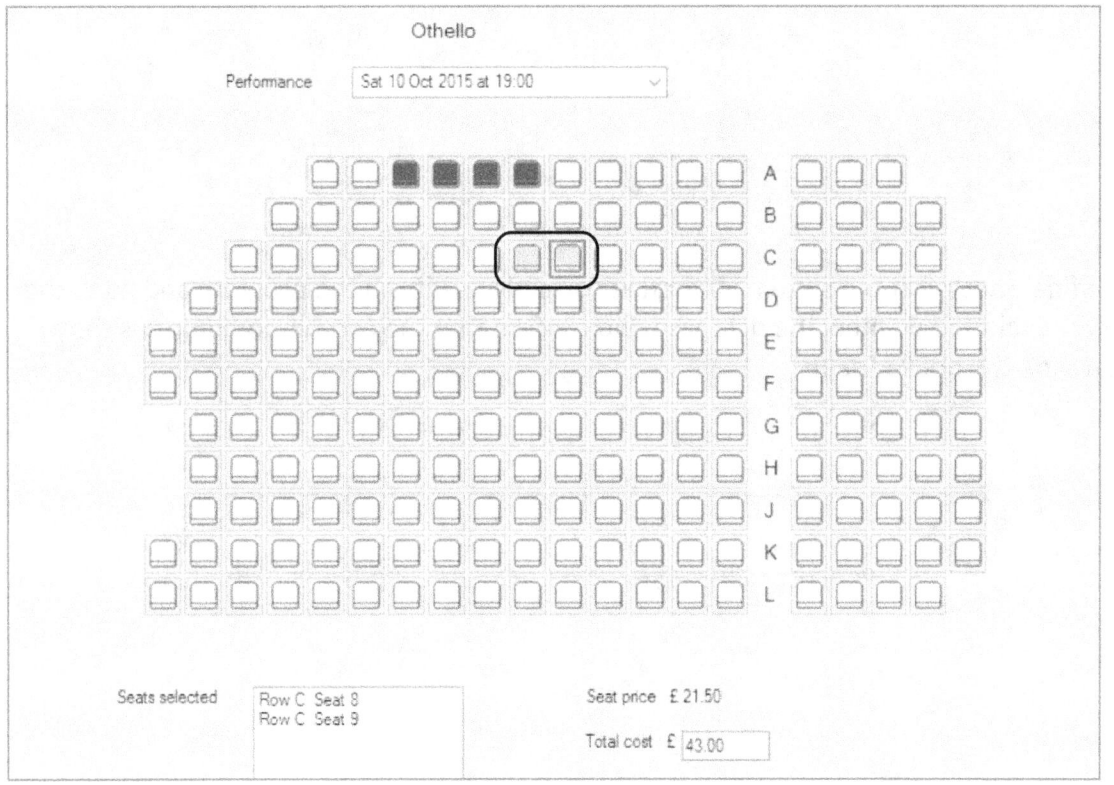

Complete the booking

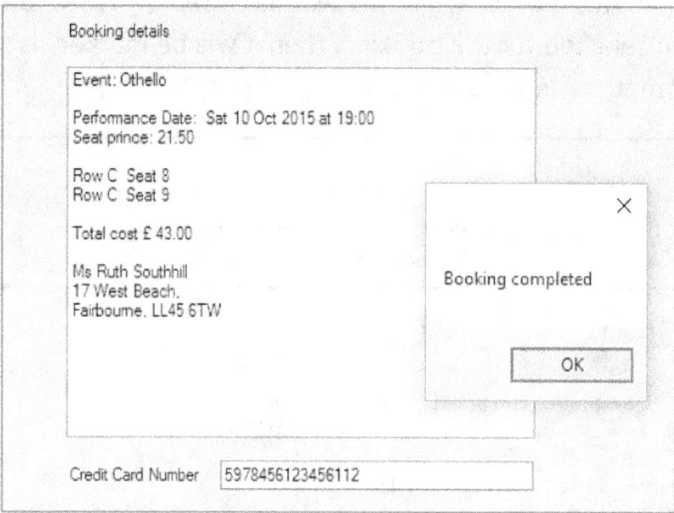

Return to the same performance and confirm that the seats selected previously are now displayed as '**booked**'.

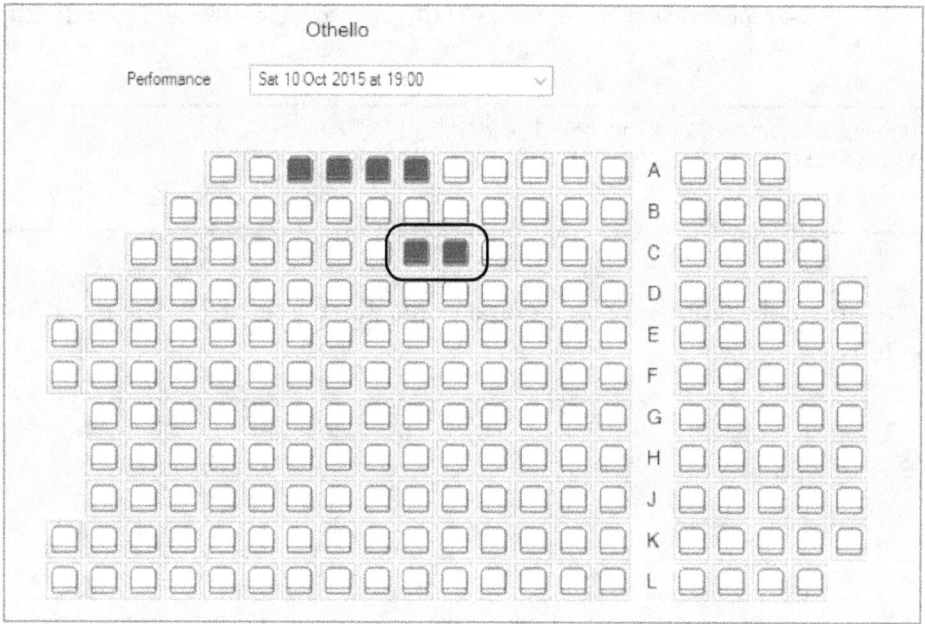

As a final check that the system is working correctly, exit from the program and go to the Server Explorer. Connect the database and confirm that the correct **bookingID** is shown alongside the booked seats.

seatRow	seatNumber	performanceID	available	bookingID
C	7	2	0	0
C	8	2	1	2
C	9	2	1	2
C	10	2	0	0
C	11	2	0	0

This completes the booking procedure. We have two further sections of the program to develop. These will provide information for the theatre staff about bookings received and customer contact details.

Go to the Solution Explorer window. Right-click the *theatreBookings* program icon to add a new *Windows Form*. Give this the name *TicketSales*.

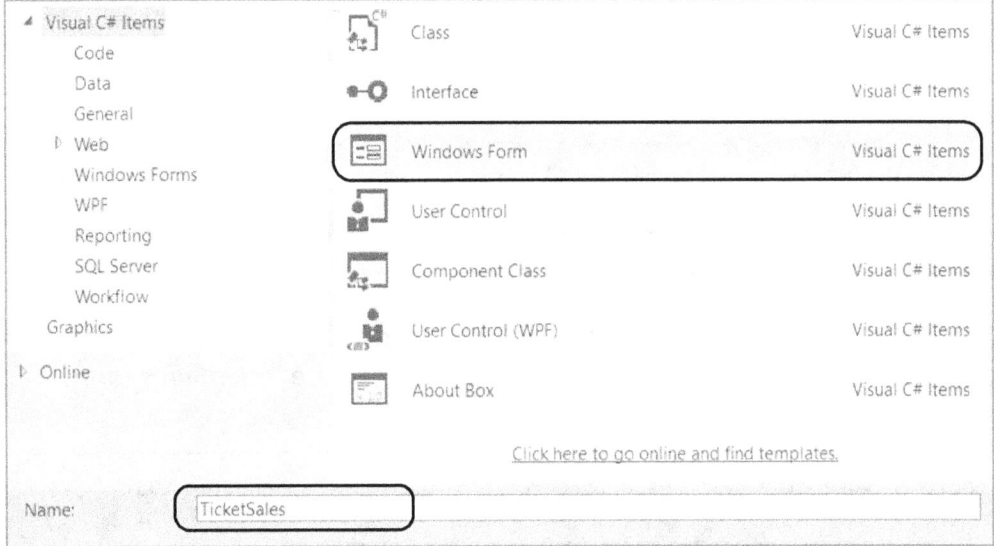

Add components to the form.

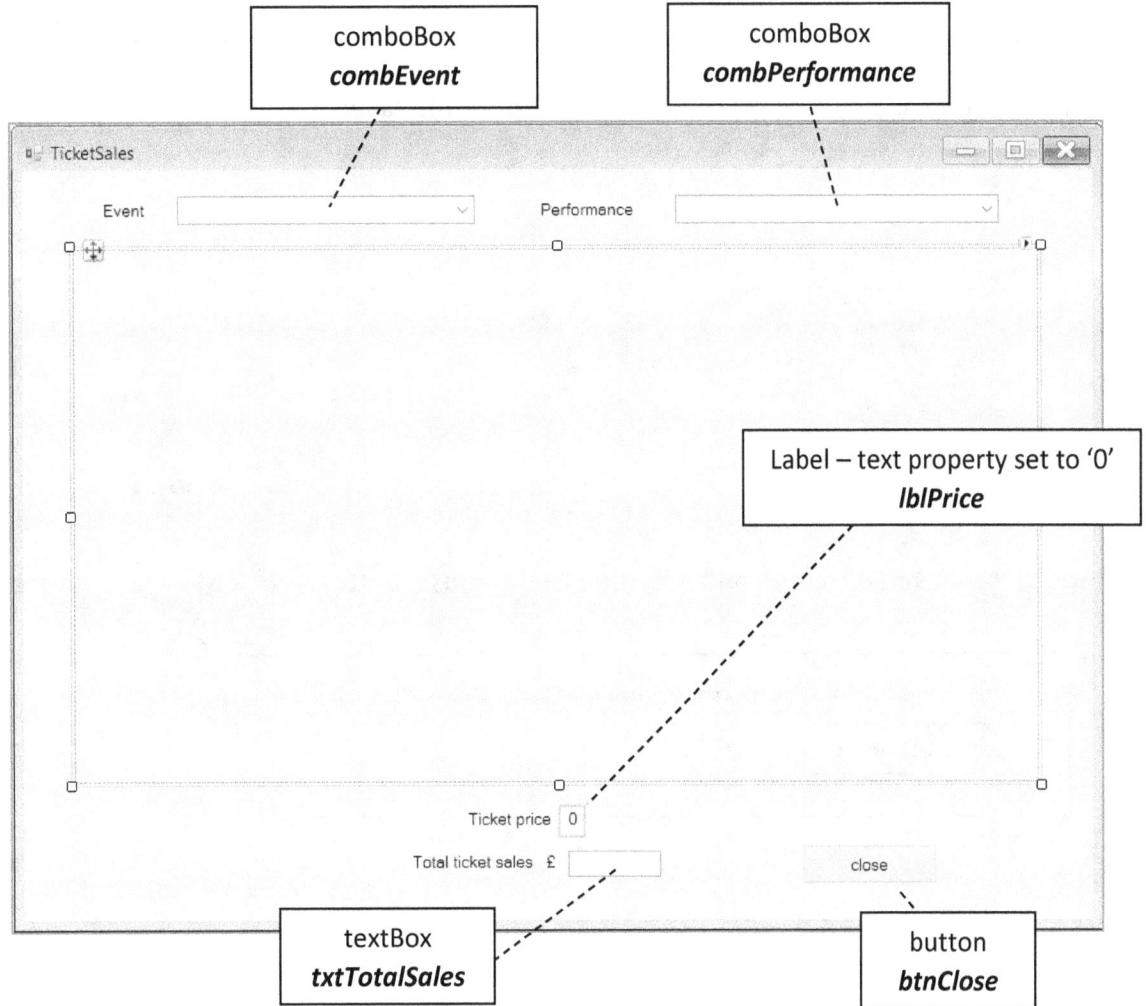

Open the code window for the *TicketSales* form and add lines to the *TicketSales( )* method to load the titles of theatre events into the comboBox.

```
public TicketSales()
{
    InitializeComponent();

    combEvent.Items.Clear();
    string eventTitle;
    for (int i = 0; i < theatreEvent.eventCount; i++)
    {
        eventTitle = theatreEvent.eventObject[i].getTitle();
        combEvent.Items.Add(eventTitle);
    }
}
```

Go to the *DisplayEvents* form and double click the *'Display ticket sales for performance'* menu option. Add code to the menu click method to open the *TicketSales* form.

```
private void displayTicketSalesForPerformanceToolStripMenuItem_Click(
                                              object sender, EventArgs e)
{
    TicketSales frmTicketSales = new TicketSales();
    frmTicketSales.ShowDialog();
}
```

Run the program and check that a list of event titles is displayed.

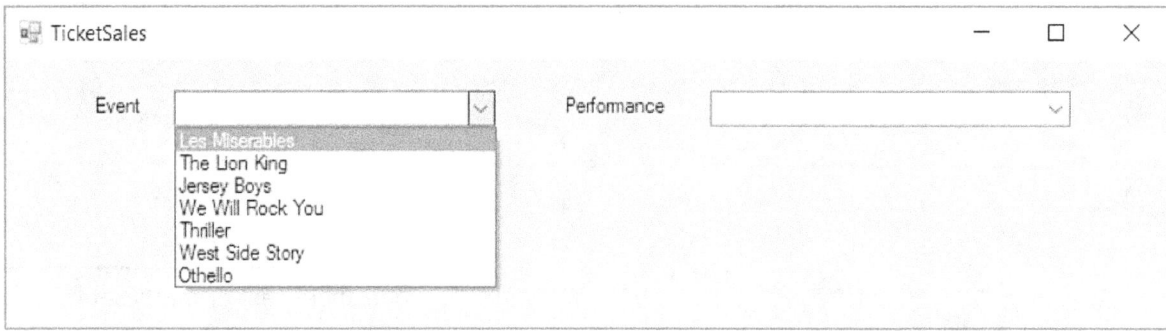

Return to the *TicketSales* form and add code to the *'close'* button.

```
private void btnClose_Click(object sender, EventArgs e)
{
    this.Close();
}
```

Double click the **event comboBox** to create a method. Add code which will load performance dates and times for the selected event.

```
private void combEvent_SelectedIndexChanged(object sender, EventArgs e)
{
    int i = combEvent.SelectedIndex;
    int eventID = theatreEvent.eventObject[i].getEventID();
    performance.loadPerformances(eventID);
    combPerformance.Items.Clear();
    for (int p = 0; p < performance.performanceCount; p++)
    {
        DateTime performanceDate = performance.performanceObject[p].getDate();
        string format = " ddd d MMM yyyy";
        string performanceDateString = performanceDate.ToString(format);
        string performanceTime = performance.performanceObject[p].getTime();
        combPerformance.Items.Add(performanceDateString + " at " +
            performanceTime);
    }
}
```

Run the program to check that performance details are displayed correctly.

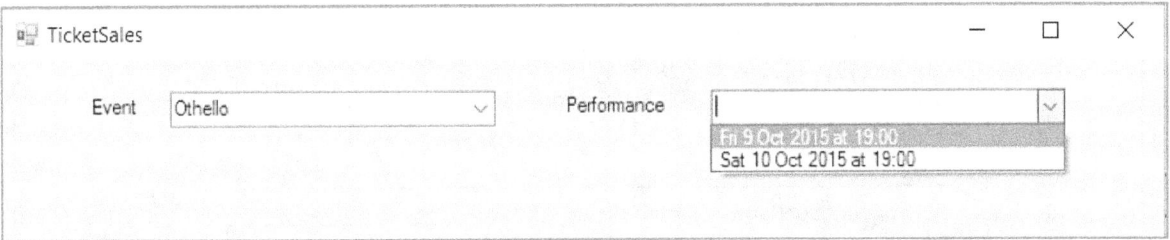

We can make use of the **drawPlan( )** method which we wrote earlier for the **TheatrePlan** form.

Begin by adding the **button**, **label** and **seatStatus** arrays at the start of the **TicketSales** form.

```
public partial class TicketSales : Form
{
    Button[,] btnSeat = new Button[22, 12];
    Label[] label = new Label[12];
    int[,] seatStatus = new int[21, 12];
```

Copy the **drawPlan( )** method from **TheatrePlan** into the **TicketSales** form.

The seat plan will be for display only, and it is not necessary for the seat buttons to be interactive. Remove the lines of code which allocate names to the seat buttons and create button_Click methods, as indicated on the next page.

```
private void drawPlan()
{
    int offset;
    int seatMax;
    for (int j = 1; j <= 11; j++)
    {
        seatMax = 20;
        if (j == 1) seatMax = 14;
        if (j == 2) seatMax = 16;
        if (j == 3) seatMax = 17;
        if (j == 4) seatMax = 19;
        if (j >= 7 && j <= 9) seatMax = 19;
        if (j == 11) seatMax = 19;
        for (int i = 1; i <= seatMax; i++)
        {
            offset = 0;
            if (j == 1) offset = 4;
            if (j == 2) offset = 3;
            if (j == 3) offset = 2;
            if (j == 4) offset = 1;
            if (j >= 7 && j <= 9) offset = 1;
            btnSeat[i, j] = new Button();
            btnSeat[i, j].Width = 28;
            btnSeat[i, j].Height = 28;
            btnSeat[i, j].Left = ((28 * i) + (28 * offset));
            if ((i + offset) > 15)
                btnSeat[i, j].Left += 28;
            btnSeat[i, j].Top = (28 * j);
            btnSeat[i, j].Image = Image.FromFile("../../seat1.png");
            if (seatStatus[i, j] == 1)
                btnSeat[i, j].Image = Image.FromFile("../../seat2.png");
            String buttonName = "btn";
            if (j <= 9)
                buttonName += " ";
            buttonName += j;
            if (i <= 9)
                buttonName += " ";
            buttonName += i;
            btnSeat[i, j].Name = buttonName;
            btnSeat[i, j].Click += new EventHandler(seat_Click);
            pnlTheatre.Controls.Add(btnSeat[i, j]);
            int rowNumber = j;
            if (j > 8)
                rowNumber++;
            string tooltipText = Convert.ToChar(rowNumber + 64).ToString()
                + (i).ToString();
            ToolTip buttonToolTip = new ToolTip();
            buttonToolTip.SetToolTip(btnSeat[i, j], tooltipText);
        }
        label[j] = new Label();
        label[j].Size = new System.Drawing.Size(24, 30);
        char c = Convert.ToChar(64 + j);
        if (j > 8)
            c = Convert.ToChar(65 + j);
        label[j].Text = Convert.ToString(c);
        label[j].Font = new System.Drawing.Font("Microsoft Sans Serif", 10F,
            System.Drawing.FontStyle.Regular, System.Drawing.GraphicsUnit.Point,
            ((byte)(0)));
        label[j].Location = new System.Drawing.Point(455, 4 + 28 * j);
        pnlTheatre.Controls.Add(label[j]);
    }
}
```

Remove these lines of code (the block from `String buttonName = "btn";` through `btnSeat[i, j].Click += new EventHandler(seat_Click);`)

Double click the *performance comboBox* and add code to load the seat data for the selected performance. This data is transferred to the *seatStatus array*, using code values of 0 for an available seat and 1 for a booked seat. At the same time, the total cost of tickets for all booked seats is being calculated.

When seat data has been processed, the previous pattern of seat buttons are removed from the form, and the *drawPlan( )* method is called to create the seating plan display.

```
private void combPerformance_SelectedIndexChanged(object sender, EventArgs e)
{
    int p = combPerformance.SelectedIndex;
    int performanceID = performance.performanceObject[p].getPerformanceID();
    double seatCost = performance.performanceObject[p].getPrice();

    seat.loadSeats(performanceID);
    double totalSales = 0;
    for (int i = 0; i < seat.seatCount; i++)
    {
        char c = seat.seatObject[i].getSeatRow();
        int r = ((int)c) - 64;
        if (r > 8)
            r--;
        int s = seat.seatObject[i].getSeatNumber();
        int available = seat.seatObject[i].getAvailable();
        seatStatus[s, r] = available;
        if (available == 1)
        {
            totalSales += seatCost;
        }
    }
    int totalButtons = pnlTheatre.Controls.Count;
    for (int i = 0; i < totalButtons; i++)
    {
        pnlTheatre.Controls.RemoveAt(0);
    }
    drawPlan();
    lblPrice.Text = seatCost.ToString("f2");
    txtTotalSales.Text = totalSales.ToString("f2");
}
```

Run the program and check that seat plans can be displayed for any performance.

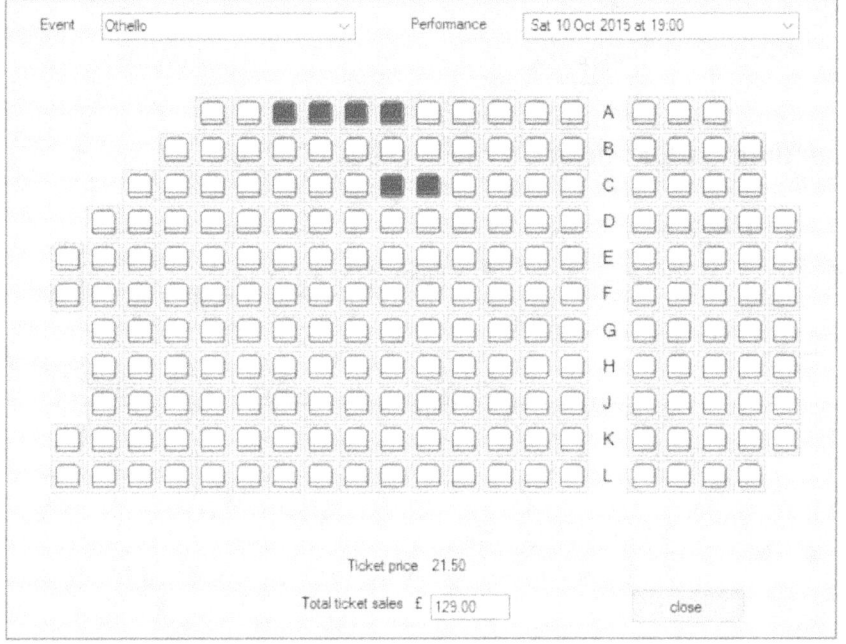

The final option we will include in our program is to view customer records.

Add another Windows Form with the name '**CustomerRecord**'. Add components to the form as shown.

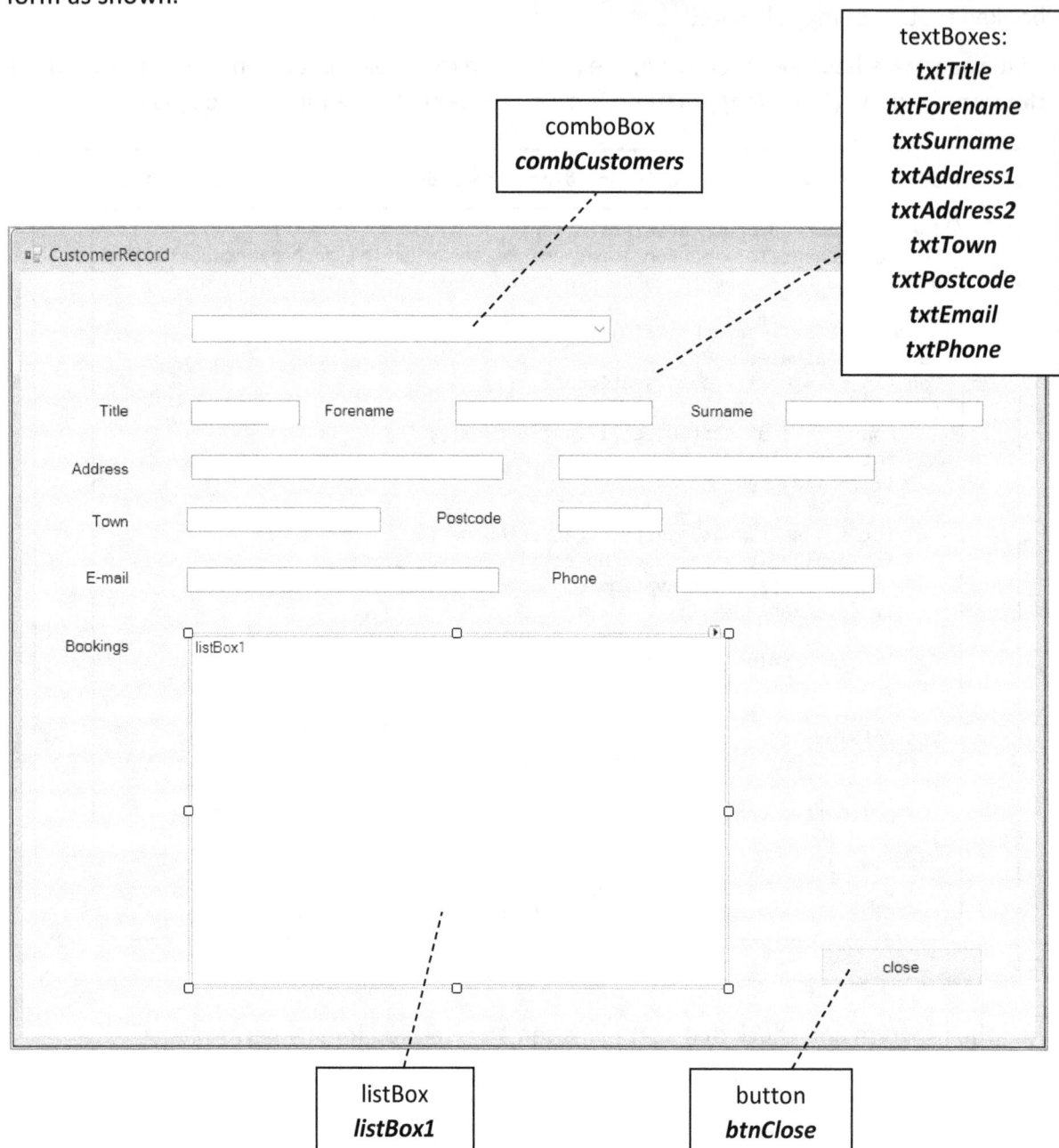

Double click the '*close*' button and add a line of code.

```
private void btnClose_Click(object sender, EventArgs e)
{
    this.Close();
}
```

Create a *loadCustomers( )* method which will load customer names into the drop-down *comboBox* list. Call this method from the *CustomerRecord( )* method.

```
public CustomerRecord()
{
    InitializeComponent();
    loadCustomers();
}

private void loadCustomers()
{
    customer.loadCustomers();
    combCustomers.Items.Clear();
    for (int i = 0; i < customer.customerCount; i++)
    {
        string customerName = customer.customerObject[i].getSurname() + ", "
            + customer.customerObject[i].getTitle() + " "
             + customer.customerObject[i].getForename();
        combCustomers.Items.Add(customerName);
    }
}
```

Go to the *DisplayEvents* form and add code to the '*View customer records*' menu option to load the *CustomerRecord* form.

Run the program and check that customer names are listed correctly in the *comboBox* on the *CustomerRecord* form.

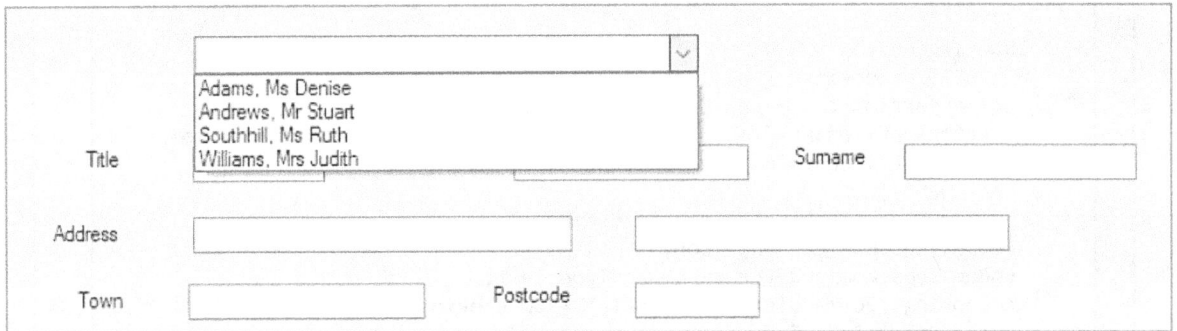

Return to the CustomerRecord page and double click the *comboBox*. Add code to the method.

```
private void combCustomers_SelectedIndexChanged(object sender, EventArgs e)
{
    int i = combCustomers.SelectedIndex;
    int customerID=customer.customerObject[i].getCustomerID();
    txtTitle.Text = customer.customerObject[i].getTitle();
    txtForename.Text = customer.customerObject[i].getForename();
    txtSurname.Text = customer.customerObject[i].getSurname();
    txtAddress1.Text = customer.customerObject[i].getAddress1();
    txtAddress2.Text = customer.customerObject[i].getAddress2();
    txtTown.Text = customer.customerObject[i].getTown();
    txtPostcode.Text = customer.customerObject[i].getPostcode();
    txtEmail.Text = customer.customerObject[i].getEmail();
    txtPhone.Text = customer.customerObject[i].getPhone();
}
```

Run the program and select a customer from the comboBox on the **CustomerRecord** form. The customer name, address, e-mail and phone number should be displayed.

The final step is to display the details of the bookings made by the selected customer. Before doing this we must add a method to the booking class.

Open the **booking class file** and create a **loadBookings( )** method. Also add a **bookingCount** variable, and an array to hold **bookingObjects**.

```csharp
    private double totalCost;
    private string creditCardNumber;

    public static int bookingCount;
    public static booking[] bookingObject = new booking[16];

    public static void loadBookings(int customerID)
    {
        bookingCount = 0;
        DataSet dsBookings = new DataSet();
        SqlConnection con = new SqlConnection(@"Data Source=.\SQLEXPRESS;
          AttachDbFilename=" +databaseLocation + "Integrated Security=True;
          Connect Timeout=30; User Instance=True");
        con.Open();
        SqlCommand cmBookings = new SqlCommand();
        cmBookings.Connection = con;
        cmBookings.CommandType = CommandType.Text;
        cmBookings.CommandText = "SELECT * FROM Booking WHERE customerID = '"
          + customerID + "'";
        SqlDataAdapter daBookings = new SqlDataAdapter(cmBookings);
        daBookings.Fill(dsBookings);
        con.Close();
        bookingCount = dsBookings.Tables[0].Rows.Count;
        for (int i = 0; i < bookingCount; i++)
        {
            bookingObject[i] = new booking();
            DataRow dataRow = dsBookings.Tables[0].Rows[i];
            bookingObject[i].setBookingID((int)dataRow[0]);
            bookingObject[i].setPerformanceID((int)dataRow[2]);
            bookingObject[i].setTotalCost(Convert.ToDouble(dataRow[3]));
            bookingObject[i].setCreditCardNumber(Convert.ToString(dataRow[4]));
        }
    }
```

Return to the **CustomerRecord** form and add code to the Customers **comboBox IndexChanged( )** method. This loads the booking records and uses a loop to check if each booking has been made by the selected customer. If so, the details of the booked performance will be displayed in the listBox on the **CustomerRecord** form.

```
txtTown.Text = customer.customerObject[i].getTown();
txtPostcode.Text = customer.customerObject[i].getPostcode();
txtEmail.Text = customer.customerObject[i].getEmail();
txtPhone.Text = customer.customerObject[i].getPhone();

booking.loadBookings(customerID);
listBox1.Items.Clear();
for (int b = 0; b < booking.bookingCount; b++)
{
    int performanceID = booking.bookingObject[b].getPerformanceID();
    performance.performanceDetails(performanceID);
    DateTime performanceDate = performance.performanceObject[0].getDate();
    string format = "ddd d MMM yyyy";
    string performanceDateString = performanceDate.ToString(format);
    string performanceTime = performance.performanceObject[0].getTime();
    int eventID = performance.performanceObject[0].getEventID();
    for (int j = 0; j < theatreEvent.eventCount; j++)
    {
        int eventIDfound = theatreEvent.eventObject[j].getEventID();
        if (eventID == eventIDfound)
        {
            string eventTitle = theatreEvent.eventObject[j].getTitle();
            listBox1.Items.Add(eventTitle);
        }
    }
    listBox1.Items.Add("EventID: " + eventID);
    listBox1.Items.Add("");
    listBox1.Items.Add("PerformanceID: " + performanceID);
    listBox1.Items.Add(performanceDateString + " at " + performanceTime);
    listBox1.Items.Add("");
    int bookingID = booking.bookingObject[b].getBookingID();
    listBox1.Items.Add("BookingID: " + bookingID);
}
```

Run the program and check that the performances booked are displayed.

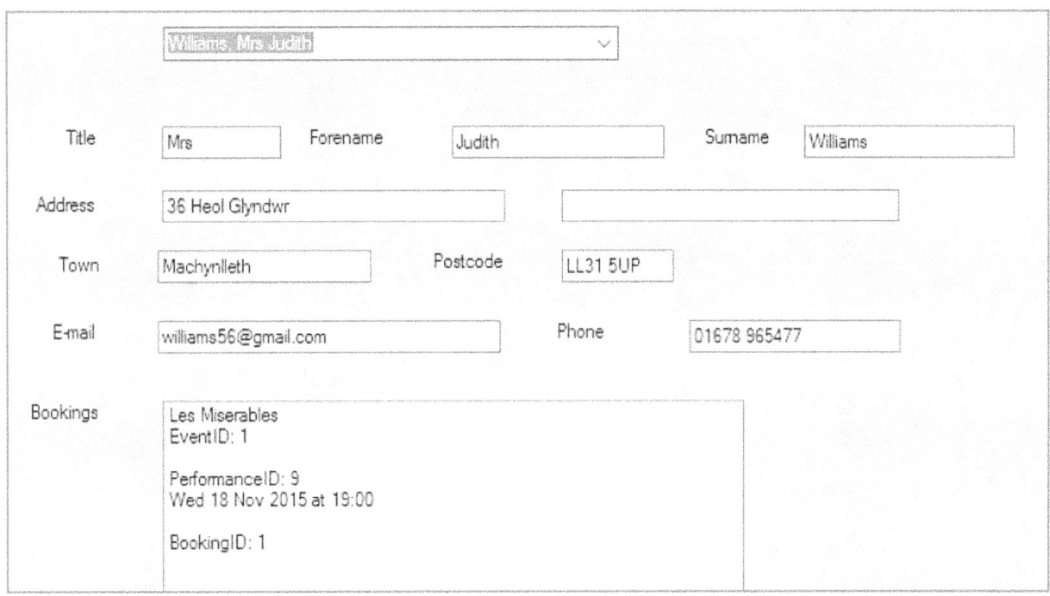

The only thing to now add is a list of the seats booked by the customer and payment details. Add code to the Customers *comboBox IndexChanged( )* method to do this.

```
listBox1.Items.Add("PerformanceID:  " + performanceID);
listBox1.Items.Add(performanceDateString + " at " + performanceTime);
listBox1.Items.Add("");
int bookingID = booking.bookingObject[b].getBookingID();
listBox1.Items.Add("BookingID:  " + bookingID);

listBox1.Items.Add("Seats booked:");
seat.loadSeats(performanceID);
for (int k = 0; k < seat.seatCount; k++)
{
    int bookingIDfound = seat.seatObject[k].getBookingID();
    if (bookingID == bookingIDfound)
    {
        char seatRow = seat.seatObject[k].getSeatRow();
        string seatBooked = Convert.ToString(seatRow)
            + Convert.ToString(seat.seatObject[k].getSeatNumber());
        listBox1.Items.Add(seatBooked);

    }
}
listBox1.Items.Add("");
double totalCost = booking.bookingObject[b].getTotalCost();
listBox1.Items.Add("Total cost:    £ " + totalCost.ToString("f2"));
listBox1.Items.Add("");
string creditCardNumber = booking.bookingObject[b].getCreditCardNumber();
listBox1.Items.Add("Payment by credit card " + creditCardNumber);
listBox1.Items.Add("_____");
listBox1.Items.Add("");
}
```

Run the program and check that seats booked are now listed.

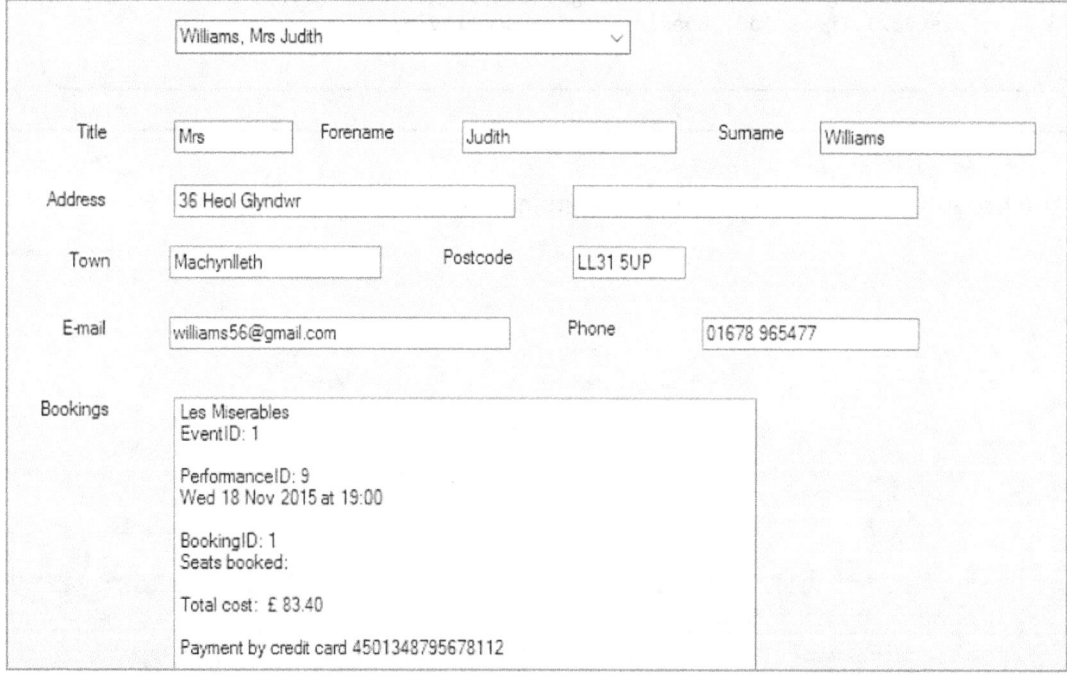

Congratulations on completing this final project successfully.

www.ingramcontent.com/pod-product-compliance
Lightning Source LLC
Chambersburg PA
CBHW081045170526
45158CB00006B/1864